Shusterman's Somaesthetics

Studies in Somaesthetics

EMBODIED PERSPECTIVES IN PHILOSOPHY,
THE ARTS AND THE HUMAN SCIENCES

Edited by

Richard Shusterman (*Florida Atlantic University, USA*)

Editorial Board

Roger Ames (*University of Hawaii, USA*)
Else Marie Bukdahl (*University of Aalborg, Denmark*)
Pradeep Dhillon (*University of Illinois, USA*)
Yanping Gao (*Chinese Academy of Social Sciences, Beijing, China*)
Mathias Girel (*École Normale Supérieure (Paris), France*)
Kristina Höök (*Royal Institute of Technology, Stockholm, Sweden*)
Mark Johnson (*University of Oregon, USA*)
Leszek Koczanowicz (*University of Social Sciences
and Humanities, Wroclaw Campus, Poland*)
Hans-Peter Krüger (*University of Potsdam, Germany*)
Tanehisa Otabe (*University of Tokyo, Japan*)
Paul Taylor (*Vanderbilt University, Nashville, USA*)
Bryan Turner (*Australian Catholic University, Sydney, Australia*)
Eva Kit Wah Man (*Hong Kong Baptist University, Hong Kong*)
Krystyna Wilkoszewksa (*Jagiellonian University, Krakow, Poland*)

VOLUME 4

The titles published in this series are listed at *brill.com/sis*

Shusterman's Somaesthetics

From Hip Hop Philosophy to Politics and Performance Art

Edited by

Jerold J. Abrams

BRILL

LEIDEN | BOSTON

Cover illustration: Yann Toma, *Somaflux with Richard Shusterman Performing as the Man in Gold: Mooring Meditation*, 2012. Photo Courtesy of Yann Toma and Richard Shusterman.

The Library of Congress Cataloging-in-Publication Data is available online at https://catalog.loc.gov
LC record available at https://lccn.loc.gov/2021049267

Typeface for the Latin, Greek, and Cyrillic scripts: "Brill". See and download: brill.com/brill-typeface.

ISSN 2451-8646
ISBN 978-90-04-47054-5 (paperback)
ISBN 978-90-04-46879-5 (hardback)
ISBN 978-90-04-46880-1 (e-book)

Copyright 2022 by Jerold J. Abrams. Published by Koninklijke Brill NV, Leiden, The Netherlands.
Koninklijke Brill NV incorporates the imprints Brill, Brill Nijhoff, Brill Hotei, Brill Schöningh, Brill Fink, Brill mentis, Vandenhoeck & Ruprecht, Böhlau and V&R unipress.
Koninklijke Brill NV reserves the right to protect this publication against unauthorized use. Requests for re-use and/or translations must be addressed to Koninklijke Brill NV via brill.com or copyright.com.

This book is printed on acid-free paper and produced in a sustainable manner.

Contents

Acknowledgments   VII
List of Figures   VIII
Notes on Contributors   IX

Introduction   1
   Jerold J. Abrams

PART 1
Pragmatism and Somaesthetics

1   Shusterman's Pragmatist Philosophy   23
       Stefán Snævarr

2   From Pragmatism to Somaesthetics as Philosophy   44
       Alexander Kremer

3   Somaesthetics, Somapower, and the Microphysics of Emancipation   61
       Leszek Koczanowicz

4   Living Beauty, Rethinking Rap: Revisiting Shusterman's Philosophy of Hip Hop   74
       Max Ryynänen

5   Somaesthetics and Pathic Aesthetics   86
       Tonino Griffero

6   Eating as an Aesthetic Activity: Somaesthetics and Food Studies   106
       Dorota Koczanowicz

PART 2
Performative Philosophy and the Man in Gold

7   Somaesthetics, Photography, and the Man in Gold   125
       Jerold J. Abrams

8   An Exquisitely Beautiful Longing: A Lacanian Reading of *The Adventures of the Man in Gold*   149
     Diane Richard-Allerdyce

9   Shusterman as Philosopher and the Man in Gold   166
     Yvonne Bezrucka

10   The Golden Turn in Shusterman's Somaesthetics: The Magical Figure of the Man in Gold   177
     Else Marie Bukdahl

11   On Shusterman's Somaesthetic Practice: The Case of the Man in Gold   209
     Yang Lu

12   Somaesthetics and Cinema: The Man in Gold in the Film *Walk the Golden Night*   219
     Jerold J. Abrams

PART 3
Shusterman in His Own Words

13   Somaesthetics, Pragmatism, and the Man in Gold: Remarks on the Preceding Chapters   243
     Richard Shusterman

14   On the Path of Somaesthetics: An Interview with Richard Shusterman   261
     Yanping Gao

Abbreviated Bibliography and Filmography of Richard Shusterman   279
Name Index   282
Subject Index   285

Acknowledgments

During this unique historical time the writers collected in the present volume have been unflagging in their professionalism and kindness, and I am grateful and honored to have worked with all of them: Stefán Snævarr, Alexander Kremer, Leszek Koczanowicz, Max Ryynänen, Tonino Griffero, Dorota Koczanowicz, Diane Richard-Allerdyce, Yvonne Bezrucka, Else Marie Bukdahl, Marit Benthe Norheim, Claus Ørntoft, Yang Lu, Yanping Gao, and, of course, Richard Shusterman who thoughtfully responded to all the essays about his work. For all of us, Richard has been an ongoing source of inspiration and encouragement, generously giving of his time over the years in innumerable ways, in teaching, conferencing, writing, editing, attending performances, performing in the arts, curating art exhibitions, establishing centers of somaesthetics, and collaborating with artists and scholars. We have all benefitted greatly from a philosopher whose theories of art are nourished and tested by his own artistic practice, and whose kindness to friends and artists and philosophers sets a standard few if any of us could have thought possible prior to seeing it lived.

Richard often insists that the success of his work in somaesthetics owes an immeasurable debt to the Schmidt Family Foundation that generously funds his chair at FAU and supports the Center for Body, Mind, and Culture he established there. He told me he would like to thank the Schmidts again for their support, which also greatly benefitted this book. I join him in thanking them for this generosity.

Last but not least, I am deeply grateful to Elizabeth F. Cooke for her ever-present support and philosophical conversation on pragmatism and aesthetics over the years and throughout the editing of this volume (in time of pandemic), and for more good things than I can ever hope to count.

Figures

1. Yann Toma, *Somaflux with Richard Shusterman performing as the Man in Gold.* Photographic still from the film, *A Night with Richard Shusterman.* Paris, 2010. Photo courtesy of Yann Toma and Richard Shusterman.   183
2. Man Ray, *Space Writing (Self Portrait)*, 1935. Gelatin silver print on paper. 8.1 × 5.9 cm. Bowdoin College Museum of Art, Brunswick, Maine Museum Purchase, Lloyd O. and Marjorie Strong Coulter Fund, and The Artist Rights Society. Courtesy of Bowdoin College of Museum of Art.   188
3. Yann Toma, *Somaflux with Richard Shusterman performing as the Man in Gold: Currents of the Seine*, 2012. Photo courtesy of Yann Toma and Richard Shusterman.   193
4. Yann Toma, *Somaflux with Richard Shusterman performing as the Man in Gold: Sunset in Vesterklit*, 2014. Photo courtesy of Yann Toma and Richard Shusterman.   195
5. Yann Toma, *Somaflux with Richard Shusterman performing as the Man in Gold: The Lion's Altar.* Hirtshals, North Jutland, Denmark, 2014. Photo courtesy of Yann Toma and Richard Shusterman.   197
6. Claus Ørntoft, *Small Tectonic Space.* Granite slabs and sculpture are floating on light and smoke after dark. Hirtshals, North Jutland, Denmark, 2016. Photo courtesy of Eigil Kirkegaard.   199
7. Claus Ørntoft, *Three Lions and Nine Hearts*, 2012. Granite, Marselisborg Palace Park, Aarhus, Jutland. Photo courtesy of Claus Ørntoft.   201
8. Marit Benthe Norheim, *Life-boats.* Three sailing sculptures in ferrocement, 2017. Photo courtesy of Claus Ørntoft.   203
9. Yann Toma, *Somaflux with Richard Shusterman performing as the Man in Gold: Ship of Longing*, 2014. Photo courtesy of Yann Toma and Richard Shusterman.   205
10. Yann Toma, *Somaflux with Richard Shusterman performing as the Man in Gold: The Look of Love*, 2014. Photo courtesy of Yann Toma and Richard Shusterman.   206

Notes on Contributors

Jerold J. Abrams
is Professor of Philosophy at Creighton University in Nebraska. He is the editor of *The Philosophy of Stanley Kubrick* (2007). Recent articles include "*2001* as Philosophy," in *The Palgrave Handbook of Popular Culture as Philosophy* (2020); and "Ancient Chinese Cave Paintings as Cinema: The Volcanos and Dragons of Mogao Cave 249," in *International Communication of Chinese Culture* (2021).

Yvonne Bezrucka
is Professor of English Literature at Verona University in Italy. Recent publications include "Nature as Oikos and Kepos," in CRIER X (2013), "Utopia, Homeland, Occupiert," in *Polemos* (2020), "The Well-Beloved: Thomas Hardy's Manifesto of 'Regional Aesthetics,'" in VLC (2008); and *The Invention of Northern Aesthetics in 18th-Century English Literature* (2017).

Else Marie Bukdahl
is Affiliated Professor at the University of Aalborg and former Rector of the Royal Danish Academy of Fine Arts She is the author of *Diderot, critique d'art* (1980), *Johannes Wiedewelt* (1993), *The Baroque* (1998), *Caspar David Friedrich's Study Years at the Royal Danish Academy of Fine Arts and his Importance for Danish Art* (2005), *The Golden Age in Spain* (2006), *The Re-enchantment of Nature and Urban Space* (2011), and *The Recurrent Actuality of the Baroque* (2017).

Yanping GAO (高砚平)
is Associate Professor in the Institute of Literature at the Chinese Academy of Social Sciences in Beijing. She is the author of *Winckelmann's Vision of Greek Art* (in Chinese, 2016), the translator of Suzanne Langer's *Feeling and Form* (2013) and Shusterman's *Act and Affect* (2018), and coeditor of the (Chinese) journal *International Aesthetics* (published by the Chinese Academy of Social Sciences).

Tonino Griffero
is Professor of Aesthetics at the University of Rome "Tor Vergata" in Italy. He is the author of *Il corpo spiritual: Ontologie "sottili" da Paolo di Tarso a Friedrich Christoph Oetinger* (2006), *Atmospheres* (2014), *Il pensiero dei sensi* (2016); *Quasi-Things* (2017), *Places, Affordances* (2019).

Dorota Koczanowicz
is Professor of Cultural Studies at the University of Wroclaw, Poland. She is the author of *Experience of Art, Art of Living* (in Polish, 2008), *Positioning Taste* (in Polish, 2018), and coeditor of *Between Aestheticization and Emancipation* (in Polish, 2010), *Shusterman's Pragmatism: Between Literature and Somaesthetics* (2012), and *Discussing Modernity: A Dialogue with Martin Jay* (2013).

Leszek Koczanowicz
is Professor of Philosophy and Political Science in the Faculty of Psychology at the SWPS University of Social Sciences and Humanities. He is the author or editor of twelve books, including *Politics of Time* (in English, 2008), *Modern Fear: Essays on Democracy and its Adversaries* (in Polish, 2011, *Lek nowoczesny: eseje o demokracji i jej adwersarzach*), *Politics of Dialogue* (in English, 2015), and *Anxiety and Lucidity* (in English, 2020).

Alexander Kremer
is Habilitated Associate Professor of Philosophy at the University of Szeged, Hungary. He is the author of *Chapters from the History of Western Philosophy from Thales to Hume* (in Hungarian, 1997), *Why Did Heidegger Become Heidegger?* (in Hungarian, 2001), *Basic Ethics* (in Hungarian, 2004), *Philosophy of the Late Richard Rorty* (in Hungarian, 2016), and "Martin Heidegger's Influence on Richard Rorty's Philosophy" (in English), in *Pragmatism Today*, vol. 2, no. 1, summer 2011 (pragmatismtoday.eu). He is Editor-in-Chief of *Pragmatism Today*, and Head of the Hungarian Forum of Somaesthetics.

Diane Richard-Allerdyce
is Chair of the Faculty of the Humanities & Culture (HMS) concentration of the Ph.D. Program in Interdisciplinary Studies at Union Institute & University, in Cincinnati, Ohio. She is author of *Anaïs Nin and the Remaking of Self* (1998). Recent work appears in *The Journal of Somaesthetics* (2017) and the *North American Review* (2019).

Max Ryynänen
is Senior Lecturer of Theory of Visual Culture at Aalto University in Espoo, Finland (since 2006). He is, with Falk Heinrich, Coeditor-in-Chief of *The Journal of Somaesthetics*, and Coeditor of *Popular Inquiry* (with Jozef Kovalcik). Recent publications include (with Zoltan Somhegyi) *Learning from Decay* (2018), and "From Haunted Ruin to the Most Touristified of All Cities," in *Philosophical Perspectives on Ruins, Monuments and Memorials* (2019).

Richard Shusterman
is the Dorothy F. Schmidt Eminent Scholar in the Humanities, Professor of Philosophy and English, and Director of The Center for Body, Mind, and Culture at Florida Atlantic University. A select list of his books appears at the end of this volume. The most important books for understanding his approach to pragmatism and somaesthetics include *Pragmatist Aesthetics, Practicing Philosophy, Performing Live, Body Consciousness, Thinking through the Body, The Adventures of the Man in Gold*, and *Ars Erotica: Sex and Somaesthetics in the Classical Arts of Love*.

Stefán Snævarr
is Professor of Philosophy at the Inland Norway University in Lillehammer. He is the author *Ostraka* (Icelandic Edition, 1997), and *Metaphors, Narratives, Emotions: Their Interplay and Impact* (2010).

Yang Lu (陆扬)
is Professor of Literature in the Department of Chinese at Fudan University in Shanghai, China. He is the author of *Medieval and Renaissance Aesthetics* (1999), *Derrida and Foucault* (2000), *An Introduction to Cultural Studies* (2006), *Aesthetics of Death* (2006), and *Critique of Aestheticization of Everyday Life* (2012). He has also translated several books (fiction and nonfiction), including the Chinese edition of Shusterman's *The Adventures of the Man in Gold*.

Introduction

Jerold J. Abrams

Pragmatist philosopher Richard Shusterman's works in aesthetics may be divided into three successive periods: analytic aesthetics, pragmatist aesthetics, and somaesthetics. In the first period, having trained in analytic philosophy, Shusterman developed his "analytic aesthetics" with a focus on literary interpretation, culminating in *T. S. Eliot and the Philosophy of Criticism* (1988).[1] While, within this early work, he explored elements of classical American philosophy in relation to Eliot, Shusterman's thinking remained firmly within the tradition of analytic philosophy, and apart from pragmatism (classical or contemporary). In fact, Shusterman in his book on T. S. Eliot had criticized Richard Rorty's pragmatist view of interpretation, in general, and, more particularly, the very idea that language is an instrument that creates descriptions of texts without end. At the time, Rorty, as the author of *Philosophy and the Mirror of Nature* (1979), was, and continued to be, a towering figure on the landscape of American and European philosophy, not least for disavowing analytic epistemology for pragmatism.[2] Not unexpectedly, the analytic guard opposed Rorty's disavowal of hard-edged thought for what they considered a clouded and now outdated philosophical perspective; but not everyone within analytic philosophy would remain so opposed. In fact, it was Rorty, in conversation, who would convince Shusterman (despite his prior criticisms) to reconsider the tradition

---

1 At the time, when scholarly studies had generally neglected the poet and literary critic's work in philosophy, and his analytically-minded philosophy, in particular, despite Eliot's own studies in analytic thinkers of the age; most notably Bertrand Russell. Richard Shusterman corrected that view in *T. S. Eliot and the Philosophy of Criticism* (New York: Columbia University Press, 1988), arguing that Eliot had been widely misunderstood as championing an "Anglo-American parochialism and narrow aesthetic formalism," and deserved appreciation for his philosophical historicism and hermeneutics (4).
2 Richard Rorty in *Philosophy and the Mirror of Nature* (Princeton: Princeton University Press, 1979) drew on Thomas Kuhn's view of paradigm shifts, from *The Structure of Scientific Revolutions* (1962), to argue that philosophy had enchanted itself with a powerful metaphor for the mind as a "mirror of nature"—which lay at the center of modern epistemology's representationalist theories of knowledge—and that this enchantment constituted an exhausted paradigm, which the pragmatists had already overcome with an alternative set of images for language, like the "tool" (understood artistically) for creating new poetic descriptions of things. For an excellent study of Rorty's philosophy, see Christopher J. Voparil, *Richard Rorty: Politics and Vision* (Lanham: Rowman & Littlefield, 2006).

of classical American pragmatism, and delve deeper into the writings of John Dewey, especially *Reconstruction in Philosophy*.

The recommendation of *Reconstruction in Philosophy* was a good place to start, and one can see in that work the path that had led Rorty safely out of the strictures and dogmas of analytic epistemology and philosophy of language. But as a young philosopher working primarily in aesthetics, Shusterman's reading in Dewey's writings would soon run to the philosopher's major work in the philosophy of art, *Art as Experience*. That work would have a powerful effect on Shusterman's thinking in aesthetics, and complete his turn to pragmatism, which was not quite the kind of turn Rorty must have envisioned. As the two philosophers continued their conversation, Shusterman would find that Rorty never really liked Dewey's *Art as Experience*, and for two main reasons. One reason was that Rorty didn't really like "aesthetics," in general, as a discipline of philosophy, particularly as it had been shaped by Kant in the *Critique of Judgment*; the other reason was that Rorty had rejected outright the concept of "experience," in all disciplines of philosophy, and especially as it continued to appear in Dewey; "experience" meant as something nonlinguistic, i.e., a perceptual engagement with things apart from, and prior to, language. By contrast, Shusterman would find *Art as Experience* to be the crowning achievement in Dewey's pragmatism, and in no small part for its brilliant unfolding of an integrated view of human life and art, in which nondiscursive aesthetic experience played a central role.

Perhaps Rorty's concerns about nonlinguistic "experience," within the context of some philosophical disciplines, for example, epistemology, are not so difficult to understand, particularly considering his rejection of what founding pragmatist C. S. Peirce once called "certain faculties claimed for man," and what American philosopher Wilfrid Sellars had called the "myth of the given," in *Empiricism and the Philosophy of Mind*, for which Rorty later wrote an instructive Introduction.[3] But Rorty's lack of appreciation of aesthetics has always been more difficult to understand, considering his firm embrace of romanticism which sets the creative and artistic power of the imagination (together with the emotions and the arts) over reason. As Rorty writes in "Pragmatism and Romanticism," "At the heart of romanticism, is the thesis of the priority of imagination over reason—the claim that reason can only follow paths that imagination has broken."[4] That was the later Rorty of *Philosophy*

---

3 Wilfrid Sellars, *Empiricism and the Philosophy of Mind*, Introduction by Richard Rorty, Study Guide by Robert Brandom (Cambridge: Harvard University Press, 1997).

4 Rorty, "Pragmatism and Romanticism," in *Philosophy as Cultural Politics: Philosophical Papers*, vol. IV (Cambridge: Cambridge University Press, 2004), 105.

as Cultural Politics; but early on as well, and not long after his own break with analytic philosophy appeared in *Philosophy and the Mirror of Nature*, a quite romantic and artistic picture of language and culture was vividly unfolding.

In fact, it was right around the time he had persuaded Shusterman to turn from analytic philosophy and reconsider pragmatism, that Rorty's *Contingency, Irony, and Solidarity* (1989) would place a seemingly very aesthetically-oriented pragmatist view of creative, linguistic self-fashioning on the philosophical map, and, in the process, help to reanimate romanticism (with its deep love of art and nature) from the foregoing analytically-oriented age. A more open appreciation of philosophy of art would seem so natural to Rorty's philosophical perspective, and for so many reasons: if not for his romantic views that language is art, and the "priority of imagination over reason," then perhaps for his many writings on literature and literary self-fashioning, or perhaps his early love of orchids, discussed in "Trotsky and the Wild Orchids," or even his later love of birdwatching, or simply as a beautiful writer. But such was not to be.[5] As a consequence, for any pragmatist philosopher of art, and certainly Shusterman himself, Rorty's distance to aesthetics (and Dewey's aesthetics, in particular) would always feel a little strange.

And yet Rorty's writings in aesthetics—even if he wouldn't call them that—would, like Dewey's *Art as Experience*, have a considerable impact on Shusterman's thought. In fact, Shusterman would find Rorty's Deweyan project of creative self-fashioning to be a brilliant step forward in aesthetics, even as it subtly channeled a tradition of masterworks like Michel de Montaigne's *Essays* and Ralph Waldo Emerson's Montaigne-inspired (and aptly-titled) *Essays: First Series* and *Essays: Second Series*. As he set out developing his own project in the aesthetics of self-fashioning, the influence of Rorty's pragmatism on Shusterman's pragmatism would became increasingly apparent; as would their differences, especially with Shusterman's groundbreaking *Pragmatist Aesthetics: Living Beauty, Rethinking Art* (1992 and 2000), and numerous articles and volumes to follow. If in *T. S. Eliot and the Philosophy of Criticism*, Shusterman had found Rorty's pragmatism to be problematic from an *analytic* perspective, now Shusterman had found Rorty's pragmatism to be problematic from a *pragmatist* perspective. Still caught in the snares of a linguistic essentialism, held over from analytic philosophy, Rorty's romantic project of aesthetic self-fashioning—despite its pragmatism—seemed to operate almost entirely at the level of writing, and to be reserved for the most elite class of writers. His paradigmatic self-fashioners were Friedrich Nietzsche, with his character

---

5   Rorty, "Trotsky and the Wild Orchids," in *Philosophy and Social Hope* (New York: Penguin, 1999).

(and alter-ego) Zarathustra, the philosopher sage residing on a mountain, high above society, in *Thus Spoke Zarathustra*, and G. W. F. Hegel, whom Rorty took to be the central character (*Geist*) in the *Phenomenology of Spirit*, a genius unfolding and creating himself through history; along with several other brilliant writers like Emerson, William James, Vladimir Nabokov, and Marcel Proust. Of course, Rorty had, in *Contingency, Irony, and Solidarity*, presented self-fashioning (in the private sphere) as merely one side of the contemporary cultural coin, allowing for a richly egalitarian, democratic culture, on the other side (in the public sphere). But if anyone could, and ideally everyone would, participate in an open and creative democratic culture, it was always a little hard to see how anyone outside an elite circle of writers could ever hope to participate in self-fashioning—at least as Rorty described it—except perhaps vicariously or in admiration of the masters.[6]

In advancing his own pragmatist aesthetics of self-fashioning, Shusterman would rectify both of these shortcomings, i.e., the erasure of lived embodied experience, and a narrowly exclusive focus on the most elite practitioners of the Western tradition. Rather than finding the pragmatist art of self-fashioning exhausted in literary self-creation, as Rorty had done, Shusterman conceived the project more pragmatistically: as ongoing, experiential, experimentalist, pluralistic, culturally open, and grounded in the lived and naturally artistically expressive human body. Literary self-fashioning would, by no means, be excluded from Shusterman's pragmatist aesthetics, but neither would his pragmatist aesthetics of self-fashioning be exclusively literary. In fact, as part of his pragmatist aesthetics, Shusterman steadily unfolded a comprehensive philosophy of the popular arts, as they appeared in contemporary popular culture, and which had become so prominent in America and throughout the world in the twentieth century. With richly pluralistic tastes in the arts, and an expansive philosophical palate, as Shusterman embraced and explored everything from hip hop music and country musicals to movies and dance and popular theatre, pragmatist aesthetics became a vast and wide-ranging philosophical

---

6 Shusterman, "Pragmatism and Culture: Margolis and Rorty," in *Surface and Depth: Dialectics of Criticism and Culture* (Ithaca: Cornell, 2002); see 203–207 for Shusterman's discussion of his differences with Rorty. Shusterman also discusses his points of convergence and differences with fellow pragmatist Joseph Margolis: "Both forms of pragmatism—the descriptive metaphysics of Margolis and the constructive-genealogical approach I favor—challenge the argument that invariant realism deserves it dominance because it is conceptually necessary for the very possibility of coherent discourse and knowledge" (194). Margolis and Shusterman, old friends, taught together for many years at Temple University, before Shusterman moved to Florida Atlantic University to become the Dorothy F. Schmidt Eminent Scholar in the Humanities.

enterprise, seemingly capable of absorbing and synthesizing all the arts, and understanding them in rich new ways.

As the project continued to evolve, pragmatist aesthetics also continued to distinguish itself from other views within pragmatism, most notably Rorty, but also from other views within aesthetics, especially analytic aesthetics, most notably Arthur Danto, one of the most prominent and influential philosophers of art of the twentieth century. Like Rorty, Danto would also prove to be a powerful influence on Shusterman's thought, although for different reasons. All three American philosophers had trained in the analytic tradition, but whereas Rorty and Shusterman broke with that tradition to embrace Deweyan pragmatism (in different ways)—yet each retaining analytic philosophy's virtues of clarity and logical precision—Danto remained firmly within the analytic tradition. As for Dewey's pragmatism, Danto had little taste for it, distinguishing himself from Rorty on precisely this point, in "The Cosmopolitan Alphabet of Art," in Giovanna Borradori's *The American Philosopher*. Like any analytic philosopher, Danto had what he refers to as a "taste for the architecture of philosophical thought," but in Dewey he could find no "structure."[7] So, while *Art as Experience* would play an essential role in Shusterman's pragmatist aesthetics, that work would have no more impact on Danto's philosophy of art than on Rorty's pragmatism. Even though a pragmatist, Rorty could reject Dewey's aesthetics because it was aesthetics, while Danto, even though a philosopher of art, could reject Dewey's aesthetics because it lacked structure. To be fair, it wasn't just Dewey; very little of the American tradition appears in Danto's philosophy of art, although he did write a fine Introduction to George Santayana's *The Sense of Beauty: Being the Outlines of Æsthetic Theory*.[8]

On the other hand, Danto does acknowledge a turn within his analytic philosophy of art. The year was 1964. Andy Warhol's *Brillo Boxes* exhibit was on display at the Stable Gallery in Manhattan. Danto was there. But what he saw in the *Brillo Boxes* was very different to anything anyone else seemed to see. If some saw genius but could not explain why, then others saw a set of wooden boxes painted and stacked to look exactly like boxes of Brillo brand dishwashing scrubbers that anyone might find down the street in a grocery store and

---

7 Giovanna Borradori, "The Cosmopolitan Alphabet of Art" (Interview with Danto), in *The American Philosopher: Conversations with Quine, Davidson, Putnam, Nozick, Rorty, Cavell, MacIntyre, and Kuhn*, ed. Borradori, tr. Rosanna Crocitto (Chicago: University of Chicago, 1994), 90–91.

8 Arthur Danto, "Santayana's *The Sense of Beauty*: An Introduction," for George Santayana's *The Sense of Beauty: Being the Outlines of Æsthetic Theory*, Critical Edition, ed. William G. Holzberger and Herman J. Saatkamp, Jr. (Cambridge: MIT Press, 1988), xv–xxviii.

therefore wonder at the relevance of this so-called work of art. Danto, for his part, saw and understood the genius of the boxes, and knew that while others would dismiss them for their exact resemblance to mere everyday utilitarian things, therein lay their genius. Beginning with "The Artworld" (1964, the same year as Warhol's exhibit), and in many works to follow, Danto described the philosophical brilliance of the *Brillo Boxes* with analytical precision and focus, but also a deep sensitivity to the history of art and the history of philosophy as well.

According to Danto, the *Brillo Boxes* are the completion of a logically unfolding developmental trajectory of modern painting that began with the rise of cinema, and which had now come to an end. Painting in the nineteenth century had enjoyed a seemingly royal status among the visual arts, partly for its unique ability to capture reality in fine detail, and partly for its unique ability to document or narrate actions in visual images. One thinks, for example, of Jacques-Louis David's *Napoleon Crossing the Alps* (1801; Château de Malmaison, Rueil-Malmaison) or Eugene Delacroix's *Liberty Leading the People* (1830; Louvre, Paris). But then moving pictures appeared on the scene; and that changed everything. As Danto writes in *The Philosophical Disenfranchisement of Art*, art could now "directly represent motion by means of moving images, thus facilitating narrative representation in a way closed off to painting." It's true that painting could indicate or suggest motion and time, but not *show* it, not directly anyway, and certainly not in any way like film. So, all of a sudden, the once supreme visual art, painting, found itself not so much challenged in a battle to be fought nobly by marshalling a finer style, but completely outdone and dethroned: "Painting was therefore required to redefine itself or collapse into a secondary activity."[9]

Of course, painting did not "collapse into a secondary activity," and did indeed "redefine itself." But redefining itself meant reinventing itself; and reinventing itself required knowing itself; and if knowing itself entailed inquiring into itself, then painting would inquire into itself in the only way open to it: by experimentation with its medium. So painting turned inward, and went in search of its foundations and its limits, almost like a philosopher searching for the foundations and limits of thought or experience by setting reason to interrogate reason. This search would give rise to what Danto in *The Philosophical Disenfranchisement of Art* calls "the astonishing sequence of convulsions that have defined the art history of our century."[10] The phrase "astonishing sequence

---

9   Danto, *The Philosophical Disenfranchisement of Art* (New York: Columbia University Press, 1986), 118 (see also 206).
10 *Ibid.*, xv.

of convulsions" refers to the rapid succession of varied artistic styles in painting appearing in the late nineteenth century and the twentieth century, e.g., Impressionism, Expressionism, Post-Impressionism, Cubism, Futurism, etc. At the time, the variation in styles did not seem to reveal anything like an underlying logic or a developmental order, except perhaps a pattern of indirection: each new genius sought to outdo the last by exploring the medium anew, searching for some hidden chamber of the canvas, only just glimpsed by any before. The astonishing convulsions proceeded in this manner through the first half of the twentieth century, and part of the second half, one after another, and all seemingly without end in view; until, at last, the sequence did come to an end, in 1964, and in a way no one could have quite expected, with the *Brillo Boxes*.

This end of the sequence of movements in painting, culminating in philosophical self-knowledge, is what Danto means with his justly famous thesis of the "end of art." But this concept of the "end of art," appearing in works like "The End of Art: A Philosophical Defense" and *After the End of Art*, has led to some confusion.[11] By "end" Danto never meant that art, e.g., painting, sculpture, or cinema, would somehow come to a stop. The concept of an "end" (or *telos*) is a philosophical term meaning the culmination of a series of stages of development, or the fulfilment of a trajectory in a completed condition; the classic example being the acorn that develops toward its end in the form of an oak tree. Applying that example to modern painting, if film's light and flowing images (like sunlight and water) had triggered painting (like an acorn) to unfold rapidly, then the succession of movements in modern painting (like the growth of an oak tree) would be an artistic—and largely unconsciously philosophical—search for the medium's essence, and the *Brillo Boxes* (as the completed oak tree) would be the achievement of self-knowledge that painting had sought, though could hardly have foreseen.

The *Brillo Boxes* were visually indiscernible from their "lookalikes" in the grocery store, "mere real things," as Danto would call them, but precisely this visual indiscernibility effectively raised the question of their difference to these "mere real things." If no difference could be detected by sight alone—for one is not permitted to lift and handle objects in a museum or gallery—then how would any difference be known? The mysterious exactness of the three-dimensional copies of the "mere real things," together with the confusion they

---

11   Danto, "The End of Art: A Philosophical Defense," *History and Theory*, vol. 37, no. 4, Theme Issue 37 on "Danto and His Critics: Art History, Historiography, and After the End of Art" (December 1998); and Danto, *After the End of Art: Contemporary Art and the Pale of History* (Princeton: Princeton University Press, 1997).

raised, would have been, understandably, unlike anything so many viewers, at the time, would have seen in the artworld. But these sorts of questions were not at all unknown to philosophy, questions like, "Which one of these is real, and which is the copy?" and "How exactly might one distinguish between them?" and "What discipline or sphere of thought or culture does this object inhabit anyway?" In epistemology, for example, one of the most fundamental questions regards our knowledge of the external world; in particular, whether the appearances of the world reveal an actual world, or perhaps only a representation (or image) of an actual world, possibly a dream or a vast deception; questions which then lead one to wonder whether any actual world truly exists at all (beyond what the mind may construct).

Art now posed a related problem: namely, the problem of distinguishing between one set of boxes from the grocery store, and another set of boxes that are perfect visual copies constructed by art. This problem would, in turn, raise a further question. If visual perception cannot distinguish between the two sets of boxes, then what exactly makes one set of boxes "art," and the other not art? Perhaps both are art, or perhaps neither is art? And then, why? In other words, the *Brillo Boxes* had effectively raised the fundamentally philosophical question of their own self-identity, almost like a young person growing up and becoming reflectively self-conscious, and wondering who she is, and what she is, and how she might even begin to answer these sorts of questions. Of course, she cannot begin to answer these sorts of questions except from within the sphere of philosophy, the sphere from which they naturally arise; nor could art begin to answer its own questions of self-identity, except from within philosophy. In posing questions of what they are, and whether they are art at all, and what art is—all in relation to other things with which they are identical, and which are not art—art, in the form of the *Brillo Boxes*, had, at last, come to speak the language of philosophy.

Moving pictures had spurred painting into an identity crisis, causing painting to turn inward in search of its essential nature. That inquiry took shape as a dynamic self-interrogation resulting in all the various styles and movements of modern painting. But eventually the convulsions came to an end and for the most natural reason: art had finally completed its inquiry; art had uncovered its essential nature, albeit in a strange and paradoxical way. Art had discovered its nature to be something that is and is not art; certainly something that was not, historically speaking, painting. Painting had discovered its true nature to be philosophy, and its true nature as philosophy to be historically extended. Painting could not have achieved what it achieved except by struggle of inquiry into itself, into its own foundations and limits; nor would this investigation have unfolded in the way it did unless painting had been challenged from without, by cinema. So, what painting had found, in discovering itself, was not only that it was philosophy, but also that it was an historically unfolding entity whose nature could not be separated from its development, which had proceeded by self-interrogation, which, in turn, resulted in a unique form of philosophical and historical and artistic self-consciousness. The true nature of painting, then, would be nothing other than the developmental sequence by which the acorn of the medium had unfolded dynamically to become aware of itself as philosophy, and philosophy "speaking" in a unique way, namely, in the form of exact replicas of mere real things.

Art had now passed over into the higher sphere of philosophy, having passed over, as it were, into itself, having found that it, art, had always been philosophy, only that that nature had not, before Warhol, been fully actualized. Art then found itself, in Danto's sense, always to have been on the way to knowing itself as philosophy—philosophy as a sphere whose very nature is recursive, and, indeed, the only sphere of thought whose subject matter is itself. That is what Danto saw in the *Brillo Boxes*, not a stop to art, but the whole history of modern art revealed (all at once) as a unified and developing organism, having finally unfolded (by logic of self-interrogation), to achieve its ultimate end in a unique form of philosophical self-consciousness. Danto also saw in the *Brillo Boxes*, the outlines of a philosophy of art that had already been advanced, in the nineteenth century, by German philosopher G. W. F. Hegel in his *Lectures on Fine Art*, Hegel who had already described art as an historically developing organism passing through a series of stages, until, finally, coming to end, as it "passes over into higher forms of consciousness."[12]

Danto's philosophy of art stands as one of the great achievements in contemporary aesthetics. But there are some concerns with it. As Shusterman would write in *Pragmatist Aesthetics*, Danto's philosophy of art was the first among the analytic aestheticians to define art in terms of history, and social and cultural contexts.[13] But however historical it proposed to be, as Shusterman would write, Danto's aesthetics remained too "narrow, internalistic, and rarified"—in a word, too "analytic"—compared to Dewey's no less historical yet far more wide-ranging, transactional, and socially-engaged view of art.[14] With his turn to Darwinian evolutionary naturalism, which lays at the center of all

---

12 G. W. F. Hegel, *Hegel's Aesthetics: Lectures on Fine Art*, vol. I, tr. T. M. Knox (New York: Oxford, 1975), 102.
13 Shusterman, *Pragmatist Aesthetics*, *Pragmatist Aesthetics: Living Beauty, Rethinking Art* (Oxford: Blackwell, 1992), 21–22; second edition (New York: Rowman and Littlefield, 2000), with a new introduction and an additional chapter.
14 *Ibid.*, 22.

pragmatism, Dewey retained the Hegelian insight into the historical nature of art, while separating himself from the Hegelian view of art as an entity teleologically unfolding its end according to its own internal logic—like an acorn becoming an oak tree—in favor of a view Shusterman in *Pragmatist Aesthetics* calls "the integration of art and life."[15] Recapitulating Dewey's separation from Hegel's aesthetics, Shusterman distinguishes his pragmatist aesthetics from Danto's Hegelian aesthetics with its view of art as an organism that develops within its own historically structured artworld that is not really integrated with human life in its naturally transactional relations with its environment and culture. The artworld, in Danto's aesthetics, is still a fairly self-enclosed entity; internally dynamic, to be sure, but not exactly dynamically interactional with everyday human life.

Of course, in a way, Danto's philosophy of art may seem to be not so self-enclosed; and his view of art may seem to be expansive and integrated with everyday life. After all, Danto sets pop art at the center of his philosophy of art, and, in particular, Warhol's work, which depicts "commonplace" objects, and "mere real things," like Campbell Soup cans or grocery store boxes of Brillo brand scrubbers. But "pop art" is not the same thing as "the popular arts," and philosophers who like to highlight the popular arts, such as Dewey in *Art as Experience* with his critique of Hegel,[16] and Shusterman with his Deweyan critique of Danto's Hegelian aesthetics, are careful about distinguishing "popular arts" as a legitimate field of inquiry in aesthetics, and about recognizing how a seemingly popular theme may suggest cultural openness or availableness, when, in fact, what is really happening in a work, like the *Brillo Boxes*, for example, can be something quite exclusive. So, while it's true that the *Brillo Boxes* are replicas of "mere real things," indeed, things that could hardly be more "commonplace," to use Danto's terminology, yet their place in the history of art, in general, and pop art, in particular, and their relation to society as a whole, and their philosophical brilliance, could hardly be less "commonplace." What Warhol achieved with the *Brillo Boxes* was astounding, but it was also a work about as available to all but a select few as the *Critique of Pure Reason* or the *Philosophical Investigations*.

As Shusterman writes in *Pragmatist Aesthetics*, Dewey in *Art as Experience* had a very different view of the artworld to the one found in Hegel and Danto; one no less historically dynamic or intellectually engaging, yet far more human.

---

15   *Ibid.*
16   John Dewey, *Art as Experience* (New York: Penguin, 2005), 158.

> For him the artworld was not an abstract, autonomously aesthetic notion, but something materially enmeshed in the real world and significantly structured by its socioeconomic and political factors. He saw art history as similarly conditioned by such factors, not as the essentially autonomous 'internal development' portrayed by Danto and his analytic cohorts. Most significantly, Dewey realized that not only the concepts of art and aesthetic about which we theorize, but also our very concepts of theory and philosophy are themselves structured and conditioned by the social practices and institutions which inform our lives and thought, and thus by the contingencies and struggles of history which in some way shape those structuring practices and institutions.[17]

Art is not a logically and teleologically enclosed entity unfolding its true form of self-consciousness by passing over into philosophy. Rather art is "something materially enmeshed in the real world," writes Shusterman, something organically open to social, economic, cultural, and political spheres of human life, and something, in turn, shaping those spheres through and through, and, ultimately, shaping all thought about those spheres, including art itself.

Art is everywhere. It pervades all life and society. Art shapes what Dewey calls the "live creature" from its very beginnings and throughout life. Art is there with our first words, as we behold colored shapes and hear musical sounds, with our first steps in the surrounding environment, in all interactions with the natural world, with flowers and trees and other creatures. Art finds outlet in the child's natural instincts to play and draw and color and explore, each new season and environment inviting new forms of creative interaction with the world, from sandcastles to snowmen to tree forts and all manner of games. Art shapes the development of the embodied mind with education and exercise, and guides the eyes and ears to beautiful forms of literature, music, paintings, and films. Within this development, the live creature also comes to take itself, more or less unconsciously at first, as a kind of art, practicing poise and self-control, learning style and fashion, the preparation of food, and table manners, the art of dialogue and rational inquiry, the art of taking walks, the art of writing letters and essays, and so on.

It's fair to say that the lived human body, as essentially artistic and part of a living and evolving artworld, has not been a major subject of philosophical discussion within the tradition, with a handful exceptions, e.g., Aristotle, Montaigne, Emerson, Nietzsche, James, Santayana, and Dewey. But, in

---

17   *Ibid.*

following this faint thread through the tradition, culminating in Dewey's *Art as Experience*, Shusterman would come to set the body, or "soma," at the center of his pragmatist aesthetics, and thereby to embark upon a third phase of his thought with "somaesthetics." If pragmatist aesthetics represented a break with his early analytic aesthetics, then somaesthetics would emerge more organically from within pragmatist aesthetics, even as somaesthetics reveals its own distinct outlines, especially as Shusterman traversed the boundary enclosing academic philosophy to become a performing artist.

The word "somaesthetics" is a combination of the words "soma" (lived body) and "aesthetics" (philosophy of beauty and art), which signifies a unique discipline in philosophy. As Shusterman writes in "Somaesthetics: A Disciplinary Proposal,"

> Somaesthetics can be provisionally defined as the critical, meliorative study of the experience and use of one's body as a locus of sensory-aesthetic appreciation (*aisthesis*) and creative self-fashioning. It is, therefore, also devoted to the knowledge, discourses, practices, and bodily disciplines that structure such somatic care or can improve it.[18]

After defining the project, Shusterman establishes "three fundamental dimensions" of somaesthetics: "analytic somaesthetics," "pragmatic somaesthetics," and "practical somaesthetics." The first, "analytic somaesthetics," is a "descriptive" dimension. Analytic somaesthetics describes the "nature of bodily perceptions and practices," and how these perceptions and practices "function in our knowledge and construction of reality." The second, "pragmatic somaesthetics," is a "normative" dimension. Pragmatic somaesthetics examines, explores, analyzes, and recommends for use all manner of somatic practices aiming at improving the body and aesthetic experience of the body. The third, "practical somaesthetics," is a dimension of physical practice. In practical somaesthetics one pursues the actual physical activities of somaesthetics: for example, sport, cuisine, Hatha Yoga, Zen meditation, weightlifting, and so on—although, of course, one may practice various somaesthetic practices without having studied them descriptively or normatively. Over the course of his career, Shusterman has engaged all three dimensions of somaesthetics, with thoroughgoing descriptions and critical examinations of various somaesthetic practices, as well as actual practice of these various practices, e.g., the Alexander Technique, of which John Dewey was a practitioner, and the

---

18   *Ibid.*, 267.

Feldenkrais Method in which Shusterman himself is a professionally trained practitioner.

Some may question whether the project of somaesthetics is relevant to social and political philosophy, or whether somaesthetics ends up being just as exclusive as Shusterman finds Rorty's project in self-fashioning to be. After all, the very idea of "meliorism" (improving oneself), which is central to somaesthetics, may suggest a culture of comfortable and leisured individuals pursuing a variety of practices to improve their health, well-being, beauty, and all manner of pleasurable experiences of the world; while so many others struggle under conditions of injustice. Shusterman has consistently engaged precisely these sorts of concerns about elitism regarding meliorism, and questions of obtuseness to the actual world all around us. While many areas of philosophy are uniquely suited, in their own ways, to address certain phenomena of social and political injustice, and many spheres of culture are formally organized to address real material needs and questions of power, somaesthetics also provides a uniquely important perspective and methodology for examining these phenomena. Any culture shapes, unconsciously, the physical actions of its members in innumerable ways, from how one sits or stands or holds one's head in the presence of others of lesser or greater power, to how and what and when and with whom one eats meals, to the conditioning of behaviors between men and women and people of different colors, to the volume and speed and tonal variation of voice, to how one walks or runs or even enters a room, or addresses friends or family or a classroom. In every sphere of human life, the embodied creature is always there, and always expressing at least something of its background conditioning, and expressing too whether one is self-consciously at ease with that background conditioning or perhaps somehow reacting to it and attempting to revise it. For too long philosophy has set these phenomena, in particular, and the body, in general, to the side, as if questions of mind, knowledge, being, and art, might be handled separately from the body, each somehow elevated onto a plane of pure inquiry to be examined abstractly and without recourse to everyday contingency and change that permeates all life.

But questions of social and political equality, freedom, solidarity, and order arise for all living human bodies, and one important way in which philosophy, especially in the form of somaesthetics, may explore these questions is by exploring the manner in which bodies have been shaped, and how bodies experience their worlds, and how, ultimately, melioristically, individuals may take hold of their shaping, and respond to their social, political, and cultural backgrounds, hopefully to understand themselves better by combination of study and actual somaesthetic practice. By experimenting with various somaesthetic practices, the individual may explore a variety of forms of somaesthetic experience, while simultaneously opening oneself to a more experimental way of living, which, in turn, may open the mind to different cultures and ways of life. Opening one's mind to other forms of cultural practice can also uncover other forms of practice and cultural conditioning in oneself, enabling a deeper somatic and somaesthetic form of self-consciousness, possibly also leading the individual to expand this somaesthetic self-consciousness by experimentation with alternative cultural practices, and even to liberate oneself, to the extent one can, from socially, culturally, and politically oppressive somatic practices. If the body is shaped by social, cultural, and political practices, and oppressed by many of these practices, from the overt and violent to the subtle and unconsciously mediated forms of conditioning, so too must resistance and liberation come through the body.

Shusterman has explored this project for over two decades now, carrying somaesthetics beyond the United States into Europe and Asia and South America, immersing himself in these cultures, exploring their various and unique somaesthetic practices, and engaging philosophy and the arts as they emerge in different ways. One of the most stunning of these explorations of the arts and other cultures appears with Shusterman's book, *The Adventures of the Man in Gold: Paths Between Art and Life* (2016).[19] The *Adventures* is a philosophical narrative about a figure known only as "the Man in Gold." In fact, this figure is the philosopher Richard Shusterman himself, and yet the Man in Gold is not Richard Shusterman *as* himself. Following a lifechanging event, discussed openly in the work, and an increasingly felt need to step beyond the position of philosopher of art and into art itself, Shusterman, in collaboration with his friend the Paris photographer Yann Toma, began creating a new way of doing philosophy.

The narrative of the *Adventures* begins in France at the Royaumont Abbey and records a meeting between Toma and Shusterman. If Shusterman had planned to explore the medium of photography philosophically with a photographer, and perhaps even pose for a series of shots, Toma surprised him with a golden bodysuit costume, one of two worn by Toma's parents who performed in the Paris Opera Ballet. Shusterman was understandably hesitant about, and even, at first, resistant to, the very idea of donning a golden bodysuit for a photoshoot. In general, philosophers working in aesthetics tend to be comfortable focusing on an artwork, examining it critically, and then speaking and writing about it; but actually becoming the work of art—*that* was an entirely different

---

19   Shusterman, *The Adventures of the Man in Gold: Paths Between Art and Life, A Philosophical Tale*, tr. English to French, Thomas Mondémé, with Somaflux Photography by Yann Toma (Paris: Hermann Éditeurs, 2016).

matter. Or was it? After all, Shusterman was a pragmatist philosopher devoted to the arts and the spirit of experimental creativity, and a vision of human life as a form of artistic performance. So how different could (or should) direct engagement and performance in the arts really be?

Shusterman bravely set his ego aside and stepped out of the traditional and comfortable academic role of the detached and critical philosopher, and put on the golden bodysuit—and not just for the sake of a few photographs (as a favor for a friend and to say he'd done it), only to quickly remove the thing and return to his academic persona. No, it wasn't like that at all. Shusterman took the experimental photography shoot (and the technique of "light drawing") very seriously, and did something, frankly, few if any philosophers would do. He threw himself completely into a character of his own creation, a character that had not existed except from the moment of its coming into being in that photoshoot. The character was and is somewhat strange, and not least because the character was both Shusterman and not Shusterman. Somehow, Shusterman had simultaneously created and inhabited this new golden character, and yet this golden man, as Shusterman would later write, also seemed somehow to create himself (to "give birth to himself"), and, in so doing, had also taken temporary possession of the somatic form of the living philosopher. But amidst this possession, Shusterman remained self-conscious and aware of the possession, and, as a result, was able to behold himself as another even as that other had animated his form—indeed, sufficient for Shusterman later to recall and record what occurred during those periods of his possession and animation by the Man in Gold.

Some philosophers, and perhaps even some philosophers of art, may find the very idea of becoming someone else by means of art absurd or contrived, perhaps even a clever literary trick not to be taken too seriously. But artists themselves seem always to have understood this kind of experience of possession, and to have found within this experience a powerful channel of creativity; the experience is one of becoming another, temporarily, of entering a state of mind in which the art itself seems to take over and direct the living artist's hand. Stage actors and dancers, for example, will recognize this experience of becoming another, when one inhabits the role of a character, and yet also feels that the character has somehow inhabited the actor or dancer, even taken possession of the individual on stage or in the film, as if the actor were, for a time, little more than a vehicle for Oedipus or Jocasta or Hamlet or Cleopatra, and yet capable of beholding oneself as an actor and a character at the same time.

Writers throughout history have also described experiences of possession and even presented themselves as conduits or vehicles of language. Homer, for example, begins the *Iliad* by declaring himself a medium of the Muse: "Sing, goddess, the anger of Peleus' son Achilleus and its devastation."[20] Homer begins the *Odyssey* in the same way: "Tell me, Muse, of the man of many ways, who was driven far journeys, after he had sacked Troy's sacred citadel."[21] Plato was astounded by this phenomenon and devoted an entire dialogue, the *Ion*, to the experience of possession of poets like Homer and rhapsodes like Ion, and the kind of genius that arises from these forms of possession, with its power sufficient to overwhelm thousands of listeners and to shape the very thought of cultures. In fact, Socrates in the *Ion* even claims of the *Iliad* and the *Odyssey* that "these beautiful poems are not human, not even *from* human beings, but are divine and from gods," and, further, that the supreme "poets are nothing but representatives of the gods, possessed by whoever possesses them."[22] Ralph Waldo Emerson in his essay "Beauty" (in *The Conduct of Life*) similarly wrote of the experience of possession: "The ancients believed that a genius or dæmon took possession at birth of each mortal, to guide him; that these genii were sometimes seen as a flame of fire partly immersed in the bodies which they governed." If at the height of romanticism the realm of spirits had already (and by then, some time ago) given ground to nature—for as Emerson writes of a change in terminology, "we give it our own names"—still the old stories would illuminate much of a certain kind of experience, and one which, for Emerson as for Plato, had shaped history through and through.[23]

To clarify this strange and unique kind of aesthetic experience (much as we can), possession does not appear to be a state of mind whereby the artist has somehow temporarily "left his mind," so to speak, in order to make room for another inhabitant (as if such a thing were possible anyway). And yet an alternate state of mind, and one apparently quite different to what we typically experience as waking self-consciousness, appears to be essential to the work of many great artists. Perhaps the aesthetic experience of artistic creativity in possession is something comparable to a waking dream or a trance, like that in which Samuel Taylor Coleridge composed *Kubla Kahn: or, A Vision in a Dream* (1816). Similar states of mind may also be known to musicians, and perhaps especially virtuosos in piano or violin or guitar, in which the artist somehow

---

20 Homer, *The Iliad of Homer*, tr. Richmond Lattimore (Chicago: University of Chicago, 1951), Bk. I, 59.
21 Homer, *The Odyssey of Homer*, tr. Richmond Lattimore (New York: HarperPerennial, 1991), Bk. I, 27.
22 Plato, *Ion*, tr. Paul Woodruff, in *Plato: Complete Works*, ed. John M. Cooper (Indianapolis: Hackett, 1997), 534b–e, 942.
23 Ralph Waldo Emerson, "Beauty," in *The Conduct of Life*, ed. Joseph Slater, Douglas Emory Wilson, with an Historical Introduction by Barbara Packer, vol. VI of *The Collected Works of Ralph Waldo Emerson* (Cambridge: Harvard University Press, 2003), 153.

becomes "one" with the music she is also creating, and feels as if the music were somehow creating itself through her, as if she were also an instrument. It is this kind of state of mind that seems to appear in the *Adventures*, one in which a self-conscious philosopher, Shusterman, is aware of his possession by the equally self-conscious Man in Gold, who is also a philosopher; a possession which, as Shusterman himself points out, is not at all easy to describe; nor is the strangely speechless Man in Gold himself. Perhaps, in the end, the nature of the Man in Gold simply cannot be known, any more than the nature of artistic possession can ever be fully understood. But among those who would explore these questions, and attempt their answers, few are so well-suited as the writers collected here, art critics and philosophers of art who know Shusterman well, and who have engaged his pragmatist aesthetics and somaesthetics over the years with rich aesthetic sensitivity and depth of focus.

• • •

Part 1 begins with Stefán Snævarr's critique of Shusterman's pragmatist and non-essentialist view of the self. According to Snævarr, Shusterman fails to develop anything approaching a sufficiently ontological view of the self; a problem which may, however, be solved from within pragmatist aesthetics beginning with Shusterman's otherwise correct view of the aesthetic self. By contrast to this critical view of an ontology-less philosophy, Alexander Kremer argues that Shusterman sets an ontologically naturalistic and dynamic view of the "soma" right at the center of his pragmatism, and, in the process, returns philosophy to the various practices in the arts of living common to ancient Greek and Chinese philosophy such as Confucianism. These arts of living, as they appear in the ancient world, in the East and the West, and as Shusterman describes them, reveal unique ethical and aesthetic perspectives of the body and its relation to society, as well as unique relations to political power. As Leszek Koczanowicz writes in his chapter, Shusterman's project of somaesthetics is a powerful philosophical framework for understanding how individual and social somatic resistance to oppressive power in everyday life can operate as vehicles of emancipation.

These themes of resistance and liberation from oppression have long been central to Shusterman's thought, appearing in his social and political writings, but also in his writings on hip hop music and culture. As Max Ryynänen demonstrates, while early scholarly debates focused on the cultural and political import of rap music, Shusterman also focused on the aesthetics of hip hop as a unique poetic and musical art form, situating rap within the broader movements of postmodernism and philosophy as a way of life, while showing how its aesthetics and technologies of creation empower its social and cultural politics. For example, hip hop's artistic techniques of technological recycling and appropriation, reveal its postmodern philosophical underpinnings expressive of early stages of a soon-to-be burgeoning computer-oriented and ultimately digital popular culture that would set these artistic practices to work everywhere and throughout the arts. Taking a less sympathetic approach, Tonino Griffero finds Shusterman's pragmatism and somaesthetics, with its melioristic vision of self-development of the body and experience, to be misguided, and favors a "pathic-atmospherological aesthetics" by which the individual is phenomenologically and aesthetically passive to what surrounds her in the form of aesthetic "atmospheres." By contrast to Griffero's critical opposition, Dorota Koczanowicz expands the range of somaesthetics, within the context of food studies, by building on Shusterman's prior work in the field in "Somaesthetics and the Fine Art of Eating."[24] With its focus on the body, somaesthetics naturally (and even inevitably) raises questions regarding the arts of cuisine, food preparation, dining, ingestion, health, and taste; and Koczanowicz explores these questions with rich studies of gustatory art, the complexity of taste, eating as performance art, and the role of cultural and historical understanding in the top restaurants.

Part 2 of the volume is devoted to *The Adventures of the Man in Gold*. Here Abrams explores the concept of "transfiguration" in Shusterman's *Adventures*, in relation to Danto's *Transfiguration of the Commonplace*, and Emerson's "Literary Ethics," before turning to the relation between the Man in Gold and Philip K. Dick's novella *The Golden Man*, two deeply philosophical science fiction stories about speechless golden men each of whom is part-photography. If Abrams finds the *Adventures* to be a work of science fiction, then Diane Richard-Allerdyce finds it to be a joyous celebration of paradox, impermanence, vulnerability, and affective freedom attained in embrace of human limits and loss. According to Richard-Allerdyce, the Man in Gold is presented as a fictional character on temporary loan to the social self; and one from which arises joy in Jacques Lacan's sense of *jouissance*, joy in embodied wisdom achieved by what Shusterman elsewhere calls "thinking through the body." Yvonne Bezrucka similarly explores the nature of subjectivity in the *Adventures*, and finds not only Shusterman to be possessed by the Man in Gold, but the Man in Gold also capable of being inhabited by spectators who unexpectedly encounter him and treat him as a form on which they project their own beliefs and prejudices. As he engages in artistic performances, the Man in Gold invariably provokes the witnessing viewers to react in ways that express their own

---

24   Shusterman, "Somaesthetics and the Fine Art of Eating," in *Body Aesthetics*, ed. Sherri Irvin (New York: Oxford University Press, 2016), 261–280.

values and imaginative propensities or biases. Art historian and theorist Else Marie Bukdahl has seen several of these improvisational performances and her chapter examines in detail Shusterman's transformation from a philosopher of art who engages with the arts into an actively engaged practitioner of performance art. A friend to both Shusterman and the Man in Gold, Bukdahl is also a character in the *Adventures*, and here relates their many engagements with the Danish sculptors Claus Ørntoft and Marit Benthe Norheim, who also appear in the *Adventures* as themselves, and as their mythical counterparts in the Man in Gold's vision. Bukdahl's chapter includes explanatory texts by these same artists whose works also form a key part of the climax of the tale of the Man in Gold.

The *Adventures* takes place in France, Florida, Colombia, and Denmark, and is written with two running columns, one in English and the other French, each side translating the other; but Chinese philosophy and culture are also essential to the work as a whole, for example, in discussions of the philosophy of the Chinese sage Laozi; and, in fact, one of the main characters of the work is the magical glowing sculpture known as Wanmei, whose name in Chinese means "perfection." By the time of the publication of the *Adventures*, Shusterman's main works had all been translated into Chinese, and his philosophy has been widely studied in China; but a translation of the *Adventures*, at the time, was still needed. Intrigued by the work, Yang Lu took on the job of translating the *Adventures* into Chinese, which, in turn, led to its warm reception in China. In his chapter for this volume, Yang Lu argues that the *Adventures* exemplifies Shusterman's somaesthetic practice (in a way that is very different from his practical body consciousness workshops). Besides being somaesthetics in action, the Man in Gold's *Adventures* exemplifies Shusterman's pragmatist practice, more generally, as a form of doing philosophy in a different and experimental way, namely, through imaginative literature and by combining philosophical themes with a fairytale sense of innocence and adventure. In the final chapter on the Man in Gold, Abrams examines Yann Toma's film of the Man in Gold entitled *Walk the Golden Night* as a detective mystery that investigates itself by raising questions of its own philosophical self-consciousness, in the tradition of Andy Warhol's *Empire* (1964).

Part 3 concludes the volume with two chapters, one with Shusterman's "Remarks" on the chapters preceding, and the other an interview of Shusterman by Yanping Gao. Conducted at a distance during the Coronavirus Pandemic (2020), the two discuss key aspects of Shusterman's pragmatist philosophy and somaesthetics (such as meliorism, soma, affect, proprioception, disability), and the reception of his work in China.

PART 1
Pragmatism and Somaesthetics

∴

CHAPTER 1

Shusterman's Pragmatist Philosophy

Stefán Snævarr

> The light and shade, the curious sense of body and identity.
> WALT WHITMAN, *Leaves of Grass*[1]

∴

1   The Soma and Somatism

Richard Shusterman has for decades been a daring philosophical maverick, challenging dogmatic assumptions concerning aesthetics and embodiment. It is high time we celebrate his achievements, albeit in a critical fashion. Beginning with an outline of Shusterman's thinking concerning the body and the self, I shall discuss his relationship with the thought of Maurice Merleau-Ponty's philosophy, and Shusterman's relationship with his fellow pragmatist John Dewey on the self, followed by a discussion of Shusterman's conception of the aesthetic self. Finally, I shall criticize some of Shusterman's ideas, while, at the same time, suggesting how his philosophy may be defended against such criticisms, and how his view of the aesthetic self may be enhanced.

I shall call Shusterman, Merleau-Ponty, Dewey, and others, "somatists." A somatist is one who thinks that the sentient body is primordial to consciousness and constitutes the ground of our coping with, and cognition of, the world. While many materialists tend to focus on the inside of the body, and especially on the brain and the nervous system, somatists tend to be more interested in the outside of the body, not least the limbs, and the way in which the sentient body as a whole interacts with its environment. "I sing the body electric,"[2] writes the American poet Walt Whitman in *Leaves of Grass*, anticipating the somatists' celebration of corpo-reality. Writing in this same tradition, Shusterman in *Body Consciousness: A Philosophy of Mindfulness and*

---

1   Walt Whitman, *Leaves of Grass*, vol. 1 of 3 (New York: Doubleday, 1920), 260.
2   *Ibid.*, 113.

Somaesthetics defines his philosophical project of "somaesthetics" as "the critical meliorative study of one's experience and use of one's body as a locus of sensory-aesthetic appreciation and creative self-fashioning."[3] While such a definition may seem limited to aesthetics, it is important to bear in mind that somaesthetics has a normative side, and aims at improving bodily experience and bodily existence.

To understand this project, we must start by taking a look at one of the most important concepts in Shusterman's thinking, the "soma," roughly "the body." According to Shusterman in "Soma, Self and Society: Somaesthetics as Pragmatist Meliorism," the "soma" is not merely the physical body but "the living sentient, intentional body that involves mental, social and cultural dimensions.'"[4] The soma is not merely an object of consciousness, but a lived conscious subjectivity displaying multiple levels of consciousness and unconsciousness. The soma includes both body and mind because it is capable of mental embodied acts, such as intentional physical movement, discriminating perception, explicit awareness, and self-monitoring. The soma minds and reacts to various events in its environment while being capable of minding itself. Shusterman thinks that it is not very fruitful to use the word "mind" as a noun denoting a substance, but rather as a verb denoting a process or characteristic: "The body expresses the ambiguity of human being as both subjective sensibility that experiences the world and as an object perceived in that world."[5]

Further, Shusterman claims that our somas are essentially shaped by culture as well as by nature. A fetus, for example, can be shaped by cultural factors, becoming limited in abilities if the low social status of the mother means that she starves during the pregnancy. Habits are created by culture and are essentially embodied. They govern not only most of our motor actions, but also most of our processes of thinking. The social shaping of the soma makes it a key site for instilling obedience to norms; obedience itself being a kind of habit.[6]

---

3   Shusterman, *Body Consciousness: A Philosophy of Mindfulness and Somaesthetics* (Cambridge: Cambridge University Press, 2008), 19.
4   Shusterman, "Soma, Self and Society: Somaesthetics as Pragmatist Meliorism," *Metaphilosophy*, vol. 42, no. 3 (April 2011), 315. See also Shusterman, *Body Consciousness*, 1.
5   Shusterman, *Body Consciousness*, 3.
6   For an analysis of habits as central to human life, see Pierre Bourdieu, "Physical Space, Social Space, and Habitus," in *Rapport 1, Institutt for sosiologi og samfunnsgeografi* (Universitetet i Oslo, 1996), 7–22. Habitus refers to the generative principles of given practices, for example, what a typical worker eats and how he eats it. See also Shusterman, *Thinking through the Body: Essays in Somaesthetics* (Cambridge: Cambridge University Press, 2012), 53–54. As we later shall see, John Dewey's theory of habits is also important to Shusterman's somaesthetics.

Shusterman does not situate his thinking concerning the soma within any grand metaphysical or ontological theory. He is critical of metaphysics on grounds that it is largely superfluous because it is suited mainly to examining a world of stable and fixed essences; and, according to Shusterman in "Pragmatism and Culture: Margolis and Rorty," we have no reason to think the world contains any essences at all.[7] Practices and language games speak for themselves, and there is no need to find any deeper metaphysical underpinning for them. After all, we can only do metaphysics by taking part in some linguistic practices, but those practices would then in their turn need metaphysical underpinning.[8] Moreover, these linguistic practices are in a state of flux; and inventing new ways of speaking and acting are some of the pragmatist practices engaged by Shusterman himself, e.g., "somaesthetics." In fact, it seems plausible that Shusterman's theory about the soma is an attempt at inventing a new way of speaking about the body and the mind, and perhaps also an attempt at a description of the concepts of the body and mind as they actually function in our everyday language games, far removed from metaphysical speculation.

2 *Körper* and *Leib*

The concept of soma owes a lot to the phenomenologists Edmund Husserl and Maurice Merleau-Ponty[9] (and as we shall see later, Husserl's student Helmuth Plessner). In the view of the French phenomenologist, and arch-somatist, we *are* our bodies. But the body does not entirely belong to the realm of *res extensa*. It is by necessity shot through with subjectivity, and subjectivity is suffused with somatic moments. Merleau-Ponty tries to show this mutuality between body and subjectivity with the aid of the following example: I try to find out how hard a tennis ball is by squeezing it with my right hand. Then I use my left hand to study the contraction of the muscles in the right hand, which

---

7 Shusterman, *Surface and Depth: Dialectics of Criticism and Culture* (Ithaca: Cornell University Press, 2002), 191–207.
8 One may wonder whether looking for such metaphysical underpinnings leads to an infinite regress. If every underpinning is a part of a linguistic practice, which needs a metaphysical underpinning, which is a part of yet another linguistic practice, and so on, there appears to be no end view. In fact, Shusterman here is criticizing Joseph Margolis's pragmatist metaphysics, and not necessarily metaphysics in general.
9 For a statement of his view of Merleau-Ponty's philosophy of the body, see Shusterman's "The Silent, Limping Body of Philosophy: Somatic Attention Deficit in Merleau-Ponty," in *Body Consciousness*, 49–76.

is still squeezing the ball. In this case, the right hand is simultaneously the subject and the object of experience. These "two" right hands are fundamentally different. The one (the object) is simply a collection of bones, muscles and sinews; the other (the subject) is in some sense neither visible nor touchable. The subject one is that which constitutes the relationship to objects in general. The body is a subject before it becomes an object for us. The body is that which constitutes our relations to objects. To be sure, the bodily subject cannot exist without the body *qua* material object. However, at the same time, the former constitutes the latter *qua* object of knowledge; we cannot know that we have a material body unless we have a body *qua* subject.

We can use our left hand to touch the right hand and thereby the right hand feels the touch while the left one is the object of this touch. But the left hand feels the touch of the right hand, which means that the object of the touch is also a site of subjectivity, in stark contrast to what ordinary objects of touch are. This means that we relate to our bodies in a different way than to other objects. More precisely, our body is simultaneously an object and a subject for us. Furthermore, we cannot prove that our feeling really is in the brain or the mind, what is given is the feeling in the hands. So if subjectivity is an irreducible part of who we are, then our body is an irreducible part of us, being the site of subjectivity (but that does not mean that we know how subjectivity is situated in it, or whether it makes sense to talk about it being situated in anything).

Merleau-Ponty thinks that emotions are not only something subjectively felt, but that they have intentional objects and are something corporeal; my angry gestures and red face are part of my anger just as are angry thoughts. My anger is not only in my head but in my face.[10] For Merleau-Ponty, the body is far from an ordinary material object. It has almost a transcendental function: we can only see things from a point of view, and the body (a material body in space and time) provides these points of view, and therefore the conditions for the possibility of seeing. Something similar holds for the other senses as well. In fact, corpo-reality provides the conditions for the possibility of perception in general: the body is the horizon for all possible experiences.

This meaningful and transcendental side of the body is the "*le corps proper*" (the proper body), in contrast to the anatomical "*le corps objective ou reel*" (the objective or real body), a distinction that originates in Husserl's discrimination

---

10   Ludwig Wittgenstein's view is not dissimilar: feeling, in his view, is not only something subjectively experienced but something behavioral as well. Pain-behavior is part of what pain really is. See, for example, Wittgenstein's *Philosophical Investigations*, tr. G. E. M. Anscombe (Oxford: Blackwell, 1958), §244, 89.

between the *Leib* (the living, feeling body) and *Körper* (the anatomical body).[11] Even though our *Körper* has rather clear boundaries, writes Merleau-Ponty, the same does not hold for the *Leib*. When a blind person uses his cane to orient himself in the world, the cane is not an object that exists between him and the world. It is a sort of sense organ, an extension of the blind man's *Leib*. Merleau-Ponty states as follows: "The blind man's stick has ceased to be an object for him, and is no longer perceived for itself; its point has become an area of sensitivity, extending the scope and active radius of touch, and providing a parallel to sight."[12]

Merleau-Ponty rejects both subjectivism and materialism concerning consciousness; it is neither an immaterial substance nor part of the brain, but something that exists at the meeting-point between the *Leib* and the world. It is a part of our practices. The *Leib* is intentional and consciousness permeates it and vice versa. When I touch things, my consciousness is in my fingers. My consciousness is part of my active relationship with the world; in fact, a practical "I can" is even deeper than the Cartesian "I think." This means that consciousness is a part of our practices. The actions of the *Leib* and its practical relations with the world constitute our thoughts. This constitution is not performed by any disembodied consciousness. Being conscious is being open to the world.

Knowing means doing, the activities of the *Leib* and its understanding of the world cannot be separated. Most of our knowledge, for Merleau-Ponty, is tacit knowledge, know-how. My fingers know how to type even though I cannot explain how they know their way about the keyboard of my computer: the know-how resides *in* the fingers. Similarly, when solving a problem, my whole *Leib qua* intentional body is focused on it, thrown towards it, but only partly consciously. My corpo-real competence plays a crucial role; an experienced carpenter sees, or, more precisely, feels diverse possibilities, without much conscious reflection. In contrast to a person without much experience (or tacit knowledge) in carpentry, she would hardly be able to discover these possibilities.

Far from a mere machine, the body is something suffused with subjectivity and intentionality, and subjectivity and intentionality have a lived corporeality. Meaning has its roots in our bodily gestures, the gestures of the *Leib*, and, in its turn, meaning takes part in constituting the *Leib*; and the *Leib* and

---

11 Edmund Husserl, *Zur Phänomenologie der Intersubjektivität: Zweiter Teil 1921–1928*, ed. Iso Kern (The Hague: Martinus Nijhoff, 1973), 3–6.
12 Maurice Merleau-Ponty, *Phenomenology of Perception*, tr. Colin Smith (New York: Routledge, 2002), 165.

the self are interwoven.¹³ Moreover, Merleau-Ponty's thinking about the body has an aesthetic side: the unity of the body's diverse parts is like the unity of an artwork; in a similar fashion the *Leib* is aesthetically unified. And all our corporeal actions, our emotions and perceptions are like artworks.¹⁴ If he was a materialist, then he could be called "an aesthetic materialist."

Shusterman certainly does not agree with everything in Merleau-Ponty's thinking. For example, Shusterman criticizes Merleau-Ponty for thinking that somatic sensations are strictly separated from conscious thinking. In Shusterman's view, there are modes of somatic sensation, which may be called " 'lived conscious reflection,' that is, concrete but representational and reflective body consciousness."¹⁵ Such a representational and reflective somatic consciousness can help us correct bad bodily habits. For example, if one unconsciously acquires the habit of unhealthy postures, then becoming conscious of them can improve one's health. Feeling pain is an example of somatic awareness and paying attention even to vaguely felt pain can help us detect injuries and prompt a search for remedies.¹⁶

Now, one might ask how Shusterman appropriates the *Leib/Körper* distinction. The answer is that Shusterman maintains that the concept of soma extends over both *Leib* and *Körper*.¹⁷ Like Plessner, Shusterman in "Soma and Psyche" regards the *Leib* as "an aspect or form of behavior rather than a thing. It is the form of lived, experiential behavior that is differently lived and interpreted in the variety of cultures in which it is expressed."¹⁸ Furthermore, Shusterman apparently agrees with Plessner that the "the *Körper/Leib* distinction is clearly not a primordial, permanent ontological duality but, rather, a pragmatically functioning distinction in the practical behavior of persons."¹⁹

There is time for every purpose under the heavens, says the Good Book. Shusterman seems to think (like Plessner) that there are situations where we are first and foremost our *Leib*, in a spontaneous, unreflecting manner. Moreover, there are other situations where we are mainly beings who have a *Körper*, because we are reflecting on it, perhaps because of some somatic

---

13 As far as I know, Merleau-Ponty never discusses the relationship between *Leib* and self, but this relationship would appear to follow from his thought.
14 Merleau-Ponty, *Phénoménologie de la Perception* (Paris: Gallimard, 1945), 184–191.
15 Shusterman, *Body Consciousness*, 63.
16 Shusterman, *Thinking through the Body*, 40.
17 Ibid., 17.
18 Shusterman, "Soma and Psyche," *The Journal of Speculative Philosophy*, vol. 24, no. 3 (2010), 210.
19 Ibid., 211.

malfunction. Therefore, it depends on practical circumstances whether the *Leib* or the *Körper* is of greatest importance to us.

Now it would be tempting to think of the self as a supervising entity, which regulates the transitions between spontaneous somatic awareness and reflective body consciousness. No, says Shusterman, the soma can regulate them itself through habits and skills; the soma does not need the self to the job. This means that Shusterman does not equate the self with the soma. As Shusterman writes in "Soma and Psyche,"

> If being a soma implies both spontaneous *Leib* consciousness and explicit awareness of the body as object, then being a self implies still more: not only consciousness of differing from other selves but also an ability to sustain a mental narrative of the continuity and development of oneself and one's relation to other selves (for instance, in terms of one's different roles as self) and an ability to act to sustain that continuity and regulate those relations.[20]

At the same time, the self is not the same as person. Personhood has to do with acquiring certain sociocultural statuses within sociocultural worlds. A human self can be denied these statuses by those who have the power to confer them upon others.

3   The Body-Mind

In addition to Husserl and Merleau-Ponty, the pragmatist and somatist John Dewey, with his theory of the body-mind, has also been an important influence on the development of Shusterman's somaesthetics.[21] In Dewey's philosophy, body and mind are intertwined and must be regarded as an integral whole. More precisely, body and mind form a unity in action. As a pragmatist, Dewey thinks it is fruitful to study phenomena as parts of actions. Rather than an interaction between body and mind, we have a transactional whole of body-mind. As Whitman writes in *Leaves of Grass*, "I have said that the soul is not more than the body. / And I have said that the body is not more than the soul."[22]

---

20   Ibid., 220.
21   John Dewey, "Anniversary Discourse: Body and Mind," *Bulletin of the New York Academy of Medicine*, vol. IV, no. 1 (January 1928), 3–19. See also Shusterman, *Body Consciousness*, 180–216.
22   Whitman, *Leaves of Grass*, 105.

In order to vindicate the theory of the transactional whole, Shusterman and Dewey point out that actions are always both mental and bodily. Take, for example, the act of eating and drinking. Though usually classified as merely physical, eating and drinking are permeated with social cognitive, aesthetic, and even spiritual meaning. Moods and thoughts affect eating, and eating, in turn, influences our moods and thoughts.

Dewey maintains that we will see how body and mind are interwoven if we scrutinize the idea of a free will. It does not make sense to think of a free will as being of a completely mental nature, existing entirely outside the realm of causal connections and matter. If a choice between hot or cold drink meant a choice wholly unconditioned by material factors, then that choice would require ignoring one's established preferences habits, desires, and so on. Such freedom of choice would only be freedom of indifference. Willing cannot be disembodied because it requires some sense of deploying available means of affordance of the environmental context of action. Voluntary action is not a product of isolated moments of purely mental decision, but relies on the habits of feeling, thinking, acting, and desiring, which makes us the selves we are. Unreflective habits spontaneously perform our will. Habits are demands for certain kinds of activity and habits constitute the self, in Dewey's view.

Shusterman adds that the research conducted by Benjamin Libet points in the direction of our motor actions being dependent on neurological events, which take place about 350 milliseconds before our conscious awareness of deciding to make a movement. Libet does not, however, deny that free will is a possibility. We have an inhibitory ability to "veto" the act between its conscious awareness and actual implementation.[23] Thus, bodily processes and conscious awareness are closely interwoven, and the bodily processes are preconditions for whatever free will we possess.[24]

Dewey did not regard the psychophysical as a special substance that is either radically different from the physical, or an addition of something psychic that is merged with the physical. Instead, the psychophysical emerges as a more complex level of organization of physical materials and energies through

---

23 Benjamin Libet, "Do We Have Free Will?" *Journal of Consciousness Studies*, vol. 6, no. 8–9 (1999), 47–57. See also Shusterman, *Thinking through the Body*, 63–64.
24 Dewey's and Shusterman's conception of the interaction between the will, material processes, and circumstances seem related to Paul Ricœur's theory of how involuntary processes and circumstances make voluntary actions possible. See, for example, Ricœur's "The Unity of the Voluntary and the Involuntary as a Limiting Idea," tr. Daniel O'Connor, in *The Philosophy of Paul Ricœur: An Anthology of His Work*, ed. Charles E. Reagan and David Stewart (Boston: Beacon Press, 1978), 3–19.

which the organism generates purposive efforts to achieve the satisfaction of its survival needs. The mind is a still higher level of organization that emerges from psychophysical experience, but only when language comes into play. Just as the mind is not opposed to the human body, but rather an emergent expression of it. Therefore, culture is not a contrast to nature, but rather its fulfilment and reshaping.

Most important for Shusterman is the fact that Dewey sees the body-mind less as ontologically given than a desired harmonious goal we should strive to attain. This suits the normative part of Shusterman's somaesthetics just fine. In addition, he emphasizes the pragmatic nature of the body-mind theory. It stresses the essential unity of body and mind, writes Shusterman in *Thinking through the Body*, while leaving "room for pragmatically distinguishing between mental and physical aspects of behavior and for the project of increasing their experiential unity."[25]

Body-mind and the *Leib* are obviously closely related, and Shusterman uses a similar pragmatic approach to both.

4 The Aesthetic Self

While suspicious of the idea of the self as a "substance," a thing-like self, Shusterman thinks that the elements that make up the self can be brought into a dynamic, developing unity of tension.[26] Like Merleau-Ponty, Shusterman thinks of the self as loosely unified. This loose unification consists in a unity of differences, which has aesthetic potentials, given that beauty is unity in variety.[27] The means for unification is narration; like so many other contemporary thinkers, Shusterman maintains that self-constitution requires self-narrative. It is not sufficient to define a self in terms of its actions because an action is without meaning unless it is seen as embedded in a narrative context. At the same time, the self is underdetermined by narratives: "For any open series of narrative events, given an indeterminate future in terms of which these events can be interpreted and also given the future revisability of past narrative interpretations, there will always be more than one narrative that can fit the facts of the individual."[28] Shusterman's analysis of narrative here raises the possibility

---

25 Shusterman, *Thinking through the Body*, 27.
26 *Ibid.*, 211–212.
27 Shusterman, *Pragmatist Aesthetics: Living Beauty, Rethinking Art* (Lanham: Rowman & Littlefield, 1992), 252–254.
28 Shusterman, *Practicing Philosophy: Pragmatism and the Philosophical Life* (New York: Routledge, 1997), 184.

of an individual having multiple and even multicultural selves. The analysis also raises the possibility of a personal way of philosophizing about the self: "If we help determine who we are by the stories we tell of ourselves, then one is surely entitled to theorize issues of the self in one's own voice and from one's own experience."[29] Thus, the concept of narrative self can be embedded in a kind of personal philosophy, a way of philosophizing in the first person singular. In fact, Shusterman philosophizes about his own narrative self. He tells the story of the complexities of his own multicultural but mainly Jewish identity, stressing that this identity can be embedded in various equally valid stories.[30]

As a poetically-minded pragmatist Shusterman in his book *The Adventures of the Man in Gold* also expresses his view of the self in a literary narrative about himself performing in gold costume as "the Man in Gold." In *The Adventures of the Man in Gold* the boundaries between Shusterman himself and this character of the Man in Gold blur.[31] The Man in Gold is Shusterman's *doppelgänger* (or "other"), and, by implication, Shusterman himself is both the golden man, and, at the same time, someone entirely different.[32]

It is important to bear in mind that Shusterman's somaesthetics is normative, aesthetic, and melioristic: we should not focus one-sidedly on understanding what the self is, but also improve our selves, for instance, by making them center around the ideals of harmony, order, and grace.[33] Since the self is embodied, one of the main roads to its improvement is the use of such somatic techniques as the Feldenkrais Method and various kinds of meditation.[34] Striving for this kind of improvement is at the heart of Shusterman's somaesthetics.

In addition to Dewey, Merleau-Ponty, and Moshe Feldenkrais, Michel Foucault has also inspired Shusterman's normative view of the soma and the self. In his early works, Foucault tended to write as if human beings were

---

29　*Ibid.*, 182.
30　*Ibid.*, 179–195. On multiculturalism and identity, see Shusterman's *Performing Live: Aesthetic Alternatives for the Ends of Art* (Ithaca: Cornell University Press, 2000), 182–200.
31　Shusterman, *The Adventures of the Man in Gold: Paths Between Art and Life* (Paris: Éditions Hermann, 2016).
32　For an illuminating analysis of Shusterman's *Adventures of the Man in Gold*, see Catherine F. Botha's "Rethinking the Ego/Reconceptualizing Philosophy: Shusterman's 'Man in Gold,'" *Pragmatism Today*, vol. 8, no. 2 (2017), 80–87.
33　See Botha, "Rethinking the Ego/Reconceptualizing Philosophy," 83. In the text quoted by Botha, Shusterman is talking about aesthetic life. But it makes sense to reconstruct his implicit view of the self this way, lives are led by selves whether aesthetically or not. See also Shusterman, "Postmodernist Aestheticism: A New Moral Philosophy?" *Theory, Culture & Society* 5 (1988), 348; and Shusterman, *Pragmatist Aesthetics*, 236–261.
34　See Shusterman, *Thinking through the Body*, 25–46.

forever incarcerated in the prison houses of language and power. As Foucault writes, "The individual is the product of power."[35] Furthermore, according to Foucault, "The soul is an effect and instrument of political anatomy; the soul is the prison of the body."[36] For Foucault, a subject is created through subjection.[37] It and/or the individual is something that was created in the course of human history and might very well disappear again.[38] It exists in an intersubjective way, interwoven with others.[39] Therefore, it is not unreal, however fleetingly it might exist.[40] It is not dead but decentered; the unity of the self is an illusion. It only appears on the surface as being unified; deep down it is fragmented.

However, in his later writings Foucault modified his view and put forth an aesthetic theory of the self. To be sure, the self is fragmented, but it can bounce back and refashion itself (without any aid of rules), as a modernist work of art, celebrating its fragmented and quasi-illusory character in the process. This aesthetic view of the self was inspired by Nietzsche, who thought of the self as a kind of artwork that each individual could create, a harmonious whole like a classical work of art. As Nietzsche writes in *The Gay Science*, "*wir aber wollen die Dichter unseres Lebens sein*" ("but we want to become the poets of our lives").[41] In some contrast to Nietzsche's view here, however, Foucault's own poem was a modernist one; our selves can become modernistic artworks.[42] The modernist part means that there are no rules for this artistic creation of oneself. Refashioning is only possible because the individual is already

---

35 Michel Foucault, "Preface" to Gilles Deleuze and Félix Guattari, *Anti-Oedipus*, tr. Robert Hurley, Mark Seem, and Helen R. Lane (Minneapolis: University of Minnesota Press, 1983), xiv.
36 Foucault, *Discipline and Punish: The Birth of the Prison*, tr. Alan Sheridan (Harmondsworth: Peregrine, 1986), 30.
37 This theme appears in many places in Foucault's writing; see, for example, "Le sujet et le pouvoir," *Dits et écrits 1954–1988, Tome II: 1976–1988* (Paris: Quarto Gallimard, 1994), 1041–1062.
38 Foucault, *The Order of Things*, tr. Alan Sheridan-Smith (New York: Vintage Books, 1973), 387. Here Foucault talks about the possible disappearance of man, but seems to be thinking about the individual subject or self.
39 Foucault, *The Order of Things*, 351.
40 Friedrich Nietzsche, *Die Fröhliche Wissenschaft* ("*La gaya scienza*"), *Das Hauptwerk II* (Munich, 1990), IV, §29, 523. See also Roger Alan Deacon, *Fabricating Foucault: Rationalizing the Management of Individuals* (Milwaukee: Marquette University Press, 2003), 239.
41 My translation.
42 Foucault, "On the Genealogy of Ethics: An Overview of a Work in Progress," in *The Foucault Reader*, ed. Paul Rabinow (Harmondsworth: Penguin Books, 1984), 350–351.

fragmentary, the fragments can be put together in new ways, while some new fragments are added.

But Shusterman criticizes Foucault for one-sidedly advocating aesthetic self-creation as a total innovation, something radically different from that which is ordinary, something spectacular and dazzling like a daring avant-garde artwork. Unfortunately, as Shusterman points out in *Practicing Philosophy*, Foucault "was unable to recognize the possibility of a popular aesthetics of simplicity that can be beautiful without being dazzling and radically original."[43] Shusterman adds that Foucault did not give any argument in favor of the contention that a popular aesthetic was impossible or inadequate for the purposes of self-creation.

Despite these differences, Shusterman and Foucault share an aesthetic view of the body and the self, and a normative view of them, regarding each as intertwined and shaped by cultural and social forces. The self and body have aesthetic potentials which can be realized with the aid of somatic training and meditation.[44]

To summarize the reconstruction of Shusterman's more or less implicit theory of the self, so far, the self is: (a) a function of the soma, perhaps more the *Leib* than the *Körper*; (b) conscious of its differing from other selves; (c) capable of sustaining a mental narrative of its own continuity and relations to other selves; (d) everchanging and has unclear boundaries with its *Körper*, other selves, society, and its general environment; (e) in some ways the sum of its habits; (f) essentially social in virtue of being a function of the soma, which is culturally embedded; (g) loosely unified, mainly through narratives; (h) without any ultimately "correct" narrative; while several narratives for one self may be equally correct, or incorrect; (i) a unity of opposites, like an artwork; (j) a well of aesthetic potentials, again like an artwork; and (k) something that can and should be improved, both aesthetically and otherwise by meditation and somatic techniques.

5 Critiquing and Defending Shusterman

Shusterman's theory of the soma and the self are certainly interesting and thought provoking. But his theories are not without concerns. The first three concerns to follow regard possible inconsistencies, while the fourth regards a

---

43   Shusterman, *Practicing Philosophy*, 60.
44   See, for example, Shusterman's *Body Consciousness*, 68–90.

question of empirical science, and the additional three have to do with ontological issues:

1. As we have seen, Shusterman defines "soma" as "the sentient, intentional body," and, at the same time, maintains that the soma encompasses both *Leib* and *Körper*. But only *Leib* can be called "a sentient, intentional body." So the question arises whether Shusterman is being entirely consistent.

2. Shusterman also says that the self is more than the soma and implies consciousness of differing from other selves, ability to sustain a mental narrative, etc. But if the self is also a consciousness that transcends the soma, then this consciousness must have a mental and nonphysical existence. However, that seems to go against the grain of Shusterman's whole somatist approach, and again raises the question of consistency.

3. Shusterman rejects essentialism, but, at the same time, writes as if the soma is the essential element of a human being. Here, too, a question of consistency arises.

4. Shusterman uncritically accepts Libet's conclusions of his own experiments concerning free will. However, Libet's conclusions are not accepted by all scientists and scholars in the relevant fields. According to some critics, the neurological events that he thought controlled our decisions can also be understood as being related to the wrist to be moved or the button to be pushed, and not the decision at all. Furthermore, the experiment relied on the participants own recording of when they felt the intention to move. Nevertheless, there may be a delay between the impulse to act and the recording of it, recording requiring a shift of attention from the intention to act.[45] And if that is the case, as Steve Taylor writes in "Benjamin Libet and the Denial of Free Will: How Did a Flawed Experiment Become so Influential?" then Libet has not been able to show that the brain "makes the decision" before becoming aware of it. Moreover, as Jürgen Habermas points out "The Language Game of Responsible Agency and the Problem of Free Will," Libet only asked people to decide swiftly and randomly about performing such trivial acts as moving one finger. Libet seems to have neglected the importance of deliberative decisions about what course of life to choose or what party to support in the upcoming election, and so on. In such decisions, reasons play an important role and they cannot be reduced to causes. There is an irreducible, logical link between reasons and decisions, says Habermas. Now, some philosophers claim that our reasons for believing in arguments are only epiphenomena, while the real action is the set

---

45   Steve Taylor, "Benjamin Libet and the Denial of Free Will: How Did a Flawed Experiment Become so Influential?" *Psychology Today* (2017), www.psychologytoday.com/us/blog/out-the-darkness/201709/benjamin-libet-and-the-denial-free-will.

of causally determined processes in the brain. Habermas replies by saying that we are products of evolution, and it would be strange if nature used so much energy to produce such purported epiphenomena. Usually nature is austere, so it is not likely that reasons are mere epiphenomena.[46]

5. Many contemporary philosophers working in metaphysics do not think of themselves as looking for metaphysical underpinnings of everyday linguistic practices. Inspired by developments in modal logic and possible world semantics, these thinkers have rejuvenated the field of metaphysics within area of analytical philosophy. One part of this rejuvenation is the rebirth of essentialism.[47] Some analytic metaphysicians even talk as if metaphysics were the only game in philosophical town.[48] Shusterman, however, does not address this issue of metaphysical essentialism.[49]

Moreover, just stating that there are language games and practices means saying that there are states and objects in the world of a certain kind, which implies an ontology of sorts, however minimal. Besides, Shusterman's emphatic rejection of essentialism and of dualism concerning body and mind certainly must imply some ontological commitments, even though this rejection is thought to be pragmatic, and as a part of a reinvention of our descriptions of these issues. Therefore, there is an ontological moment in his thinking, however minimal.

6. In light of this, it is only fair to ask Shusterman to address possible ontological issues concerning the soma. One of the issues is the question whether the body really is indispensable for selfhood. There might be functionalist arguments against the indispensability of the body for selfhood. Just as a mousetrap is nothing but a set of functions that can be realized in different materials, the self can be regarded as such a set, multiply realizable, and just contingently realized in a human body.[50] Let us assume that in the future people may be able to upload their selves and minds into computers and leave their bodies behind. At the same time, their minds and their selves would function exactly as they did when embodied. The functions that the body has hitherto taken

---

46 Jürgen Habermas, "The Language Game of Responsible Agency and the Problem of Free Will: How Can Epistemic Dualism be Reconciled with Ontological Monism?" tr. Joel Anderson, in *Philosophical Explorations*, vol. 10, no. 1 (2007), 13–50.
47 See, for example, Saul Kripke, *Naming and Necessity* (Oxford: Blackwell, 1970).
48 See Eric T. Olson, *The Human Animal: Personal Identity without Psychology* (New York: Oxford University Press, 1997).
49 My fifth, sixth, and seventh worries concern what could be called "instances of the metaphysical and ontological deficiency of somaesthetics."
50 For the mousetrap analogy, see Thomas W. Polger's entry "Functionalism," *The Internet Encyclopedia of Philosophy* (www.iep.utm.edu/functism/).

care of would be taken over by machines. Let us further assume that a substantial number of people will choose to do so. Would they become beings without selves? If the answer is no, then the body is not essential to selfhood.[51]

Shusterman could say that, for the time being, theories like that remain pure speculation; we do not know whether it will be possible to upload selves and minds, and not even whether this alleged possibility makes any sense. Then he could add that he is interested in real human beings, not some logical abstractions that may only make sense in a world of theories without any relevance for the real world and ordinary people.

7. Another possible ontological problem concerns the alleged non-separability of body and mind, i.e., the anti-dualistic contention that they are but parts of a whole, and that the whole is the soma. This theory seemingly has all the trappings of an ontological theory. In order to vindicate this theory, Shusterman might have to counter the important eliminative materialist view of the mind, or the powerful immaterialism of philosophers such as Alvin Plantinga. There is no place for body-mind or *Leib* in these two opposite views, immaterialism and eliminative materialism.

Paul Churchland and Patricia Churchland may be the best-known proponents of eliminative materialism; they deny the existence of consciousness, mind, and self. These concepts can be eliminated, matter is all that matters, even all there is, the eliminativists say.[52] Patricia Churchland maintains that the self is nothing but its brain.[53] Now, if this were true, then we could easily eliminate the mind part of the purported body-mind and the *Leib*, leaving only the *Körper* as being real.

Plantinga's immaterialism may not be as well known, so I will allot more space to it. Plantinga maintains that it is impossible for material objects to think and have other kinds of mental activities. If a belief is material, then it must be a neuronal event or structure. Now, if this is what beliefs are, then they will have two very different sorts of properties. On the one hand, there will be electrochemical or neurophysiological properties; and, on the other hand, semantic content. It is in virtue of having such a content that a belief can be true or false. For example, the belief that all men are mortal has true content. We can examine the neuronal event or structure as carefully as we please, yet

---

51 See Joseph Margolis, *Persons and Minds: The Prospect of Nonreductive Materialism* (Boston: D. Reidel Publishing Company, 1978).

52 Paul Churchland, *Matter and Consciousness: A Contemporary Introduction to the Philosophy of the Mind*, rev. ed. (Cambridge: MIT Press, 1988).

53 Patricia Churchland, "Self-Representation in Nervous Systems," *Annals of the New York Academy of Sciences* (November 2003), 31–38.

we nowhere find anything resembling content. Physical activity cannot constitute content any more than a number can have weight, or an elephant be a proposition. Now, is it not equally difficult to understand how an immaterial object can think as a material object can? At least we can form representations of the operation of material objects when they are engaged in thinking. But Plantinga points out that even if we cannot form a representation of the number 79 being a prime number, it does not follow that it is not a prime number. To ask the question how an immaterial self produces thought is to ask an improper question, analogous to such improper questions as "How does an electron manage to have a charge?" and "How do sets manage to have members?" Having a negative charge is simply something an electron has and is (as far as we know), not a result of any activity of any possible parts of electrons (they do not seem to have any parts). According to Plantinga's immaterialism, thinking is just an activity of an immaterial self, not a result of activities of any immaterial bits of the self.[54] A self is an immaterial, noncomposite whole. What about all the indicators that this or that mental activity takes place in this or that part of the brain, or that physical events and states are necessary for mental activity?

Plantinga has a pretty powerful answer. When you run, or wag your finger, something typically happens in your brain: some parts of it are activated when you run, while another part of the brain is activated when you wag your finger. But you would not seriously say that running and wagging your fingers are activities of the brain and nothing else, not activities of your legs and fingers. Digestion will occur only if a brain is in the right condition, but it certainly does not follow that digestion is really an activity of the brain, and not an activity of the digestive system. The functioning of the brain depends on blood flow and on the proper performance of the lungs, but that does not mean that brain function is really circulatory or pulmonary activity. All of our activities depend upon ingesting enough of and the right kind of food, but it hardly follows that Ludwig Feuerbach was right about us being just what we eat. Even though the appropriate brain activity is a necessary condition for mental activity, it simply does not follow that the latter is just the former. Furthermore, because electrons and quarks cannot think, it is difficult to see how an object, composed of them, can be a thinking being.[55] Such a nonmaterialist (and

---

54 Alvin Plantinga, "Against Materialism," *Faith & Philosophy*, vol. 23, no. 1 (January 2006), 3–32.
55 Habermas's defense of reasons as irreducible to material configurations accords with nonmaterialism.

dualist) view inevitably opposes the theory of the body-mind, or that of the *Leib*.⁵⁶

Shusterman could point out that ontological problems are notoriously thorny, and that we have no conclusive evidence for the correctness of any attempted solutions to the ontological problem of the self, be it the immaterialist solution, or the one of eliminative materialism. In fact, we do not have any conclusive evidence in favor or against any given ontological view. Shusterman might add that this problem should be tackled in a pragmatist manner, and say that there are contexts in which it may be helpful to talk about the mind/body problem, or the problem of the self, while there are other contexts in which these issues have no bearing. In everyday life, these ontological problems are not problems at all. Somaesthetics might be regarded as being mainly a part of everyday practices, far away from the theoretical world where the mind/body problem is of importance.

Now, it makes sense to say that theoretical activities of both immaterialists and eliminative materialists are only empirically possible given a host of everyday practices, including going to the office, turning on the computer, looking for books in bookshelves, and interacting with others and oneself in various ways. Maybe it can be shown that our everyday practices involve essentially us regarding people (including ourselves) as somatic beings, mainly *Leib* or body-minds, not pure material objects, or dualistically split beings. The *Leib* could be regarded in this context as having a similar kind of existence as colors or artworks, not entirely objective in the theoretical sense, but not entirely subjective, and definitely objective enough, for the intents and purposes of practical life. The *Leib* certainly is objective in many ways; I can discriminate between the body language of someone who is deeply disappointed and someone who is not, just as I can discriminate between red and blue. Consider the Argentine star soccer player Lionel Messi and his body language after Argentina's loss against Germany in the 2014 World Cup Finals. It spelled deep disappointment, unless Messi is a fantastic actor who pretended to be disappointed, but was jubilant because of the loss. In stark contrast to him, the German victors showed jubilation with their entire bodies, unless they are also brilliant actors.

---

56 Plantinga ignores the possibility of matter having not yet discovered properties. If they exist, then these properties may turn out to be that which we now call "consciousness," "the subjective," and "the self." Furthermore, some kind of property dualism might be a better tool for explicating dualist intuitions than Plantinga's substance dualism. Perhaps the self consists of both mental and material properties, or is emergent from a number of such properties.

(We can even talk about "the beauty of body language," the beauty of the German players' pure joy, and the ugliness of Messi's sore loser body language.)

Eliminative materialists might be right that feelings are only material processes; by implication, the feelings expressed by the soccer stars would solely be such processes. Just as the experience of red and blue could be explained as illusions that arise out of material processes. And artworks could be regarded as similar illusions. Nevertheless, in the workaday world, we can successfully test propositions about colors, and about feelings expressed through the body. We can also test propositions about the existence of artworks, looking in vain for Mahler's twelfth symphony is a proof good enough that it does not exist. Playing his fifth symphony is likewise an acceptable proof that it really exists. These kinds of tests show that colors, body language and artworks have the necessary objectivity needed for our workaday purposes. Something similar holds for the self.

Icelandic philosopher Kristján Kristjánsson in *The Self and Its Emotions* advocates a soft realism concerning the self. The opposite of soft realism is hard realism. Its proponents believe that the self is substantive, for instance a soul or some material objects. In contrast, the soft realist maintains that we do not need to regard it as a substance: it is rather something like "the voter," something real but not substantive.[57] We can add that simple empirical tests can show who is a voter and who is not, and therefore it makes sense to say that voters exist, given that empirical tests can ascertain existence and non-existence. Moreover, if selves are like voters, then it makes sense to say that we can ascertain their existence. It also makes good practical sense to say that a seriously demented individual, who does not seem to know of her own existence, and has lost her memory and linguistic abilities, has lost her self. By implication, she can be said to have possessed a self before she became demented; she could also be said to have lost her free will, on a soft realism concerning free will.

We can add that artworks and *Leib* are real but not substantive. The fact that selves and artworks exist on the same ontological level increases the plausibility of an aesthetic approach to selfhood, given that everything else is equal. This does not mean that we need to build an ontological system in order to vindicate this, a minimal ontology will do, such as a fallibilist ontology, which pragmatically and tentatively separates that which is real in a substantive way from that which is real in a soft manner.

---

57   Kristján Kristjánsson, *The Self and Its Emotions* (Cambridge: Cambridge University Press, 2010), 46–52.

Joseph Margolis certainly builds ontological edifices. Moreover, he argues forcefully in favor of the self and artworks sharing a host of important properties. Both are embodied and culturally emergent entities. Being thus emergent means that they are being created and exist in the dimension of the meaningful, or "the intentional," in Margolis's sense in *Historied Thought, Constructed World*, which encompasses intentionality, its objects, and the intentional.[58] Selves or persons are artifactual by being culturally emergent as if they had been created by someone by what Margolis calls "artifactualization."[59] But they are, at the same time, thoroughly natural and products of natural evolution; they are hybrids. Selves are hybrids because they possess both intentional properties and material properties. The evolution of human beings is strongly impacted by cultural processes: selves and even the entire cultural world of which they are part, including artworks, are products of artifactualization.

Margolis points out that the identity of the self has a thing or two in common with the identity of artworks. Both selves and artworks possess a kind of identity that is hardly the common Leibnizian $A = A$ kind, i.e., strict identity. A self can develop and change, and, therefore, it is not self-identical in any strict sense. We are talking about a kind of non-strict identity, but not the kind of non-strict self-identity a given body has through a long life-span, say, seventy years (the body changes a lot, but in a sense remains the same); rather, a softer kind of non-strict self-identity, of the kind that Margolis calls "unicity." Neither selves nor artworks are static but depend upon various changeable interpretations. Their mode of existence is that of being interpreted.[60] Despite being critical of Margolis's metaphysics, Shusterman's view of the unity of selves and artworks is similar, in some respects, to the one Margolis holds.[61]

In fact, Margolis's view of the aesthetic and hybrid self may be fused with Kristjánsson's "soft realism," and with Shusterman's somaesthetic theory of the self, as a dynamical unity of variety (and opposites); the hybrid aesthetic self view may be added to the narratives that partly constitute the self, and which may be evaluated aesthetically. After all, a narrative is a unity of opposites

---

58 Margolis, *Historied Thought, Constructed World* (Berkeley: University of California Press, 1995), 197–199.
59 Margolis, "Towards a Metaphysics of Culture," in *Pragmatism, Metaphysics and Culture-Reflections on the Philosophy of Joseph Margolis, Nordic Studies in Pragmatism* 2, ed. Dirk-Martin Grube and Robert Sinclair (Helsinki: Nordic Pragmatist Network, 2015), 3–5.
60 See Margolis, "Reinterpreting Interpretation," *Journal of Aesthetics and Art Criticism*, XXXXVII, no. 3 (1989), 247.
61 Shusterman, *Surface and Depth: Dialectics of Criticism and Culture* (Ithaca: Cornell University Press, 2002), 195.

which can be judged aesthetically to be, for example, awkwardly comic while at the same time a sublime drama, and so on.

So, it makes sense to say that the self can be regarded as an aesthetic object. More precisely, there is nothing absurd about aspecting it (seeing-it-as) such an object; seeing the self as something aesthetic can provide us with food for thought and some pleasurable, aesthetic experiences. Certainly, the self can be aspected in different non-aesthetic ways. But that does not make the aspecting of it as something arbitrary or entirely subjective. Not any arbitrary way of seeing a duck-rabbit picture as something is justifiable. I can see it as a duck or a rabbit, but if I think I see it as a mathematical equation, then I am probably a victim of some illusion. In light of the arguments put forward here, it is perfectly justifiable to see the self as an aesthetic object.

Shusterman is right about our everyday practices involving selves and the body/mind issue functioning usually quite well, but wrong about them not needing any ontology at all. We need a minimal ontology, and doing such ontology "light" can mean doing it my way: namely, showing that ontological materialists and immaterialists are bound in practice to accept the validity of the workaday view of selves and body/mind.

6   A New Fusion

Shusterman is a somatist who has an interesting view of the self as being embodied, without having a systematic or fully explicit theory of the self. But it can be reconstructed as a theory that maintains that the self is, to a large degree, a function of the soma, besides being shaped by habit and culture. At the same time, the self is conscious of its differing from other selves, even though it has somewhat blurred boundaries with others and with its own *Körper*. In addition, it has the ability to create mental narratives. Narratives take part in the constitution of the self, but the self is underdetermined by given narratives. The self is loosely unified through narratives, it is a unification of opposites, just like an aesthetic object, and like objects of that kind, it can be improved.

Shusterman develops his somatist ideas in actual and virtual dialogues with other thinkers including Merleau-Ponty, Dewey, and Foucault. Merleau-Ponty differentiates between two aspects of the body, the *Körper*, and the *Leib* as the precondition for thought and perception. Shusterman is also influenced by Dewey's idea of the body-mind, while critically appropriating Merleau-Ponty's and Foucault's conception of the aesthetic self. However, the question arises whether his conception of the self is entirely consistent. And he is somewhat uncritical of Libet's research. Furthermore, Shusterman is critical of metaphysics and ontology, while not discussing powerful modern analytical ontological theories. At the same time, there is an ontological moment in his theorizing. Because it is not elaborated and systematically defended, there is an ontological deficiency in Shusterman's thinking about these issues. Although, hat is needed is not an ontological system, but a minimal pragmatic ontology.

Immaterialism and eliminative materialism represent powerful challenges to Shusterman's conception of soma and body-mind/*Leib*. And while he has not discussed these ontological theories, being skeptical of metaphysics, Shusterman could give a pragmatist answer, recognizing ontological questions are notoriously difficult to answer. Instead of trying to answer them, one could focus on the self as it appears in practical contexts. Moreover, it makes sense to talk about soft realism concerning the self because it exists in a similar manner as the voter or the artwork. As Margolis points out, the self shares some important properties with artworks such as having unicity and being culturally emergent. By fusing Shusterman's somaesthetics with soft realism and the hybrid theory of the aesthetic self, we can justify the aspecting of the self as an aesthetic object.

CHAPTER 2

From Pragmatism to Somaesthetics as Philosophy

Alexander Kremer

Aesthetics is usually taken as part of philosophy. Alexander Baumgarten (1714–1762) and Immanuel Kant (1724–1804) classified aesthetics as an important new part of philosophy, and even Hegel lectured about it in this sense. Nevertheless, if we understand both philosophy and aesthetics in a new way, we have to apply this traditional classification in a new form. I am convinced that this is the case in Richard Shusterman's writings. Shusterman not only changed the approach of aesthetics, but he also broadened the meaning of philosophy by revitalizing the old approach of it. If we want to see Shusterman's achievement in the field of aesthetics and philosophy clearly, it is worth looking at the history of pragmatism and that of pragmatist aesthetics for a moment, before developing our main argument.

1

In origin, pragmatism is an American philosophy, and it is flatly opposed to European philosophy. It has never been a canonized philosophical movement, but a loose set of philosophers with a wide scope of interests, along with some shared principles and values. Pragmatism is radically oriented to practice (life is problem-solving; everything is a tool: scientific and philosophical theories as well). "Truth" means what is good for the community, what is useful. The most important theories of truth are the correspondence, coherence, and pragmatist theories, but the representatives of the last one are not concerned with ultimate metaphysical or epistemological "truth." Naturalism is fairly prevalent in pragmatism, but the common denominator is radical empiricism. Richard Rorty (1931–2007) is an exception since he welcomed the linguistic turn and saw empiricism as a metaphysical reminiscence. Anti-essentialism, pan-relationism, and meliorism are also features that characterize pragmatism in general.

The main representatives of the classical American pragmatism are Charles Sanders Peirce (1839–1914), William James (1842–1910), and John Dewey (1859–1952). Neopragmatism was founded by Rorty when he converted to pragmatism from analytic philosophy in 1989 with his book *Contingency, Irony, and*

© ALEXANDER KREMER, 2022 | DOI:10.1163/9789004468801_004

Solidarity. But Rorty had already changed his mind by 1967, as is evident in his Introduction to his edited book, *The Linguistic Turn*.[1] From this Introduction, the reader feels that already Rorty is dissatisfied with analytic philosophy, even if he emphasizes it in more detail in *Philosophy and the Mirror of Nature* (1979) where he refuses the representationalism and ahistoricism of analytic philosophy. Besides Robert Brandom, who was Rorty's doctoral student, and Richard Shusterman, who was persuaded by Rorty of the usefulness of pragmatism, some analytic philosophers like Willard van Orman Quine and Donald Davidson have also advanced neopragmatist views.

Nowadays, pragmatism takes different forms, but—according to one of the possible classifications—the three main groups of pragmatists are neoclassical pragmatism, analytic pragmatism, and postanalytic pragmatists. *Neoclassical pragmatists* (e.g., Larry Hickman, Susan Haack, John McDermott, John Ryder, Jacquelyn Kegley, Kenneth Stikkers, and James Campbell) combine their naturalism first of all with the importance of scientific methods, and see themselves as the truest intellectual heirs of Peirce, James, and Dewey. *Analytic pragmatists* (e.g., Robert Brandom, Huw Price, Donald Davidson, Hilary Putnam, and the early Rorty) take the linguistic turn with deadly seriousness, and see the future of philosophy in a combination of pragmatism and analytic philosophy. *Postanalytic pragmatists* (e.g., the later Rorty, Daniel Dennett, and Richard Shusterman) do not insist on the primacy of the analytic philosophical method, and prefer only the analytic style. Nevertheless, the post-analytic pragmatists also take seriously the development of the 20th century Continental philosophy (e.g., phenomenology and hermeneutics), and preserve several basic pragmatist principles.

2

If we focus now on pragmatist aesthetics, in general, then we have to mention first of all Dewey, Rorty, and Shusterman. Pragmatist aesthetics is mostly naturalistic, but its details depend on the given philosopher. Dewey, who was also influenced by Darwinism, saw the human being as a result of its continuous transactions with the environment. He based his science-centered thinking on radical empiricism and liked to use the methods of induction and experimentalism. Dewey was also a famous educator, whose educational theory proved to

---

[1] Richard Rorty (ed.), *The Linguistic Turn: Recent Essays in Philosophical Method* (Chicago: University of Chicago Press, 1967).

be more influential after the "death" of traditional pragmatism (from the 1930s to the end of the 1970s), than his pragmatism. As a Social Democrat, Dewey also became *the* philosopher of democracy.

In his book on aesthetics *Art as Experience* (1934) Dewey opposed the "museum conception" of art by which people remove works of art from their historical and cultural contexts, and then pile up these works of art in galleries and museums as symbols of public or private "greatness." The museum conception of art is a historical product—it is a product of capitalism—that Dewey condemned. In his opinion, the contradiction between real life and art is not necessary, as the representatives of *"Erlebniskunst"* thought.[2]

In his philosophy of art, Dewey finds art to be embedded within the very practices of human life. Everyday life and its experiences ("anaesthetic experiences") are mostly incomplete, random, fragmentary, and chaotic; for example, think of an everyday morning, when we are rushing to work, but we are already late, and it turns out that our child has a fever, plus our mother-in-law also calls at the same moment. By contrast, an aesthetic experience ("consummatory experience," or, more simply, *"an experience"*) is unified, integrated, harmonious, and satisfactory, one which can have either a positive or negative value. Nevertheless, in Dewey's opinion, everyday life experience always contains the possibility of aesthetic experience (again, "an experience"); for example, a nicely set table, a becomingly furnished flat, a beautiful building, or the sublimity of the mountains, or the sea, can result in aesthetic experience. As Dewey wrote,

> A piece of work is finished in a way that is satisfactory; a problem receives its solution; a game is played through; a situation, whether that of eating a meal, playing a game of chess, carrying on a conversation, writing a book, or taking part in a political campaign, is so rounded out that its close is a consummation and not a cessation.[3]

For Dewey, unified, integrated, and satisfactory everyday-life experiences *are already aesthetic experiences*, capable of offering aesthetic consumption even on the simplest days. In Dewey's view, *experience is already understanding* (it is important for both artistic creation and aesthetic appreciation), and *art should not stand in contradiction to everyday life*.

---

2 See Friedrich Schiller's *On the Aesthetic Education of Mankind*, tr. Reginal Snell (Mineola: Dover, 2004; original, 1795).

3 John Dewey, *Art as Experience*, in *The Later Works of John Dewey, 1925–1953*, vol. 10: 1934, ed. Jo Ann Boydston (Carbondale and Edwardsville: Southern Illinois University, 1980), 42.

As an heir to Dewey, Rorty criticized analytic philosophy on several points[4] and yet replaced the Deweyan pragmatist concept of experience with language as the center of his neopragmatist philosophy.[5] Together with this philosophical turn, Rorty also made a political turn. He refused his family's Trotskyist heritage, became a liberal (Social Democrat), and this new political attitude saturates his later philosophy. This change manifested itself in *Contingency*, where Rorty envisions a utopian liberal democracy, and a new type of human being, the "liberal ironist." Liberals, writes Rorty, "are the people who think that cruelty is the worst thing we do."[6] Rorty then defines the ironist:

> I use 'ironist' to name the sort of person who faces up to the contingency of his or her own most central beliefs and desires—someone sufficiently historicist and nominalist to have abandoned the idea that those central beliefs and desires refer back to something beyond the reach of time and chance.[7]

The public-private split is also essential, for Rorty, with Harold Bloom's model of "the strong poet," the creator of the new social vocabularies, serving as the ideal of a liberal-ironist culture, rather than the priest or warrior or scientist.[8]

Summarizing his philosophy of art, we can say that Rorty takes the linguistic turn in dead earnest, and that is why he deals only with literature within his philosophy of art. However, Rorty deals with everything within the literature that promotes the realization of his own liberal democracy (i.e., the public sphere), or the personal development (i.e., the private sphere) of the liberal ironist, e.g., Ralph Waldo Emerson, Walt Whitman, Charles Dickens, Harold Bloom, Milan Kundera, etc. (see Rorty's Vladimir Nabokov chapter, and the George Orwell chapter in *Contingency*). Rorty, as a good pragmatist, also handles literature (as he does science, philosophy, etc.) as a tool. That is, everything is a tool, for Rorty, from a practical and moral point of view. Thus, apart from its aesthetic value, literature becomes good, in Rorty's view, as it promotes his purposes for the public and the private dimensions of life. Rorty prefers the type of literature that shows conflicts between the rich and the poor, or which shows the richness of human life forms and sociopolitical possibilities.

---

4   See Rorty, *Philosophy and the Mirror of Nature* (Princeton: Princeton University Press, 1979).
5   See Rorty, *Contingency, Irony, and Solidarity* (Cambridge: Cambridge University Press, 1989).
6   *Ibid.*, xv.
7   *Ibid.*
8   *Ibid.*, 53.

Shusterman, although born in Philadelphia, was an Israeli analytic aesthetician before Rorty suggested he look more thoroughly into Dewey's *Reconstruction in Philosophy*. Shusterman, who received his Ph.D. from Oxford, St. John's College, after some years of teaching at different Israeli universities, resettled in the U.S. Shusterman became a professor of philosophy at Temple University, and served as Chair of the Philosophy Department from 1998 to 2004. Based on his personal experiences, and philosophical readings of texts, Shusterman changed his mind (signs of which appear already in his second book, *T. S. Eliot and the Philosophy of Criticism*), and became a pragmatist in 1988. Shusterman started to work out his project of somaesthetics, on the basis of Dewey's aesthetics, in the second half of the 1990s.[9]

Shusterman became internationally famous with the publication of *Pragmatist Aesthetics* (1992), which has been translated into fourteen languages (and many of his subsequent works have also been translated into multiple languages). Shusterman strengthened his philosophical position in several important volumes to follow: *Practicing Philosophy* (1997), *Performing Live* (2000), *Surface and Depth* (2002), *Body Consciousness* (2008), *Thinking through the Body: Essays in Somaesthetics* (2012), and *The Adventures of the Man in Gold* (2016). As Shusterman developed further his interpretation of the pragmatist tradition, his many books provoked both significant criticism and enthusiasm among professional philosophers. In 2005 Shusterman became the Dorothy F. Schmidt Eminent Scholar in the Humanities, Professor of Philosophy and English at Florida Atlantic University, where a year later he established The Center for Body, Mind, and Culture, which he continues to direct as a research hub for developing his philosophy of somaesthetics. As somaesthetics has become an international movement, partner centers of somaesthetics have appeared in Europe and East Asia.

If we want to define Shusterman's general theoretical standpoint, we can say that it is a *philosophical aestheticism* that is saturated with *democratic political intentions*. This standpoint appears especially in Shusterman's *naturalistic somaesthetics*, which is colored by a pragmatist *meliorism*, according to which society should be *democratized* as much as possible. Shusterman started his pragmatist career partly with a theory of interpretation, but his

---

9 Shusterman introduced the notion of somaesthetics in *Vor der Interpretation* (Vienna: Passagen, 1996), 132; a revised German translation of Shusterman's *Sous l'interprétation* (Paris: L'éclat, 1994). Shusterman published "Somaesthetics: A Disciplinary Proposal," *Journal of Aesthetics and Art Criticism*, vol. 57, no. 3 (Summer 1999); and later added that essay as a chapter to the second edition of *Pragmatist Aesthetics* (2000).

general standpoint is a "meta-theoretical interpretive pluralism"[10] where practice is not determined by theory, but the challenges of practice reveal new directions for interpretive development. If—as Shusterman thinks as well—understanding and interpretation (which usually follows understanding) are necessary parts of human life, then we live in a permanent condition of self- and world-understanding, and a permanent condition of self- and world-interpretation. When its object happens to be our life and existential being, then this self- and world-understanding becomes philosophy. That occurs in Shusterman's somaesthetics since the self is always an embodied self; that is, the *soma* always has a distinguished role in his philosophy. That is why Shusterman—contrary to Rorty—brings back the central role of experience and non-conceptual understanding.

Why has this naturalistic philosophy of art been given the name of "somaesthetics"? On the one hand, our body is "the tool of tools" (as Shusterman often uses this expression). On the other hand, only a living, body can have such a central place. In Hungarian we do not clearly distinguish the living body from the dead body. However, in the German language, this difference is clear: "*der Leib*" and "*der Körper.*" The "*Leib*" is the living body, and the "*Körper*" means the body in the physical sense. The expression "soma," however, means the living body, already in the ancient Greek language, and Shusterman combines "soma" with the word "aesthetics," in the word "somaesthetics." As we know from "The Invention of Pragmatist Aesthetics: Genealogical Reflections on a Notion and a Name," Shusterman was also the first pragmatist philosopher to call—consciously and intentionally—this naturalistic philosophy of art a "pragmatist aesthetics." Dewey never used the expression "pragmatist aesthetics:"

> Aesthetics is one such field where pragmatism's impact has recently been most strongly felt. Yet aesthetics was initially a very marginal field for pragmatist philosophy. Neither Peirce nor James wrote any books or articles on this field, and John Dewey turned to it only late in his career, publishing his massive masterpiece, *Art as Experience*, in 1934, the year he turned seventy-five. Though understandably regarded as the founding document of pragmatist aesthetics, Dewey's book, in fact, never advances any theory with that name. Not only does Dewey refrain from using the term 'pragmatist aesthetics' (or cognate terms like 'pragmatic aesthetics'

---

10   Wojciech Małecki, *Embodying Pragmatism: Richard Shusterman's Philosophy and Literary Theory* (New York: Peter Lang Publishing, 2010), 99.

or 'aesthetic pragmatism'), he does not even deploy the term 'pragmatism' in that book.[11]

Shusterman's somaesthetics has *three historical* and *two genealogical* roots. The historical roots are, as he mentions them in my interview, Dewey, ancient Greek philosophers, and Confucius. When he read Dewey's *Art as Experience* the second time, Shusterman appropriated it more deeply. As Shusterman recalls, "by the end of the 1980s Dewey was my principal pragmatist inspiration."[12] The ancient Greek practice of philosophy is not only different but also more authentic than our approach today. Shusterman recalls his study

> *of the ancient (Greek) idea of practicing philosophy as an embodied way of life rather than simply a merely theoretical academic pursuit of reading and writing texts.* We should always remember that Socrates established philosophy not by writing any books or articles (for he authored none) but by his exemplary way of living and dying in the search for the wisdom to guide the quest for the good life.[13]

Last, but not least, ancient Asian wisdom also privileges embodiment: "somaesthetics has been especially inspired by Asia's rich tradition of deploying somatic disciplines for philosophical and spiritual enlightenment along with better health and harmony."[14] Shusterman also notes,

> Confucius for his emphasis on embodiment and pleasure and the importance of the arts for the ethical aim of self-cultivation in which the self and its cultivation are always seen as essentially socially constituted through one's relations with others rather than being narcissistically autonomous.[15]

As to genealogical roots, Shusterman claims,

---

11 Shusterman, "The Invention of Pragmatist Aesthetics: Genealogical Reflections on a Notion and a Name," in *Practicing Pragmatist Aesthetics: Critical Perspectives on the Arts*, ed. Wojciech Małecki (Amsterdam: Rodopi, 2014), 14.
12 Kremer, "Shusterman in Budapest: An Interview," *Pragmatism Today* (Winter 2014), 8.
13 Shusterman, *Szómaesztétika és az élet műészete: Válogatás Richard Shusterman írásaiból* (Szeged: JatePress, 2014), 4.
14 *Ibid.*, 4.
15 Kremer, "Shusterman in Budapest," 10.

> Genealogically, somaesthetics has its roots in philosophy and more particularly in pragmatist aesthetics. Somaesthetics emerged from the following two ideas: Because *the body is crucial both to the creation of art and to its appreciation*, a pragmatist approach (which also means a meliorist approach) to aesthetics should try to improve the body's perceptual and performative capacities so that it can improve our aesthetic experience. Moreover, because *pragmatist aesthetics*, as I conceive it, is also centrally concerned with *the ethical art of living* and because the body is the necessary medium through which we live, then it follows that a pragmatist, meliorist approach to living should work on cultivating our key tool or medium of living, namely our soma. These two philosophical arguments, which originally inspired the idea of somaesthetics, continue to inspire it and to shape the approaches of non-philosophers who are working in this field. I believe that philosophical thinking is not confined to professional philosophers with Ph.D.'s in this subject. This brings me to a further point about the somaesthetics-philosophy relationship. If we conceive *philosophy broadly as an ethical art of living that is guided by critical inquiry aimed to promote a more aesthetically satisfying form of life for both self and society*, then the various disciplines and forms of knowledge that contribute to this art of living (even if they are not distinctively or professionally philosophical) can be related to the broad philosophical project of the quest for wisdom in how to live better lives. Somaesthetic research in forms outside the normal disciplinary bounds of philosophy surely can contribute to this overarching philosophical project.[16]

Shusterman developed and expanded upon Dewey's naturalistic philosophy of art, and brought together those historical and present thoughts and practices which focus on the "soma." While there are slightly different formulations of his definition of somaesthetics, I take the following definition from Shusterman's *Thinking through the Body*. Somaesthetics is

> *the critical meliorative study of the experience and use of one's body as a locus of sensory-aesthetic appreciation (aesthesis) and creative self-fashioning.* In examining the forms of knowledge and disciplines of practice that structure such somatic care or can improve it, somaesthetics involves the critical study of society's somatic values and comportment, so as to redirect our body consciousness and practice away from the

---

16   *Ibid.*, 10–11.

oppressively narrow and injurious stereotypes of somatic success that pervade our advertising culture and to focus instead on exploring more rewarding visions of somatic value and fulfillment and better methods for attaining them.[17]

It is clear as day from this definition that Shusterman is aware that *soma* is both *subjective* and *objective*. Shusterman is also aware of the differences between his standpoint and Maurice Merleau-Ponty's views (1908–1961).[18] Shusterman also knows that the "creative self-fashioning" is both *external* and *internal* (the latter is connected to proprioception and psychosomatic phenomena: pleasure, excitement, stress, depression, etc.). It is also clear Shusterman seeks to improve society with somaesthetics within the context of a democratic meliorism. Thus, Shusterman's somaesthetics is a permanent self- and world-understanding, and a pragmatist meliorism with three main parts. (1) Analytic somaesthetics (theory) explains the nature of our bodily perceptions and practices, and that of their role in our knowledge and construction of the world. (2) Pragmatic somaesthetics (method) explores specific methods of somatic improvement and their comparative critique. (3) Practical somaesthetics (practice) is disciplined bodywork aimed at somatic improvement.[19]

3

Why can we say that Shusterman's somaesthetics is a philosophy?[20] Summarizing our arguments, there are at least five reasons.

1. Shusterman's approach is not a substance-oriented but a process-and-practice-oriented approach. Ancient and medieval European philosophies were mostly ontologically based philosophies. Philosophers used to look for the substance of the world (e.g., Ideas, the Form of Forms, God, or the Absolute),

---

17   Shusterman, *Thinking through the Body: Essays in Somaesthetics* (Cambridge: Cambridge University Press, 2012), 182–183 (emphasis added).
18   Cf. Shusterman, *Body Consciousness: A Philosophy of Mindfulness and Somaesthetics* (Cambridge: Cambridge University Press, 2008), Ch. 2.
19   Cf. Shusterman, *Pragmatist Aesthetics: Living Beauty, Rethinking Art*, 2nd ed. (Lanham: Rowman & Littlefield Publishers, Inc., 2000), Ch. 10.
20   In my terminology, aesthetics is merely a branch of philosophy (as ontology, epistemology, ethics, logic, social philosophy, philosophy of language, etc.) dealing with art, beauty, and aesthetic properties. I regard philosophy as concerned more widely with the human being's self-understanding and self-interpretation in the world and thus an understanding of that world.

and then tried to deduce the other things from the substance. Only in modernity do problems of recognition and epistemological questions become more important than ontological questions (cf. Continental Rationalism and British Empiricism). Shusterman is not interested in the substance of the world, but instead he views the world as a conglomerate of ever-changing processes and relations, where contingency makes possible the effective functioning of human actions. As evidence, I quote Shusterman's dense but extremely important confession, "What Pragmatism Means to Me: Ten Principles." Describing his first principle ("1. The changing, open, and contingent nature of reality"), Shusterman says:

> The world that we know through human experience is a world without absolute fixity or permanence. Not only our personal experience, but the external world is a world whose regularities and stabilities exist in a framework of change, much of which is not noticed. Even our images of permanence, such as mountains, are the products of change and continue to change through erosion and other natural and human forces. Contingency means that chance is an integral part of life, that behavioral and social processes and even natural laws are matters of probability rather than of absolute necessity that admits of no surprises, exceptions, or aberrations. The fact that the things and events of our lives and social world are contingent does not mean that they are entirely random or arbitrary and thus not subject to predictable regularities that can be known and utilized.[21]

Shusterman speaks here not only about his views on nature, but also right away draws the consequences of this view regarding human actions and fallibilism:

> One consequence of the pragmatist vision of an open, changing universe is that facts are not just there to be discovered but are largely made through human activity, which can have significant (including baneful) effects not only on the social world but also on the natural environment. The open, malleable nature of the world, moreover, encourages the idea of freedom for positive action that can make a real difference. A further consequence is that philosophy, as a human activity that engages with the changing world, can also help change it. In that sense, pragmatism

---

21   Shusterman, "What Pragmatism Means to Me: Ten Principles," *Revue Française Ançaise d'Études Américaines*, no. 124 (2010), 60.

provides support for the idea that philosophy should engage not only with concepts but also in praxis. This has encouraged my efforts to revive the ancient idea of philosophy as an embodied way of life. I should mention here that the pragmatist notion of contingency and a changing world evolving through contingent occurrences owes much to the influence of Charles Darwin. The idea of a changing world also implies the important pragmatist idea of fallibilism: that our currently warranted beliefs or established knowledge are always subject to improvement or revision in light of future experience. This is different from skepticism in that for fallibilism there is no reason to cast doubt or question our beliefs unless we have encountered in experience a specific reason to do so.[22]

It is clear as day that Shusterman embraces not only Darwinian evolutionary theory but also the tradition of American pragmatism, whose representatives created their process-and-practice-oriented approach chiefly by radicalizing British empiricism. From our point of view, that means that we are not on the aesthetic, but on the philosophical level, of thinking.

2. Shusterman replaces mind and rationality with the soma as the center of philosophical research. From Socrates to the 20th century, "reason" dominated European philosophy as the central idea. The recognition that the self is always embodied was emerged only in the last third of the last century. It is beyond question, however, that some philosophers (e.g., Montaigne, the British empiricists, and Friedrich Nietzsche) already acknowledged the importance of experience and the body, but generally the rationalist philosophies dominated the intellectual landscape of Europe. In particular, not only religious theories but also theologies, and even the Enlightenment, supported this tendency, since their representatives did not want to accept that the mind is decisively determined by the body. In the 20th century, Merleau-Ponty and Michel Foucault (1926–1984) were the main figures who emphasized the distinctive role of the living body in our mental and rational life. Nevertheless, Shusterman was the first thinker to offer a theoretical framework for the dominantly somatic approaches to human life. Having illustrated the primacy of human action and purpose in the above-mentioned text ("2. The primacy of human action and purpose in even our most rational and cognitive pursuits and concepts"), Shusterman now emphasizes the particular importance of naturalism in "3. A non-reductive, embodied naturalism."

---

22   Shusterman, "What Pragmatism Means to Me," 60.

> The Deweyan pragmatism I favor (and one to a very considerable extent shared by William James and to a somewhat lesser extent by C.S. Peirce) understands human intelligence and reason as grounded in our natural equipment for survival and improvement rather than a supernatural gift from God or some other-worldly source. Reason is a product of evolution, and it can evolve and change further. Classical pragmatism has an essentially embodied view of human nature. It rejects the traditional radical dualism of body/mind. For Peirce, the organism (with its embodied feeling) is what distinguishes a man from a sign. James also explains not only emotion but the sense of self, coherent thought, attention, and the very unity of consciousness in terms of a structuring background of bodily feeling. For James, only the will remained other than bodily, while Dewey went further, insisting that also the will was a function of somatic habit (Shusterman 2008). That classical pragmatism emphasized the embodied nature of human experience and cognition has been very helpful to me in developing my project of somaesthetics.[23]

Without going into the details of the ongoing body-mind debate, Shusterman summarizes his emergentist standpoint, which makes evident that the living soma dominates his view:

> Pragmatist naturalism is not aimed to reduce mental phenomena to mere neuronal reactions in the brain; mental life is rather seen as emerging from though not reducible to mere physical, molecular reactions. Indeed, for pragmatism, even spirituality can be likewise seen as a real, experiential phenomenon, though it again emerges from the natural and represents a dimension of experienced meaning and behavior rather than a separate other-worldly substance, totally divorced from embodied, material existence. This idea of mind evolving and emerging from below can also be linked to Darwin's influence. The essential continuity of bodily nature and mind is complemented by the continuity of nature and culture. Mind is not an isolated psychic substance but rather incorporates energies and elements from the natural and social environments. In the full-blown human sense, the mind is essentially social and reflects a network of communication and meanings enabled by language. The embodied nature of mind is reflected in the importance that pragmatism gives

---

23   *Ibid.*, 61.

to habit, which is shaped by and incorporates elements from both the natural and social environment to guide human thought and action.[24]

Having criticized the traditional dominance of mind and rationality, Shusterman does not, however, fall into the other extreme position that only the living soma is able to offer us an explanation for our philosophical problems. Shusterman works out in several different texts a sophisticated and defensible standpoint regarding the relationship between the body and the mind. As we can see from the quotation above, Shusterman summarizes his emergentism in a short form, within the context of his Pragmatist Principles, but gives us a detailed description of his view in other texts, for example, Shusterman's Dewey chapter in *Body Consciousness* (2008), and the first chapter of *Thinking through the Body*, entitled "Thinking through the Body: Educating for the Humanities." Here Shusterman writes,

> We humanist intellectuals generally take the body for granted because we are so passionately interested in the life of the mind and the creative arts that express our human spirit. But the body is not only an essential dimension of our humanity, but it is also the basic instrument of all human performance, our tool of tools, a necessity for all our perception, action, and even thought. Just as skilled builders need expert knowledge of their tools, so we need better somatic knowledge to improve our understanding and performance in the arts and human sciences, and to advance our mastery in the highest art of all—that of perfecting our humanity and living better lives. We need to think more carefully through the body in order to cultivate ourselves and edify our students because true humanity is not a mere genetic given but an educational achievement in which body, mind, and culture must be thoroughly integrated. To pursue this project of somatic inquiry, I have been working in the interdisciplinary field called somaesthetics, whose disciplinary connections extend beyond the humanities to the biological, cognitive, health sciences, which I see as valuable allies for humanistic research.[25]

I do not want to go into a thorough reconstruction of the argumentation in this chapter, but here Shusterman emphasizes the dominant role of the naturally and socially determined soma in its mutually interconnected relationship with

---

24   Shusterman, "What Pragmatism Means to Me," 62.
25   Shusterman, *Thinking through the Body*, 26.

the mental life. What is more—and this is much more significant for my present argumentation—we should recognize that Shusterman's "somatic turn" could not be achieved on the mere aesthetic level: it is a more general philosophical act, a more general philosophical decision and change.

3. Somaesthetics is a permanent self- and world-understanding, and a permanent self- and world-interpretation, which is manifested, first of all, in the analytic part of somaesthetics. If we are focusing on the question, What is philosophy? then we can expect a kind of answer. Thousands of different philosophies have been born since its Greek beginnings, but in some form, directly or indirectly, every philosophy addresses the relationship between the human being and the world, in general. That seems to be self-evident from ancient Greek philosophy, through medieval Christian philosophy, to the end of the modern period, and our present situation. We can always find some ontology—usually in a latent form, and without elaboration—within a contemporary philosophy. For example, Karl Jaspers, Jean-Paul Sartre (on individual existence), Bertrand Russell, Ludwig Wittgenstein, J. L. Austin, and even the early Rorty, all based their work on an ontology, ultimately arising from one basic question: *"Who is the human being in the world?"* I am persuaded that this is the main question of philosophy because every philosophical theory has been produced by a finite and historical human being who, first of all, wanted to understand himself in the world. Philosophy can be defined in several concrete ways, but I think the essential structure of philosophical thinking does not change. The formal structure of this thinking works not only in the traditional metaphysical philosophies but also in contemporary analytic and continental philosophies. *The formal structure of philosophical thinking might be regarded as the theoretical and historical self-reflection of the human being that is the permanent condition of existential inquiry. However, if philosophy is a permanent, theoretical self- and world-understanding and interpretation*, then the ontological question must be dominant within every philosophy. The reason this is so is that the main structure of the world and our place in the world can only be comprehended on the basis of an *ontological principle* (which is always an answer to the question "What is the world like?"), and it can be found already in the worldview of the individual. This is a precondition of every form of ontology because ontology can be expounded only from this kind of principle. I consider this ontological principle so general that every individual uses it. I am convinced that analytic somaesthetics deals, at least partly, with this question as well, because somaesthetics is not only an aesthetics but a general philosophy.

4. Somaesthetics has significant relationships with every art and science and human activity (e.g., the fine arts, politics, education, history, the social

sciences, health sciences, technology, etc.). One of the basic theoretical questions regarding somaesthetics is its place of among the disciplines, a question which is connected to our question, *Why can we say that somaesthetics is a philosophy?* In my interview at the Somaesthetic Conference of Budapest in 2014, Shusterman said,

> When the idea of somaesthetics first came to me, I thought it would be a subdiscipline of philosophical aesthetics, but, as you say, my thinking was wrong. Somaesthetics has become an interdisciplinary field because the body—as our tool of tools and the central site of our experience—is crucially related to the many disciplines that concern human flourishing: not only the arts but politics, education, historical and social sciences as well as health sciences and even technology.[26]

Shusterman also advances this kind of argument in *Thinking through the Body*:

> Just as skilled builders need expert knowledge of their tools, so we need better somatic knowledge to improve our understanding and performance in the arts and human sciences, and to advance our mastery in the highest art of all—that of perfecting our humanity and living better lives. We need to think more carefully through the body in order to cultivate ourselves and edify our students because true humanity is not a mere genetic given but an educational achievement in which body, mind, and culture must be thoroughly integrated. To pursue this project of somatic inquiry, I have been working in the interdisciplinary field called somaesthetics, whose disciplinary connections extend beyond the humanities to the biological, cognitive, health sciences, which I see as valuable allies for humanistic research.[27]

It is well-known that from the 2010s, somaesthetics became an international philosophical movement. I am convinced that is partly based on its interdisciplinary features, which, again, constitute not an aesthetic, but a philosophical, challenge.

5. Somaesthetics also renewed the ancient Greek understanding of philosophy. It is not only writing and lecturing, but firstly, and above all, somaesthetics is a way of life. Shusterman, in arguing for philosophy as an embodied "ethical art of living,"[28] also finds support in ancient Asian thought.

---

26   Kremer, "Shusterman in Budapest," 10.
27   Shusterman, *Thinking through the Body*, 26.
28   Kremer, "Shusterman in Budapest," 11.

> Confucius repeatedly insists that fine words are not enough, that they require fine action to make them convincing, and that without such action words in themselves are suspicious. 'What can possibly be done with people who find pleasure in polite language but do not draw out its meaning, or who comply with model sayings but do not reform their ways?' ... 'Exemplary persons would feel shame if their words were better than their deeds' (AC 9:24, 14:27). Moreover, right action for Confucianism is not merely performing the proper act but also requires performing it with the 'proper countenance' or 'demeanor' that expresses the proper attitude (AC 2:8, 8:4).[29]

However, Shusterman takes the idea of philosophy as an art of living in a radically new direction when he performed as the Man in Gold.[30] As Shusterman writes in the *Adventures*,

> my work with *L'homme en Or* also enlarged my sense of personal identity as a transactional philosopher of the art of living to embrace this golden, free-spirited, aesthetic avatar who, by extending my experience into new roles and contexts that initiate new gestural responses and new feelings, further expands my philosophical self and self-knowledge by including *L'homme en Or* as a philosopher without words.[31]

In other words, this new approach of philosophy expands from the practice of somaesthetics in art into Shusterman's whole life. It follows from this that Shusterman's somaesthetics has become so broad that it is already a philosophy, a "traditionally new" type of philosophy. As he puts it,

> If philosophy is more than merely words, if it can be creatively embodied, then it provides a twofold challenge as an art of living. It is not enough to compose our texts and refine our language with logical and literary skill; we must also take real pains, in practicing philosophy, to give careful composition to our character, behavior, and bearing, and to refine them

---

29 Shusterman, "The Philosopher without Words," in *Unsettled Boundaries: Philosophy, Art, Ethics East/West*, ed. Curtis L. Carter (Milwaukee: Marquette University Press, 2017), 49.
30 Cf. Shusterman, *The Adventures of the Man in Gold: Paths Between Art and Life, A Philosophical Tale*, tr. English to French by Thomas Mondémé, Somaflux Photography by Yann Toma (Paris: Éditions Hermann, 2016).
31 Shusterman, "The Philosopher without Words," 48.

through harmonizing grace and attractive style and expressive gesture that are artfully appealing though not artificial or insincere.[32]

---

[32] *Ibid.*, 50.

CHAPTER 3

Somaesthetics, Somapower, and the Microphysics of Emancipation

Leszek Koczanowicz

In 1999 the Chinese Communist Government began to crack down on Falun Gong.[1] Falun Gong is a cross between a religious sect and a corporeal practice healing movement. Commenting on the event in *The New York Times*, Ian Buruma wrote:

> From a historical perspective, Falun Gong looks very familiar. Secret societies, religious movements and faith-healing sects, based on a mishmash of Buddhism, Taoism and millenarian folk beliefs, have been part of the Chinese scene for thousands of years. They tend to grow—and grow violent in times of crisis and transition.[2]

What was characteristic of Falun Gong was that the movement never questioned Communist power, presenting itself instead as promoting well-being through bodily practices and spiritual meditations. Buruma identified Falun Gong as the last incarnation of the long line of Eastern sects that combined physical exercises with a more or less elaborate spiritual message. But such movements are by no means unique to the East. Similar tendencies are easily observed in the West as well.

Most of them begin without any political agenda, but some are forced by the state to take a political stand, as was the case with Falun Gong. As a rule, such movements become popular with the oppressed, giving them a chance to convert their lives and achieve some level of independence from their oppressors, or at least the illusion (the false sense) of it. Sometimes, as exemplified in martial arts, which are so popular across cultures, the body itself becomes an instrument of opposition against state power, for example, by breaking the state's monopoly on violence, as the sociologist Max Weber once defined the state. In this way, martial arts and other social practices and movements come

---

1 The text has been written in the framework of National Science Center Grant no. 2018/29/B/HS2/00041.
2 Ian Buruma, "The Sect That Became an Enemy of the State," *New York Times*, July 25, 1999.

to embody the very idea of emancipation, as was the case with, for instance, capoeira, which is a mixture of ritual, dance, gymnastics, and religion. As Matthias Röhrig Assunção writes in *Capoeira: The History of An Afro-Brazilian Martial Art*, "one of the reasons capoeira fascinates young people all over the world is that it still seems to epitomize resistance: against the slave owner, the police, the establishment."[3]

In my paper, I will focus on how such movements can be conceptualized within the humanities and social sciences. The difficulty is that they are located at the intersection of two important, but inadequately researched, theoretical fields: the body as a vehicle of social critique, and the relation between everydayness and politics. I would like to address these two issues by discussing briefly the debates on them unfolding in the contemporary social sciences and humanities. This will enable me to identify the existing gaps and suggest, sketchily I'm afraid, how they could be bridged. My main argument is that we need an adequate understanding of the relations between the body and power, emerging from the pragmatist tradition, and which appears in Richard Shusterman's pragmatist philosophy.

After Michel Foucault's seminal work on biopolitics, biopower, and the microphysics of power, to speak about the political significance of the body may sound like a platitude. In a way, Foucault changed the focus of political thought by integrating the corporeal side of the human into it. Before Foucault, political theory had been preoccupied mainly with pure ideas, in which the body "evaporated" even if human physicality was clearly referenced or targeted, as for instance in revolutionary terror. Of course, a great deal of political and social theory is still like this, but there is also a growing recognition of the relevance of the body to the understanding of politics. However, as Lemke writes: "Foucault's concept of biopolitics assumes the dissociation and abstraction of life from its concrete physical bearers. The objects of biopolitics are not singular human beings but their biological features measured and aggregated on the level of populations."[4] This strategy was, of course, justified by the purpose of Foucault's work, which was to show the distinctiveness of modern politics. At the same time, however, Foucault's strategy makes it much more difficult to forge a link between his concept of biopolitics and his concept of the social body as shaped by the mechanisms of power.

---

3 Matthias Röhrig Assunção, *Capoeira: The History of An Afro-Brazilian Martial Art* (London: Routledge, 2005), 2.
4 Thomas Lemke, *Biopolitics: An Advanced Introduction*, tr. E. F. Trump (New York: New York University Press, 2011), 5.

Trying to construct such a link, we encounter one more problem. The significance of Foucault's work consists in depicting how bodies are shaped and controlled by power. But, as many have noticed, his theory is problematic in that it treats the body almost exclusively as a passive material to be transformed and subordinated into docility. Obviously, in his later work, Foucault introduced the concept of the "technologies of the self," which attributed far more agency to the body, but its conceivable power-opposing potency still remained very individualistic as it enabled "individuals to effect by their own means or with the help of others a certain number of operations on their own bodies and souls, thoughts, conduct, and way of being, so as to transform themselves in order to attain a certain state of happiness, purity, wisdom, perfection, or immortality."[5]

This flaw has also plagued Foucault-inspired efforts to combine biopower with biopolitics, as exemplified in an influential paper written by Paul Rabinow and Nikolas Rose entitled "Biopower Today," where biopower is defined in the following terms:

> The concept of biopower seeks to individuate strategies and configurations that combine three dimensions or planes—a form of truth discourse about living beings and an array of authorities considered competent to speak that truth; strategies for intervention upon collective existence in the name of life and health; and modes of subjectification, in which individuals can be brought to work on themselves, under certain forms of authority, in relation to truth discourses, by means of practices of the self, in the name of individual or collective life or health.[6]

Although this approach has produced many interesting works on empowering patients in health systems, especially those from oppressed groups, it did not actually expand the field of social theory.[7]

There are two main reasons for this failure. One of them is that a distorted image of the relation between politics and everyday life prevails in the humanities and social sciences. The other is that an adequate concept of the body is

---

5   Michel Foucault, "Technologies of the Self," in *Technologies of the Self: A Seminar with Michel Foucault*, ed. Luther H. Martin, Huck Gutman, and Patrick H. Hutton (Amherst: University of Massachusetts Press, 1988), 17.
6   Paul Rabinow and Nikolas Rose, "Biopower Today," *BioSocieties*, vol. 1, issue 2 (June 2006), 203–204.
7   See, for example, Maren Klawiter, *The Biopolitics of Breast Cancer: Changing Cultures of Disease and Activism* (Minneapolis: University of Minnesota Press, 2008).

lacking, which would combine its social character with the appreciation of its emancipatory potential.

Admittedly, research on everydayness is robustly developing and studies on various dimensions of everydayness are proliferating across disciplines, from history to sociology and cultural studies, yet the political significance of everydayness still remains less than discernible. The everydayness-politics relations are usually framed in three models. The first posits their radical separation. In this framework, politics is an autonomous sphere not reducible to any other elements of social life. This independent dimension of politics is often conceptualized as a division between politics and the political (in French *la politique* and *le politique*). As Paul Ricœur elucidates this difference in his seminal paper "The Political Paradox," "political alienation is not reducible to another, but is constitutive of human existence, and, in this sense, that the political mode of existence entails the breach between the citizen's abstract life and the concrete life of the family and of work."[8] Although social theory boasts a range of various conceptualizations of the political division, each valorizing it differently, they all share the idea that politics is above any muddling with social reality of everyday life.

However, regardless of how we separate politics from everyday life, it is clear that much political pressure is exerted in petty mundane activities. The extreme cases of such influence are, of course, totalitarian regimes with their obsession with control, but even in democratic societies politically motivated changes in legislation can alter everyday life engagements and pursuits. The evidence that politics has an impact on everyday life and that this impact can be, by general consensus, unjust, lays at the foundation of what may be called the *"critique of everyday life."* As Henri Lefebvre writes in *Critique of Everyday Life*,

> Everyday life includes political life: the public consciousness, the consciousness of belonging to a society and a nation, the consciousness of class. It enters into permanent contact with the State and the State apparatus thanks to administration and bureaucracy. But on the other hand, political life detaches itself from everyday life by concentrating itself in privileged moments (elections, for example), and by fostering specialized activities. *Thus the critique of everyday life involves a critique of political life, in that everyday life already contains and constitutes such a critique:* in that it *is* that critique.[9]

---

8 Paul Ricœur, "The Political Paradox," in *History and Truth*, tr. Charles A. Kelbley (Evanston: Northwestern University Press, 2007), 260.
9 Henri Lefebvre, *Critique of Everyday Life* (London: Verso, 2014), 114.

This type of critique has been widely practiced by the left wing, beginning with Friedrich Engels's seminal *The Condition of Working Class in England*, and Karl Marx's *Economic and Philosophic Manuscripts*.[10] More recently, Pierre Bourdieu has shown in his monumental oeuvre how class divisions shape almost all facets of everyday life, including the body, as in his famous category of habitus.

Though without a doubt immensely significant, this type of critique has a crucial flaw. It is focused on *reproduction* of social inequalities, and largely ignores human agency, while arguably people are not just objects in the reproduction of social structure. Crucially, they can also develop a critical approach to the existing social order by drawing on their everyday life experience. Luc Boltanski was the most important sociologist to demonstrate the mechanism of this critique. In contrast to Bourdieu's critical sociology, Boltanski in *On Critique: A Sociology of Emancipation* calls his ideological agenda a pragmatic sociology of critique, and emphasizes that

> The *actors* whom these works have made visible were very different from the *agents* who feature in the critical sociology of domination. They were always active, not passive ... They made their demands, denounced injustices, produced evidence in support of their complaints, or constructed arguments to justify themselves in the face of the critiques to which they were themselves subjected. Envisaged thus, the social world does not appear to be the site of domination endured passively and unconsciously, but instead as a space shot through by a multiplicity of disputes, critiques, disagreements and attempts to re-establish locally agreements that are always fragile.[11]

According to Boltanski, every successful concept of social critique must draw on individuals' experiences and on the ways they feel the injustice of their social systems:

> Critical theories feed off these ordinary critiques, even if they develop them differently, reformulate them, and are destined to return to them, since their aim is to *render reality unacceptable*, and thereby engage the people to whom they are addressed in action whose result should be to change its contours. The idea of critical theory that is not backed by the

---

10   Karl Marx, *Economic and Philosophic Manuscripts of 1844*, tr. Martin Milligan (Amherst: Prometheus Books, 1988).
11   Luc Boltanski, *On Critique: A Sociology of Emancipation*, tr. Gregory Elliott (Malden: Polity Press, 2011), 26–27.

experience of a collective, and which in some sense exists for its own sake—that is for no one—is incoherent.[12]

Boltanski insists that critique is founded on individuality that opposes the system and the disembodied institution. Individuality, which is inexorably bound up with the body and submerged in everydayness, can stand up to the ubiquity of the institutional order. Boltanski is certainly right to observe that the ritualization of the institutional order may also be channeled through bodiliness and though emotions which are implicated in the ritual. This strategy may be effective for some time, but as the totalitarian experience has shown, it loses its allure the moment it is confronted with existential tests, which are ascribed a major role in Boltanski's concept of critique. They are "based on experiences, like those of injustice or humiliation, sometimes with the shame that accompanies them, but also, in other cases, the joy created by transgression when it affords access to some form of authenticity."[13] Nevertheless, "these experiences are difficult to formulate or thematize because there exists no pre-established format to frame them, or even because, considered from the standpoint of the existing order, they have an aberrant character."[14] Given this, a critique powered by this perspective has some distinctive features, since its originary experiences "are situated on the margins of *reality*—reality as it is 'constructed' in a certain social order—these existential tests open up a path to the *world*. Hence they are one of the sources from which a form of critique can emerge that might be called *radical*, in order to distinguish it from *reformist* critiques intended to improve existing reality tests."[15] Of course, existential tests form only a part of a possible critique of the existing reality, but, in my view, they are extremely interesting in that they highlight the relevance of individual, often bodily, experience to devising political agendas.

Nevertheless, it seems that such critique must lie at the origin of all types of social critique if they are to be effective. In terms of my argument, the most important issue is in how far corporeal/visceral/emotional reactions can serve as a vehicle of critique, and also how far bodily activities can serve as a vehicle of emancipation, at least at the individual level.

To define emancipation at this level, we must reflect on emancipation as such. Emancipation has to be understood not only as a certain general movement toward a greater freedom and/or equality, but also as a set of everyday

---

12   *Ibid.*, 5.
13   *Ibid.*, 107.
14   *Ibid.*, 107–108.
15   *Ibid.*, 108.

life activities that enable people to obtain more autonomy in their actual social relations. This latter aspect of social and political life, which I call "microphysics of emancipation," is largely overlooked by the pundits of political theory. They tend to concentrate on "big" issues related to power struggle. At the same time, researchers of everyday life history or culture usually attend to the influence of politics on everyday life, and not the other way around. This situation in social theory reinforces the popularity of the "political division" between politics and the political. While the division does indeed help highlight the conflictual nature of the public and private spheres, it also precludes understanding the potential inherent in dialogue and cooperation, without which society as such simply cannot exist.

This "microphysics of emancipation" can be multifaceted, as Jeff Goldfarb insists in *The Politics of Small Things*,[16] a book devoted to cultural resistance in Communist Poland, and as Li Bennich-Björkman has found in his research on existential resistance in the Baltic States and Western Ukraine. Generally speaking, such emancipation does not have a political character; originally, it is a-political or even anti-political, and its politicization is a secondary development triggered by the pressure of the totalitarian state. Goldfarb describes unexpected places of freedom, such as the kitchen in a small Polish apartment:

> Our first picture is of a general but significant location: the kitchen table in Poland and elsewhere in the old bloc. During the Soviet period, small circles of intimate friends were able to talk to each other without concern for the present party line around the kitchen table. ... Any denigration of private space was viewed with suspicion. Any attempt to make private questions political seemed exactly wrong.[17]

Goldfarb convincingly argues that such islands of freedom created a climate of unofficial opinion, which, in turn, resulted in founding Solidarity in 1980, which became the first independent organization in a communist country since the October Revolution.

Bodily, corporeal practices hold a prominent place among various forms of micro-emancipation. Their specific nature can be grasped in light of the theories of the body evoked above, which highlight its social constructedness, and, at the same time, foreground its emancipatory potential. One can observe three distinctive, albeit interconnected, trends in the theoretical conceptualization

---

16   Jeffrey Goldfarb, *The Politics of Small Things: The Power of the Powerless in Dark Times* (Chicago: University of Chicago Press, 2006).
17   *Ibid.*, 10.

of the body. The first trend has originated in the phenomenological approach of Maurice Merleau-Ponty whose work is a turning point in the philosophical discussion on the body.[18] However, Merleau-Ponty interprets the body as an agent of perception rather than the agent of action. Therefore, his great oeuvre has only a limited significance for research on the body as a vehicle of emancipation, although it has inspired an interesting investigation in philosophical medicine.[19] The second trend is focused on political and social construction of the body. Here, Foucault's seminal discussion of the body as a vehicle of social oppression is of great importance. He shows convincingly that modernity developed various methods of shaping and controlling bodily activities. Moreover, Foucault forged a link between the concept of the social body and his notion of power as a ubiquitous phenomenon which permeates all social and political relationships. To some extent Foucault's idea of the body can be supplemented by Pierre Bourdieu's investigations on the shaping the body by class divisions.[20] His notions of *habitus* and *hexis* serve as tools for analyzing how everyday bodily practices are influenced by the place which an individual has in the social hierarchy. However, despite the greatest significance of their work, they perceive the body as a rather passive object of the social influence.

A third trend appears in the pragmatist view of the body, as formulated by John Dewey and George Herbert Mead, and developed by Richard Shusterman, whose view is of primary importance to our discussion. In their early writings, both Dewey and Mead show convincingly that, broadly conceived, our mental phenomena are merely moments in a complicated co-ordination between the organism and its environment, which is, rather than mere adaptation, first of all a complex process of interaction, where the organism is able to change its environment and also itself. The emphasis Dewey and Mead placed on the role of bodiliness was a response to the excessive intellectualism of introspective psychology, which was prevalent in the early 19th century. To a degree, they both followed in the footsteps of William James, who despite his generally dualist psychological approach, frequently referred to bodily activities as the foundation of mental life. In their mature works, Dewey and Mead reveal the mechanisms through which the body manages its relations with its surroundings. Dewey, for example, in his social psychology explores how intelligent bodily habits work in order to construct and reconstruct our relationships with

---

18   Maurice Merleau-Ponty, *Phenomenology of Perception*, tr. Donald Landes (London: Routledge, 2012).
19   Drew Leder, *The Absent Body* (Chicago: University of Chicago Press, 1990).
20   Pierre Bourdieu, *Distinction: A Social Critique of the Judgement of Taste*, tr. Richard Nice (Cambridge: Harvard University Press, 1984).

social settings. Mead's sophisticated theory of the social self locates the self as originating in biological co-ordinations through gestures. Furthermore, in his later years, Dewey developed an interest in the Alexander Technique as a way of improving the quality of life through bodily practices.

Still, the concepts of the body developed by Dewey and Mead only have a limited significance. They were interested not so much in the body as such, as rather in the body as a vehicle of relations with the social and natural environment. It took quite a while for the potential of the pragmatist idea of what bodiliness is to fully flesh out in the work of Richard Shusterman. Of course, Shusterman has been able to build on a rather different theoretical background, featuring the breakthrough studies of Merleau-Ponty and Foucault, in which the body is elevated into an independent agent of knowledge or social relations. Shusterman has shown that, from the pragmatist perspective, both their frameworks call for an essential corrective. Nevertheless, it was a critical scrutiny of the concept of the body in John Dewey in "Redeeming Somatic Reflection: John Dewey's Philosophy of Body-Mind"[21] that served Shusterman as the starting point. Shusterman is aware that Dewey's concept of the body is partially flawed and in need for correction. Here I am not going to examine in detail his account of Dewey's philosophy of the body, but I will note that Shusterman acknowledges a troubling dilemma inherited through Dewey's thought.

> Here then is the core practical dilemma of body consciousness: We must rely on unreflective feelings and habits—because we can't reflect on everything and because such unreflective feelings and habits always ground our very efforts of reflection. But we also cannot entirely rely on them and the judgments they generate, because some of them are considerably flawed and inaccurate. Moreover, how can we discern their flaws and inadequacy when they are concealed by their unreflective, immediate, habitual status; and how can we correct them when our conscious, reflective efforts of correction spontaneously rely on the same inaccurate, habitual mechanisms of perception and action that we are trying to correct?[22]

In the text in question, Shusterman does not give a definite answer to this problem, but he hints that despite our technological progress we are still

---

21 Richard Shusterman, *Body Consciousness: A Philosophy of Mindfulness and Somaesthetics* (Cambridge: Cambridge University Press, 2008), 180–216.
22 *Ibid.*, 212.

heavily dependent on our bodies, which, in turn, are inscribed in our social and cultural practices.

> Despite our evolutionary progress of rational transcendence (including the technological advancements that some regard as rendering us posthuman cyborgs), we still essentially and dependently belong to a much wider natural and social world that continues to shape the individuals we are (including our reasoning consciousness) in ways beyond the control of our will and consciousness. As oxygen is necessary for the functioning of consciousness in the brain, so the practices, norms, and language of society are necessary materials for our processes of reasoning and evaluation. It is not moral perfectionism but blind arrogance to think otherwise.[23]

Seeking inspiration for his research, Shusterman explores the Eastern philosophies of Confucius and Mencius, showing that they vividly depict how the progress of our mental faculties is closely linked with the state of our bodies. These diverse sources, however, share one important conviction: namely, the more we concentrate on the body, the more we realize that the body cannot be considered apart from the environmental contexts, both natural and social, in which it develops and progresses. Therefore, the exercise of the perfection of our bodies can bring about a better relationship with the outer world as well as a better understanding of ourselves. So Shusterman writes in the conclusion:

> By enabling us to feel more of our universe with greater acuity, awareness, and appreciation, such a vision of somaesthetic cultivation promises the richest and deepest palate of experiential fulfillments because it can draw on the profusion of cosmic resources, including an uplifting sense of cosmic unity. Enchanting intensities of experience can thus be achieved in everyday living without requiring violent measures of sensory intensification that threaten ourselves and others. And if we still prefer more dangerous psychosomatic experiments of extreme intensity, our somaesthetically cultivated sensory awareness should render us more alert to the imminent risks and also more skilled in avoiding or diminishing the damage.[24]

---

23 *Ibid.*, 214.
24 *Ibid.*, 216.

Ponderings on the status of the body in various philosophies in general and on the pragmatist theory of the body in particular led Shusterman to conclude that it was expedient to found a new interdisciplinary research field. He called it "somaesthetics," and defined its pursuits and goals as follows:

> Beyond reorienting aesthetic inquiry, somaesthetics seeks to transform philosophy in a more general way. By integrating theory and practice through disciplined somatic training, it takes philosophy in a pragmatist meliorist direction, reviving the ancient idea of philosophy as an embodied way of life rather than a mere discursive field of abstract theory.[25]

The essential objective of somaesthetics is thus to look for the ways of making our lives richer and fuller through engaging in bodily practices and exercises. This approach clearly presupposes that the body bears an emancipatory potential which can be activated by means of social and individual somatic practices. Of course, harmonious development is optimally fostered when these two dimensions are aligned with each other. This, however, is not always the case. Individual aspirations for development may collide with social conditions, which opens an avenue through which somaesthetics can enter the political field. Somaesthetics, as Shusterman explains, aims at

> studying the ways we use our soma in perception, performance, and self-fashioning; the ways that physiology and society shape and constrain those uses; and the methods we have developed or can invent to enhance those uses and provide newer and better forms of somatic awareness and functioning.[26]

In the political field, the major task of somaesthetics would be to reveal how the body could be both a vehicle of emancipation and a site of resistance against an oppressive regime. Given the weight of the problem, I propose introducing a separate concept of somapower to capture this particular discipline. Somapower refers to Foucault's notion of biopower, the difference being that I underline the operative body engaged in action and capable of resisting external pressures. This concept vitally affirms that while the body is shaped by social relations of power, it can also shape these relations. In this sense, somapower is intimately intertwined with the concept of the microphysics

---

25　Shusterman, *Thinking through the Body: Essays in Somaesthetics* (Cambridge: Cambridge University Press, 2012), 3.
26　Ibid., 188.

of emancipation I evoked above. The development and liberation of bodies from oppression produces a niche of freedom even if the external conjuncture is averse to it. Such niches of freedom may vary widely, depending both on the strategies of somapower and on the possibilities afforded by the political circumstances and by the cultural rules in place. One thing is constant among this variety; specifically, somapower always means the resistance of the concrete against an abstract and oppressive ideology. In fiction, this clash is impressively rendered in an episode of an apocryphal version of the Gospel created by Mikhail Bulgakov in his masterpiece *The Master and Margarita*, when the famous dialogue between Jesus Christ and Pontius Pilate takes an unexpected turn (compared to the canonical version). Pilate asks, "What is truth?" The answer he receives is astonishing:

> The truth is, first of all, that your head aches, and aches so badly that you're having faint-hearted thoughts of death. You're not only unable to speak to me, but it is even hard for you to look at me. And I am now your unwilling torturer, which upsets me. You can't even think about anything and only dream that your dog should come, apparently the one being you are attached to. But your suffering will soon be over, your headache will go away.[27]

It is rather easy to read in this text a hardly disguised critique of abstract ideology, which is always in service of an oppressive power. Yeshua opposed to the ornamented splendor of Rome the logic of the suffering body, which is the one and only true reality.

Emotionally powerful though it is, Bulgakov's literary vision is not a research treatise, of course, and as such begs a commentary. It is through its materiality that the body can become a vehicle of emancipation, but also a site of oppression and violence. Its palpability is alluring, because it seems easy to instrumentalize. Totalitarian regimes relish all kinds of gymnastic shows and promote sports, particularly those that have military applications. Physical activity helps trigger feelings which channel identification with the regime. Terrorist movements use the body as an instrument of violence, a practice drastically illustrated by suicide bombings. Somaesthetics and somapower provide a clear criterion in this matter: the soma becomes a site of emancipation only on condition that bodily activity and somatic practices are autonomous

---

[27] Mikhail Bulgakov, *The Master and Margarita*, tr. Richard Pevear and Larissa Volokhonsky (New York: Penguin Books, 2007), 97.

and do not serve any purpose exterior to the soma itself and the development of its potential. Ultimately, this translates into intellectual growth, increased emotional sensitivity, and richer and more complete social relationships. The criterion of bodily autonomy engenders value judgments on political systems. A system can only garner a positive appraisal if it ensures conditions for development and does not seek to harness the corporeal in the service of ideology or violence.

CHAPTER 4

Living Beauty, Rethinking Rap: Revisiting Shusterman's Philosophy of Hip Hop

Max Ryynänen

1   From the Bronx to Finland

Twenty-six years ago, during the winter of 1993/1994, I enrolled in Väinö Kirstinä's (1936–2007) poetry course. Kirstinä was post-Dadaist, but also a precise minimalist writer whose work I admired. In Northern European literary modernism, which, at that time, still haunted us, rhymes were "banned." I used rhymes in my poems though, inspired as I was by my encounters with Latin American poets. I was the only one in the course who did. I remember in our feedback session Kirstinä went silently through my pile. I sensed he was uneasy with my choice to use rhyme and that he did not really know what to say. In the end, the poet removed his glasses, took a deep breath, and said: "I have heard that in America poets are out in the streets performing their work. They use rhymes again. This is called rap music." It was petrifyingly cold that morning in snowy mid-Finland. Geographically and culturally, we were light years away from the birthplace of rap, the block houses at Sedgwick Avenue in the Bronx, New York, where DJ Kool Herc had looped breakbeats at his sister's birthday party twenty years earlier, on August 13, 1973. Far away from Finland, some years ago my wife and I made a pilgrimage to the Bronx to see the graffiti-covered site where it all began. Rap must have been already "in the house," if even elderly modernist poets like Kirstinä knew about it.

2   Rap's Struggle for Scholarly Recognition

Rapping started with Nigerian Yoruba galas with abusive female poems, and with the work of the griots, i.e., musicians working on oral poetry, in Ivory Coast. With slavery, rap traveled to America where it produced new poetics and rhyme-based linguistic techniques, for example, in Harlem, New York, and the "signifying songs" of New Orleans, Louisiana.[1] As Gladney Marvin writes

---

[1] David Toop, *The Rap Attack: African Jive to New York Hip Hop* (London: The Works, 1984), 31–33. Claudia Mitchell-Kernan, "Signifying, Loud-Talking and Marking," in *Rappin' and Stylin'*

in "The Black Arts Movement and Hip-Hop," rap could be seen already to be part of the black arts movement, in tendencies within the Harlem Renaissance such as seeking for autonomy and a balance between artistic freedom and commercialism.[2] Rap also took as much from the world of pop and soul as it took from the tradition of inversion in Afro-American communication, and the classical dynamics of an Afro-American audience.[3] The use of breakbeat loops—from today's perspective, a quite dry rhyming on the beats—and the way early rap often did not base much of its musical agenda on melody, caused many to speak of a new art form. Rap was like the platypus, hard to categorize when academics "found it."

When musicians, cultural journalists, and public intellectuals were not nagging about how rappers only spoke but did not really sing, and that rap was not "real music," and that it was not "composed" but created by appropriation of other people's songs, and, generally, what Kirstinä may have had in mind mentioning these "America poets" who "are out in the streets performing their

---

Out: Communication in Urban Black America, ed. Thomas Kochman (Urbana: University of Illinois Press, 1972), 315–335.

2 Marvin Gladney, "The Black Arts Movement and Hip-Hop," in *African American Review* 29 (1995), 291–301, 293. See also Herbert Grabes, "The Revival of Pragmatist Aesthetics," in *Pragmatism and Literary Studies: Yearbook of Research in English and American Literature*, ed. Winfried Fluck (Tübingen: Narr Verlag, 2002), 137–149. Grabes criticizes Shusterman to say rap could also survive in the consumer society, and that it did not need support like some highbrow arts (146). But Grabes's analysis is misguided. We also have painting and poetry which receive no support from cities, societies, or theorists, e.g., marketplace painting and rhymes in advertisements. We know support and legitimization make it possible to find a wider array of possibilities inside any art form. Why keep anything narrow and just for markets alone? Interestingly, it looks like neither Marvin nor any other African-American philosophers and theorists who touched upon rap music, dug up older African American classics, like W. E. B. DuBois or Alain Locke for support to work on the philosophy of rap music. In "From Natural Roots to Cultural Radicalism: Pragmatist Aesthetics in Alain Locke and John Dewey," in *Surface and Depth: Dialectics of Criticism and Culture* (Ithaca: Cornell University Press, 2002), Shusterman discusses Locke's openly somatic approach to the arts (129); the philosophy of DuBois (which is touched upon) may also be of interest, e.g., DuBois's most famous work, *The Souls of Black Folk* (New York: Bantam Classics 1989; orig. 1903). Here Dubois aspires to show a very simple thing: African Americans also have a soul. This is shown through analogies between them and white people. One could say, that in some sense, as an aficionado of African-American music, Shusterman pedagogically also explained in the same way to the (white) highbrow intellectuals of the early 1990s that rap is an art form too—a work which has since then been increasingly important in the field of postcolonial cultural studies. To straighten up things from an intercultural point of view we sometimes need to show similarities between traditions.

3 Anette Powell Williams, "Dynamics of a Black Audience," in *Rappin' and Stylin' Out*, 101–106; William Labov, "Rules for Ritual Insults," in *Rappin' and Stylin' Out*, 265–314; and Grace Simms Holt, " 'Inversion' in Black Communications," also in *Rappin' and Stylin' Out*, 152–159.

work," doing this thing "called rap music."[4] The American pragmatist philosopher Richard Shusterman commented on the state of the art and its criticism in his groundbreaking essay, "The Fine Art of Rap," collected in *Pragmatist Aesthetics: Living Beauty, Rethinking Art* (1992): "Rap is today's fastest growing genre of popular music, and the most maligned and persecuted."[5] At the time, in Finland, I think this really was as true as it was in America.[6]

If Rap and Hip Hop Studies today have a strong focus on gender, identity, politics, and religion,[7] early scholarly debates often accentuated, if not the textual side, then the widely held idea that rap was a new form of music or a new form of art or culture.[8] Today the family of highbrow practices which has

---

4   Interestingly the lack of "traditional" and/or "original" (read: Central European highbrow) composition, vs. improvisation, was also a problem for some early European philosophical commentaries on jazz; see, for example, Henry Parland's critique of jazz in *Säginteannat: Samlad Prosa* (Helsinki: Söderström, 1970; orig. 1929); Shusterman, *Pragmatist Aesthetics: Living Beauty, Rethinking Art* (Oxford: Blackwell, 1992), 201. Everywhere Shusterman's early work on rap music was discussed at the time of its publication and in its early reception, the analysis of the lyrics of Stetsasonic's *Talkin' All That Jazz* (1988) in *Pragmatist Aesthetics* was at the forefront.

5   Shusterman, *Pragmatist Aesthetics*, 201. See also Shusterman, "The Fine Art of Rap," *New Literary History*, 22 (1991), 613–633; and Shusterman, "The Fine Art of Rap," Part 1, in *JOR Quarterly: The Journal of Rap Expression and Hip Hop Culture*, 2:2, 36 (1992), 13–15, 36; "The Fine Art of Rap," Part 2 in *JOR Quarterly: The Journal of Rap Expression and Hip Hop Culture*, 2:4, 10–11, 15–17; Shusterman, "Ghetto Music," in *JOR Quarterly: The Journal of Rap Expression and Hip Hop Culture*, 2, 1, 11–18; Shusterman, "L'esthétique postmoderne du rap ["The Postmodern Aesthetic of Rap"], *Rue Descartes* 5.6 (1992), 209–228. Ex-Black Panther George Ware served as Editor-in-Chief of *JOR Quarterly: The Journal of Rap Expression and Hip Hop Culture* in the 1990s, at the time when rap legend Chuck D wrote for the journal, and when Shusterman himself published some of his first essays on rap. See also Shusterman, "Rap Remix: Pragmatism, Postmodernism and Other Issues in the House," *Inquiry* 22, no. 1 (1995), 150–158; Shusterman, "Art Infraction: Goodman, Rap, Pragmatism," *Australasian Journal of Philosophy*, 73, 2, 269–279; and Massimo Bortolotti, "Colloquio con Richard Shusterman," *Juliet Art Magazine* 95 (1995), 24–25. See also Herbert Gans, *Popular Culture and High Culture* (New York: Basic Books, 1974).

6   Of course, any new art form, whether rap or "techno" music will stimulate scholarly debate, but rap appears to be the last popular art to have gained serious institutional and theoretical support for being Art with a capital "A." See also Gilbert Seldes, *The 7 Lively Arts* (New York: Harper & Brothers Publishers, 1924).

7   Bettina L. Love, *Hip Hop's Li'l Sistas Speak: Negotiating Hip Hop Identities and Politics in the New South* (New York: Peter Lang, 2012); and Inka Rantakallio, "Muslimhiphop. com: Constructing Muslim Hip Hop Identities on the Internet," *Cyber Orient* (2013), 7, 2.

8   For an early statement of this work, see Esa Sironen's essay " 'Hip-hop don't stop:' Katujen uutta kulttuuria" (1987), in *Aistimellisuus, sivistys ja massakulttuuri: Fragmentteja eräästä projektista 1977–1987*, ed. Lauri Mehtonen and Esa Sironen (Jyväskylä: Jyväskylän yliopisto,

become the major framework for arts throughout the world, and by colonialization and diaspora, can make some Central European scholars feel uneasy due to complicated connections to gender, class, and colonial history. At the time rap theory began, belonging to this "family of practices," or, at least, gaining acceptance as a satellite, was often the best one could do. By contrast, the contemporary art world is so open to different methods and practices that one hardly struggles in the same way for recognition and legitimacy for alternative practices and methods in the arts. For example, Halil Altindere's music videos featuring rap (produced as community art) have been at the front of central exhibition forums like the Berlin Biennale (2016) and the Museum of Modern Art. The growth of popular culture and the rise of Popular Culture Studies have also dramatically decreased the need for traditional practices of legitimation of an art as truly "art."[9]

According to Frederic Jameson in *Postmodernism, or The Cultural Logic of Late Capitalism*, and other works, the postmodern culture of the 1980s and 1990s is permeated by collage and a sense of cultural schizophrenia. Such fragmentation and confusion render difficult any project of determining the foundations and boundaries of modernity, and therefore justifying any project of emancipatory politics or radical cultural critique.[10] No less difficult within the fragmentation of late twentieth century postmodernism, with the ever-widening divisions of art, science, morality, and politics, was determining any way to see in popular culture, in general, and popular music, in particular, and rap especially, any kind of normative critique of culture.

1987). I translate the title of the article into English as " 'Hip Hop Don't Stop:' New Street Culture." Sironen's essay is a sociological interpretation of hip hop, examined in relation to the movies of the time. There we find a broader analysis of the holistic combination of music, text and dance, which together with graffiti, according to Sironen, signifies a positive take on mass culture, street life and commercialism. Sironen, in his sociological aesthetic approach, even claims that the fast moves of hip hop dance resonate with the destiny of the singing of some urban birds. Some birds are singing shorter melodies because of their fast-paced and noisy environment, e.g., Sironen mentions the great tit (*parus major*). Sironen thought that breakdancing embodied this. Mtume Salaam in "The Aesthetics of Rap" also discusses rap's essential features as a new musical art, discussing, for example, concepts like "flow" (*African American Review* 29, 2 [1995], 303–323, 305).

9 One reason may have been that it was hard to see rap as music; another may have been that there was not yet any commonly known scene of noise music.

10 In the late 1990s, scholars were asking if new cultural formations had already brought this forth; to this day, I do not understand why nobody asked why we had to wait for modernism to open its doors, as the world outside was full of art too.

3 Shusterman on Rap

Despite the confusion and with a sharp eye to the sheer genius of rap, Shusterman's philosophical analysis of rap and hip hop, in essays like "The Fine Art of Rap" and "Form and Funk: The Aesthetic Challenge of Popular Art" (both collected in *Pragmatist Aesthetics*), was nothing short of revolutionary. Building primarily on the American philosophical tradition of pragmatism, and especially the works of John Dewey like *Art as Experience*, Shusterman set aesthetic experience at the very foundation of democracy and thereby found a doorway out of the Ivory Tower to see cosmopolitan culture, in particular, and ultimately the world as a whole, as shaped through and through by art. But by examining popular art like hip hop as "fine art," and rendering hits like "Don't Believe the Hype" philosophy, inevitably Shusterman's works revealed their own "hit potential," and by implication greatly expanded the audience of American pragmatism. In fact, Shusterman's works on rap and hip hop have been central and formative to the entire evolving discourse on these topics in philosophical aesthetics and cultural studies, ultimately transforming these fields in deep ways; specifically, by including that which was theretofore so vehemently dismissed as unphilosophical.

In some ways the concept of "aesthetic experience" is not entirely new. After all, Aristotle sets the idea catharsis of the emotions of pity and terror at the center of his analysis of tragedy in the *Poetics* 4, not to mention making poetry philosophical in the *Poetics* 9. And certainly Shusterman draws in many ways upon Aristotle's naturalism and philosophy of art, but Dewey was arguably the first philosopher to make aesthetic experience the central dimension of his philosophy of art and experience in general. Dewey developed his pragmatist philosophy with art as a central element, following the earlier founding pragmatists Charles S. Peirce and William James, drawing more on James's creative view of experience, than Peirce who did little at all with art, but did make logic to depend on ethics and ethics to depend on aesthetics. But Dewey went beyond both in his aesthetic view of experience, and followed the argument where it led, to take seriously, in philosophical terms, the popular arts and popular culture of the age. In *Art as Experience*, for example, Dewey laments how the general population consumes comic books and jazz music, but somehow do not really think they are taking pleasure in art.[11] Unfortunately, Dewey does not provide a full and concrete analysis of any popular art form, or even any

---

11 John Dewey, *Art as Experience* (New York: Perigree Books, 1980), 5–6.

popular work of art, which he might have explored in what Shusterman calls Dewey's "pragmatist aesthetics."

For Dewey, aesthetic experience with the arts is one of the key motors in life and always has been, whether in hunting and gathering, or cultivating the land, or playing the flute. Historically the arts permeate all forms of life and add enjoyment and meaning. In the modern world, however, culture seems to have lost touch with the power of the arts, and in the process lost touch with what it is to be human. In his critique of the museum, for example, Dewey writes that in museums like the Louvre in Paris works of art have been taken from their original contexts of everyday human life, to be displayed as experientially shallow trophies. Deprived of their original roles in human culture, such works, according to Dewey, appear as shadows of their real nature and potentials.

In contrast to this detached view of aesthetics, found, for example, in Immanuel Kant's definition of "taste" as "the faculty for judging an object or a kind of representation through a satisfaction or dissatisfaction without any interest," in the "Analytic of the Beautiful," in the *Critique of Judgment*, Dewey advances a livelier and engaged and embodied relation to the arts, and one necessary for integrating human experience. In contemporary culture, everyday experience is fragmented: memories, aesthetic skills, organic energies, and all the other human faculties are constantly being pulled apart; but genuinely engaged aesthetic experience is capable of integrating human experience again. According to Dewey in *Art as Experience*, by engaging with an aesthetic object, e.g., a work of art, we accumulate, intensify, and bring together our capacities, and enter a flux, which in the end brings us aesthetic fulfillment.[12] We crave for a dynamic aesthetic event, writes Dewey in *Art as Experience*: we crave for a dialogical engagement with an aesthetic object through which we achieve a unique intellectual, emotional, and imaginative pleasure.[13] Virtually anything, from organized sports to hiking and camping can be a productive dialogical encounter in our aesthetic life.

Following Dewey, and building upon this theory of aesthetic experience, Shusterman in "Art as Dramatization" develops "the idea of art as dramatization," and then further defines dramatization: "In its more technical meaning, to dramatize means to 'put something on stage,' to take some event or story and put it in the frame of a theoretical performance or the form of a play or scenario." But, he adds, " 'dramatize' also has another main meaning that

---

12   Ibid., 132, 137.
13   Ibid., 158–159. See also Dewey, *Experience and Nature* (New York: Dover, 1958), 8–12.

suggests intensity."[14] Here Shusterman draws a connection to Dewey: "For, as Emerson, Nietzsche, Dewey, and other life-affirming aestheticians have realized, there is something in the vividness and intensity of art's aesthetic experience that heightens our natural vitality by responding to deeply embodied human needs."[15] As Dewey's pragmatism, in general, and aesthetics, in particular, accentuates the lived body, it was quite natural that rap music would evoke a need for rethinking Dewey, as Shusterman has done.[16]

4 Talkin' All That Rap

Today, it is difficult to remember how original rap once sounded with its "talkative" quality. But in any culture we may find musical pieces with spoken words, and certainly in African-American culture already the prefigurations of rap could be heard in musically and poetically in the "talkative" and "rappish" acts of James Brown, Pigmeat Markham, Amiri Baraka, Gil Scott-Heron, and Isaac Hayes. Still, this talkative and rappish quality would sound even more radical for rap's unique use of record players and readymade music, even if, in its early phases, this use was not always particularly melodic.

Shusterman in an essay entitled "L'esthétique postmoderne du rap," published in the French cultural journal *Parachute*, took up the theme of "cannibalism" as an image for explaining how rap consumed readymade music, and, in the process, transformed the music of other non-rap artists.[17] And in "The Fine Art of Rap" Shusterman refers to early and brilliant "rap DJs" as the "musical cannibals of the urban jungle."[18] This cannibalism proved a uniquely postmodern strategy, in contrast to romanticism and modernism. Romanticism and modernism, writes Shusterman in "The Fine Art of Rap," are both trapped

---

14 Shusterman, "Art as Dramatization," *The Journal of Aesthetics and Art Criticism*, 59, 4 (Autumn 2001), 363–372, 367.
15 *Ibid.*, 366.
16 After all, Dewey for decades had been a major thinker in American philosophy of art education circles, bringing his democratically oriented thought about culture made it easy to discuss culture at all levels of society. See also Jacques Ranciere, *Five Lessons in Intellectual Emancipation* (Stanford: Stanford University Press, 1991) on the need to develop intellectual democracy (e.g., we should listen to the poor and the less privileged, not explain things to them).
17 Brazilian writer Oswald de Andrade in his *Manifesto Antropófago* [The Cannibalist Manifesto], in *Third Text*, vol. 13, no. 46 (1999), celebrated 1928 Brazil's history of "cannibalizing" other cultures as its strength (92–95).
18 Shusterman, *Pragmatist Aesthetics*, 203.

in an "ideology of originality," deriving from a "sharp distinction between original creation and derivative borrowing." Postmodern art, in general, and rap, in particular, are entirely different. "Postmodern art like rap undermines this dichotomy by creatively deploying and thematizing its appropriation to show that borrowing and creation are not at all incompatible."[19] As a postmodern form of art, rap draws on contemporary technologies in its appropriation of readymade material.

According to Tim Brennan in "Off the Gangsta Tip: A Rap Appreciation, or Forgetting about Los Angeles," Shusterman was appropriating rap into philosophical and artistic postmodernism, and thereby bringing it into the context of white middle class America.[20] But, as Shusterman writes, African-Americans were no strangers to the concept of postmodernism; and several black American intellectuals had, like Shusterman, also found rap to express the new postmodern philosophy. Yet, if rap music expressed postmodernism, then postmodernism (as a philosophy) would also help to illuminate various dimensions of rap music, as aesthetically challenging, intellectually penetrating, and socially critical. We take for granted that European painting and classical music develop historically in dialogue with philosophy, each examining the other for its complexity and intellectual force. With the emergence and development of rap music as well, we need theoretical analysis and critique if we are to appreciate the new form of art and the culture in which it grows.

Part of the task of this ongoing critical and theoretical project is to explore the diverse landscape of rap studies. In general, popular culture does not tend to unify its analyses and discussions, e.g., in film, television, comics, or music, like rap music. Perhaps part of the reason for this pluralism is that there are still rather few forums and archives and experts in the field of popular culture studies (although, certainly, this is changing). As Mtume ya Salaam writes in "The Aesthetics of Rap,"

> After reading many articles supposedly concerning rap music—about the social aspects of rap music, the criminal elements in rap music, the lawsuits caused by rap music, sampling in rap music, gossip concerning rap musicians, how other musicians feel about rap music, etc.—I realized that I had yet to read about the music itself. In other words, I had not read about the 'aesthetics' of rap, about the qualifiers which made particular

---

19   *Ibid.*, 205.
20   Tim Brennan, "Off the Gangsta Tip: A Rap Appreciation, or Forgetting about Los Angeles," *Critical Inquiry* 20 (1994), 663–693.

examples of rap music good music—not necessarily good rap music, but simply good music.[21]

Of course, this point is overdrawn. After all, there *were* scholars writing about the aesthetics of rap, most prominently Shusterman himself in essays like "The Fine Art of Rap."[22] But if "The Fine Art of Rap" entered the academic mainstream in 1991 in a literary journal, the essay had a far greater impact collected and expanded as a chapter in Shusterman's *Pragmatist Aesthetics: Living Beauty, Rethinking Art*, which included a full-scale philosophical analysis and fierce defense of popular culture, together with sharply focused and thoroughgoing critique of the landscape of critical and often rather cynical texts against popular culture. At the time, nothing of the sort existed, not in philosophy or popular culture studies.

Some may claim such a defense as Shusterman's in *Pragmatist Aesthetics* to be an unnecessary task considering so many of the old charges against popular art, e.g., that it offers no real cultural satisfaction, or that it would never last, were absurd.[23] But as Shusterman writes in "From Natural Roots to Cultural Radicalism: Pragmatist Aesthetics in Alain Locke and John Dewey," the problem with many of these early critiques—together with charges of commercialism and violence leading even to censorship—is that they had the potential to undermine rap's struggle for recognition as a real form of art.[24] That is not to say these earlier critiques were without value, even if they were wrong, for they provided the philosophical occasion for critical debate, in which philosophers like Shusterman could reveal various assumptions about mass culture to be wrong, and effectively reset the debate. In this way, Shusterman and others have helped to clear a space to think through the complexities of popular culture, in general, and rap, in particular, for example, with regard to the technological poetics of recycling and appropriation of readymade material, and the

---

21 Salaam, "The Aesthetics of Rap" (1995), 303.
22 But if there were not many scholars of rap at the time, over the last several years the academic scene has improved dramatically, with more and more academic journals dedicated to popular culture and a growing community of scholars of popular culture. Cultural studies had already broken away from highbrow thinking, in the 1950s; and then (as now) many of their perspectives came from identity, class, and gender questions, and not from questions of artistry and aesthetics.
23 Bernard Rosenberg and David Manning White, *Mass Culture: The Popular Arts in America* (Glencoe: The Free Press, 1963).
24 Shusterman, "From Natural Roots to Cultural Radicalism: Pragmatist Aesthetics in Alain Locke and John Dewey," in *Surface and Depth: Dialectics of Criticism and Culture* (Ithaca: Cornell University Press, 2002), 201.

more ethically complicated issues surrounding rap's images of violence, which have haunted the art form for so long.

5 Rap and Violence

Shusterman addresses the issue of violence in rap head-on in his essay "Rap Aesthetics: Violence and Keeping it Real," collected in Derrick Darby and Tommie Shelby's edited volume *Hip Hop and Philosophy: Rhyme 2 Reason* (with its Foreword by Cornel West). According to Shusterman, violence is not unique to rap but pervades the fine arts:

> The sculptor who chisels, the ballet dancer who leaps, the shrieking soprano playing the Queen of the Night in Mozart's *Magic Flute*, all exhibit physical violence, just as do hip-hop artists, whether they are tagging graffiti, whirling and popping in breakdancing, frantically scratching vinyl as DJs, or busting rhymes and moves as MCs. Great art further works through violence not simply by representing it as in *Oedipus, King Lear, Crime and Punishment*, or *The Stranger*, but by effecting it in the flow of our experience: through the swift, enthralling power of aesthetic experience, which even when not pleasant is relished for its explosive intensity. So much of our routine experience of life is humdrum and boring that we relish art for sweeping us away by the power of its intense experiences.[25]

Keeping with the image of rap music as a violent echo from the street, Shusterman emphasizes that there was already antiviolence in rap music early on (like KRS-One, Guru, and others), but this antiviolence had not caught the attention of the media as much as gangsta rap.[26] But even though rap's violence has a negative side, it also has a positive side: part of rap's violence is to be found in its breaking down of oppressive social patterns, to reveal our own natures and the nature of society itself.[27] Arguably our entire postmodern digital culture is one of ongoing borrowing, cutting-and-pasting, and

---

25   Shusterman, "Rap Aesthetics: Violence and Keeping it Real," in *Hip Hop and Philosophy: Rhyme 2 Reason*, ed. Derrick Darby and Tommie Shelby, Foreword by Cornel West (Chicago: Open Court, 2005), 56–57.
26   *Ibid.*, 59.
27   Morgan Marcyliena does the same with rap battles, searching for analogies to philosophy, in "After ... Word! The Philosophy of the Hip Hop Battle," in *Hip Hop & Philosophy*, 205–212.

appropriation, like rap itself. Today we all see every kind of cultural form being borrowed, recycled, and reused in so many different ways, that it is hard to react very much anymore when one sees it. Most of us today cut-and-paste, edit, filter, and recycle/appropriate culture with the help of computers, smartphones, and other contemporary tools. Something about that practice is inherently violent, and rap illustrates this postmodern culture, and shows us what we are. Dewey spoke of culture as a process and the arts as ever changing.[28] As our postmodern and technological culture continues to change, by appropriating and recycling, adaptation to new changes is essential.[29] For those of us living in a culture where everything is appropriated, recycled, cut-and-pasted, and repeated mechanically, Shusterman's philosophy of rap, with its own rich musical and hip hop style, continues to illuminate rap music, popular culture, and our everyday lives.[30]

6   Recycling the Past, Reinventing the Future

On March 28, 2019, the European Union voted for a new copyright law, which cuts down the free play of memes and pulls a tighter string around people who work in appropriating media. I cannot but think that we might also be at the end of an era. Culture policies may be taking a step back regarding the aesthetic strategies discussed in this essay. The era that rap music so forcefully started might soon be coming to an end, and that is very sad. Hip hop (or rap) music is a brilliant living example of how culture in its postmodern form appropriates a past hidebound with habits, cuts the past and pastes it, again and again, to breathe life into the present, and to reanimate that past, to show how its original groovy potentials might shine through once again in new

---

28   Dewey, *Experience and Nature*, 14, 81.
29   Martti Honkanen in "Tien estetiikka ja tietaide" *Ympäristö, arkkitehtuuri, estetiikka*, ed. Arto Haapala, Martti Honkanen, and Veikko Rantala (Helsinki: Gaudeamus, 1995), that rap music is often created to resonate with the experience of driving. I think the same could be said of Shusterman's works. They are good company for rap music, company which can deepen and enrich the dialog with the aesthetic object. Equally good company is Shusterman's essay "Moving Truth: Affect and Authenticity in Country Musicals," *Journal of Aesthetics and Art Criticism*, 57, 2 (Spring 1999), 221–233. Here Shusterman turns to American country musicals to write the same open minded attention he consistently brings to bear on everything from pragmatism to rap to Chinese and Japanese philosophy.
30   In some sense, one could say that Dewey, one of the most boring writers in philosophy, became appropriated in a hip hop style by Shusterman.

and fresh form. Especially for people struggling with their cultural past, and struggling underneath oppression, the power of rap with its liberating energies stands ready to speak in its unique philosophical voice, appropriating and synthesizing all the various spheres of culture, and all the cultures, all peoples from America to Finland to China the burgeoning feminist hip hop scene in Chile.[31] All over the world, rap seems to be more vital than ever.

---

31   Philosophy-wise I dedicate my essay to Richard Shusterman, and rap-wise I dedicate it to Driemanskap, Kanyi Mavi, MV Bill, Reverie, Gavlyn, Princess Nokia, Sofa, Pastoripike, Vafe Jhous and Dania Neko, who recently made rap meaningful to me again.

CHAPTER 5

Somaesthetics and Pathic Aesthetics

Tonino Griffero

1   Opening the Dialogue

In my chapter in this volume, I want to celebrate the philosopher Richard Shusterman's contributions to pragmatist philosophy and somaesthetics, while, at the same, identifying some of our disagreements, and what I see as possible points of convergence: specifically, between somaesthetics and my own philosophical perspective of "pathic-atmospherological aesthetics," based in objective-spatial atmospheric feelings and a rigorous first-person felt-bodily awareness. Despite their different backgrounds, i.e., somaesthetics in pragmatism, and pathic aesthetics in phenomenology, respectively, these two philosophical projects have fundamentally shared interests and objectives. For example, both pathic aesthetics and somaesthetics set the living human body as the locus of aesthetic experience at the center of their philosophies. Somaesthetics offers much that is right, but some of its limitations may also point in the direction of an alternative aesthetic approach to the body, and this alternative approach to aesthetics, namely, pathic aesthetics is in some respects truer to the nature of aesthetic perception.

2   Pathic Aesthetics

Some background of pathic aesthetics may be helpful. If aesthetics were really "only" a philosophy of art, then aesthetics today might no longer even be necessary. Indeed, aesthetics would be a form of reflection, which—after reaching its height in the 19th century against a background of an upper-bourgeois culture inclined to see the artworld (considered then to be autonomous) as an authentic surrogate of faith—may well have lost its *raison d'être*. Such diagnosis could quite reasonably be applied to any aesthetics whose only subject matter was the work of art, while that same diagnosis certainly does not apply (or should not be applied) to aesthetics in the wider sense. Indeed, such diagnosis would not adversely affect an aesthetics that re-evaluates (*cum grano salis*) the discipline's 18th century genesis, i.e., Alexander Gottlieb Baumgarten's

Ästhetik, and is perhaps better conceived as a philosophy of sensible knowledge (or sensibility *tout court*), or even the "thought of the senses" (meant in both the subjective and the objective sense of the genitive).

Over the past several years, my thinking has moved steadily from an "aesthetics of atmospheres" to an ontology and phenomenology of "quasi-things,"[1] within a wider project of a "pathic aesthetics."[2] By "pathic" I do not mean "pathetic" or "pathological," but rather the affective and *lebensweltlich* involvement that the perceiver feels, when that perceiver is unable to react critically, or mitigate its intrusiveness. This very involvement, this non-distancing complicity with the atmospheric world, is, I believe, the core of the aesthetic sphere (in the etymological sense of *aisthesis*), much more so than art or beauty; and further I believe that this pathic aesthetics withstands all projectivistic criticisms. Philosophically rehabilitating pathicity means valorizing the ability to "let oneself go,"[3] a skill as rare today as it is relevant and needed. This skill of "pathicity" is the ability to be a means of what happens to us rather than subjects of what we do.

Such a skill was underestimated in the rationalistic post-Enlightenment age which privileged subjective autonomy and individual agency and action; and now, even more so in the present biotechnological age, with every attempt to remove any and all kinds of contingency. Against this Enlightenment and biotechnological thinking, pathic aesthetics embraces our natural ability to welcome what happens to us (whether we like it or not), and to resist the temptation to transform the "given" into something that is "done" (by us), that is, resisting the temptation to transform nature understood as spontaneous evolution into artifice, or to seek shelter from contingency into so many forms of late-Romantic nostalgic "culture."

Only if we philosophically valorize what happens in the world, and to us, can pathic aesthetics—liberated from the nineteenth and twentieth-century view of art as religion and politics by other means—truly adopt Baumgarten's

---

1 Tonino Griffero, *Atmospheres: Aesthetics of Emotional Spaces* (2010; New York: Routledge, 2014). See also Griffero, *Quasi-Things: The Paradigm of Atmospheres* (2013; Albany: SUNY Press, 2017); Griffero, "Atmospheres and Felt-bodily Resonances," in *Studi di estetica*, XLIV, 4, 1 (2016), 1–41; Griffero, "Felt-Bodily Resonances: Towards a Pathic Aesthetics," in *Yearbook for Eastern and Western Philosophy*, 2 (2017), 149–164; Griffero, "Is There Such a Thing as an 'Atmospheric Turn'? Instead of an Introduction," in *Atmosphere and Aesthetics. A Plural Perspective*, ed. T. Griffero and M. Tedeschini (Basingstoke: Palgrave Macmillan, 2019), 11–62.
2 Griffero, "Something More: Atmospheres and Pathic Aesthetics," in *Atmospheres: Testing A New Paradigm*, ed. T. Griffero and G. Moretti (Milan: Mimesis International, 2018), 75–89; and Griffero, *Places, Affordances, Atmospheres: A Pathic Aesthetics* (New York: Routledge, 2019).
3 Gernot Böhme, *Ethik leiblicher Existenz* (Frankfurt: Suhrkamp, 2008).

vision of aesthetics as "also" a theory of sensible knowledge, and even the "thought of the senses,"[4] as a non-gnostic but pathic phenomenology, in Erwin Straus' sense.[5] In "pathic aesthetics" aesthetics frees itself from what was really only ever just one of its many projects, specifically, the philosophy of art. Unfortunately, classic aesthetics tends to be (a) narrow in its focus on the work of art (with its supposed autonomy); (b) metaphysical in considering art and beauty *sub specie aeternitatis*; (c) bourgeois in its adherence to the values of a European elite; and (d) overly intellectual in its focus on judgment or interpretation rather than "experience," and in its corresponding misunderstanding of the role of felt-bodily sensitivity in the name of (Kantian) disinterested pleasure. In short, classic aesthetics is governed by the same estrangement from nature we find in the natural sciences, and the Enlightenment's overinflated view of the autonomous subject.

But as soon as one abandons this aesthetics "from above," and then begins to trace artworks back to instances of everyday sense perception, one sees how it is possible to avoid falling into Kantian transcendentalism with its excessive subjectivity and detachment, on the one hand; while avoiding, on the other hand, hermeneutics (and semiotics) which prizes seemingly limitless interpretability of any work of art, privileging an apparently unavoidable deferred sense at the expense of "presence."[6] Pathic aesthetics, as an alternative remains as faithful as possible to presence, that is, to the way "appearances" resound in our lived bodies, without the usual temptation to defer feeling them over time. Pathic aesthetics prescinds from special "things," such as artworks as well as the traditional categories of aesthetics, e.g., the beautiful, the sublime, genius, etc., and, following Hermann Schmitz[7] and Gernot Böhme,[8] investigates instead

---

4   Griffero, *Il pensiero dei sensi: Atmosfere ed estetica patica* (Milano: Guerini & Associati, 2016).

5   Erwin Straus, *The Primary World of Senses: A Vindication of Sensory Experience* (New York: Free Press of Glencoe, 1963), 367–379.

6   Griffero, "Come Rain or Come Shine … The (neo)phenomenological Will-to-Presentness," *Studi di estetica*, XLVI, 4, 2 (2018), 57–73.

7   Hermann Schmitz, *System der Philosophie*, Bd. III.2, *Der Gefühlsraum* (Bonn: Bouvier, 1968); "Situationen und Atmosphären: Zur Ästhetik und Ontologie bei Gernot Böhme," in *Naturerkenntnis und Natursein: Für Gernot Böhme*, ed. M. Hauskeller, C. Rehmann, et al. (Frankfurt: Suhrkamp, 1998), 176–190; Schmitz, "Entseelung der Gefühle," in *Gefühle als Atmosphären: Neue Phänomenologie und philosophische Emotionstheorie*, ed. K. Andermann, U. Eberlein (Berlin: Akademie Verlag, 2011), 21–33; Schmitz, *Der Leib* (Berlin/Boston: De Gruyter, 2011); Schmitz, "Atmosphäre und Gefühl—Für eine Neue Phänomenologie," in *Atmosphären: Dimensionen eines diffusen Phänomens*, ed. C. Heibach (München: Fink, 2012), 39–56; and Schmitz, *Atmosphären* (Freiburg-München: Alber, 2012).

8   Böhme, *Leibsein als Aufgabe: Leibphilosophie in pragmatischer Hinsicht* (Kusterdingen: Die Graue Edition, 2003). See also Böhme, *Atmosphäre: Essays zur neuen Ästhetik* (Frankfurt: Suhrkamp, 1995); Böhme, *Anmutungen: Über das Atmosphärische* (Ostfildern v. Stuttgart:

our "atmospheric feelings" within the context of today's aestheticization of the lifeworld, and the so-called diffuse design typical of late capitalist societies. The analysis of situations and atmospheric perceptions constitutes the first step in the project of pathic aesthetics, serving to establish entities (or quasi-things), which, without being full and measurable objects, are present, and act on us, primarily by populating our *Lebenswelt* and creating an experiential and nonthematic horizon not yet purified of any subjectivity.

Our ordinary, naïve, involuntary sensible experiences form the basis of an aesthetics of reception, with its fundamental criterion of affectivity, or self-affection, which means how "one feels" when experiencing the co-presence of oneself and a thing (or quasi-thing). Hermeneutics and constructionism exclude the very idea that you can have direct access to the world, and for this reason these views are committed to identifying what may be the media that guarantee this access, the pathic aesthetic, no: it implies a direct felt-bodily relationship with the world, and that "access" is a misleading notion. In pathic aesthetics experience does not presuppose an interpretive and constructivist approach in which the world is given through some reflective "access."[9] Rather, pathic aesthetics supposes that there is a sensory realm that is always already sedimented outside of us and can be verified through our felt-bodily and pre-reflexive communication with the world. We experience impressions radiated by spaces inhabited by things and quasi-things, and by entities that fully coincide with their felt-bodily appearance "in act" (active and effective; indeed, *wirklich*),[10] and with the generation of the affective situation (*Befindlichkeit*) in which we find and feel ourselves.

Both natural phenomena, e.g., twilight, luminosity, darkness, the seasons, the wind, the weather, the hours of the day, the fog, etc., and relatively artificial phenomena, e.g., townscape, music, soundscape, the numinous, dwelling, charisma, the gaze, shame, etc., are expressive qualities, which, by radiating atmospheres, become quasi-things. These expressive qualities are salient not despite being apparent and ephemeral, but precisely *because* of their ephemerality—provided this becoming isn't understood as anomalous. Western thought too

---

Tertium, 1998); Böhme, *Architektur und Atmosphäre* (München: Fink, 2006); Böhme, *The Aesthetics of Atmospheres* (New York: Routledge, 2017); Böhme, *Atmospheric Architectures. The Aesthetics of Felt Spaces* (London et alia: Bloomsbury, 2017); and Böhme, *Critique of Aesthetic Capitalism* (Milan: Mimesis International, 2017).

9   See Lambert Wiesing, *The Philosophy of Perception: Phenomenology and Image Theory* (London: Bloomsbury, 2014).

10 Böhme, *Aisthetik: Vorlesungen über Ästhetik als allgemeine Wahrnehmungslehre* (München: Fink, 2001).

often considers these expressive qualities devoid of reality, in contrast to what are thought to be full things because they are endowed with borders and separated from other such full things with their persistence through time (and typical inactivity provided they not physically moved). Pathic and atmospherological aesthetics emphasizes a cooperative and integrated relation between sense perception and the surrounding radiating atmosphere of quasi-things.[11]

Pathic aesthetic experience is an in-between space experienced by the felt- or lived body (*Leib*), and one not reducible to any physiological or anatomical dimension of experience. Pathic aesthetic experience also always presents itself as a task insofar as it is something for which we are daily responsible, and all the more so today because the very possibility of pathic experience is threatened by countless technological modifications to the human form such as technological prostheses. The theory of atmospheres and quasi-things presupposes investigation of human felt-bodily living and understanding of the need to rehabilitate certainty in aesthetics, considered as an *experientia vaga*, without rules, in its rich lifeworldly meaning, irreducible either to an etiological or a genetic approach. This experiential and sensible certainty, however vague, attests to our natures better than other, traditionally privileged states (including the *cogito*).

We must learn to "experience pathically," no longer regarding goal-directed and object-related thinking as a phenomenologically privileged path. By paying less attention to our role as subjects—pathologically overestimated in modernity (and its various problems of detachment and dualism)—and more attention to our nature as pathic (i.e., the pathic "me"), which is prior to our subjectivity. Human beings are not so much "subjects of" but "subjects to," not so much independent and autonomous, in the modern sense, but sovereign and mature just insofar as they are educated to resiliently face what happens to them, in the right way. What happens to us, according to a pathic aesthetic view, all the more determines us as we oppose it, or try to manipulate it, than when we abandon ourselves to it (*cum grano salis*), thereby allowing for greater affective involvement, and potentially greater freedom (rather than an illusory sense of freedom in control of what opposes us).

This view of pathic aesthetics holds much with Hermann Schmitz's New Phenomenology and Gernot Böhme's aesthetics as a general theory of perception. There is much too in pathic aesthetics that agrees with Shusterman's

---

11   *Ibid.*, 37–54.

somaesthetics, which he describes as a "program of philosophical self-perfection in the art of living."[12]

3   Shusterman on Pragmatism and Popular Art

Despite their differences, somaesthetics and pathic aesthetics agree that aesthetics has to do with the many practices and experiences so often snubbed by traditional aesthetics, and that the discipline of aesthetics should aim at demystifying hackneyed distinctions like beautiful/functional, form/content, and so on. In this regard, Shusterman's pragmatist aesthetics has been truly inspiring for its criticisms of the fetishization of artworks, and a welcome stress on the experience of producing and enjoying them, but also for the unearthing from within the so-called great works of art several characteristics typical of popular art. Such characteristics of art include, for example, transience of value, as well as historical-economic conditioning; but Shusterman demonstrates how popular works of art (more or less consciously) also reveal many of the characteristics attributed to what are thought to be great works of art: for example, deep semantics, ethical and political commitment, and problems of knowledge of reality. Indeed, Shusterman encourages a full rehabilitation of popular art, beginning with what is sometimes considered a borderline case, i.e., with rap music, and with amazing results. And yet, while pathic aesthetics finds much with which to agree in pragmatist aesthetics, questions inevitably arise.

(1) Shusterman in *Pragmatist Aesthetics* acknowledges that we do not "need to be fully outside something in order to criticize it effectively."[13] I worry, however, that this strategy of rehabilitating popular art may give too much ground to traditional aesthetics, in allowing some of art's traditional binding criteria to apply to popular art, perhaps underestimating America's anti-aristocratic and egalitarian tendencies, which Shusterman himself defends.[14] For example, in his well-known brilliant defense of the artistic value of rap entitled "The Fine Art of Rap" (in *Pragmatist Aesthetics*), Shusterman suggests that rap is less radical than it actually is, which, in turn, seems to moderate the artistic value of traditional fine arts, e.g., Ludwig von Beethoven's *Ninth Symphony*. As a further and related concern, one wonders whether Shusterman's defense of popular art effectively reduces the meaning or value of the art to a product arising from

---

12   Richard Shusterman, *Pragmatist Aesthetics: Living Beauty, Rethinking Art* (Lanham: Rowman & Littlefield, 2000), 263.
13   Ibid., 214.
14   Ibid., 197.

the synthetic unity of interaction between the work and its audience. In other words, does greater popularity of art somehow indicate greater artistic value? For example, could the television show *Dallas* (1978–1991, created by David Jacobs) be judged to be more artistic than Dante Alighieri's *Comedy* (1320)?

(2) A second main concern regards Shusterman's defense of enduring and even everlasting features in popular art. For example, while he articulates and explores several features of postmodern art, such as recycling, hybrid style, and the use of modern technologies, found in rap, Shusterman also highlights in rap several everlasting features of art, such as polysemy, inner allusion, and political critique. The value of these everlasting features, and the related claim that they have some sort of enduring validity, seems problematic; and problematic too even from within Shusterman's account, for (elsewhere) he criticizes traditional aesthetics for elevating precisely these features in the fine arts.

Furthermore, anything that is deeply interpreted, and overinterpreted, even a newspaper article about a sporting event, to borrow an example from Stanley Fish's essay *Is There a Text in This Class?*, may take on the appearance of a deep work of art.[15] Shusterman's rehabilitation of rap relies too much on decontextualization, which gives rap the appearance of a poem deserving a deep exegesis; and Shusterman recognizes those who perform this kind of exegesis as artists themselves: interpreters of art (or even sport) create their own works of art through interpretation and overinterpretation.

Moreover, despite his claim that the artistry of the work, such as a track of rap music, is confirmed by listening and dancing to it, Shusterman's view remains too entangled in the tradition with its priority given to language and semantic meaning as criteria of artistic quality. By rejecting this priority, Shusterman's view of rap may then become more consistent with his own philosophical projects of pragmatist aesthetics and somaesthetics. By rejecting a residual linguistic essentialism, and embracing the bodily effects and emotional involvement intrinsic to rap, a more fully somaesthetic perspective of rap (exploring its many somaesthetic meanings) may thereby be achieved.

(3) A third concern with Shusterman's aesthetics lies in its fluidity, its ephemerality; although there is much with which to agree in this account. On the one hand, Shusterman's rehabilitation of popular art rightly opens a way to the recognition of the value of the ephemeral. Aesthetic values, and the concept of art as such, cannot be fixed once and for all, and thereby appear to be just instrumental and transitory concepts. This also means that the artistic

---

15   Stanley Fish, *Is There a Text in This Class? The Authority of Interpretive Communities* (Cambridge: Harvard University Press, 1980).

means may be enjoyed as such, regardless of their ends, or the relation between means and ends, since temporary aesthetic satisfaction is not less authentic than lasting aesthetic satisfaction. Against the old Platonic view of the body, Shusterman argues that even using the body as an instrument doesn't exclude the possibility of enjoying it also as an end. On the other hand, however, the Heraclitean ephemerality of Shusterman's aesthetics risks a version of nihilism whose consequences should not be underestimated. If art exists only in the exact simultaneity of reception, one can, strictly speaking, never determine how aesthetically pleasing was a past experience, even a quite recent one. Without some identity to art, we do not seem to be able to have works of art, not in the true sense of the word; instead, we would have only quasi-works of art. Or, in words Shusterman uses to describe Richard's Rorty pragmatism, we would have something "essentially romantic picaresque."[16]

Again, none of this is to say that elevation of ephemerality is altogether problematic. Like Shusterman's abolition of the hierarchical distinction between high art and popular art, ephemerality is also quite welcome, despite some limits in regard to the definition of the work of art. Indeed, both perspectives, in Shusterman's pragmatist aesthetics, or, at least variations of these perspectives, once transformed, open the way to a pathic aesthetics of atmospheres, understood as an aesthetics of intermittent and ontologically vague aesthetic-emotional situations. For example, aesthetic ephemerality may be saved from a certain kind of nihilism by relinquishing our desire to fetishize the work of art, as a thing. In regard to Shusterman's aesthetics, however, one wonders why the fetishized work of art (which he rightly criticizes) must be devalued at all, particularly considering his view in *Pragmatist Aesthetics* according to which "we must feel a work's artistry and aesthetic power impress itself on our senses and intelligence."[17] Such aesthetics seems to move in the direction of a thing-ontology of the work of art, prevalent in modernist aesthetics, while Shusterman's acknowledgment of the "positive pleasures of self-limiting self-mastery"[18] no less separates the subject from the object, again in quite modernist manner. Those perspectives may lead philosophy to wonder why Shusterman criticizes purist modernist asceticism in the first place, e.g., why an aesthetics combining the private and the public—particularly given that an ethical-aesthetic project is never really private and completely free from influences and public consequences—should be thought any better than an

---

16 Shusterman, *Pragmatist Aesthetics*, 248.
17 *Ibid.*, 215.
18 *Ibid.*, 252.

aesthetics oriented exclusively to the private sphere, one even taking pleasure from this elite's self-restraint?

4 The Limits of Somaesthetics

Shusterman sets his project of somaesthetics (the experiential aesthetics of the body) at the center of his pragmatist philosophy. This project of somaesthetics is certainly one of the most important contributions to contemporary aesthetics. At the center of his somaesthetics, Shusterman sets the distinctly pragmatist view, drawn primarily from the classical American philosopher John Dewey, that "a good definition of art should effectively direct us toward more and better aesthetic experience."[19] Neither Dewey nor Shusterman, in making lived bodily experience the center of aesthetics, aims at an hedonistic enhancement of the bodily dimension; nor does atmospheric or pathic aesthetics. In fact, there is much pathic aesthetics shares with somaesthetics, and pragmatist aesthetics in general. For example, pathic aesthetics shares somaesthetics' rejection of the centuries-long disqualification of popular art and the corresponding separation of mind and body, and the view that detached mental aesthetic inquiry is superior to "more somatic forms of effort, resistance, and satisfaction,"[20] and the somaesthetic perspective that what one enjoys superficially may also be enjoyed more deeply; enjoying more deeply a pleasure can be understood in the sense of Kant's *Beförderung des Lebens*. Pathic aesthetics also shares with somaesthetics what Shusterman calls a "joyous return of the somatic dimension which philosophy has long repressed ... as irrational regression from art's true (i.e., intellectual) purpose."[21]

But certain concerns arise with Shusterman's definition of the project somaesthetics as "the critical, meliorative study of the experience and use of one's body as a locus of sensory-aesthetic appreciation (*aisthesis*) and creative self-fashioning."[22] I raise these concerns in philosophical friendship and ongoing dialogue.

(1) We may ask, how exactly did the idea of the body, as a forgotten, repressed, and misunderstood dimension of human life, reappear in philosophy sufficient for self-correction, that Shusterman with his disciplinary project of somaesthetics may write of how we may begin to "aesthetically enrich our

---

19   Ibid., 57.
20   Ibid., 184.
21   Ibid., 184.
22   Ibid., 267.

lives in terms of an enhanced quality and awareness of felt experience"?[23] If the answer to that question is that the critical attitude does not "require an external, autonomous standpoint—altogether detached and disinterested," as Shusterman writes, then is that answer sufficient?[24] After all, what exactly drives critique in a culture pervaded by repression of the felt bodily dimension?

(2) The pathic aesthetic perspective, no less based in bodily experience, demands a firmer position in the tradition of phenomenology (and neophenomenology) with its distinction between the felt body (*Leib*) and the physical body (*Körper*). Shusterman speaks of soma instead of body in order to express "the living, feeling, sentient, purposive body."[25] Shusterman in *Body Consciousness* also refers to the Japanese term *shintai*, which means "a living, perceptive, sentient, dynamic, intelligent corporeality that involves intentionality, mind, and the spiritual rather than being a brute material counterpart from which mind and spirit must be distinguished and opposed."[26] Shusterman then goes on to refer to "the beautiful experience of one's own body from within,"[27] which brings us very close to the *Leib/Körper* distinction. But one wonders whether Shusterman's "soma" and bodily experience (from within) refer to *Leib*, or, perhaps that Shusterman thinks of somaesthetics as effectively overcoming several of the problems highlighted by that phenomenological distinction between *Leib* and *Körper* (possibly even the distinction itself).

As a related question, Shusterman, following Dewey, argues that the body-mind unity is something that we should continually strive to attain,[28] but then does the soma appear to be something of a regulative idea, something we are forever trying to become?

(3) According to Shusterman in *Body Consciousness*, "our bodies really function best when we most ignore them rather than mindfully trying to guide their functioning."[29] This also plays a central role in Maurice Merleau-Ponty's philosophy in *Phenomenology of the Body*, as Shusterman acknowledges. In fact, Shusterman reminds us that, according to Merleau-Ponty, the body is a "background of silence," it is "the 'silent consciousness' of 'primary subjectivity'

---

23   Ibid., 261.
24   Shusterman, *Thinking through the Body: Essays in Somaesthetics* (Cambridge: Cambridge University Press, 2012), 230.
25   Shusterman, *Body Consciousness: A Philosophy of Mindfulness and Somaesthetics* (Cambridge: Cambridge University Press, 2008), xii.
26   Shusterman, *Thinking through the Body*, 227.
27   Shusterman, *Pragmatist Aesthetics*, 262.
28   Shusterman, *Body Consciousness*, 187.
29   Ibid., xi.

and 'primordial expression,'" acting as an "unreflective lived body."[30] Much the same idea appears already in William James, who, as Shusterman also points out, "feared that somaesthetic introspection would inhibit action and destroy the energies, spontaneity, and positive attitude he considered crucial for success in practical life."[31] James's concern is a legitimate one. Whenever I, for example, consider the body as a medium, i.e., an object of reflection, its efficiency seems greatly reduced. Because there is an ongoing and dynamic striving inhabiting a body that may successfully execute various movements in everyday life without consciously controlling them.

One may say accordingly that human behavior and action are extensions of capabilities already present in the body and which don't need to be improved. However, this view is partly at odds with Shusterman's melioristic stance and requires some explanation of his view of non-inhibiting reflection. According to Shusterman in *Body Consciousness*, "we cannot properly know how to smooth the brow, if we cannot feel that our brow is furrowed or know what it feels like to have one's brow smooth."[32] Even if that were true, somatic awareness would seem to have no autonomy and would require an "external" judgment, which, in turn, presupposes an insurmountable gap between a felt-bodily movement and its felt-bodily awareness.

Shusterman rejects this proposal of "latent body." Whoever considers the reflection on the body to be an obstacle to its fluency and grace, writes Shusterman, is simply defending the "traditional unquestioning faith in divine or natural providence."[33] On the contrary, a wise passiveness is ultimately the best path to our atmospheric harmony with the world, and tangibly shows how every perception requires a previous passive (already atmospheric) synthesis. The right everyday "exercise" is a strategically unprepared and unplanned art of living, and this seems to us entirely sufficient.[34]

(4) Following James' view that "reflective somatic self-consciousness" can generate "psychological and moral problems of depression,"[35] Shusterman suggests we "distinguish between introspection that is depressive, obsessive, and focused on the negative (designated as rumination) and other, more positive, forms of introspection that are distinguished as self-awareness or

---

30   *Ibid.*, 49, 57, and 63.
31   *Ibid.*, 169.
32   *Ibid.*, 168.
33   *Ibid.*, 13.
34   I think that body-sculpting, even in the nontrivial sense suggested by Shusterman, is fairly useless.
35   Shusterman, *Body Consciousness*, 11.

self-reflection."³⁶ But what exactly is the criterion for distinguishing these two forms of self-reflection? And is the criterion determined according to the external consequences (even the physiognomic ones) that are observable only from a third person perspective, and therefore somehow objectified?

A similar problem arises with Shusterman's view that the habit-body of sedimentation is not free from errors. According to Shusterman in *Body Consciousness*, "once bad habits are acquired how do we correct them? We cannot simply rely on sedimented habit to correct them—since the sedimented habits are precisely what is wrong."³⁷ Shusterman adds that the somaesthetic attention, which is supposed to be a part of everyday experience, "does not need (nor is meant) to be a permanent focus that distracts from other goals."³⁸ Somaesthetics, according to Shusterman, would thus be able to teach individuals how to replace faulty with good movements until these new movements "can be habituated and then allowed to slip into unreflective but intelligent habit,"³⁹ provided that a "mindful consciousness is important for learning new skills and necessary for properly identifying, analyzing, and rectifying our problematic bodily habits."⁴⁰ One would simply have to render these habits "more appropriate to our changing conditions, tools, and tasks," writes Shusterman, more in harmony with "transformations in bodily use and experience,"⁴¹ and thus be aware that "one can be self-consciously absorbed in one's feelings."⁴²

But does this mean that somaesthetic attention must and can operate only occasionally? And, if so, then when do we get the urge to correct bad habits? According to Shusterman, following Frederick Matthias Alexander, who developed the Alexander Technique, "most people ... suffer from 'debauched *kinaesthetic* systems,'" which causes "lack of somatic self-awareness," and hinders "their performance by making them the unconscious victims of unthinking habits of bodily misuse."⁴³ When do we become aware of the need to correct for "unthinking habits of bodily misuse"? Shusterman's answer to these questions is not entirely clear. Attention to our somatic sensations can provide useful information, writes Shusterman in *Body Consciousness*, but first one must "learn how properly to read one's own somaesthetic signs."⁴⁴ Reading those

---

36   *Ibid.*, 175, fn. 53.
37   *Ibid.*, 62.
38   *Ibid.*, 123.
39   *Ibid.*, 123.
40   *Ibid.*, 13.
41   *Ibid.*, 13–14.
42   *Ibid.*, 70.
43   *Ibid.*, 191.
44   *Ibid.*, 121.

signs, writes Shusterman (following Dewey), requires distinguishing "between 'routine,' unintelligent habit and 'intelligent or artistic habit.'" But what exactly allows me to properly consider what is, in Shusterman's terms, a "flexible, sensitive habit,"[45] and more generally to bypass bad bodily habits? It is true that Shusterman's conclusions on this matter are provisional, and based on a kind of "respect and suspect" toward our habits and sensory feelings,[46] but with all due respect, I think it is a slightly evasive answer from a theoretical point of view.

(5) Shusterman in *Body Consciousness* also acknowledges the possibility that "to focus on the body implies a retreat from the social."[47] Shusterman responds to this concern that "any acutely attentive somatic self-consciousness will always be conscious of more than the body itself."[48] In other words, better somaesthetic awareness brings with it better sensing of one's environmental background. For example, better somaesthetic awareness can help to reduce prejudices, writes Shusterman, which are often "somatically expressed or embodied in vague but disagreeable feelings that typically lie beneath the level of explicit consciousness," and for this reason "resist correction by mere discursive arguments for tolerance."[49] Of course, sometimes disagreement can be quite explicit, as in the case of international conflict negotiations, but here too somaesthetic practices may serve to ease tensions between opposing parties. As Shusterman writes in *Body Consciousness*, "mutual understanding is greatly improved once the negotiators [before hostile] actually spend enough agreeable time together to get somaesthetically comfortable with each other."[50]

A closely related view appears in *Thinking through the Body*, where Shusterman demonstrates how architectural spaces are somaesthetically socially generated. Here Shusterman writes that "the soma is the crucial medium through which architecture is experienced and created."[51] Shusterman's somaesthetic view that good somatic awareness connects in a better way the perceivers with their lived environment is actually quite close to the pathic aesthetics view of atmospheres as feelings poured out within our surrounding lived space and resounding in our felt body. And if, as Shusterman himself acknowledges, the somaesthetic view still "deserves extended analysis,"[52] then

---

45 *Ibid.*, 205.
46 *Ibid.*, 212.
47 *Ibid.*, 25.
48 *Ibid.*, 8.
49 *Ibid.*, 25.
50 *Ibid.*, 130, fn. 19.
51 Shusterman, *Thinking through the Body*, 227.
52 *Ibid.*, 232.

perhaps this idea of architectural space and how it is generated by individual somatic forms, may be one point of extended analysis; for architecture, in particular, is a central (if not canonical) example of an intersubjectively produced social atmosphere, within pathic aesthetics.[53] Perhaps by broadening somaesthetics to include atmospheres in general—and not merely the most visceral feelings—a rich aesthetics may be developed as based in what is truly "felt-bodily."

To be fair, Shusterman in *Thinking through the Body* does consider the "turn to atmosphere" in aesthetics, when he writes that

> the post-critical turn to atmosphere is also a serious critical response to the perceived limits of earlier views of architecture that denigrated or neglected the atmospheric as irrelevant to architecture's disciplinary practice and mission, and that defined architecture's disciplinarity (and criticality) in terms of autonomy.[54]

By "atmosphere" Shusterman means an "experienced quality of a situation," something "resistant to conceptual definition and discursive analysis," as well as "grasped before [a] situation is divided into its objective and subjective elements."[55] That is correct, but one wonders whether Shusterman is prepared to take the further steps, found in pathic aesthetics, and extend the idea to all the humanities, and to accept atmospheric feelings (beyond the felt-bodily effect of atmospheres) as objective-spatial rather than subjectively projected feelings. One wonders whether Shusterman would instead promote only the atmospheres that improve felt-bodily conditions and the habits that are waiting to become unconscious in order to be effective. Lastly, given his robust acceptance of Dewey's idea of a transactional self, i.e., the symbiotic body,[56] would Shusterman explain, as Hermann Schmitz does, any relationship with external form and expression as an *ad hoc* form of felt-bodily (*leiblich*) communication?[57] Embracing these points would mean bringing somaesthetics closer to a neophenomenological pathic aesthetics and thus overcoming our (sometimes merely lexical) differences.

---

53 Griffero, *Places, Affordances, Atmospheres*, 99–136.
54 Shusterman, *Thinking through the Body*, 233.
55 Ibid., 234.
56 Shusterman, *Body Consciousness*, 214.
57 Griffero, "Felt-bodily Communication: A Neophenomenological Approach to Embodied Affects," *Studi di estetica* XLV, 4, 2 (2017), 71–86.

(6) According to Shusterman in *Body Consciousness*, a too rigid opposition between reflection and action would force us to admit that "the philosopher of the body [is] the farthest removed from her own lived body, because she is overwhelmingly absorbed in struggling with all her mind to analyze and champion the body's role."[58] Shusterman's telling reflection leads one to wonder about the reasons that might motivate any philosopher to take a special interest in the body. One reason might be their bodily health; one thinks, for example, of Friedrich Nietzsche or William James writing about their physical well-being and even their infirmities (and taking even theoretical inspiration from them). According to Shusterman, the biographical character of these philosophies of James and Nietzsche in no way discredits them. After all, writes Shusterman, a "heightened personal interest can generate better theory by promoting more penetratingly vigilant attention, more subtle awareness, and keener sensitivity."[59] But one concern with this perspective is that apparently better somatic performances would then make these philosophers of the body perhaps somewhat less acute, and potentially diminish the need for a new thoroughgoing philosophy of the body; which is certainly contrary to somaesthetics' intentions.

(7) This last point returns the discussion to the central difference between somaesthetics and pathic aesthetics, which is, again, the meliorism of somaesthetics. Shusterman insists in *Body Consciousness* that an "improved body consciousness can help relieve [problems of attention, overstimulation, and stress] and enhance one's knowledge, performance, and pleasure."[60] But does philosophy really have the goal of an "ameliorative self-mastery,"[61] as if to "know yourself" meant to "know better your body," and, as a consequence, also to "improve [your] body functions," as well as your "capacities for pleasure"?[62] Such a view might even seem consistent with the present culture's tendency to overstimulation, which dulls the senses to the point of anaesthesia, and hardly seems to allow cultivating "a somaesthetic sensitivity to detect and deal with threats of stressful overload."[63] We should be careful about any oversimplified equating of pragmatist meliorism and the "acritical or post-critical attitude" (or, worse, postmodern frivolity).[64] And, anyway, as Shusterman writes, "post-critical should not be confused with acritical."[65]

---

58 Shusterman, *Body Consciousness*, 74.
59 Ibid., 138.
60 Ibid., ix.
61 Ibid., 123.
62 Ibid., 6.
63 Ibid., 13.
64 Shusterman, *Thinking through the Body*, 229.
65 Ibid., 233.

According to Shusterman in *Thinking through the Body*, somatic self-examination

> provides a model of immanent critique where one's critical perspective does not require being entirely outside the situation critically examined but merely requires a reflective perspective on it that is not wholly absorbed in the immediacy of what is experienced; a perspective better described as positionally eccentric (or decentered) rather than as external.[66]

Shusterman's somaesthetics wrongly elevates, quite optimistically, somatic efficiency, somatic improvement, and an all-too-modern critical, detached, and reflective self-awareness. While he maintains that "somaesthetics ... clearly refuses to exteriorize the body as an alienated thing," and that somaesthetics does not "tend to impose a fixed set of standardized norms," Shusterman's "positionally eccentric" view with its ideal of reflective somatic self-knowledge would appear to resemble a fixed norm—and for pathic aesthetics too the ideal is just an external fixed norm.[67] This ideal, fixed or not, certainly resembles the classical and modern ideal of detached self-knowledge where "pleasure in knowing" is the pleasure of knowing oneself, of always learning more about oneself.[68] Such a melioristic perspective inevitably excludes the unique and deep pleasure of feeling our vulnerability, and thereby ignores the rich pathic aesthetic possibilities that our weakness, and even our illness, may and do sometimes provide. While, according to Shusterman, "bodily finitude does not entail the futility of working on our somatic selves,"[69] precisely bodily finitude, our limits, our weaknesses, vulnerabilities, are also deep sources, at least sometimes, of aesthetically pleasurable experiences.

Somaesthetic training aimed at improved somatic self-understanding may even dull bodily awareness, i.e., in a too efficient and trained body. Shusterman himself acknowledges in *Body Consciousness* how "sensory appreciation is typically dulled when blasted with extreme sensations."[70] But excessive body training might do much the same. Frankly, I'm not sure that a well-trained body is really able to feel the emotional and medium-intensity affordances of our environment, i.e., atmospheres in their essential vagueness and multiple

---

66 *Ibid.*, 231.
67 Shusterman, *Body Consciousness*, 28.
68 *Ibid.*, 42.
69 *Ibid.*, 44, footnote 39.
70 *Ibid.*, 37.

nuances. If, as Shusterman writes in *Body Consciousness*, "any real appreciation of unreflective perception depends on its distinctive contrast from reflective consciousness, just as the latter clearly relies on the background of the former,"[71] by contrast, I think a stimulation leading to bodily efficiency, to a successful and reflective performance, could be so strong as to prevent any potentially softer sensation that may otherwise come next.

Pathic aesthetics does not simply define the body as the "great reason," in Nietzsche's terms, potentially leading us to *amor fati*; nor does pathic aesthetics repeat a critique of a civilization whose grounding is the removal of the felt-bodily presence in favor of the physical one.[72] Against somaesthetics' meliorism,[73] and, to some extent, Eastern meditation and other somatic techniques,[74] many authentic and deep aesthetic experiences—especially the felt-bodily perception of atmospheres and quasi-things—typically arise from sensory deficits, inaccuracies, and ambiguities, in the perceiver and the perceiver's perceived reality (i.e., *de dicto*/*de facto* deficits). For example, aesthetic (sensory) weakness, weariness, perceptive inaccuracy, even everyday careless mistakes, can often be more aesthetically fruitful than sensorial intensification and analytical precision. One finds precisely this sort of atmospheric (and almost morbid) fascination in Marcel Proust's *Remembrance of Things Past*.[75] A too precise and "healthy" perception sometimes even destroys an aesthetic pleasure and nullifies every atmospheric affordance. Accordingly, somaesthetics is, for me, too bound to an energetic program of sensory intensification and performance, and thus risks being unable to pathically recognize the right intrinsic aesthetic value of perceptive experience's nuances and ambiguities.

It's clear that the pathic and barely reflexive ability to feel and know how atmospheres felt-bodily resonate must be inevitably a lived but, to some extent, still a retrospective reflection on the felt-body.[76] In other words, it, as

---

71   *Ibid.*, 67.
72   I should also note that the felt body is able to change in order to respond with explorative innovations to unforeseen (also bodily-physical) challenges.
73   Shusterman, *Body Consciousness*, 28, fn. 17.
74   A criticism to be taken *cum grano salis*, because, for Eastern thought and practices, the goal is obviously not something to be attained, but something that rather makes itself known exactly when the thetic desire to know is neutralized. See David Edward Shaner, *The Bodymind Experience in Japanese Buddhism: A Phenomenological Perspective of Kūkai and Dōgen* (Albany: SUNY Press, 1985), 132.
75   Marcel Proust, *Remembrance of Things Past*, tr. C. K. Scott Moncrieff (Hertfordshire: Wordsworth Editions Limited, 2006).
76   Indeed, the introspective contemplation of how one feels oneself in one's environment (drawing on Schmitz) also remains a reflection, even if without completely breaking with the pathic. This is what Thomas Fuchs in *Leib, Raum, Person. Entwurf einer*

a philosophy, cannot have anything to do with the absolutely pre-reflexive experience of the felt-bodily mine-ness, as is better expressed by a simple (and unphilosophical) exclamation of "A-ha!" Nor can *Leib*-phenomenologists claim to have that skill *de jure*. Often inactive and apparently stressed-out, the new phenomenologists sometimes look like tourists failing to adopt the local rhythms of a foreign land. They seem to be having, and even describe, a seemingly disembodied experience, content as they are with a faded objectivity, which is little more than a by-product of the more original lived richness of the *Leib* and absolute subjectivity (which are, ultimately, two sides of the same coin).

Only when the phenomenologist focuses precisely on the felt-bodily resonance of atmospheric feelings can he or she avoid the risk of experiencing the world in anesthetized terms. As Albert Borgmann writes in *Technology and the Character of Contemporary Life*, the risk to "have not felt the wind of the mountains, have not smelled the pines, have not heard the red-tailed hawk, have not sensed the slopes in their legs and lungs, have not experienced the cycle of day and night in the wilderness."[77] Otherwise, if the atmospheres one describes are disembodied and not really felt-bodily involving, they are perhaps ersatz-feelings rather than true atmospheric feelings. On this view, a philosophy of the body aiming at being a pioneering work and not repeating a rear-guard approach has to confine reflection to a minimum.

(8) According to Shusterman in *Body Consciousness*, central to somaesthetics is a "robust sense of the real body as a site for practical disciplines of conscious reflection that aim at reconstructing somatic perception and performance to achieve more rewarding experience and action."[78] Starting from a pragmatic pluralism, Shusterman draws from a wide range of somatic practices and technique, and adopts a richly interdisciplinary project that includes "the best of contemporary scientific knowledge."[79] With respect to the range of somatic practices and techniques, Shusterman laudably advances moderate alternatives to extreme approaches to the body in philosophy. For example, in *Body Consciousness* Shusterman criticizes Michel Foucault's limitation of the somaesthetic pleasures to the "most intense delights" of the body,[80] not least

---

phänomenologischen Anthropologie (Stuttgart: Klett-Cotta, 2000) rightly defines a paradoxical "simultaneous reflection" (273).

77 Albert Borgmann, *Technology and the Character of Contemporary Life: A Philosophical Inquiry* (Chicago: University of Chicago Press, 1984), 56. See also G. Csepregi, *The Clever Body* (Calgary: University of Calgary Press, 2006), 4.
78 Shusterman, *Body Consciousness*, 75.
79 Ibid., 203.
80 Ibid., 36.

for their detriment to "everyday somatic pleasures."[81] As Shusterman writes, Foucault unfortunately falls into a traditional "anhedonia," and despite critical diagnosis of the age, unwittingly cooperates with "our culture's sensationalist extremism."[82]

With respect to Shusterman's interdisciplinary methods, from the perspective of pathic aesthetics, the embrace of the natural sciences is somewhat problematic. Physicalism and neuroscience, in particular, tend to deny (in a fairly reductionist sort of way) the value of both the philosophical and practical approaches to the lived body, bringing the quantitative and third-person perspective to the fore, so incorporating them may ultimately undermine somaesthetics. Acknowledging the concern of dividing first and third person perspectives, Shusterman writes that "the pragmatic distinction between the perceiving I and the perceived me should not be erected into an insurmountable epistemological obstacle."[83] In place of that seemingly insurmountable obstacle, Shusterman sets a fruitful third option, lived somaesthetic reflection, but any wide-ranging interdisciplinary pluralistic approach will have tensions among its perspectives, and distinctions within itself.[84] Of course, such distinctions are not always problematic, and are very often necessary for any comprehensive aesthetic perspective; and on this point, pathic aesthetics is no different, e.g., differences in kinds of atmospheres mirror differences in kinds of outside feelings. Perhaps ultimately neither of these two approaches, somaesthetics or pathic aesthetics, is superior; neither "the only useful critical perspective or the best one," to use Shusterman's own remarks about architecture.

5 An Ongoing Dialogue

In the end, somaesthetics offers much that is correct, and while some of its limitations may point in the direction of an alternative aesthetic approach

---

81 Ibid., 37.
82 Ibid., 39.
83 Ibid., 73.
84 Shusterman, *Body Consciousness*, 63. As Shusterman acknowledges in "Somaesthetics: A Disciplinary Proposal," *Journal of Aesthetics and Art Criticism*, vol. 57, no. 3 (Summer 1999), "Somaesthetics has three fundamental dimensions." (1) "Analytic somaesthetics" is "descriptive" (and regards the "nature of bodily perceptions and practices," and how they "function in our knowledge and construction of reality." (2) "Pragmatic somaesthetics" is "normative" in its examination and recommendation of various practices and disciplines for somatic improvement. (3) "Practical somaesthetics" (in contrast to analytic and pragmatic somaesthetics) regards the actual doing of bodily practices (304–307).

to the body, perhaps ultimately somaesthetics and pathic aesthetics may be held in some unique pluralistic unity. After all, both share so much.[85] Duke Ellington released "It Don't Mean a Thing (If it Ain't Got that Swing)," a music of body and motion, of swing. Almost a century later, at the center of somaesthetics, no less of pathic aesthetics, we may say in the spirit of the Duke, that aesthetics doesn't mean a thing either, if it hasn't got that swing, the swing of the living human subject. The question remains however, who or what exactly is doing the swinging of aesthetic feeling: the individual filled with his own melioristic music, imposing it on the world, or the individual resonating with atmospheric music and feeling it all around.

85 For a more detailed comparison between somaesthetics and New Phenomenology see Griffero, "Corporeal Landscapes: Can Somaesthetics and New Phenomenology Come Together?" *The Journal of Somaesthetics*, vol. 7, no. 1 (2021), 15–28.

CHAPTER 6

Eating as an Aesthetic Activity: Somaesthetics and Food Studies

Dorota Koczanowicz

1   **Food and Philosophy**

American pragmatist Richard Shusterman proposes an original framework for analyzing the art of eating. While culinary art tends to be equated with a skillful harmonization of flavors and compelling dish presentation, Shusterman focuses first and foremost on the bodily processes involved in the act of food ingestion, which can become art only if it triggers the subject's somatic engagement. This requires special mindfulness and sensitivity. In this way, Shusterman expands the philosophical aesthetics of taste to include the art of eating. This essay addresses somaesthetics in the context of food studies, a field committed to exploring the biological and cultural meanings of the cooking and sharing of food.

The proclaimed goal of food studies is to explore and highlight the relevance of food to the interpretation of human existence. Until recently, food, cooking, and eating were objects of scholarly interest only within the natural sciences. However, food, without a doubt, far exceeds the bounds of biology and physiology. As a matter of fact, everyday bodily activities, while seemingly mundane, carry powerful social, cultural, and political resonances.

The disciplinary history of food studies may be rather short, but the history of the study of food studies is certainly long. As is the case with many humanities and social sciences, food studies boasts a complex genealogy. An interest in food and the ways it affects the operations of the body and the soul alike can be traced back to antiquity. Greek historian Plutarch insisted that a good physician relied on diets as a cure rather than using medications or the knife. Scribonius Largus, the physician of Emperor Claudius, also subscribed to this view. Watchful practices of dietary moderation were similarly advocated by Socrates, Petronius (the author of *The Satyricon*), and the physician Galen who claimed that a good medical doctor should also be a good cook. Unsurprisingly Galen's writings are interspersed with cooking recipes.

The thoughtful choice of meals was believed to attest to one's prudent judgment and to reflect a strong will capable of resisting the desires of the flesh.

Simplicity and temperance while dining were deemed an unmistakable sign of the person's proper choice of path in life. By the same token gastronomic decisions were simultaneously ethical decisions, exemplifying people's dutiful responsibility for their bodies and their communities. Such views were shared, for example, by the Stoics and Socrates who was wary of sophistication in the kitchen because he believed that preoccupation with luxury was a prelude to social injustice and war.[1]

Scholarly discourse on the origins of food studies goes back to early twentieth century anthropology. Indeed, one would be hard-pressed to conceive of anthropological research into family, social structure, or religion, without attention to food and practices of eating.[2] In fact, nutritional customs and habits are inevitably linked to virtually all cultural practices and very often offer rich insights into them. Exploring existing, and devising new, methodologies and theories for understanding the communicative and symbolic importance of food, and the cultural and philosophical meanings inherent in practices of eating, are still very much works, if fast growing works, in progress. Interest in the cultural importance of food production and consumption has steadily migrated from anthropology and ethnography into several other scholarly disciplines such as sociology and history, culminating in a major shift in the field of food studies in the late 1990s.

Today anthropological research still holds sway in the field of food studies with research programs investigating food as a central element of cultural rituals and social behaviors.[3] But the classic anthropological and historical research frameworks have been substantially augmented by scholarly voices from other disciplines, such as philosophy, communication sciences, art,

---

1 Cf. Louise Foxcroft, *Calories and Corsets: A History of Dieting Over Two Thousand Years* (London: Profile Books, 2013), 14–20. The interconnections between the stomach, ethics, and politics were equally pronounced in the Enlightenment when the diction of taste wandered into aesthetics. The corporeal taste became a useful metaphor for depicting beauty and discussing choices of an ethical nature. The 18th century is often referred to as the age of taste. It was also a time when the stomach became the locus of the operations of power.
2 Cf. James L. Watson and Melissa L. Caldwell, Introduction to *The Cultural Politics of Food and Eating: A Reader*, ed. James L. Watson and Melissa L. Caldwell (Oxford: Blackwell Publishing 2011), 1.
3 See E. N. Anderson, *Everyone Eats: Understanding Food and Culture* (New York: New York University Press, 2005); Joanna Davidson, *Sacred Rice: An Ethnography of Identity* (New York: Oxford, 2016); David E. Sutton, *Remembrance of Repasts: An Anthropology of Food and Memory* (New York: Berg Publishers, 2001); David E. Sutton, *Secrets from the Greek Kitchen: Cooking, Skill, and the Everyday Life on an Aegean Island* (Berkeley: University of California Press, 2014); R. Wrangham, *Catching Fire: How Cooking Made Us Human* (New York: Basic Books, 2009).

psychology, education, political science, gender studies, economics, the health sciences, theology, social justice, literature, film studies, architecture, and tourism, to name only a handful—and the number of these fields continues to grow. Among these fields, I focus on how food and eating are addressed within philosophy, in particular, the philosophical discipline known as "somaesthetics," which has been pioneered by Shusterman. Theoretically inclusive and purposefully integrative as it is, somaesthetics offers a promising perspective for philosophical explorations of food, eating, and the aesthetics of taste.[4]

2 *Der Mensch ist was er isst*

In the history of philosophy, a discipline dedicated to the quest for ultimate, eternal truth, there is a dearth of serious debate on food and eating. Lisa Heldke emphasizes how paradoxical this state of affairs actually is: philosophy is, after all, a "discipline that, more than any other, concerns itself with questions of meaning and value in human life," and yet it is "silent about food, a primary source of meaning and value."[5] Of course, Plato, David Hume, and Friedrich Nietzsche do offer some remarks on food, but only very recently have dietary choices become prominent in philosophy.[6]

Consistent with the dominant analytical trend of American philosophy, Heldke contends that the major focus in philosophy of food should fall on clarification of terms and concepts presently used in scholarly and public discussions on food. Heldke urges philosophers to abandon the habit of making pronouncements on particular issues, and to focus on unveiling those hidden preconceptions too often unreflectively adopted by participants in these debates. According to Heldke, this goal of conceptual clarification may be achieved by relying on four strategies.[7] First, established philosophical

---

4   For a detailed discussion of the premises of somaesthetics and the prospects for the development of the field, see Richard Shusterman's "Somaesthetics: A Disciplinary Proposal," in *Pragmatist Aesthetic: Living Beauty, Rethinking Art* (Lanham: Rowman & Littlefield, 2000).

5   Lisa Heldke, "Philosophy and Food," in *Routledge International Handbook of Food Studies*, ed. Ken Albala (London and New York: Routledge, 2013), 135. To redress this gap, Heldke and Deane W. Curtin's edited volume *Cooking, Eating, Thinking: Transformative Philosophies of Food* (Bloomington: Indiana University Press, 1992) offers a compilation of texts, which are capable of reshaping fundamental philosophical problems, if only we began to take seriously humans' relationships to food.

6   Heldke, "Philosophy and Food" (2013), 135.

7   Heldke's *Philosophers at Table: On Food and Being Human* (Chicago: University of Chicago Press, 2016), coauthored with Raymond Boisvert, discusses several philosophical issues and combines the strategies she has listed. These two philosophers sit down at the table

categories may be used to investigate food-related issues. Second, general philosophical discussions may be reframed as referring to food. Third, classic philosophical studies may be reexamined for their reflections on food. Fourth, philosophical discussions of food may be analyzed in terms of potential impacts on how we comprehend questions posed by philosophers.[8]

While employed within and across traditional philosophical disciplines, ethics especially would seem to benefit from these four strategies, particularly given well-established and impassioned debates on animal rights and ethical vegetarianism.[9] There are also compelling examinations of the ethical ramifications of new biotechnologies for food modification, and philosophical studies of the exceptionally disturbing problem of hunger.[10] Though directly focused on quite narrow, specialized issues, such studies (set within a broader perspective) concern nodal aspects of environmental ethics, one of the most important fields of contemporary philosophy. Environmental ethics is essentially interlocked with social philosophy, political philosophy, and feminism, particularly as regards their most topical concerns, such as globalization, colonialism, post-colonialism, domination, and oppression.[11]

3 Food, Art, and Aesthetics

When exploring the social circumstances of food and eating, social scientists attend to the activities and positions of male and female cooks, to cookbooks, to the contents of women's magazines, and to exhibits in museum cabinets; they delve into excessive food consumption, food shortages, and abuses

---

and ask, "How should we eat?" in order to discuss the ethics of dietary choices, aesthetics of eating, and tasting as a tool of knowledge.

8 Heldke, "Philosophy and Food" (2013), 137–141.

9 See, for example, Andrew Light and Erin McKenna, *Animal Pragmatism: Rethinking Human-Nonhuman Relationships* (Bloomington: Indiana University Press, 1999); Peter Singer, *Animal Liberation: A New Ethics for Our Treatment of Animals* (New York: HarperCollins, 1975); Peter Singer and Jim Mason, *The Ethics of What We Eat: Why Our Food Choices Matter* (New York: Rodale Books, 2006).

10 See F. Kirschenmann, *Cultivating an Ecological Conscience: Essays from a Farmer Philosopher* (Lexington: University Press of Kentucky, 2010); P. B. Thompson, *The Agrarian Vision: Sustainability and Environmental Ethics* (Lexington, University Press of Kentucky, 2010); S. George, *How the Other Half Dies: The Real Reasons for World Hunger* (Lanham: Rowman & Littlefield, 1989).

11 See Susan Bordo, *Unbearable Weight: Feminism, Western Culture and the Body* (Berkeley: University of California Press, 1995); Heldke, *Exotic Appetites: Ruminations of a Food Adventurer* (New York: Routledge, 2003).

of food; and they investigate the global flows, and the local peculiarities, of taste. So far, however, they have displayed little interest in the meal as such, the meal understood as a social event.[12] Georg Simmel's "The Sociology of the Meal" (1916) is a notable exception in this respect.[13] Simmel considers the meal within the framework of the nature-vs.-culture opposition, analyzing the ways in which "the exclusive egoism of eating"[14] is socialized and thus promoted into "the sphere of higher and spiritual charms."[15] These processes are crucially mediated by aestheticization which governs the ritual of the shared meal. But does the aesthetic component of food bring it closer to the status of a work of art? Simmel resolves this dilemma claiming, "Whereas the beauty of an artwork has as its essence in its untouchability, which keeps us at a distance, it is the refinement of the dining table that its beauty should still invite us to disturb it."[16] Simmel's article was written in a time of tectonic changes within art, which resulted in a redefinition of the very idea of the work of art, effectively reducing, if not altogether abolishing, the distance between the work of art and the audience, and in the process opening up new opportunities for redrawing the position of culinary art in culture.

Recent years have seen heated debates in food studies surrounding the sense of taste, a topic grievously neglected in theory before.[17] Aestheticians, culture scholars, anthropologists, and art critics have inquired about the status of taste among the other senses and about the possibilities of an aesthetic valorization of culinary practices; in many cases, artists working with food themselves have stirred the theorists to address these issues. While artistic representations of food and eating in art date from the dawn of culture, the 1930s marks an essential breakthrough as food products came to be used not only as the subject

---

12 See William Alex McIntosh, "The Sociology of Food," in *Routledge International Handbook of Food Studies*, 14.
13 Michael Symons, "Simmel's Gastronomic Sociology: An Overlooked Essay," *Food and Foodways*, vol. 5, no. 4 (1994), 333–351, especially 340–350. Simmel's "The Sociology of the Meal" (1910) is also published in *Simmel on Culture*, ed. David Frisby and Mike Featherson (London: Sage Publications, 1997).
14 In Symons's "Simmel's Gastronomic Sociology," 345.
15 *Ibid.*
16 *Ibid.*
17 Some of the weightiest philosophical explorations of taste are to be found in the work of the American feminist Carolyn Korsmeyer's work such as *Making Sense of Taste* (Ithaca: Cornell University Press, 1999), *Gender and Aesthetics: An Introduction* (New York: Routledge, 2004), and *The Taste Culture Reader: Experiencing Food and Drink* (New York: Oxford University Press, 2005).

matter of artworks but also as the very materials of works of art. The acts of food and drink sharing served firstly to extend the boundaries of art, and then secondly to offer critical commentary on culture by posing questions about consumption, ecology, hospitality, identity, gender, etc.

Today, contemporary art abounds with examples of the successful coupling of the artistic and the gastronomic. Tellingly, artists such as Gordon Matta Clark and Daniel Spoerri have also been restauranteurs. Clark founded his restaurant in New York in 1970, and Spoerri in Dusseldorf in 1968. Two years later Spoerri opened an art gallery in the same house where he put on display among other exhibits his famous assemblages known as "trap-pictures," which he had been composing of meal leftovers since the 1960s. When considering restaurant spaces, we should also mention *The Identical Lunch*, a performance by Alison Knowles at the Riss Diner in New York. Knowles visited the diner regularly for lunch, ordering and eating exactly the same meal every time; and the practice evolved into a performance exhibition. But while many artists cook, and many cooks and chefs create art, there is one celebrated chef and conceptualist the artworld has embraced as its own. *Ferran Adrià,* founder of molecular cuisine, in 2007 received the unique honor of invitation to attend *documenta* in Kassel, Germany—one of the most prestigious international art events—where he participated on equal footing with all other artists in attendance.

Explorations of similarities and overlapping patterns of food and art tend to take two basic forms: first, by analyzing the work of the cook in terms of aesthetic and artistic values, and second by scrutinizing the practices of artists who discern artistic potential in culinary techniques, or use food products as a material for art. Either of these forms inevitably generates questions about how culinary art is related to Art with a capital "A," for example, whether, when talking about the art of cooking, the art of serving food, or the art of tea-making, we are speaking metaphorically or not. Is there an idiom which captures the aesthetic status of food, and which, at the same time, helps us to examine food and cooking as meaningful and profound aesthetic experiences? In other words, one central question is whether art and everyday life can be brought into proximity, and, then if so how may be that be achieved.

Carolyn Korsmeyer in *Making Sense of Taste* challenges the culturally entrenched models of ascribing value to the senses, and ousting the bodily senses from philosophical inquiry. At the same time, Korsmeyer maintains other fundamental premises of Western thought, for example, that art should be disinterested, and that it should avoid familiarity with the audience in order for aesthetic experience to be founded on detachment. So while she denounces the degradation of taste, and makes a convincing case for taste as multidimensional, relevant, and indispensable to aesthetics, Korsmeyer is adamant about denying any possibility of regarding food as art. Korsmeyer admits that meals bear symbolic, representational, cognitive, and expressive meanings, but all of this is not enough to render a meal (no matter how conceptually impressive or visually spectacular it might be) a work of art. Culinary practices, insists Korsmeyer, may at most aspire to the status of an applied or decorative art, which is an art of a lower order. Nevertheless, Korsmeyer believes that this end of decorative art is not exactly the ideal gourmets should pursue. The cooking and sharing of meals do not require any external emblems of art, for they are—in and of themselves—an autonomous, essential, and compelling cultural phenomenon which "has aesthetic importance in its own right."[18]

Arnold Berleant takes an even bolder position *vis-à-vis* the disciplinary past in his *Re-Thinking Aesthetics* when he proposes to discard the notional remnants of the old historical approaches in order to radically reappraise aesthetics, and thus to recast and rechannel the flow of concepts.[19] Berleant critically surmounts the Kantian tradition, which is founded on the exclusion of aesthetics "from the natural and moral realms and [on granting it] its independent jurisdiction in a separate domain."[20] Berleant believes Kant's tenets concerning the nature of beauty, in the *Critique of Judgment*, are shaped by presuppositions from outside aesthetics as such. In Berleant's view, Kant's theory is neither adequate to capture contemporary art nor even traditional art. In place of these traditional ideas of aesthetic autonomy and disinterestedness Berleant advocates a new project of engaged aesthetics. A work of art (and the cultural sphere of art, in general), writes Berleant, should not be philosophically framed as an independent object external to the will of the viewer. Instead, Berleant emphasizes the continuity of art and experience, and consequently argues that art "functions ... as a present and active factor in the participatory engagement that is the sign of the aesthetic. Any object that acts in this way is art or artlike; any experience that joins object and perceiver in a nontranscendent perceptual unity is aesthetic."[21] On this model,

---

18   Korsmeyer, *Gender and Aesthetics*, 100.
19   *Ibid.*, vii.
20   Arnold Berleant, *Re-Thinking Aesthetics: Rogue Essays on Aesthetics and Art* (New York: Routledge, 2016), viii.
21   Berleant, *Re-Thinking Aesthetics*, 109.

the sphere of art extends beyond the so-called fine arts to the applied arts, the various crafts, and all other "practices of creative making that are the locus of creative human activity,"[22] even culinary art. Working within the traditions of American philosophy and phenomenology, and owing much to John Dewey and Maurice Merleau-Ponty, Berleant makes experience the fundamental category of aesthetics.

The first book to ask explicitly whether food is art was Elizabeth Telfer's 1996 *Food for Thought: Philosophy and Food*. In Heldke's classification, Telfer's work belongs to the first category of studies, namely, those applying the familiar notions entrenched in philosophy to new fields of inquiry. Building on the tradition of fine arts, Telfer grants culinary art a place among the lower order arts, side by side with applied art, likewise incapable of inducing profound emotions.[23] By contrast, again within Heldke's classification, Korsmeyer's *Making Sense of Taste* belongs to the fourth category, as Korsmeyer observes that there is a dearth of analysis of the sense of taste in the history of philosophy, and, consequently, makes it her aim to identify and explore the reasons behind this neglect for palatal taste, in particular, and bodiliness, in general, which so many otherwise great thinkers have consistently exhibited.

While some philosophers ponder various food-related issues, and espouse various theoretical positions and methods, the pragmatists, not surprisingly, stand out in the field. As Heldke writes in "Philosophy and Food," "Pragmatist philosophy begins from the understanding that philosophical questions begin in, and return to, the concerns of everyday human life."[24] Pragmatism undercuts the dichotomies which have traditionally propelled the exclusion of food from philosophical investigations. Dewey, for example, even avails himself of culinary examples which he then turns into arguments for his pragmatist view of the nature of aesthetic experience. Heldke, Shusterman, Boisvert, Nicola Perullo, Russell Pryba, Glenn Kuehn, and I draw on Dewey's pragmatist insights to explore the aesthetic potential of food.[25] Shusterman's pragmatist somaesthetics, in particular, is especially conducive to integrating all four of Heldke's strategies for the philosophical scrutiny of the cooking and sharing

---

22 *Ibid.*, 2.
23 Elizabeth Telfer, *Food for Thought: Philosophy and Food* (London and New York: Routledge, 1996).
24 Heldke, "Philosophy and Food," 142.
25 See also D. Koczanowicz, "Regimes of Taste and Somaesthetics," *The Journal of Somaesthetics*, Issue on *Somaesthetics and Food*, vol. 2, nos. 1 and 2 (2016), 102–112; and Dorota Koczanowicz, "John Dewey: Culinary Perspective," *Pragmatism Today*, vol. 7, no. 2 (Winter 2016), 88–94.

of food. Furthermore, because it transcends the narrow bounds of classical philosophy, somaesthetics is a site where several different approaches to the study of food as a biological and cultural phenomenon may be brought together.

4   The Somaesthetic Art of Eating

I believe we are now witnessing the rise of a specific intellectual climate that promotes the development of cultural mechanisms fostering the emancipation of taste, which dovetails with renegotiations of the boundaries of art in order to include cooking and eating within the arts. It is not only possible but necessary to reappraise the relations between aesthetic and culinary experiences with a focus on the presence of taste in art practice and the exploration of culinary culture. Many chefs approach menus as multilayered communications with eaters through the sense of taste, while also engaging the eater's intellect; and not only her knowledge but often her sense of humor as well. For example, dinners at South America's best restaurant, Central, or at Europe's best restaurant, Osteria Francescana, are known to provide outstanding gustatory experiences but also to serve as lessons in geography and history.[26]

It is important to reestablish the position of taste because the sense of taste fell victim to the traditional dualistic vision of culture in which body and mind are separated and pitted against one another. In this philosophical view, found, for example, in Plato, mind is distinguished from and elevated over body.[27] Such a division persists throughout the tradition of philosophy and still persists today. As Dewey writes in *Art as Experience*, "For many persons an aura of mingled awe and unreality encompasses 'spiritual' and 'ideal' while 'matter' has become by contrast a term of depreciation, something to be explained away or apologized for."[28] Partly following Dewey, Shusterman's somaesthetics also seeks to overcome this opposition, close examination of the philosophical

---

26   The menu composed by Virgilio Martinez (Central) reflects the diversity of Peru's ecosystems. Massimo Bottura (Osteria Francescana) designs innovative dishes based on the traditional Italian products. His most famous dish is "five ages of Parmigiano Reggiano," devoted to Italy's best-known cheese produced in Emilia-Romagna.

27   Cf. Korsmeyer, *Making Sense of Taste*, 13. According to Plato, the only chance of retrieving the divine knowledge we forget upon being born lies in the effort of the rational soul, which must "conquer" the mortal body and regulate the senses and emotions. The subduing of the body is the only path to knowledge and virtue.

28   John Dewey, *Art as Experience* (New York: Perigee Books, 1980), 6.

importance of the aesthetic experience of the body in everyday activities,[29] and rich analyses of perception, awareness, sentience,[30] and the kinetic aspect of human functioning. Shusterman has also extended somaesthetics to food and the art of eating with his article entitled "Somaesthetics and the Fine Art of Eating."[31] Before examining his somaesthetics of food and eating, however, I will highlight those elements of Shusterman's pragmatism integral to the establishment of gastronomic practices as forms of art.

Shusterman's writings are permeated with the idea of integrated human experience in which the aesthetic, the ethical, the political, the practical, the cognitive, and the corporeal interpenetrate and condition each other. Revisiting the ancient ideal of philosophy as an art of living,[11] Shusterman in *Practicing Philosophy* proposes an holistic approach to human existence. He believes that combining philosophy as a theoretical inquiry with philosophy as an artful life-practice yields optimal effects. In this way, Shusterman overcomes the repudiation of the body which has so long haunted philosophy. Reflecting on one of the most pertinent queries that philosophy poses, "How to make life better?" Shusterman contemplates ethical, political, and aesthetic questions, but assigns equal importance to proper bodily posture, appropriate nourishment, and adept regulation of one's breathing. Hence his philosophy is not simply another attempt at valorizing "the body" *vis-à-vis* "the mind," but rather a descriptive and normative project of recognizing "the sentient soma" with the totality of its operations. As Shusterman writes in "Somaesthetics and the Fine Art of Eating," somaesthetics must include theoretical reflection alongside "practical bodily disciplines to enhance our experience and performance while increasing our tools for self-fashioning."[12]

Let us now consider the somaesthetics art of eating. Shusterman contrasts the "act" of eating with the "art" of eating, and investigates the conditions under which the one can transition into the other. Shusterman distinguishes several degrees of engagement and expertise in the somatic art of eating. He locates the starting point at the level of the simple satisfaction of hunger, which we share with animals. Even if the human act of eating is reduced to

---

29 This theme is also insightfully discussed by Yuriko Saito, who calls for combining the "what" and the "how" the way Eastern philosophical tradition have been doing. Cf. Saito, *Aesthetics of the Familiar: Everyday Life and World-Making* (New York: Oxford University Press, 2017).

30 Shusterman, *Thinking through the Body: Essays in Somaesthetics* (Cambridge: Cambridge University Press, 2012), 3.

31 Shusterman, "Somaesthetics and the Fine Art of Eating," in *Body Aesthetics*, ed. Sherri Irvin (New York: Oxford University Press, 2016), 261–280.

an instinctive, unmindful, and "crudely insensitive" response to the hunger-triggered need, the satisfaction of this need always takes place in a cultural context. This context is produced in part by cooking techniques and by the capacity to name things, that is, to talk about the products and sensations they induce. As Shusterman writes in "Somaesthetics and the Fine Art of Eating,"

> Human culture, through its use of language, enables us to name or identify what we eat and thus better select, communicate, acquire, and critically evaluate our food choices. We can thus organize our ingestion of them in an orderly form or a sequence that adds meaning to the art of eating.[32]

According to Shusterman, the top of the gourmet pyramid is occupied by those who have mastered the art of dining. They are people who have cultivated tastes, knowledge about composing meals, the ability to derive pleasure from eating them, and the capacity to analyze the entire complex process of eating. Additionally, writes Shusterman, "they know how to eat aesthetically."[33]

The art of eating consists of three intertwined and interdependent components: the art of cuisine, the art of food appreciation and criticism, and the art of eating in the strict sense. In Shusterman's typology, the art of cuisine encompasses the processes of preparation and presentation of food. The art of food appreciation concerns the choice of dishes and the selection of ingredients, the judgments on which hinge the knowledge of both the quality and the gustatory properties of foods as well as their nutritional and health-related value. Additionally, as the adequate composition and apt assessment of meals are also linked to the sociocultural meanings of food, they require a cultural competence.[34]

In his discussion of the relevance and cultivation of gastronomic art, Shusterman often refers to the insights of the French epicure Jean Anthelme Brillat-Savarin. For example, concurring with Brillat-Savarin, Shusterman writes in "Somaesthetics and the Fine Art of Eating" that when describing pleasures of the table, we should not stop at the level of smell and taste, but also explore "the visual beauties of food-presentation and the auditory harmonies of music that often accompany our dining to enhance its overall satisfaction."[35] Specifying the conditions that foster harmonious and intense pleasures

---

32 *Ibid.*, 263.
33 *Ibid.*
34 *Ibid.*, 264.
35 *Ibid.*, 267.

of the table, Shusterman focuses on the state of the senses traditionally evoked in such circumstances, i.e., taste, smell, sight, and hearing, as well as the role of touch and proprioceptive sensations in shaping our culinary experiences, again with compliments to Brillat-Savarin's celebrated observations. For example, Shusterman stresses tactile delights that arise from sensing various surfaces and textures of food products and utensils used while eating. We touch foods and accessories with our hands, lips, teeth, tongues, mouths, and palates. Pleasure can be occasioned by the warmth that washes over our bodies or the refreshing coolness of chilled drinks, cooled fruit, cold dishes, ice cream, and other desserts. Tactile stimuli are provided by the chopsticks placed between fingers, by the weight, shapes, and surfaces of cutlery we hold in our hands, or by the texture of the napkin cloth we use to wipe our lips and fingers. When tearing off a piece of baguette, we find out whether it is crispy, whether its crust is hard and crunchy, and the flesh firm or soft.

Cooking sections of bookstores and libraries are full of volumes devoted to cooking techniques, recipes, food products, and the history of cuisine, as well as the history of cookbooks themselves, kitchen equipment, restaurants, chefs, and food migrations. Scarcer are studies addressing the aesthetics of eating, which is associated with appealing dish presentation and the delightful blending of savors. The originality of Shusterman's methodological approach lies in his adoption of a third and highly unconventional perspective on the art of eating. Specifically, Shusterman passes over the creative aspects of cooking, and instead chooses a less obvious field of exploration, focusing on the aesthetic dimensions of food ingestion. In doing so Shusterman delves beneath the surface of the body, looking into the abyss of the mouth, the throat, the stomach and the intestines. In "Somaesthetics and the Fine Art of Eating" Shusterman calls this object of inquiry the art of eating in the strict sense, defining it narrowly as the "modes and manners of ingestion."[36]

Shusterman defines the art of eating in the strict sense of the term as based on the following criteria: the posture at the table, eating dynamics, eating implements, the kinds of dishes, the timed sequence of serving them, the way in which the foods and drinks are appreciated, and the pleasure offered by both festive banqueting and everyday meals. Shusterman also stresses how important it is to know when to stop eating and drinking.

Discussing the first dimension of the somaesthetic art of eating, Shusterman wonders which body postures optimize eating experience and maximize its aesthetic potential. He envisages the benefits and discomforts of various

---

36   Ibid., 262.

positions our bodies adopt while eating meals, bearing in mind historical variants and contemporary norms distinctive to various cultures. Shusterman's analysis highlights the deeply contextual nature of the art of eating, which depends on the styles and norms embraced in particular cultures, with all the subtleties behind the endorsement or nonendorsement of various behaviors both across and within cultures.

Exploring movement as part of the act of eating, Shusterman focuses on two aspects: internal and external motions. The motions of the arms, the hands, and the fingers are necessary to bring food to our mouths, when we use various table accessories, or when assisting our co-banqueters by passing them dishes or spices. Arm motions are associated with the movement of the entire body which we initiate when bending or turning. Volitional internal movements, such as biting, chewing, swallowing, drinking, smelling, etc., are no less important because people who are aware of these factors can influence the rhythms of their motions to harmonize with the rhythms of the bodies and the needs of other people at the table. Regarding internal movements, breathing involves respiratory movements linked to eating processes.

Evoking examples from a range of cultures, Shusterman focuses on the appropriate selection of cutlery and other eating implements, which depend on the context in which the meal is served and on the type of dishes included. The choice of the physical properties of the utensils—their materials, sizes, shapes, etc.—significantly affects tactile and proprioceptive pleasures of eating. The selection of foods and the sequencing of dishes form another important aspect of the art of eating. These selections are formed by the culture in which we grow up as every culture has its own specific table customs and meal-related conduct forms. Shusterman highlights differences between the West and the East modes of food serving, and differences within the West, for example, between European and American styles of food serving and eating. The intricacy of refined eating is enhanced by the expediency of bringing food in alignment with the time of day, the season of the year, the diner's health condition, the occasion of the meal, etc. The choice of food items also involves eliminating some ingredients or dishes from the menu "for aesthetic reasons other than mere taste."[37]

The fifth dimension, which Shusterman calls "perceptions," overlaps with the previous four. "Perceptions" are generated by operations of the "complex sensorimotor systems" within our bodies. These systems perform varied functions. For example, they control our postures, coordinate limb movements,

---

37   Shusterman, "Somaesthetics and the Fine Art of Eating," 272.

and determine the gustatory, olfactory, tactile, and proprioceptive sensations. At the same time, writes Shusterman, they also "enable appropriate recognition and handling of eating accessories; and they govern our selection and sequencing of foods by identifying them and their qualities through diverse sensory perceptions."[38]

Shusterman recommends "cultivating and sharpening perceptions of inner bodily space, especially those within the mouth, nose, and throat where biting, tasting, chewing, smelling, and swallowing take place,"[39] as this could optimize culinary experiences through enhanced intensity, complexity, and satisfactoriness. A greater alertness to proprioceptive sensations coming from the body's posture and its physical contact with food will be instrumental both in deriving enjoyment from eating and in timely deciding to finish the meal when the body produces signals of satiety.

According to Shusterman, we must reappraise the functions and roles of the senses in relationships between humans and their environments. In this way, Shusterman's concepts inscribe themselves in the already mentioned conceptual movement mobilized around the idea of the new aesthetic sensorium. The sensorium is a combination of the body's perceptions and the space in which the environment is experienced and interpreted. Part of the complexity intrinsic to this issue arises from the complex nature of the senses themselves. On the one hand, the senses are private and subjective experiences; while, on the other hand, the positions and potentials of the senses are defined by culture, and regulated by social and cultural norms.

In the new sensorium, the integrated senses are viewed as autonomous, which makes it possible to recast the production of world images, including the social world image, such that the senses are treated as equal to discursive language. Defined in these terms, the sensorium overcomes very many of the old prejudices and anxieties that contributed to instituting the hierarchy of the senses in which the bodily senses, and taste in particular, were discriminated against. The new phenomenon is largely defined through aesthetic qualities, enhanced by self-reflection and heightened ethical awareness.

Taste can be defended in two different ways. One strategy involves proving that taste is closer to the more appreciated senses than common opinion would have it. Another bolder and pathbreaking strategy, which Shusterman adopts within his study of the art of eating, examines the sensual aspect of eating without focusing on its visual, symbolic, and cognitive facets. By the

---

38 *Ibid.*, 273.
39 *Ibid.*

same token, Shusterman emphasizes that the sensuality of eating is a value in and of itself.

5 The Culture of Sensory Experience

Without doubt the position of food studies within the humanities and social sciences is consolidating, and food studies is gradually carving out its own place as a subdiscipline of culture research. Nevertheless, the theoretical status of the field, and the reasons for the growing popularity of food studies, are still open to debate. For example, upsurge of interest can be recognized as a symptom of a shift both in culture and in the ways of studying culture. Following a longstanding preoccupation with the text, and the focus on cultural developments as discursive systems, scholarly attention is turning towards sensory experiences. As a consequence, food naturally makes its way toward the center of culture research. And as a result of this change, the search for universal mechanisms that order the social world are increasingly set aside for the sake of vernacular accounts of individual experiences. Still, intimate taste sensations are always, at least in part, expressions of collective experience, and grow out of culture even as they unfold within culture. The thematic field explored by food studies is also comprised of meanings and values, which, above and beyond individual variance, organize the mechanisms of making pronouncements on and the rules that regulate the operations of the *sensus communis*, and consequently foster the feeling of belonging to a given community of taste.

At the same time, the influx of food-related themes into culture research embodies a general tendency of valorizing this sphere of experience in the globalizing consumer society. Culture research thus seeks to identify and produce an account of cultural activities which ensue from the meeting of hunger-caused needs. Such activities come in a broad and varied array of forms, which depend on the culture-specific contexts and the culture-determined goals. However, the responsibilities of food studies are not limited to impartial descriptive efforts: dedicated to analyzing art practices as the field is, its pursuits also accrue an analytical-critical dimension.

A considerable investment of food studies lies in revealing and critiquing the ramifications of unreflecting consumerism. Considerations of the ethical-aesthetic aspects of nutritional behaviors are a response to this ensemble of attitudes and propose alternative approaches. This reaction, and such proposals, are perhaps best exemplified in Shusterman's somaesthetics, a framework which is committed to sensory experiences, without however allying with consumerism, and without catering to the hedonistic needs artificially induced by the consumer industry. Calling for perfecting sensory appreciation, Shusterman recommends due care, specific moderation, and mindful attention to the needs of the body and the environment alike. He treats the meal as a holistic and multimodal sensory experience in which the sensual, the intellectual, and the emotional mutually condition and reinforce each other. Rather than an aesthetics of pure form, the pragmatist aesthetic model developed by Shusterman foregrounds an aesthetics of experience which does not relinquish ethical obligations and makes it its main goal to maximize experience. This intensification, however, is neither equated nor coupled with the proliferation of stimuli, luxuriousness, excess, or unending feast; rather, it originates in the skill of bringing one's needs into tune with the capacities of the environment and from the willing readiness to systematically work on improving the quality of every minute experience. The point lies thus in cultivating and optimizing somatic mindfulness. Somaesthetics, writes Shusterman, "building on the pragmatist insistence on the body's central role in artistic creation and appreciation ... highlights and explores the soma—the living, sentient, purposive body—as the indispensable medium for all perception."[40] Revisiting and reembracing *aisthesis*, somaesthetics is a helpful tool for culture research-inflected foods studies interested in the historically changeable norms and regulations of sensory experiences.

40   Shusterman, *Thinking through the Body*, 3.

PART 2

Performative Philosophy and the Man in Gold

∴

CHAPTER 7

Somaesthetics, Photography, and the Man in Gold

Jerold J. Abrams

> Speech is silvern, Silence is golden.
> THOMAS CARLYLE, *Sartor Resartus*[1]

∴

1 The Adventures of the Man in Gold

Richard Shusterman's book *The Adventures of the Man in Gold* is a work of philosophy, photography, and fiction, about a figure known only as "the Man in Gold."[2] Shusterman narrates the adventures of the Man in Gold from the perspective of a philosopher whose body (and whose philosophy) has somehow been possessed by the mysterious golden figure. The Man in Gold inhabits and experiences the world through the conduit of the philosopher, but Shusterman is still able to observe these experiences sufficient to narrate them in English, French, and Chinese. These experiences must be narrated by Shusterman, if they are to be told at all, because the Man in Gold himself is as silent as a photograph; which is strange because the Man in Gold is also a philosopher, and philosophy, traditionally, is a spoken and written form of art. The Man in Gold understands language, but chooses not to speak or write because he understands, and feels in a very powerful way, the limits of language in its various attempts to describe the nature of aesthetic experience. In fact, the Man in Gold is so critical of the pretensions of language that he even appears at times to be critical of Shusterman's own philosophical descriptions of these very aesthetic experiences of the Man in Gold.

---

1 Thomas Carlyle, *Sartor Resartus*, ed. Kerry McSweeney and Peter Sabor (New York: Oxford University Press, 2008), 165.
2 Richard Shusterman, *The Adventures of the Man in Gold: Paths Between Art and Life, A Philosophical Tale*, English/French text by Shusterman, tr. Thomas Mondémé, Somaflux Photographs by Yann Toma (Paris: Éditions Hermann, 2016).

Shusterman's perspective is, therefore, quite complex. On the one hand, he narrates the experiences of the Man in Gold from the inside, as it were, because the Man in Gold inhabits the philosopher's body. On the other hand, this perspective (from the inside) is not the first person perspective singular perspective, the "I see," or "I experience," of the Man in Gold, nor a first person plural perspective of Shusterman and the Man in Gold; for example, the "We see," or "we aesthetically experience." Shusterman narrates from his own first person perspective, as an "I," and a third person perspective on the Man in Gold, the "He" (referring to the golden figure); and yet in narrating in this manner, Shusterman is recalling what it was like to be there, inhabited, possessed, seeing simultaneously with his own eyes, and the eyes of the Man in Gold, two first person perspectives ambiguously intertwined, a mysterious form of intersubjectivity.

Paris photographer Yann Toma also "narrates" the adventures of the Man in Gold, from the perspective of the camera, in full-color somaflux photographs. These photographs appear throughout the *Adventures* beginning with the cover photograph of the Man in Gold holding Danish artist Marit Benthe Norheim's beautiful sculpture of a female nude whose seemingly incandescent form elegantly lights the shot from the center, setting a rich visual tone for the odyssey of philosophy and photography to follow.[3] This odyssey is philosophically challenging for its ambiguity, complexity, uniqueness, and its recognition of the limits of language to describe it. For a work so self-conscious of the limits of its multiple languages (or any other language) to articulate its own ultimately nonlinguistic subject matter, any further exploration of the *Adventures* may be well advised to proceed cautiously. Bearing that point in mind, the present chapter limits its focus to two related themes: first, the concept of "transfiguration" as it appears in Shusterman's *Adventures*, Arthur Danto's study of Andy Warhol's *Brillo Boxes*, and Ralph Waldo Emerson's "Literary Ethics;" and second, the genre of science fiction as that appears in the *Adventures* and Philip K. Dick's novella *The Golden Man* (1954). Both lines of inquiry aim to establish the *Adventures* as a philosophically self-conscious work of science fiction.

---

3 In the preface Shusterman recognizes the difficulty of the work, claiming that the *Adventures* may be "too strange a hybrid" (*Adventures*, 7) to be appreciated without preliminary explanation of three contributing factors: first, Shusterman's desire for a "more concrete and practical" exploration of his somaesthetic philosophy (*Ibid.*, 9); second, a felt need to overcome the traditional "observer's or interpreter's point of view," and fully enter the "the artist's perspective" (*Ibid.*, 10); and third, Shusterman's "encounter with Yann Toma," a photographer and Professor of Fine Art in the Sorbonne's Faculty of Fine Arts.

2 Transfigurations

In the first chapter, "A Mysterious Birth," Shusterman calls the *Adventures* a "curious tale of transfigured identities," referring to his own "transfiguration into the 'Man in Gold'" at the Royaumont Abbey.[4] The "birth" of the Man in Gold is "mysterious" because a philosopher, namely, Shusterman, effectively "gives birth" to himself in the form of a new "embryonic persona," assisted by the photographer and "midwife" Toma with his "birthing equipment: camera, lights, and body suit."[5] Shortly after this birth, in which a philosopher of art transforms into a living work of photographical art, "the Abbey's wise and wizardly mistress Marie-Christine" dubs "him as 'the Man in Gold.'"[6] If the work begins with one form of transfiguration in which the Man in Gold takes possession of the philosopher, the *Adventures* ends with yet another form of transfiguration in which the Man in Gold is himself transfigured by Norheim's newly animated and glowing sculpture of the female nude, followed by a separation of the Man in Gold from the philosopher. As Shusterman recalls in the last chapter, "The Magic Vessels of the Viking Queen," the Man in Gold was "transfigured by the embrace of his beautiful lover" (whose name is Wanmei),[7] the same passionately glowing golden nude sculpture of the cover and other photographs in the work.[8]

2.1 *Danto and Shusterman*

In an essay entitled "Art and Religion," published a decade before the *Adventures*, Shusterman highlights the importance of the concept of "transfiguration" within Danto's philosophy of art. "Arthur Danto, the most influential of contemporary analytic aestheticians," writes Shusterman, "has made the concept of transfiguration the keystone of his philosophy of art."[9] If transfiguration is the "keystone" of Danto's philosophy of art; then the two sides of the arch would appear to be pop art in the 1960s, and the nineteenth century German philosopher G. W. F. Hegel's *Lectures on Fine Art* and *Phenomenology of Spirit*. In the *Phenomenology* Hegel describes a figure known as "*Geist*" (the historically unfolding collective mind of humanity) as developing over the

---

4 Shusterman, *Adventures*, 21.
5 *Ibid.*, 20.
6 *Ibid.*, 34.
7 *Ibid.*, 118.
8 Shusterman in the *Adventures* compares this fiery experience of transfiguration to the divine transfiguration of the burning bush that Moses witnessed in the book of Exodus (119).
9 Shusterman, "Art and Religion," *Journal of Aesthetic Education*, vol. 42, no. 3 (fall 2008), 8.

course of universal history to reach its own unique form of philosophical and historically reflective self-consciousness. *Geist* appears at the beginning of universal history as a potentiality, like an acorn, and develops over the course of history, actualizing its potentiality, like a developing oak tree, to achieve its ultimate philosophical end. As Danto writes in "The End of Art: A Philosophical Defense," "Hegel's hero, *Geist*, goes through an ingenious sequence of states, through which he (she?) arrives at last an idea of his or her own nature."[10]

Art is an essential part of this historical unfolding, as Hegel writes in his *Lectures on Fine Art*; and it too unfolds through history, from its beginning to its end: for "just as art has its 'before' in nature and the finite spheres of life," writes Hegel, "so too it has an 'after'"—and that "after" is seen as art "passes over into higher forms of consciousness."[11] Like *Geist* in the *Phenomenology*, Danto also describes art itself as unfolding through an "ingenious sequence of states" (within its own *Bildungsroman*), and completing itself in pop art. As Danto writes in "The End of Art," "I have certainly presented the history of art as a kind of *Bildungsroman* in which art struggles toward a kind of philosophical understanding."[12] Upon achieving this "kind of philosophical understanding," according to Danto, art comes to a philosophical "end," but here "end" is not quite the same thing as a "halt." Echoing Hegel's view that art "passes over into higher forms of consciousness," Danto writes in *The Transfiguration of the Commonplace* that even as it has come to an "end," art has not come to a stop: "It has not *stopped* but ended, in the sense that it has passed over into a kind of consciousness of itself and become, again in a way, its own philosophy: a state of affairs predicted in Hegel's philosophy of history."[13]

While the two philosophers both see art becoming philosophically self-conscious, Danto's "end of art" is not quite Hegel's "end of art." One important difference regards photography: understandably, the new medium would not feature prominently in Hegel's aesthetics, but photography and especially moving pictures are essential to understanding Danto's reconstruction of the history of art. In the mid-nineteenth century, painting had been the supreme form of visual art; but then photography appeared with its incredible realism,

---

10   Danto, "The End of Art: A Philosophical Defense," *History and Theory*, vol. 37, no. 4, Theme Issue 37 on "Danto and His Critics: Art History, Historiography, and After the End of Art" (December 1998), 135.
11   G. W. F. Hegel, *Hegel's Aesthetics: Lectures on Fine Art*, vol. I, tr. T. M. Knox (New York: Oxford, 1975), 102.
12   Danto, "The End of Art: A Philosophical Defense," 135.
13   Danto, *The Transfiguration of the Commonplace: A Philosophy of Art* (Cambridge: Harvard University Press, 1981), vii.

and soon thereafter moving pictures with their incredible power to depict both space and time. And with this power to depict space and time, moving pictures also revealed a new and powerful form of narration, and this power especially threatened painting's hold in the world of art. As Danto writes in *The Philosophical Disenfranchisement of Art*, reflecting on his Hegelian reconstruction of art, "I had in mind moving pictures, pictures which directly represent motion by means of moving images, thus facilitating narrative representation in a way closed off to painting. Painting was therefore required to redefine itself or collapse into a secondary activity."[14] If moving pictures had forced painting to redefine itself, redefining itself would first require painting to know itself; and knowing itself, as a medium, would require inquiry into itself, in the only way painting knew how. As Danto writes, this highly experimental inquiry by painting into painting was nothing short of "the astonishing sequence of convulsions that have defined the art history of our century."[15] One after another, in rapid succession, movement followed movement, e.g., Impressionism, Post-Impressionism, Fauvism, Expressionism, Cubism, Dada, Surrealism, and Abstract Expressionism. Amidst the dynamism of this period of art history, anything approaching a developmental logic or ordering of the sequence would have been terribly difficult to see; but there was, in fact, an order to the sequence. Painting had set about to know itself; and it was making progress toward that end, and would eventually achieve that end. In fact, painting would achieve this end in 1964 when Andy Warhol unveiled his *Brillo Box* exhibit at the Stable Gallery in Manhattan.[16]

The *Brillo Boxes* are wood sculptures painted (synthetic polymer paint and silkscreen ink) on wood to appear (in every detail) exactly like grocery store cardboard boxes of Brillo brand dishwashing soap pads. The subject matter alone was unique and strange: nothing grand or noble or mysterious; instead, something everyone had seen already in the grocery store, possibly even earlier that day—"commonplace" things, "mere real things," as Danto would call them. And yet, somehow, these boxes that looked so very like "commonplace" and "mere real things" were *not* commonplace, and were anything but mere real things.[17] As Danto would write in *The Transfiguration of the Commonplace*,

---

14   Danto, *The Philosophical Disenfranchisement of Art* (New York: Columbia University Press, 1986), 118 (see also 206).
15   *Ibid.*, xv.
16   *Ibid.*, 118. As Danto writes of Warhol in "The Philosopher as Andy Warhol," in *Philosophizing Art: Selected Essays* (Berkeley: University of California Press, 1999), "I have felt him to possess a philosophical intelligence of an intoxicatingly high order" (62).
17   Shusterman, "Art and Religion," 8.

by exact replication (at least to the eye), Warhol had "transfigured" these "commonplace" objects; a transfiguration that had elevated the merely real things from the plane of the commonplace to the plane of art. *The Brillo Boxes* were visually indiscernible from boxes of Brillo brand soap pads similarly stacked in the grocery store; and yet one set proposed to be art, while the other did not; and precisely this indiscernibility, according to Danto, effectively raised the question of why exactly one set of boxes was art (or not art) in relation to the other. But if art had posed the question of its own nature, as requiring determination of the difference between two identical sets of things, art alone could not answer its own question; and the reason was that the question art had posed was fundamentally philosophical. By posing a question of self-consciousness, art had now entered the higher sphere of philosophy—philosophy being the only discipline whose primary subject matter is itself. As Danto writes in "The End of Art," "My thesis was that once art raised the question of why one pair of look-alikes was art and the other not, it lacked the power to rise to an answer. For that, I thought, philosophy was needed."[18]

If art, in the form of painting, had been spurred by cinema to undertake a quest for self-knowledge, then art had at last achieved what it sought: art had attained a unique form of self-knowledge (although a form of self-knowledge art could not have foreseen). Art had at last come to behold itself, as if looking into a mirror of its own making, and found there its own essential nature; and that essential nature was philosophy. By interrogating itself, within a convulsive series of movements, art had simultaneously (and paradoxically) found itself within itself and passed beyond itself into a higher sphere of thought. That is what Danto means by his brilliant and provocative thesis of the "end of art." As Danto clarifies his thesis in "The End of Art," the "end of art" is "a theory of consciousness—of how a developmental sequence of events terminates in the consciousness of that sequence as a whole."[19] So, in the moment that art had found itself to be philosophy, and shown itself to be philosophy, art had also thereby "passed over" into philosophy. Once art had passed over into philosophy, "art" (conceived as the series of movements in late nineteenth and

---

18 Danto, "The End of Art," 134. "To use my favorite example," writes Danto, "nothing need mark the difference, outwardly, between Andy Warhol's *Brillo Box* and the Brillo boxes in the supermarket. And conceptual art demonstrated that there need not even be a palpable visual object for something to be a work of visual art. That meant that you could no longer teach the meaning of art by example. It meant that as far as appearances were concerned, anything could be a work of art, and it meant that if you were going to find out what art was, you had to turn from sense experience to thought. You had, in brief, to turn to philosophy" (134).

19 Danto, "The End of Art," 137.

twentieth century painting) had also effectively come to an "end," where "end" is defined precisely as the completion of a developmental trajectory. The history of its struggle to know itself would be the content of art's self-knowledge, everything from the advent of moving pictures to the transfiguration of commonplace mere real things in pop art.[20]

During this dynamic period of painting, cinema would not remain philosophically inert, as if enjoying its newfound fame without need of self-interrogation. According to Danto in "Moving Pictures" (in *Philosophizing Art*), after causing painting to enter into its own historical trajectory, moving pictures would unfold along a similar trajectory. If cinema with its new magical powers of narration had thrust painting aside, painting would ensure cinema too felt the sting of derision, as if from an art critic, as mere "popular art" and "mass art"—wondering at painting's newfound dynamism—painting perhaps assisted in the task of derision of film by theatre, which would, of course, also feel the power of moving pictures and no doubt sympathize with painting's disenfranchised position. Forced to evolve alongside (and in relation to) modern painting and modern theatre, the medium of moving pictures would also soon pass beyond itself, and, in so doing, would also come to know itself (as painting had) as philosophy.

One of the most spectacular things about Warhol is that what he did for painting he did for film as well, and in the same year no less. According to Danto in "The Philosopher as Andy Warhol," Warhol also brought moving pictures to a philosophical end with his film *Empire* (1964). *Empire* is a single shot, black and white, silent film of the Empire State Building, lasting just over eight hours, and with virtually no motion whatsoever. If the *Brillo Boxes* are visually indiscernible from boxes of Brillo brand soap pads, *Empire* is all but indiscernible from a black and white still photograph of the Empire State Building. A film is a moving photographical picture, in contrast to a still photograph which may capture a moment of motion or imply motion but does not show moving images. But *Empire* is a moving picture without moving pictures, which means that *Empire* raises the question of its own nature: Is it a work of film art? Or is it not a work of film art? *Empire* thereby poses the philosophical question of whether it is a moving picture at all, and what a moving picture is it all.

Danto's aesthetics had a profound impact on Shusterman's philosophical thinking on art, as he himself acknowledges.[21] In particular, the concept of

---

20 Danto's philosophy of art encompasses the whole history of art, but for purposes of the present discussion the period between the advent of moving pictures and pop art is our main focus.

21 For an important exchange between Shusterman and Danto, see Shusterman's "Art as Religion" and Danto's "Replies to Essays" in *Danto and His Critics*, ed. Mark Rollins

transfiguration (from *The Transfiguration of the Commonplace*) would come to play an essential role in Shusterman's work; although that concept of "transfiguration" would itself undergo something of a "transfiguration" in its adoption. In "Art and Religion," for example, Shusterman describes one of his aesthetic experiences in Zen meditation, in Japan, as a form of "transfiguration." A "rusty drum can" had been set purposefully in front of an otherwise magnificent view of the sea, unfortunately obstructing peaceful contemplation of a vast and beautiful horizon. Eventually, however, this commonplace object, or mere real thing, as it may be called using Danto's terminology, began to undergo what Shusterman calls "transfiguration." But this transfiguration of the commonplace mere real thing was not a form of transcendence or elevation onto a higher plane of being, of the sort Danto found in Warhol's *Brillo Boxes*; the transfiguration of the drum can was something entirely different. "Rather than being transfigured into a transcendent world of immaterial spirituality," writes Shusterman, "it transfiguratively radiated the gleam and spiritual energy with which the wondrous flow and flux of our immanent material world resonates and sparkles."[22] The drum can had changed and not changed; it was still the

---

(New York: Wiley-Blackwell, 2012). In his "Replies" Danto responds to Shusterman's critique of his view of transfiguration, while highlighting the adventurous, existential nature of Shusterman's philosophical approach with its idea of philosophy as a way of life: "Richard Shusterman, like other writers here, is concerned with promoting a pluralistic view of the arts; a concern which he addresses in terms of my notion of the transfiguration of the commonplace. True to his philosophical bent, he has approached my appropriation of the term 'transfiguration' in the existential spirit that informed and continues to inform his philosophical quest, as well as his life. By this I mean a certain courage, an openness to risks of a kind I would never have exposed myself to. The core of his paper recounts an episode that amazes me—his traveling to Japan to study, not as a scholar but as a pilgrim—the discipline of Zen meditation. I have exempted myself from meditation by saying that my mind is too restless for it—like the 'twitching of a young elephant's ear,' to use an expression that evokes ancient Ceylon, which I learned from a young Sanskritist, Robert Olsen, years ago. But I know deep in my heart that it is more than that, a kind of fear of letting go and getting lost, and hence a lack of existential courage that Richard possesses, and which lends a certain personal authenticity to his philosophical adventures" (309–310). In addition to recognition of the "existential courage that Richard possesses," Danto's last phrase in this passage, namely, the one about Shusterman's "philosophical adventures," reveals Danto's depth of understanding of Shusterman's approach to philosophy in general, i.e., that it is "an adventure" or a series of "adventures." Danto has in mind not only Shusterman's pilgrimage to Japan to study Zen meditation, but also the spirit of philosophy found throughout his writings. That spirit of a "philosophical adventure" and philosophy as adventure, appears clearly in the title and the material of the work that forms the subject matter of the present essay, *The Adventures of the Man in Gold*. (For his interaction with Danto, see also Shusterman, "Art in a Box: Danto," in *Surface and Depth*.)

22 Shusterman, "Art and Religion," 14.

same commonplace object, but the commonplace transfigured. The mere real thing began to "gleam" and "sparkle," and to channel the "wondrous flow" of energy of the "immanent material world." And within this transfiguration of the drum can, the philosopher himself, through Zen meditation, had also undergone a kind of transfiguration.

A related form of transfiguration appears in the *Adventures*, and here too Shusterman as philosopher undergoes a kind of transfiguration through a unique aesthetic experience. This new form of transfiguration appears to be quite different to the transfiguration of the drum can or the transfiguration of the Brillo boxes. If Warhol had transfigured a mere real thing, the Brillo boxes, into art, as the *Brillo Boxes*, and thereby also transfigured art into philosophy; and Shusterman in meditation beheld a mere real thing to gleam and sparkle in transfiguration; now Shusterman would himself undergo transfiguration and become a gleaming and sparkling work of art. In a way, like the drum can, Shusterman had not changed at all; but, in another way, he was entirely different. Shusterman had not left the commonplace, in Danto's sense, for philosophy; Shusterman was already part of philosophy, but by transfiguration he would now leave his commonplace existence for a new mode of being achieved by fusion with photography. If in posing for a photograph, or appearing in a film, a subject fuses her form with the medium of art—appearing in film, for example, as a glowing and animated moving image of oneself—Shusterman, in fusing his form with photography, had become a glowing image of himself, and seemed almost to have stepped out of the screen; a photographical hybrid moving within the commonplace, and known only as the Man in Gold. Always attended by the photographer Yann Toma, the Man in Gold is and is not the philosopher Richard Shusterman; a new kind of philosopher who is also a form of photographical art—not photography becoming philosophy, as in *Empire*, but philosophy becoming photography—a paradoxical work of art whose form inevitably raises the question of its nature. And just as Danto, beholding the *Brillo Boxes*, wondered at their relation to the history of painting, or, beholding *Empire* wondered at its relation to the history of photography and cinema, Shusterman, as the Man in Gold, would wonder at their relation, and proceed to reconstruct both lives, and how one had come to take possession of the other. With this unique transfiguration of a philosopher into art, art would once again raise philosophical questions of its own self-consciousness, only now those questions would arise on the side of a philosopher wondering what he had become and what kind of being he is when he is and is not himself, when he is the Man in Gold. As Shusterman writes in the *Adventures*, recalling his initial transfiguration, "By the time I reached the garden, I no longer knew what I was doing. More specifically, I was no longer I."[23]

2.2 Emerson and Shusterman

Another form of philosophical and artistic "transfiguration" appears in Ralph Waldo Emerson's essay "Literary Ethics." Like Danto, Emerson is also an important influence on Shusterman's aesthetics, and his philosophy, in general. Shusterman highlights this importance in an essay entitled "Emerson's Pragmatist Aesthetics." "Celebrating novelty as well as tradition," writes Shusterman, "Emersonian historicism means that history should be absorbed—but *not* embalmed or repeated."[24] Emersonian historicism is the absorbing and synthesizing of the tradition in a fresh new variation, so that the past continues to live in the present, while the present may stand apart in all its uniqueness. In "Literary Ethics" Emerson describes this process of absorption and synthesis of the tradition by the philosopher as "transfiguration." An inspired philosopher, writes Emerson, opposes conformity and leaves society to be alone in the wilderness, a realm prior to society and tradition, and the very ground of society (a realm increasingly forgotten in society). As he stands alone amidst the trees and mountains and flowing waters, sunlight and streaming stars, the philosopher begins to "remember," as if somehow returning to a time before conformity, a time of wonder and bravery. Nature and the tradition, too long separated, reanimate and resynthesize in "bright transfiguration."

> When he stands in the world, he feels himself its native king. A divine pilgrim in nature, all things attend his steps. Over him stream the flying constellations; over him streams Time, as they, scarcely divided into months and years. He inhales the year as a vapor: its fragrant midsummer breath, its sparkling January heaven. And so pass into his mind, in bright transfiguration, the grand events of history, to take a new order and scale from him. He is the world; and the epochs and heroes of chronology are pictorial images, in which his thoughts are told.[25]

---

23 Shusterman, *Adventures*, 30.
24 Shusterman, "Emerson's Pragmatist Aesthetics," *Revue Internationale de Philosophie*, vol. 53, no. 207 (1), Le Pragmatisme / Pragmatism (Mars 1999), 87–99.
25 Ralph Waldo Emerson, "Literary Ethics," in *The Collected Works of Ralph Waldo Emerson*, vol. I, ed. Robert E. Spiller and Alfred R. Ferguson (Cambridge: Harvard University Press, 1971), 101.

What Emerson says of the philosopher's transfiguration may be said of Shusterman's transfiguration into the Man in Gold in the *Adventures*. As the Man in Gold "stands in the world," he seems to be a "pilgrim in nature," and appears that way in several photographs early in the work, e.g., *Poppy Fields* (2010) and a still from the film *Château* (2010).[26] He seems to feel himself nature's "native king," in Emerson's sense, golden, sparkling, while the camera beholding him and ever-present "attends his steps." From him and over him stream glowing photographical lines, as the Man in Gold "inhales the year as a vapor," and all things seem to "pass into his mind, in bright transfiguration." The Man in Gold never speaks this bright new transfiguration, but Shusterman writes of these experiences, retelling what he sees and feels, and Toma records what he sees in photographs of the Man in Gold, much as Emerson's philosopher creates brilliant new "pictorial images in which his thoughts are told." As Shusterman describes Emerson's historicism, the tradition recast by the philosopher is "not embalmed or repeated" but "absorbed" and transfigured. In Shusterman's own synthesis and transfiguration of the tradition, in the *Adventures*, a vast synthesis of the arts appears, one ranging over drawing, sculpture, architecture, somaflux photography, experimental cinema, science fiction literature, and performance art, all of which appear integrated with an equally vast synthesis of the traditions of Western and Eastern philosophy, from Laozi and Heraclitus to Emerson's romantic transcendentalism, and Dewey's and Rorty's pragmatism, to Danto's aesthetics of pop art.

According to Heraclitus, all things are one, and this "one" is the *logos*; but the one is also self-opposed, and by this opposition all things are in flux (*panta rhei*), each thing becoming its opposite, in a never-ending cycle. Heraclitus describes this flux of the universe as a "fire everliving,"[27] and as an immortal "child" who eternally gives birth to himself, in order to oppose himself in a never-ending game (which is also the universe). As Heraclitus's "child" continuously gives birth to himself in his opposite, Shusterman in the *Adventures* acknowledges that "some believe" the fiery Man in Gold "gave birth to himself," apparently in the form of an opposite to the philosopher.[28] Shusterman is a discursive philosopher of art, someone who speaks and writes about his subject

---

26 After exploring "a huge field of red poppies," the Man in Gold "collapsed in intoxicated fatigue from his dizzying frolics" (35); see also the somaflux photograph, *Poppy Fields* (2010) (33). The scene recalls L. Frank Baum's *The Wonderful Wizard of Oz*, with its golden imagery of the yellow brick road.

27 Heraclitus, Fragment XXXVII, in Charles H. Kahn's *The Art and Thought of Heraclitus* (Cambridge: Cambridge University, 1979), 45.

28 Shusterman, *Adventures*, 18.

matter; but the Man in Gold is a silent philosopher, someone who is a form of art. This being of art, the Man in Gold, is also, like Heraclitus's child, a being of light and flux; not because the Man in Gold is the *logos*, rather because he is a hybrid of a philosopher and the art of photography, which is an art of light.

On the other hand, while Shusterman and the Man in Gold are opposites, one being discursive, the other being silent, the Man in Gold's silence also seems, in a way, to reflect Shusterman's philosophy of art. In his philosophy of art, Shusterman emphasizes the limits of language in articulating or capturing the nature of aesthetic experience, emphasizing this point in language, as an extension of his pragmatist philosophy. The Man in Gold also seems to hold this view, apparently not only having possessed the philosopher but also having inhabited his philosophy, so much so that the Man in Gold simply refuses to speak and instead fully inhabits the nondiscursive nature of aesthetic experience. This relation between two philosophers of flux, one discursive, the other nondiscursive, also vividly recalls Heraclitus's relation to his celebrated student, Cratylus. Cratylus not only adopted the philosophy of flux, but seems to have fully inhabited it, and lived it. If the universe is all in flux, then nothing true or meaningful could be said, reasoned Cratylus, who consequently withdrew from discourse and simply walked the city silently, only moving his finger (in continuous flux), as if in paradoxical signification of the impossibility of signification, as Aristotle records the story in his *Metaphysics* IV.5.

Two and half millennia later, the Man in Gold also walks the city silently, although not apparently because nothing meaningful can be said; rather because the Man in Gold inhabits a kind of sensory and emotional substratum of pure aesthetic experience, one seemingly unapproachable by language. As Shusterman writes in the *Adventures*, the Man in Gold "eschews discursive language, recognizing it as the glory of philosophy but also an imprisoning source of its oppressive folly—its one-sidedness."[29] But even if language's one-sidedness has a certain imprisoning quality, the *Adventures* can hardly be said to be one-sided; after all, it is narrated in both words about, and photographs of, the Man in Gold, who is himself a strange hybrid (like the book itself) of philosophy and photography. The difficulty of the work, in fact, is not so much its *one-sidedness*, but its *many-sidedness* which makes navigating its structure and seeing its outlines a philosophically difficult affair. On the other hand, this very polydimensionality would also seem to open the *Adventures* to multiple perspectives—and if the work may be understood as a transfiguration of the

---

29 *Ibid.*, 58.

tradition, in Emerson's sense, then perhaps that same tradition may illuminate one or some of these sides.

3 The Man in Gold and the Golden Man

While the *Adventures* is many things—and perhaps ultimately not one kind of thing at all—one of these things appears to be science fiction. The character of the Man in Gold especially indicates this particular genre of literature. For example, Shusterman describes the Man in Gold as an "extraterrestrial,"[30] and "a creature of light,"[31] who naturally possesses an "otherworldly perspective."[32] But as an "extraterrestrial" being, the Man in Gold is also a human-alien hybrid being because he is a hybrid of Shusterman, who is human, and another alien form. And as "a creature of light," the Man in Gold is also a human-alien-photography hybrid creature. Indeed, there is no one else quite like him in the world, and yet there is someone else somewhat like him in science fiction, someone who is also a golden, silent, human-photography hybrid being. That someone is Cris Johnson from Philip K. Dick's science fiction novella, *The Golden Man*. Set in the aftermath of a nuclear war that has caused widespread variation by genetic mutation, *The Golden Man* tells the story of DCA Agent George Baines's hunt for the mutant Cris Johnson. The storyline of *The Golden Man* is similar to that of Dick's science fiction novel *Do Androids Dream of Electric Sheep* (1968), adapted for the screen by director Ridley Scott as *Blade Runner* (1982). As "blade runner" Rick Deckard (Harrison Ford) tracks and "retires" (kills) Nexus-6 "replicants" (androids) to preserve the integrity of the human species, Baines in *The Golden Man* tracks, captures, and "euths" (euthanizes) mutants for the same reason. In *Blade Runner*, however, the Nexus-6 replicants perfectly resemble human beings, making them incredibly difficult to capture, while in *The Golden Man* the visually conspicuous golden man cannot hide in plain sight, and yet he is the most elusive mutant Baines will ever track.

The Golden Man opens with Baines sitting in a café in Walnut Creek, a small town, drinking coffee, posing as a salesman. He passes around one of his photographs of a mutant, casually making conversation about strange creatures with wings and powers of mind control. It's a common topic of conversation, and few resist sharing a story about things they'd seen or heard about in other places. But soon a young man foolishly lets slip word about something odd out

---

30 *Ibid.*, 42.
31 *Ibid.*, 94.
32 *Ibid.*, 72.

on the Johnson farm—not too far away. All at once, the locals button-up, angry and exposed, ambushed by a professional who quickly leaves the café, easily obtains directions from a policeman by posing now as the Johnsons' attorney, and drives toward the farm. Meanwhile, on the farm, Nat Johnson is watching his son Dave and daughter Jean playing horseshoes, while his other son, Cris, stands apart. "Cris stood by the porch, arms folded. He wasn't playing. He was watching. He had stood there since Dave and Jean had begun playing."[33] Eighteen years old and virtually a giant, Cris's frame appears to be physically perfect: he is brilliantly handsome, superhumanly strong and fast, and completely gold-colored, i.e., hair, skin, eyes, teeth, and nails. (Even his name, in Greek, *chrysós*, means golden.) Cris seems to live in another world, "a world of his own, a world into which none of them could come." He lives with his family, but he's never really "with" them. He doesn't even speak, not to them, not to anyone. He's just sort of *there*, alongside them, always watching, "remote, detached, aloof" (like a camera).

Setting the golden man, Cris Johnson, alongside the Man in Gold, the two share several traits. Both are silent, golden men, and both are human-photography hybrid beings, whose postures and actions, and perceptions and thoughts, reveal this strange photographical nature. The first things seen of the golden man are his color and stance: absolutely still, absolutely silent, an observer, like a camera, but a man, apparently, a man the color of sunlight. The golden man appears to be both camera-like, and photograph-like, in his stillness and silence; he seems to be photographing the world with his eyes and mind, and yet he also seems to be posing, for his glowing form appears to have been shaped as an object to behold, perhaps even photographed. The Man in Gold also appears to encompass both sides of the camera, in his nature: he is at once a silent being who seems to perceive with photographical eyes, and yet he is also a work of art, a photographical work to behold by the photographer Toma. Shusterman himself underlines this dimension of the Man in Gold, as a silently posing figure, near the beginning of the *Adventures*, recalling the initial photoshoot with Toma. "My instructions as Yann's subject were to remain perfectly still in the various poses I took in the dark Abbey chamber. My imposed motionlessness included my mouth."[34] Upon his photographical transfiguration, Shusterman, now as the Man in Gold, could move freely, but would remain silent, always; and perhaps as befits a being made of photography, he would also very often remain perfectly still, viewing his surroundings,

---

33 Philip K. Dick, *The Golden Man*, in *The Philip K. Dick Reader* (New York: Citadel Press, 1987), 35.
34 Shusterman, *Adventures*, 28.

like a photographer or a camera, or like a being posing for a photographer, which he was, for it is part of the nature of the Man in Gold that he exists in the presence of the camera.

As these two golden men, the Man in Gold and Cris Johnson, stand still and silent while viewing their worlds, they also, like cameras, seem to capture and explore their worlds in space and time, especially through the visual perception. The Man in Gold, for example, is an aesthetically sensitive and emotional "creature of light," who is open to new aesthetic experiences, and delights in the beauties of nature and the arts, especially the visual arts, like photography, cinema, sculpture, and architecture. The golden man, by contrast, may delight in the beauty of nature, but he does not appear to contemplate the arts or even to take notice of them. Instead, the golden man's perception, in the story, appears to be focused primarily on his survival which is threatened by individuals like Agent Baines as he approaches the farm in his car.

As Baines drives toward the farm, the Johnson family has no idea that a car is even approaching, but they know something is wrong when they see Cris break from his sculpture-like stance. They know to watch for these transformations in Cris, and anticipate events to come. While standing silently, Nat Johnson was watching his children, including Cris, in the present, playing a game, but Cris, standing silently, was watching Agent Baines's car approaching the present from the future. "Seeing past everyone and everything—that is, until all at once something clicked and he momentarily rephased, reentered their world briefly."[35] Almost like a photographer pressing a button for the shutter, Cris seems to "click" and "rephase," as if entering a different photographical mode or setting of a camera; and suddenly he's gone. "Like a released energy beam he bounded across the field, over the fence, into the barn and out the other side. His flying figure seemed to skim over the dry grass as he descended into the barren creek bed, between the cedars. A momentary flash of gold—and he was gone. Vanished."[36] One moment, the Johnsons see Cris standing silent and still; the next, they see him rephase—the transition, rapid—and then all they see is a golden stream of light extended from where he stood, with them, into the cedar woods miles away, as if a smooth flowing brushstroke of soundless lightning flashed at the moment he had vanished. Like the Man in Gold, who is "a creature of light," and a hybrid of photography, the golden man is also a creature of light, who at one moment, as still as a camera, captures light through

---

35 *Ibid.*, 35.
36 *Ibid.*, 36.

the aperture of his perception, and then at the next moment seems to become that very light, moves at the speed of light, escaping Baines.

When Baines arrives at the Johnson farm, he's easygoing, friendly, and visibly hot. He's a businessman, he says, the owner of the Pacifica Development Corporation, looking for a plot of land around here; and maybe a glass of water, if it's not too much trouble. Once inside the farmhouse, he slips away, and checks every room and finds what he needs. Baines quickly arrests the family and asks how Cris knew that he was coming.[37] But the family doesn't know. "He doesn't talk," they say. "He never talked to us. Ever."[38] But maybe that doesn't matter, says Jean, because DCA will never catch him anyway: he's too smart, and he's too fast; he'll see the agents coming from miles away and be gone by the time they arrive (as before). It's like they're chasing light itself, and hopelessly so. But Jean's wrong: DCA does catch Cris, and almost right away, but not because they've outsmarted him. He lets them catch him. He's protecting Jean and the rest of the family and diverting DCA away from the farm and making his escape that way. Otherwise, she's right: DCA would never have a chance, not anyway using mere instrumental rationality against a man who literally sees the future. DCA had long feared to discover "a mutant with superior intellectual powers," a creature with "a perfect semantic system," basically "a better human being."[39] What they hadn't considered was a creature like the golden man, a mutant with superior sensory powers capable of seeing them coming.

The action of the golden man, as a "released energy beam" and a "momentary flash of gold," may seem difficult to imagine. But if we bear in mind his photographical nature, a corresponding image in photography lays to hand. If any could have photographed Cris's escape, in the very instant of his disappearance, then the photograph would show Cris running and trailing a vertical golden band of light. In other words, the photograph would resemble a photograph created using a technique known as "light-drawing," which is the same technique used by Toma in photographing the Man in Gold. In a light-drawing photograph, a scene appears (and it may be still or in motion, though often still)—for example, a farm with rolling hills or an open field outside Paris—and then, amidst that stillness, one or some streams of light also appear, as if they had been "drawn" over the rolling hills or the open field, with a pencil whose lead was light. A recursive quality may be seen in light-drawings, between the content and the form of the particular photograph. Photography, in Greek, means "to draw in light," so the form of any photograph is a "light

---

37 Ibid., 38.
38 Ibid., 40.
39 Ibid., 47.

drawing," which means any photograph *of* light-drawing may be understood as a light-drawing of drawings in light.[40] Toma's photograph *Cabin à Flux* (2012), for example, shows the Man in Gold standing on a beach enclosed in a "cabin" of vibrant glittering bands of luminescence drawn around him. Toma's *Currents of the Seine* (2012) shows the Man in Gold in Paris by the Seine River seemingly emitting twirling golden streams of light from his hands at a public work of art covered in graffiti; whether he is creating that graffiti or erasing it or visually "reading" (as if by some form of photonic Braille) is not clear.

Other somaflux photographs in the *Adventures* raise different questions about the relation of the Man in Gold to light-drawing or light-writing. For example, *Bureau du Vide* (2012) shows the Man in Gold seated at a desk in front of two glowing computer screens; but here, again, whether he is reading or writing or simply perceiving the screens as glowing objects remains unclear. Of course, any computer screen displaying text or pictures would itself also seem to be a medium of "light-drawing" and "light-writing," so perhaps the Man in Gold beholds in the computer another strange "creature of light" like himself. In *Midnight Fire on the Dunes* (2014)—one of the finest photographs in the book—a night-blackened sand dune rises from the bottom to the center of a two-page full-spread photograph, against a midnight blue sky, with the Man in Gold standing on the dune and extending his arm as his hand pools with golden light, as if prepared to write upon the evening sky; and yet, once again, whether the Man in Gold would write or draw or perhaps light his own perceptual shot, these things remain unclear. Other somaflux photographs depict the Man in Gold as moving, and apparently with the same kind of speeds that appear in *The Golden Man*. In *Château* (2010), for example, the Man in Gold appears in a flower garden, in double exposure, the more transparent contrasted with the more vivid figure, suggesting duration in time, as if the Man in Gold had moved in the space of the shot, by foot or flight, leaving only a fading golden somatic signature. Similarly, in *Materialization* (2012) the Man in Gold stands with his arms extended in rapid blurring motion, up and down, almost like wings beating before a flight, as if in the next instance only a fading blur would remain. But here too, whether he is preparing to take flight is no clearer than whether he had taken flight in *Château*.

By contrast, the actions of the golden man, despite lacking a faculty of language, seem to be fairly clear. In disappearing from the farm in a golden flash, the golden man is escaping Agent Baines. The golden man can see the danger coming ten minutes ahead using a faculty DCA comes to call "prethink."

---

40 See Shusterman, *Adventures*, 22.

According to DCA, prethinking is not a faculty for "cognizing" what will happen in the future; prethinking is not precognition. In fact, prethinking is "not a development of mind" at all; it's a "pure physical *sense*."[41] Given the nature of the golden man, as a being whose form appears to be something between human and the art of photography, prethinking would seem to be something like an ontological telephoto lens. If an actual camera's telephoto lens may be used, for example, to shoot wildlife or sporting events, bringing objects faraway closer in space, the golden man's telephoto-like faculty for prethinking appears to bring objects distant in time into the present. He can extend his sight beyond the present and into the future; although, he is not really extending his sight into the future so much as expanding the range of the present. When the golden man perceives the future, "he doesn't perceive it as the future." He perceives it as "a broader present" (which it is, even if human perception cannot see it as such).[42]

In perceiving this "broader present," the golden man is not seeing blurry events in motion stabilizing into the present, and then guessing what would happen: he's not projecting subjunctive conditionals by rearranging the elements of the past, kept and recalled in memory, in relation to a moving present, in order to construct an image of a possible future. (He's not doing what human beings do.) He's perceiving scenes as they have already happened and with all the fine-grained precision of a photograph. Indeed, the golden man perceives the extended present in successive "three-dimensional still" photographs, almost as if a cannister of three-dimensional celluloid film had been rolled out before him to be viewed—only, the frames are viewed as stills, and not as a motion picture.[43] These stills reveal, for the golden man, the extended present (what humanity calls the future) with certainty, in much the same way material photographs can reveal the past with certainty. DCA discusses this point about certainty, for the golden man, in contrast to human thought. "Our present is related to the past. Only the past is certain to us. To him, the future is certain. And he probably doesn't remember the past, any more than any animal remembers what has happened."[44] That's how the golden man knew Baines was coming, and that's why he disappeared in a flash leaving only a fading blur, like a light-drawing.

By contrast to the golden man who sees into the future (as the present), and who "probably doesn't remember the past," the Man in Gold does not appear

---

41 *Ibid.*
42 Dick, *The Philip K. Dick Reader*, 48.
43 *Ibid.*, 50.
44 *Ibid.*, 48.

to see into the future, and he vividly remembers the past. The Man in Gold did not, for example, seem to see a physical threat coming upon him from the future, while he was in Cartagena, when a few rogues happened upon the silent philosopher wearing a golden suit and being photographed. The experience was startling and disturbing, and caused him to reconsider his position in the world. "I realized that misunderstanding the kind of man he was could easily lead to violent mistreatment."[45] (The golden man, however, is never surprised: he can't be.) As Shusterman recalls in the *Adventures*, "From Cartagena," the Man in Gold "learned of his love for tropical, coastal beauty, but also that many would regard him as a deviant alien, disturbing their sense of how a man should look and act."[46] The Man in Gold carries that memory with him, always, and, whenever in society, he will anticipate possible threatening scenarios emerging wherever others may judge him to be a "deviant alien."

The Man in Gold carries with him this sense of exclusion, of being a "deviant alien," and (like any human being) synthesizes what he remembers of past, and what he knows of the whole of the tradition, with his experience in the present, as it is happening, in order to adapt to the world, in a pragmatistic way. But the synthesis of the past and the present, in the *Adventures*, also appears to be quite Emersonian, specifically with respect to Emerson's view of "transfiguration" in "Literary Ethics."[47] As Emerson describes the philosopher in the wilderness beholding nature and the whole tradition as it passes into his mind in "pictorial images," all to be synthesized in art in "bright transfiguration," the Man in Gold's experiences and Shusterman's own memories of these experiences, as well as his understanding of the tradition, all now appear synthesized, alongside Toma's photographs of the Man in Gold, in new and "bright transfiguration."[48]

As Shusterman describes the experience of being judged deviant for his silence and golden appearance, DCA similarly identifies the silent golden man as a "deviant." In fact, DCA identifies all genetic mutants as "deviants," or "deeves" (for short), and seeks to eliminate them to preserve the essential wholeness of the species.[49] The golden man, however, is, for DCA, a unique

---

45 Shusterman, *Adventures*, 50.
46 *Ibid.*, 54.
47 I discuss Emerson's philosophy, and its use of photography, in relation to Shusterman's film *Walk the Golden Night* in a later chapter in this volume entitled "Somaesthetics and Cinema: The Man in Gold in *Walk the Golden Night*."
48 The golden man does not seem to "transfigure" the past or the present by art. His perception of the future is photographical; and photography is an art; which would appear to make his perception a form of art; yet, his power of prethinking appears to be more like a perfectly transparent lens of time.
49 Dick, *The Philip K. Dick Reader*, 34.

kind of "deeve" because of his new faculty of "prethinking." The golden man not only threatens the purity of the species; he threatens the dominance of the species with his superior capacity. What is even more threatening, however, for DCA, is the possibility that the golden man might reproduce and that his progeny may possess an even more powerful variation of his capacity for prethinking, expanding the perception of the present far beyond ten minutes. "Instead of ten minutes, thirty minutes. Then an hour. A day. A year. Eventually they'll be able to keep ahead a whole lifetime."[50] Humanity would be powerless against the golden line, so the sooner Cris is "euthed" the better. But whether they can euth him or not, DCA is reflective enough to know they may already be too late. The very instrument of human dominance appears to have reached an upper limit, and nature, it would seem, has begun to find a way around it. "We've carried intelligence as far as it'll go. Too far, maybe," says DCA. "We've already got to the point where we know so much—think so much—we can't act."[51] DCA is only too right, and yet has already failed to grasp the implications of its plans. In planning to euthanize a man who sees the future, they have failed to fathom his ability to see this plan and easily escape custody.

Seated in his chamber, the golden man now extends his focus to see events that have already unfolded. He sees "an unusually varied multitude of scenes for the next half hour. Much lay head. The half hour was divided into an incredibly complex pattern of separate configurations. He had reached a critical region; he was about to move through worlds of intricate complexity."[52] His mind moves from shot to shot, from scene to scene, through the corridors of an "elaborate maze," focusing on one still and then another. He sees himself in this maze interacting with others. "He was looking down into a doll's house of infinite rooms, rooms without number, each with its furniture, its dolls, all rigid and unmoving. The same dolls and furniture were repeated in many. He, himself, appeared often."[53] Leaving his chambers now, the golden man easily slips past the guards, and enters the chambers of a Class-A official and scientist named Anita.[54] Anita beholds what she calls the "golden lion," newly escaped. Anita threatens to kill him, but the golden man doesn't move. He just stands there, still and statuesque, a "great golden god." She clears her head.

---

50 *Ibid.*, 51.
51 *Ibid.*, 48.
52 *Ibid.*
53 *Ibid.*
54 *Ibid.*, 50.

She tells herself that he's a "beast" not a "god."⁵⁵ But in a moment her reason is bewitched and disarmed. They embrace in a "shimmering golden haze."⁵⁶

Now Anita plans their escape. "I have a winter home in Argentina," she says. "If worse comes to worst we can fly there. It's in the back country, away from the cities. Jungle and swamps. Cut-off from almost everything."⁵⁷ (She's forgotten that he cannot understand her.) She has to hide him somehow, and she wants to be with him. They'll be fugitives, but it doesn't matter. Anita's plan is not so different from the monster's plan in Mary Shelley's *Frankenstein*, to leave civilization and escape to the wilderness of South America once Viktor Frankenstein agrees to (and succeeds in) crafting another gigantic monster, a female, so that the two monsters can live in hiding; but Anita's plan will fail too. She watches the golden man leave her chamber. He enters the hall. The guards are waiting, and they'll assassinate him in the moment he attempts to escape. Anita's frightened. She commands the guards to part; they do (just as the golden man had seen them parting). But then, all at once, he's gone; escaped in a golden "blur of speed."⁵⁸

DCA takes stock of the situation, trying to determine what they've learned. The golden man, they say, has two powers. "One is new, the newest thing in

---

55   Ibid., 52.
56   Anita's alternating judgments of the golden man, that he is a "beast" and a "god," plainly recalls Aristotle's remarks about the "beasts" and the "gods" in the *Politics* I.2, tr. B. Jowett, *The Complete Works of Aristotle*, ed. Jonathan Barnes, vol. 2 (Princeton: Princeton University Press, 1988). As Aristotle writes, "he who is unable to live in society, or who has no need because he is sufficient for himself, must be either be a beast or a god: he is no part of a state" (1253ª27–30, 1988). Should a superhuman being appear in the state, writes Aristotle, continuing his analysis in *Politics* III.13 and III.17, the state must either assassinate, exile, or coronate the superhuman. A paler version of the threat of an overwhelming voice appears in Emerson's "Self-Reliance" with the description of a young philosophical genius who speaks with *éclat* in the middle of society, and against society, and suffers ostracism. Friedrich Nietzsche in *Thus Spoke Zarathustra* similarly describes a philosopher sage who descends to society and speaks against society; and he too suffers ostracism. Nietzsche also offers a rejoinder to Aristotle's *Politics* in *Twilight of the Idols* (tr. R. J. Hollingdale [New York: E. Penguin, 1990]): "To live alone one must be an animal or a god—says Aristotle. There is yet a third case: one must be both—a *philosopher*" (33). But in contrast to these figures in Aristotle, Emerson, and Nietzsche, who suffer ostracism for overwhelming power of voice and thought, the Man in Gold and the golden man suffer ostracism and threat of violence apparently solely for their appearance and their *lack* of speech. So long as these golden beings appear as they do, and say nothing, so many in society simply cannot bear their presence, even though neither the golden man nor the Man in Gold is violent or aggressive in any way.
57   Dick, *The Philip K. Dick Reader*, 53.
58   Ibid., 50.

survival method. The other is old as life." The one that is new is "prethinking." The one that is "old as life" is beauty: "Plumage. Bright feathers, combs for the rooster, swans, birds, bright scales for the fish. Gleaming pelts and manes for the animals." The golden man is "irresistible to human females,"[59] they say. "So all that gold, that mane, that god-like stance," DCA now realizes, "was *for* something. Not just ornament." And first and foremost, what it was *for* was temporarily and partially disabling human reason, for enchanting the imagination, as it did with Anita who now carries the golden man's genetic line.[60] Of course, DCA knows Anita can be immersed in a "sterilization tank," but the golden man, having escaped, is free to traverse the land, and DCA knows humanity's days are numbered.

Like the golden man, the Man in Gold also feels compelled to leave society, especially following the episode in Cartagena. He knows that he threatens society simply by being the kind of creature of light that he is, neither man nor art but both at once. Refusing to speak, he refuses to participate in society as others would have him do. And yet, the Man in Gold does not wish to live in isolation any more than the golden man wishes to live in isolation; he had, after all, seemed comfortable living with his family on the farm. The Man in Gold wants to be part of a society, in some way, surrounded perhaps by artists and lovers of art. In the last chapter of the *Adventures*, "The Magic Vessels of the Viking Queen," the Man in Gold appears in Denmark among Shusterman's good friends, the art critic and historian Else Marie Bukdahl, at her house on the beach, and the sculptors Claus Ørntoft and Marit Benthe Norheim, on their farm—both places sufficiently far from society. In the *Adventures* the two sculptors, Ørntoft and Norheim, appear respectively as the King of Mighty Stones and the Viking Queen of the "Magic Vessels," living and working at their "Pink Rock Castle" complex. Here in the company of the deeply sensitive art critic and the two brilliant and royal sculptors, the Man in Gold, as a philosopher of art, and a living work of art, finally feels at home. He also finds true love.

As the golden man sees through the corridors of the DCA maze—as if "looking down into a doll's house," seeing its "dolls, all rigid and unmoving," and

---

59 *Ibid.*, 55.
60 Reproducibility is essential to any surviving animal species; but it's also an essential component of the art of photography, in contrast to sculpture or painting or a performance of theatre or music. And it is the nature of the art form of photography that as its instruments improve so too may photographs themselves. The first modern camera photographs were black and white, with a good deal of grain or noise, but eventually still photographs became more vivid; and soon incorporated color, and eventually movement, in various forms, such as moving pictures, and light-drawing still photographs like those by Toma in the *Adventures*.

finally finds Anita—the Man in Gold also seems to "see" (through his imagination) a female figure in the distance. The Man in Gold now walks the Pink Rock Castle complex, amidst Norheim's beautiful female sculptures, no less "rigid and unmoving" than the "dolls" of *The Golden Man*, until finally he finds the figure he had seen in his imagination. "Near the end of the corridor," writes Shusterman in the *Adventures*, "along one of the back rows, he finally found her. Just as he imagined."[61] This figure is Norheim's elegant sculpture of a female nude; although, the Man in Gold immediately recognizes her as the Chinese goddess Wanmei (whose name in Chinese means "perfection"). As Anita, beholding the golden man, falls into a "shimmering golden haze," the Man in Gold, beholding Wanmei, also falls into a shimmering golden haze; and Toma was there to capture the scenes of light and sculpture. In his somaflux photograph *Wanmei* (2001) the Man in Gold appears with Wanmei as a golden aura pools and cascades from her incandescent stone crown like flowing phosphorescent locks. In *The Look of Love* (2014) Wanmei's vermillion glow warms upward through a delicate play of ambers and marigolds toward a blistering gleam of yellows and whites and pinks. In *La Flamme de l'amour* (2014) Wanmei's glistening form seems to overwhelm the Man in Gold, completing his final transfiguration, seemingly separating the philosopher Richard Shusterman from the Man in Gold, in preparation for flight with Wanmei among the stars.[62] The book ends with Shusterman and Toma driving back

---

61   Shusterman, *Adventures*, 112.
62   Upon his visit to Denmark to plan *The Journal of Somaesthetics* with Else Marie Bukdahl, writes Shusterman in the last chapter of *Adventures*, "The Magic Vessels of the Viking Queen," that Else wished to introduce him to her artist friends, the married couple Claus Ørntof and Marit Benthe Norheim, who live and work on a farm not far away. Ørntoft and Norheim also appear as characters in the *Adventures* as the King of Mighty Stones and the Viking Queen of Pink Rock Castle; the same Viking Queen in the chapter title, "The Magic Vessels of the Viking Queen," and whose essay, "The Artists of Pink Rock Castle," is collected in the present volume, as part of Bukdahl's chapter "The Golden Turn in Shusterman's Somaesthetics: The Magical Figure of the Man in Gold." The works of Ørntoft and Norheim are greatly admired throughout Denmark, and each sculptor was, at the time, recalls Shusterman in the *Adventures*, involved in completing a major work: "Claus had just completed a project of sculpted lions commissioned as a gift for the Queen of Denmark. Norheim was at work on an ambitious project of fashioning a series of large-scale, seaworthy Viking lifeboats made of reinforced concrete and expressing a strong but graceful feminism" (*Adventures*, 76). The "Magic Vessels of the Viking Queen" are the magnificent Viking vessels that appear throughout the third chapter of *Adventures*. The Life-boats are seaworthy concrete sculpted ships of women. As Norheim's Life-boats glide seemingly impossibly upon the sea, Ørntoft's stone sculptures of lions also inhabit an unreal realm between stone and motion. As Bukdahl writes in "To See a World in a Grain of Sand," in Ørntoft's *Tre Løver og Ni Hjerter / Three Lions and Nine Hearts* (I/S Stenshede, 2013), "these three lions are in the midst of a process" (7). Here

that night, apparently seeing the Man in Gold and Wanmei ascending and trailing starlight, their very forms "light-drawing" among the stars.

> As we were driving, I glanced out the window and saw what looked like a low, blurring shooting star. Yann saw it too but corrected me. It was simply a luminous cloud by which the Man in Gold ascended into heaven to join the immortals, propelled by the elevating energy of ennobling love, nurtured by the love of art and loving artists.[63]

> Bukdahl does not say that these three lions are in the midst of processes, but that these three lions are all in the midst of "a process," meaning "one process," as if the three lions were all three-dimensional frames in a film made of stone; and all together they form one powerful motion, one montage.

63 Shusterman, *Adventures*, 120.

CHAPTER 8

An Exquisitely Beautiful Longing: A Lacanian Reading of *The Adventures of the Man in Gold*

Diane Richard-Allerdyce

> He knew (with Rilke) that beauty is the beginning of terror since its overwhelming spell has the power to destroy us.
> *The Adventures of the Man in Gold*

∴

> Desire counts more than darkness.
> *The Adventures of the Man in Gold*

∴

In the Preface to *The Adventures of the Man in Gold/Les aventures de l'Homme en Or* (Bilingual Edition: English/French), Richard Shusterman describes the book, collaboratively produced with the Parisian photographer Yann Toma, as a "strange … hybrid."[1] This strangeness is reflected in one reviewer's comment that the volume is "refreshingly unorthodox,"[2] and in another's playful remark that it represents a "boyish prank" on the part of the author.[3] Certainly the book is not typical; its atypicality is a key to its beauty, part of its effectiveness in inspiring a liberatory reader/viewer response, and its infusion with what I will describe in the pages below as joy.

---

1 Richard Shusterman, *The Adventures of the Man in Gold: Paths between Art and Life / Les Aventures de L'Homme en Or: Passages entre L'Art et la Vie*, photographs by Yann Toma (Paris: Éditions Hermann, 2016), 8.
2 Tzachi Zamir, "Philosophy and/or Performance: A Discussion of Richard Shusterman's *The Adventures of the Man in Gold*," *Journal of Aesthetic Education* 52.4 (2018), 116–123, 116.
3 Stefán Snævarr, "Shusterman and The Man in Gold," *The Nordic Journal of Aesthetics* 54 (2017), 86–92, 86.

Sensitive, shy, and afraid of rejection, the Man in Gold is, above all, in my view, a joyful creature, full of what Shusterman calls "romantic energy," a longing for beauty, and an enormous capacity to love.[4] The story of his "adventures" as the book's title calls them, is a joyous one. "Joyous" may seem an unusual word for describing a philosopher's book. Yet from the day I received my copy the *Adventures* and began to read, that is the feeling that "possessed" me as a reader, and that is what I experience, along with curiosity, awe, and philosophical interest, upon rereading. Perhaps the question of "why" need hardly be considered, given that the Man in Gold is motivated by love, even more, I think, than by the fear that is named as his other emotional pole.[5]

The French term *jouissance* seems especially applicable: an overflowing kind of joy that can easily turn into pain, an excess of psychic energy with orgasmic connotation, and a characteristic in Lacanian psychology common to hysterics and mystics.[6] Stefano Marino's discussion of Shusterman's pursuing "living beauty," "that is, a kind of pragmatism that does not ignore the sensual bodily pleasures and the pursuit of somatic well-being, and may potentially include aesthetics of full-bodied enjoying, and aesthetic life that also cultivates the pleasure and disciplines of the body," aligns with the usage of the untranslatable term *jouissance* with its connotations of pleasure, pain, and excess.[7]

Shusterman's unusual hybrid project is a potential source and enactment of a happiness associated with the kind of joy I link to *jouissance* and to the affective freedom that is attainable when one embraces rather than defends against or denies the illusory nature of human autonomy. Inherent in the book is a spirit of receptivity to the deep reservoir of wisdom inherent in the body, as Shusterman's somaesthetic principles, his idea of "thinking through the body" promote. Such embracing—a welcoming—is itself joyous, even if laced with a certain ineffable sadness at the deal humans have to strike in order to exist. More on this will follow.

My discussion includes the following related themes, though not necessarily in this order: (1) how it is freeing to acknowledge that humans' sense of autonomy is illusory (metaphorized and thematized in the book's treatment of the

---

4 Shusterman, *Adventures*, 7.
5 "Joyful" is accurate, too, as applied to the character of the Man in Gold, while I prefer "joyous" to describe the events depicted in and comprising the book.
6 Jacques Lacan, *The Seminar, Book III, The Psychosis, 1955–56*, tr. Russell Grigg (London: Routledge, 1993).
7 Stefano Marino, "Richard Shusterman (with Yann Toma), *The Adventures of the Man in Gold/ Les aventures de l'Homme en Or* (Bilingual Edition: English/French," *European Journal of Pragmatism and American Philosophy* [Online], IX-2: 6 pages (URL:http://journals.openedition.org/ejpap/1054), 2/6).

relationships between author and character, fiction and philosophy, art and life); (2) why I consider the book as, in part, a celebratory memoir of remembered somatic experiences; (3) why embracing one's vulnerability is healthy for the individual and good for the species (points Shusterman has established as central to somaesthetic practice); and (4) why I find Lacanian theory, as one pole of the Lacanian-Somaesthetic method employed here, helpful in explicating these themes.

Shusterman describes his titular character, the Man in Gold, as an "unexpected and bizarre personality"[8] who is born from and borrows Shusterman's soma during a series of photography sessions for which Toma has Shusterman don a one-piece gold-colored bodysuit made for a dancer. It is a costume that engenders transformation, as if the everyday costume of the narrator's social self is exchanged for another in alignment with the creatively authentic yearnings of the narrator. The Man in Gold, a sensitive being whose motivating emotions are love and fear, does not speak; his having no language is significant of his character as a remembered part of the author's being (rather than a projection or alter ego) and the book itself as, in part, a memoir, rather than or in addition to philosophical autobiography. That it also contains fictional elements is apropos to its illustrating the fictionality of the self, an important theme on which I elaborate below. The Man in Gold inhabits the philosopher's body when the latter wears the gold bodysuit, but he does so on his own terms, emerging at temporal intervals over a span of four years (2010–2014) according to his sense that he will be welcome and accepted.

Shusterman states the key themes of the book explicitly as "the instability and transformational potential of the self through the powers of possession."[9] Yet what Shusterman describes here is not a possession in the ordinary sense of the word. Rather it is an opening up of the self to explore the advantages and risks of acknowledging that one's sense of autonomy in the world is largely illusory. In my view this is also a re-possession, a re-claiming of something lost from ordinary consciousness, from perceptions filtered—as they inevitably must be for us human subjects—through language. The Man in Gold is born (and borne) on the cusp of a paradox. He is without language (in my view, a remembered element of the author's psyche), and yet dependent on Shusterman's narrative's language to be known to the reader. In Lacanian terms, the Man in Gold may be said to exist in the overlap between the Real (that which is palpable but inarticulable) and the Imaginary (distinguished from imagination,

---

8 Shusterman, *Adventures*, 8.
9 *Ibid.*

the realm in human subjectivity where primordial images reside). While a full discussion of the "three orders" of Lacan's topology is beyond the scope of this chapter, in addition to the two orders or regions just mentioned (Imaginary and Real), the Symbolic represents the order of culture and language; and my contention is that Shusterman's narration ultimately negotiates and facilitates something outside its reach.

1 A Word about the Theoretical Theater in Which I Write

By now, for good or ill, my methodological stance is likely evident. My training is not as a philosopher but rather as a literary critic whose main theoretical lens is Lacanian feminism. In recent years, I have found, in a marriage between somaesthetic philosophy and Lacanian theory, an ideal basis for exploring ways the real of the body expresses itself in literature.[10] Knowing the reception among many academics that Lacanian terminology and ideas have received, particularly resistance from readers to what may appear to be a jargon-filled but soulless system, I ask the reader's forbearance in considering my approach. Despite that reception, I have seen in my mind's eye a beautiful dance of explanatory and celebratory patterns in this "theoretical theater," as I ask my doctoral students to consider the arena of our exploration when I teach Lacanian theory in my seminar on gender and identity. In light of the performative aspect of the *Adventures*, the theater metaphor seems particularly fitting.

Once, during the question and answer period following a paper I presented at a conference on somaesthetics hosted by Richard Shusterman at his Center for Body, Mind and Culture at Florida Atlantic University, a fellow presenter understandably inquired why I had chosen a Lacanian perspective to address somaesthetic themes in the stories of which I had offered analysis. My answer was probably inadequate at the time, something about my home territory in scholarship. But here, as elsewhere, that answer begs the question why the theoretical lens of Lacanian theory called me to emigrate there in the first place. The charges of jargonized complexity acknowledged, it was in the 1980s that I encountered and found an intellectual home within what to me is a shining system of topological order for understanding consciousness (Lacan was as much a philosopher and a showman as a psychoanalyst). "Every principle is an

---

10   Diane Richard-Allerdyce, "As Fragile as Tissue and as Strong: Toward a Lacanian Somaesthetic Literary Theory," *The Journal of Somaesthetics* vol. 3, nos. 1–2 (2017), 102–112.

eye to see with," wrote Ralph Waldo Emerson in his *Journals*.[11] The same may be said with philosophical theories, in general. Wed, as I am, to somaesthetic philosophy, Lacanian theory provides the apparatus through which I interpret the *Adventures*, albeit with some of the same trepidation the Man in Gold fears of rejection. I offer my reading, likewise, toward the other pole of his motivating impulse, love. Thematically and performatively, this love is a love of risk, of vulnerability, of freedom from constraints of a too-rigid identification with the signifiers of authority, and, perhaps most of all, love of the poetic spark that forged Shusterman's memoir.

At least three elements of Lacanian theory have unique explanatory power for understanding what is "really going on" in the *Adventures* (a phrase I use with some irony since the idea of a core truth about anything other than an authentic relation with one's own terms is not characterized in this theoretical approach). Here are the key elements that a Lacanian-Somaesthetic method provides:

(1) As a corrective to dualism, the oft-misunderstood "third term" interrupts the binary.
(2) A useful metaphor, in the notion of mirror stage, for the emergence of illusory autonomy in human consciousness.
(3) Following from the above two points: Celebration, rather than denial, of the self's fictional status, a recognition that offers a degree of affective freedom and the possibility of memorializing earlier versions of the fictional self in memoir.

2 Boundary-Crossing and the Move against Dualism

Several reviewers of the *Adventures* rightfully address its anti-Cartesian underpinnings. Catherine F. Botha (2017), Laura Di Summa (2018), and Stefano Marino (2019) come closest to offering a resolution to the binary beyond that thematic identification, Botha, in her citing the "life-affirming" nature of Shusterman's somaesthetic quest, in the book, "to rethink the foundations of subjectivity." Botha cites a duality between the ego and alter ego and suggests there is a parallel duality between art and philosophy. As a bridge between seeming opposites, she refers to Heidegger's "pointed rejection of Descartes' portrayal of human being as a rational mind situation in a material body," thus

---

11 Ralph Waldo Emerson, *Journals of Ralph Waldo Emerson with Annotations*, ed. Edward Waldo Emerson and Waldo Emerson Forbes, vol. 3 (Boston: Houghton Mifflin Company, 1910), 517.

highlighting the *Adventures*' rejection of the mind/body split.¹² Di Summa calls this rejection a form of the "boundary crossings" for which Shusterman is known, along with "his penchant, and talent, for individuating and questioning some of the leading dichotomies at the core of western philosophy."¹³

Related to this stance, and to the element of my discussion related to the fictional nature of the self, Botha discusses "Foucault's dissection of the grand narratives of knowledge and reason," which "... turns on his rejection of the modern, humanistic concept of the subject as a unified subjectivity."¹⁴ I include this point here to underline the paradox that to go beyond the notion of a unified, autonomous self is tied inextricably to the need to reject the idea that humans are divided into mind and body. One might ask, then, does dissecting/rejecting the idea of a totalizing selfhood mean embracing the mind/body or other split in human consciousness? How do we understand both a rejection of the Cartesian split, on one the hand, and a simultaneous rejection of the idea of a unified self, on the other hand? One answer, arising from a Lacanian-Somaesthetic perspective on Shusterman's tale, begins with Lacan's idea that all human subjectivity comes into being on the brink of a loss, and that any sense of identificatory wholeness is a fiction, albeit a useful one that can be harnessed creatively. The acknowledgment of such subjective splitting is not an endorsement of a split between the rational and the somatic but rather a receptivity to the paradox that what one considers the self is really a fictional and temporary character on loan to the combination of attributes that allow for a social self.

We can see Botha's statement that "the figure of Shusterman's Man in Gold stands as a challenge to the positivistic vision of the subject understood in terms of unity, rationality, free will and self-control" in terms of Shusterman's, and subsequently the Man in Gold's, relationship with the artist. Toma's photographic technique of using light to capture the subject's "auratic energy"¹⁵ provides a visual bridge of sorts for a crossing of boundaries between the

---

12   A Lacanian view posits the ego *as* an alter ego, both being constructions, resulting from a fundamental split in being that is foundational and inescapable. From this perspective, I do not see the narrator as ego and the Man in Gold as alter ego, but rather the Man in Gold as a remembered aspect.

13   Laura T. Di Summa, "A Review of Shusterman & Toma's *The Adventures of the Man in Gold: Paths Between Art and Life: A Philosophical Tale*," *The American Society for Aesthetics: An Association for Aesthetics, Criticism, and Theory of the Arts*, 38.2 (2018), 4–5, 4.

14   Catherine Botha, "Rethinking the Ego/Reconceptualising Philosophy: Shusterman's 'Man in Gold,'" *Pragmatism Today*, vol. 8, issue 2 (2017), 80–87, 82.

15   Shusterman, *Adventures*, 24.

photographic object and its relation to otherness, between the solidity of the soma and its unseen constant movement at the cellular and atomic level toward dissolution and transformation. Lacan's idea of a "third term" that interrupts the dyadic relationship between mother (or other primary caretaker) and infant operates similarly, but on the level of the Symbolic, that is, Lacan's order of culture and language. What Shusterman acknowledges as the risks inherent in the "art of photography" such as "its often risky rituals of posing and self-exposure,"[16] are analogous to the risks of becoming conscious of oneself in the world. Humans must do so through the linguistic systems that preexist each person's entry into this order, linguistic systems which establish roles, customs, and laws. But whether unconscious or conscious, the Real of the body's vulnerability and a concomitant subjective contingency are always present. Shusterman acknowledges this point when he writes near the book's opening that "it is risky to lose one's sense of autonomy and self-possession, as the Man in Gold taught me."[17] Yet the risk of *not* losing the illusory sense that one is autonomous, at least for the philosopher and the artist, is greater.

There is also an error, I think, in establishing an either-or approach to pairs of opposites such as mind/body, or between philosophical beliefs in somatic or other unities, on the one hand, and the resolution of such splits, on the other hand. The Lacanian notion of a "third term" provides at least one theoretical move away from such dichotomies toward a paradoxical stance akin to the Buddhist idea of the one-as-many/many-as-one. In the theoretical theater this paradox is potentially affectively liberating.

Here I turn, then, to a discussion of several dyadic pairs and perceived splits between them. Shusterman's own gender depictions such as individual agency as "manly" are largely binary;[18] they are mitigated, however, by his narrator's acknowledgment of the presence of both *yin* and *yang* energy in people of different genders. Even as the concepts of *yin* and *yang* could be said to reinforce a belief in essentialist gender binary, those Eastern philosophies upon which he draws to characterize men and women provide some ground for synthesis. The method I employ here, of course, goes beyond synthesis as the bridging element between pairs that exist on multiple planes. Reviewers of the *Adventures* discuss a number of "doublings" in the book and Shusterman's own life; and these provide thematic, analogous expression for the binary relationship between, on the one hand, the mind and body, within the mind/body split that somaesthetic philosophy and its ancestral traditions reject, and, on the

---

16   Ibid., 12.
17   Ibid., 8.
18   Ibid., 32.

other hand, the dualism of subject/object positions (*je/moi*) in the Lacanian model and its own ancestral traditions in *Saussurean* linguistics.

Botha gives examples of several "twos" in Shusterman's life to bolster the idea of a doubleness in the book—autobiographical elements to which Shusterman himself elsewhere also refers (e.g., a double major at university, two marriages with two "sets of children," his alignment with two branches of philosophy, and identification with two nationalities)—in the process, reflecting on his idea that such a life can be lived in grace and harmony, or what I identify as integrity, despite the well-known postmodern rejection of a singular true self. According to Botha, a parallel duality appears in Shusterman's book between the ego (the narrator) and the alter ego (the Man in Gold), and suggests a corresponding duality between art and philosophy, that finds resolution in somaesthetic principles: "Shusterman draws on a reading of Nietzsche (as well as Emerson and Wittgenstein) to develop his call to give 'style' to the self, and idea that is central to his Somaesthetics."[19] According to Botha, like Nietzsche, Shusterman holds that the self is not a unified entity, which, in turn, leads him to recognize, again with Nietzsche, the self as a potential self-in-being, or what I would call a self-in-becoming. Botha also uses Shusterman's phrase "embodied self-care"[20] to advance her view that the *Adventures* "stands as a daring expression of Shusterman's Nietzschean/Foucauldian impulse to live life as a work of art."[21]

Marino in his review of *The Adventures of the Man in Gold* cites another kind of doubling in identifying autobiographical-rational vs. narrative-fiction as an example of dyadic relationships among pairs. According to Marino,

> The book actually rests upon this kind of intertwinement between the autobiographical and rational perspective of the first-person authorial voice, on the one side, and the narrative-fictional and somehow mystical perspective of the Man in Gold's experiences from his first appearance until his final manifestation, on the other.[22]

---

19   Botha, "Rethinking the Ego/Reconceptualising Philosophy," *Pragmatism Today*, 85. Shusterman discusses Emerson, Ludwig Wittgenstein, and Nietzsche in "Genius and the Paradoxes of Self-Styling," in *Performing Live: Aesthetic Alternatives for the Ends of Art* (Ithaca: Cornell University Press, 2000).
20   Shusterman uses the phrase "embodied self-care," for example, in "Somaesthetics and the Body/Media Issue," in *Performing Live*, 144.
21   Botha, "Rethinking the Ego/Reconceptualising Philosophy," *Pragmatism Today*, 87.
22   Marino, 3/6.

Among these doublings, we may add Shusterman's claim that the body he lent to the Man in Gold was that of a "youthful sixty-year-old"—making the Man in Gold paradoxically both young and not young.

Zamir in "Philosophy and/or Performance" suggests another opposing pair within the *Adventures*, namely, between the performative and philosophical, while also hinting in his analysis at (what I contend is) a "third term." According to Zamir, there are "forms of knowing that appear inseparable from particular routes of discovery,"[23] and that "[e]xperiencing goes hand in hand with the ability to step back, reflect, argue, define."[24] Despite this move toward bridging, Zamir imagines Plato would criticize Shusterman for "fragmenting [him] self between [himself] as philosopher and the voiceless golden man who conducts his embodied search," thus "forfeit[ing] the hope of bringing together experiencing and thinking."[25] I say, however, that Shusterman is not fragmenting himself in the book at all; rather he is giving voice to a voiceless remembered part of the narrator's experience-in-becoming. After all, the *Adventures* brings together experiencing and thinking through the metaphorical alchemy of art. The performative and the philosophical are operative in the book, of course, but there are more than two forces at play, and they are not necessarily opposites. Rather, through embodied memoir, Shusterman's fable provides—not a synthesis—but a paradoxical and temporary artistic unity that by its nature is fleeting. Despite and/or because of its fleetingness, it is also potentially freeing.

3   Fiction, the Mirror Stage, and the "Third Term"

Thus far I have presented a perspective of the *Adventures* that positions it as the story of a negotiation and the going beyond such dyads as philosophy vs. performance, mind (thinking) vs. body (feeling), and autobiographical fact vs. fiction. It may be helpful to explore this "going beyondness" in terms of the relationship between photographic subject and object positions. This relationship is unique and yet also bears similarity to the *je/moi* relationship that occurs linguistically when someone speaks: "I" say something and hear myself, as "me," saying it, and wonder who else has heard the utterance; thus with every speech act I slide from subject ("I") into object ("me") and subsequently project a listening other whose role is dependent on a set of rules established

---

23   Zamir, "Philosophy and/or Performance," 117.
24   *Ibid.*, 121.
25   *Ibid.*

by culture, what Slavoj Žižek calls "the big Other."[26] While a deconstructionist account may posit speech as an endless string of dyadic oppositions, a Lacanian-Somaesthetic model, both poles of which anchor meaning in the body's cellular memory, forestalls the move toward deconstructive meaninglessness. From this perspective, "crossing boundaries" or "going beyond" is also a returning, a homecoming, to the body-(un)consciousness (the conscious or unconscious but palpable knowledge) that resides in the soma as much as, and primary to, the language-driven rational mind.

First, a little more about the "third term" and its anchoring function in the psyche. Another way of imagining the function of this element is to consider the impossibility of sitting on a two-legged stool; the third leg is needed to prevent falling over. A deconstructionist linguistic model, ironically like a Cartesian view, is like the two-legged stool. The Lacanian "third term" is the third leg. Also known as the paternal signifier, the "third term" is a role that, though misidentified by some feminists, is not gender-specific and can be occupied by anyone who provides the corrective to the endless back-and-forth between dyadic opposites.

The photographer Toma serves in the role of the "third term" *vis-à-vis* the *Adventures*. Described as a "midwife" to the Man in Gold, Toma must assist his birth time and again (rather than only once since intervention is required each time the Man in Gold appears). Toma's technique, as Shusterman describes it, is literally and figuratively apropos to my argument. Toma captures on film the light beams cascading through and past the physical limits of the unified body of the Man in Gold. The resultant image celebrates those limits as making possible a corporal agency in the world: the body as a work of art. At the same time, Toma's use of light exults in the conditionality of those limits, thus suggesting a transient limitlessness of the kind I have described above. The photographer's lens as "an eye to see with," to use Emerson's phrase, occupies the subjective position while the body-rendered-image occupies the objective position. We can see the operation of a "third term" in the oscillation between them as witnessed/interrupted by the viewer, whose function is held by both photographer and model as well as others, including the reader.

Such oscillation between and interruption of the binary elements of subject/object takes place in the relationship between the photographer and his model. Toma uses light and movement to "go beyond" the Man in Gold's physical, bodily boundaries. I see an analogous metaphoricity of *je-moi-autre-Autre*,

---

26   Slavoj Žižek, *How to Read Lacan*, ed. Simon Critchley (New York: W. W. Norton & Company, 2007).

as I described it above, in terms of linguistic utterances ("I" - "me" - others - the "big Other") and the photographer-photographed-viewer/reader. The *Autre* (Other) is always the order of culture and language. The narrator of the book acknowledges that while he can feel the Man in Gold's emotions, his (the narrator's) words are inadequate for expressing them; he nevertheless does so, thus creating a work of art in the livingness of their relationship. This relation is not (as I have noted), one of ego to alter ego, but that of a linguistically conscious subject to a part of the self long-forgotten and returned to awareness through the intervention of the artist.

That the Man in Gold who borrows the narrator-philosopher's body is not the same character as his host is demonstrated in the book in several places. For example, the narrator describes seeing the Man in Gold from a window in Aalborg[27] and later mentions that the Man in Gold, whose vision is "far more poetic than" that of the narrator, slept with him that night.[28] The Man in Gold and his narrator-father, Shusterman, are not parallel entities in that they are not mere images of one another. The reader thus sees that the Man in Gold is not synonymous with the narrator but exists as an "other" person. This acknowledgment that does not negate the argument that they are elements of one subjectivity when one takes into account the Lacanian idea that human subjectivity is by its very nature fundamentally split at its onset, alien. The Man in Gold's longing to find his lover and the narrator's empathy for the Man in Gold's desire not to be rejected "as a problematic alien"[29] is the yearning for wholeness that can be achieved perhaps only through art or love, and perhaps only fleetingly. The very existence of Shusterman's book highlights that by embracing the paradox that humans have to operate according to the laws of linguistics in order to exist in society and yet may remember parts of themselves that do not reside there, readers can partake in the *jouissance* that the *Adventures* celebrates.

Toma uses light and movement to "go beyond" the Man in Gold's physical, bodily boundaries. The performative aspect of posing for a camera and the relationship between the photographer and the posing subject, for me, echoes and replicates that of the subject as the perceiving entity and the object as perceived. As Stefán Snævarr points out in "Shusterman and The Man in Gold," "These experiences have a somatic aspect. This aspect includes the photographer's *mis-en-scène* of himself, the photographed subject's posing before the camera, and the critical communication between the photographer and

---

27   Shusterman, *Adventures*, 78.
28   Ibid., 83.
29   Ibid., 77.

the subject."³⁰ This relation may be explained in terms of Lacan's famous mirror stage.

4   The Mirror-Stage and the Man in Gold

I have argued so far that a Lacanian-Somaesthetic lens provides an enhanced perspective of the *Adventures*, one that "goes beyond" the dyadic relation between pairs of opposites that have been thematically central to several reviews of the book. Such extension beyond binaries entails rejection of an either/or position as well as the idea of synthesis *per se*; rather it involves a kind of living on the edge of paradox, an artistic "both/and" embracing of the body's memory of what has been lost in the subject's accession into culture and language.

The interrupting and paradoxically stabilizing "third term" provided by the Lacanian pole of this method functions in a way that allows Shusterman's reader, as well as the viewer of Toma's photography, access to a part of the self that takes form in the book's protagonist, the Man in Gold. This character's nonverbal expression places him in the overlap between regions in Lacan's topology known as the Imaginary (which is not the imagination *per se* but rather a realm in the psyche of sensory images) and the Real (that which is palpable and inarticulable, akin to the somaesthetic principle of sentient awareness). A brief overview of Lacan's mirror stage will be helpful in illustrating that what is happening in the *Adventures* is a joyous celebration of the fictional nature of the self and the artistic value of embracing paradox, impermanence, and vulnerability.

Rose writes that the mirror stage and the fictionality of the self are originally and inextricably related in "Lacan's account of subjectivity," for "in the 1930s he introduced the concept of the 'mirror stage' (*Écrits*, (1936)), which took the child's mirror image as the model and the basis for its future identifications."³¹ The image the child sees in the mirror is fictional because it gives a misperception of bodily autonomy before the development of motor skills are sufficient for the child to stand upright on her own. "But it is salutary for the child," Rose continues, "since it gives it *the first sense of a coherent identity in which it can recognize itself*."³² I suggest this is the relationship Shusterman has with

---

30   Stefán Snævarr, "Shusterman and the Man in Gold," 90.
31   Jacqueline Rose, "Introduction II," in *Feminine Sexuality: Jacques Lacan and the école freudienne*, ed. Juliet Mitchell and Jacqueline Rose, tr. Rose (New York: W. W. Norton & Company, 1985), 27–57, 30.
32   *Ibid.*, 30 (my emphasis).

the separate entity that inhabits him, that of a recognition of an unconscious part of himself. That part is rendered into art in the form of a memoir, literally a memory. The image may be fantasy, hence the term "fable" attached to the book, but it is one reconfigured in somatic form through the collaboration of two artists, Toma the photographer-shaman and Shusterman the author-host.

Juliet Mitchell in her "Introduction I" to *Feminine Sexuality* explains that

> Lacan's human subject is not a 'divided self' (that in a different society could be made whole, but a self which is only actually and necessarily created within a split—a being that can only conceptualise itself when it is mirrored back to itself from the position of another's desire).[33]

This is why the Man in Gold is "born" of Shusterman; he is born of Shusterman's desire to cross the boundaries between unconscious and conscious somatic memories, and especially from the Symbolic, or the territory where the Symbolic, Imaginary and Real overlap, to the region of the unconscious where the Symbolic is temporarily, through art, left behind like an amniotic sac. The metaphor of a conception arising from the union of Shusterman with his fantasy goddess Wu Xiaoxing thus makes beautiful poetic sense (although, Shusterman also and somewhat cynically describes "even the best of fathers as benignly irrelevant or blessedly absent").[34] The Man in Gold imagines he has no father. But he "lovingly imagines [his mother] as a tiny dancing goddess … who through a series of seductive human incarnations captured the heart and mind of Richard Shusterman."[35] The eroticism of the passage is evident, though surpassed by passages where the Man in Gold meets the incarnation of his mother in his lover, the sculpture Wanmei—passages that depict the "all-absorbing radiance of passion in their loving embrace" and the "transformative energy of their union."[36]

Yet the unifying embrace is by nature impermanent. In Lacanian terms, "[t]he very image which places the child [in the world—the order of culture and language] divides its identity into two."[37] Herein lies another of the dichotomies that Shusterman's work serves to dismantle, however gently. This dismantling allows for the artistic perspective that, according to Shusterman in

---

33   Mitchell, "Introduction I," in *Feminine Sexuality*, 1–26, 5.
34   Shusterman, *Adventures*, 18.
35   *Ibid.*
36   *Ibid.*, 118.
37   Rose, "Introduction II," in *Feminine Sexuality*, 30.

the book's preface, was missing from his somaesthetic philosophy before the birth of this book.[38]

Toma's work with the visual realm and Shusterman's emphasis in the book on seeing demonstrate the primacy of the visual realm that the mirror image, if only as a metaphor, represents. This emphasis on seeing appears in the inclusion of Toma's photography in the book, and in the Man in Gold's desire to be seen (such as when he mounts the scaffolding to a billboard), and his reluctance to be seen (such as when he runs away in fear), and in his seeing the sculptures created by Claus Ørntoft and Marit Benthe Norheim, and in the Man in Gold's finding his lover in one of them, Wanmei, the beautiful counterpart for which he has yearned. Hence my assertion that without language the Man in Gold lives in the real and the imaginary and is given linguistic expression only through the narrator's account as the work of art that operates on the brink of a paradoxical *jouissance*.

5 *The Adventures of the Man in Gold* as Memoir

The theme of crossing boundaries described above applies to the literary genre in which the *Adventures* may be classified. It is both philosophy and performance; it is, as Zamir writes, both autobiography and description. It is also a fable, a fiction, and/or, in my view, a memoir infused with awareness of the fleeting and paradoxical fictionality of a multidimensional selfhood. The *Adventures* employs the creative writer's artistic skills to honor a formerly forgotten, and, through the writer's artistry, remembered sentiency, outside of (but rendered expressible through) language. Marino identifies the bridging the book provides between theory and praxis by forging a "fruitful intersection between philosophy, narrative fiction and visual art—thus proving to be fully consistent with Shusterman's pragmatist mission of trying to use new media to do philosophy and to introduce artistic experimentation into philosophical aesthetics."[39] For me, seeing *The Adventures of the Man in Gold* as a memoir enhances its poetic beauty and its celebratory efficacy.

Alongside my aesthetic reasons for placing the *Adventures* within this genre may be understood in terms of the psychoanalytic concept of primary narcissism, which is not the ego-obsession with which the term is commonly associated. As Ellie Ragland-Sullivan writes eloquently in *Jacques Lacan and*

---

38 Shusterman, *Adventures*, 10.
39 Marino, 5/6.

the Philosophy of Psychoanalysis, negative states of being such as conflict and anxiety, which I want to emphasize, that are rooted in the body (and which Ragland-Sullivan points out are fundamental to all people) are products of "the nonpeaceful coexistence of the specular *moi* of narcissism, aware but divided from the Other (A) from which it was formed."[40] In the *Adventures* the Other itself is revealed for the narrator and, through his voice, for the reader, in the oscillation between the narrator and the character of the Man in Gold. We can consider their relationship's operation through language, which resides in the Symbolic realm, in terms of Ragland-Sullivan's point that the *moi* is "forced to verify itself through others despite the Real flux and instability of human response amid changing patterns of identification and events."[41] In this theoretical theater, there is no cure for this kind of narcissism; nor should there be. It is intrinsic to human subjectivity. However, according to Ragland-Sullivan,

> when the subject's roots in the Other (A) become apparent, an opening can be made through the speaking *je* by which one can interrogate the ... knowledge that inhabits us. ... At such times, the social subject of consciousness may glimpse the movements of the narcissistic subject of identity, briefly rendering it an object of awareness.[42]

The brevity of the encounter with the character known as the Man in Gold, rendered an object of awareness through language in the book's narration, necessarily limits the scope of Shusterman's project. We're allowed only several glimpses, over a span of four years (2010–2014), of this being who resides in the foundation of the narrator's psyche, which together form but a single glimpse. When the Man in Gold "ascended into heaven to join the immortals," at the end of Shusterman's romantic tale,[43] we can see the remembered aspect of the narrator's *moi*, having made its appearance through the narrator's ability to see the opening Ragland-Sullivan describes above that is available to Shusterman's narrator as the "speaking *je*," returning to the realm of the ineffable but palpable—the Real. Thus while Zamir suggests Shusterman fragments himself between the "philosopher" and the "golden man,"[44] I see a reunion and

---

40   Ellie Ragland-Sullivan, *Jacques Lacan and the Philosophy of Psychoanalysis* (Champaign: University of Illinois Press, 1987), 39.
41   Ibid., 39.
42   Ibid., 39.
43   Shusterman, *Adventures*, 120.
44   Zamir, "Philosophy and/or Performance," 121.

reunification of elements of the self, a self rendered not whole (for there is no wholeness to be had) but one perhaps more authentic than before.

6 A Joyous Celebration of the Fictional Nature of the Self

In this essay I have presented a Lacanian-Somaesthetic perspective on Shusterman's tale that rests on Lacan's idea that all human subjectivity comes into being on the brink of a loss and that any sense of identificatory wholeness is a fiction, albeit a useful one that can be harnessed creatively. I have posited that acknowledging such subjective splitting is not an endorsement of a split between the rational and the somatic, but that instead it opens a potential to achieve affective freedom from the constraints of rationality. Such freedom operates through the paradox that "the self" is perhaps most accurately understood as a fictional character on temporary loan to the social self. For the somaesthetic practitioner who embraces life as a work of art, the creative dancer of the self emerges to claim not a subjective wholeness but, on the contrary, a living sentiency whose potential for "life-affirming" authenticity lies in its in impermanence, its vulnerability, and the deal its author strikes with transiency. By embracing the paradox that humans have to operate according to the laws of linguistics in order to exist in society and yet may remember parts of themselves that do not reside there, readers can partake in the *jouissance* celebrated in the *Adventures*. The *Adventures* is a joyous celebration of the fictional nature of the self and the artistic value of embracing paradox, impermanence, and vulnerability. It is a volume that I believe has implications in today's world for reaching across divides to transcend binaries through its artistic advocacy for acknowledging the fictionality of ideas of selfhood that underlie identificatory fusions with divisive ideologies. The longing that is embodied in the Man in Gold's relationship with beautiful statues, and especially his lover Wanmei, is, in a way, a testament to the impossibility of reconciling a fundamental fragmentation at the heart of human existence, but which can be apprehended in art. The Lacanian idea that everyone comes into being, that humans' very subjectivity comes into being, on the brink of a loss, registers in the body and takes form in the character of the Man in Gold, an element of the narrator's experience for which he longs. So what is longing if not for something palpable that lies on the edge of verbal consciousness but resides in the cellular memory of bodies? Perhaps the Man in Gold's quest for his lover represents a way of reaching beyond the world of culture and language to bring with it the beauties of the imaginary and real back into that realm, a goal close to the heart of Shusterman's somaesthetic philosophy.

Above all, Shusterman's volume provides expression of a paradoxical and temporary artistic unity that by its nature is not sustainable but *is*, despite and/or because of its contingency, refreshing and potentially meliorative. Therein lies the joy.

CHAPTER 9

Shusterman as Philosopher and the Man in Gold

Yvonne Bezrucka

1   The Man in Gold

Richard Shusterman's *The Adventures of the Man in Gold: Paths Between Art and Life* (2016) is a novella about the experiences and artistic performances of its eponymous hero, the Man in Gold, who inhabits the body of the philosopher Richard Shusterman.[1] The novella is, however, much more than a description of art performances and their reception. The *Adventures* is a work of philosophy, and, in particular, "somaesthetics," which is a discipline focused on the aesthetics, epistemology, and language of the body. Somaesthetics is a metalanguage for reading and translating actions and performances of the body, providing philosophical insight into its often silent "actions" and seemingly mute language.

The *Adventures* is a multilayered work of art. Composed of text in English and French (English in the left column, French in the right column of text pages), the work is a descriptive and narrative record of some of the performances of the Man in Gold. The *Adventures* is also an intermedial art book that combines text with Yann Toma's somaflux photographs of the Man in Gold, and several stills from films of his performances: *Château* (2010), *A Night with Richard Shusterman* (2010), *Lights in the Dark* (2011), and *Walk the Golden Night* (2011).[2] Such combined use of text and images recalls and even rewrites the old adage of Simonides of Keos, "*Poema pictura loquens, pictura poema silens*,"[3] into photography's claimed privilege of using "real" but still not holistic reallife mimetic "documents." Nevertheless, in the *Adventures* the two artistic

---

1   Richard Shusterman, *The Adventures of the Man in Gold: Paths Between Art and Life, A Philosophical Tale*, English and French, tr. Thomas Mondémé, Somaflux Photography by Yann Toma (Paris: Éditions Hermann, 2016).
2   French photographer Yann Toma even succeeds in capturing, in photographing the performance, the performer's "aura," in any case a physical entity (warmth? temperature?) clearly detectable in the pictures of the book.
3   Simonides (c. 556–468 BCE) of Keos's famous adage on the interrelations of the arts, "Poetry is a speaking picture, painting a silent poetry," is later repeated in Horace's *Ars Poetica* (65–6 BCE) as "*ut pictura poesis*," "as is painting so is poetry," the two quotes having become axiomatic for studies on the interrelations of the arts.

media, textual and visual, also represent the material proofs of their related performances, which took place as real impromptu extemporary events, and which are now available via the text, thereby overcoming the fact that the reader is an absentee of these real performance-events. Shusterman presents these "happenings," as we would call them in the performance idiolect, in both their visual and written descriptions, testifying to the book's highly staged and multilayered elaboration.

And yet even if the sense of spontaneity of its events may be lost to the reader, the *Adventures* provides effective testimony of these actual performances. Shusterman's "translation" of the performances of the Man in Gold into the form of a philosophical novella, with photographs, also captures the fusion of genres, namely, performance and the novella. Shusterman's *a posteriori* "readings" of the performances of the Man in Gold therefore recasts those performances as if the observer/reader were actually there, at their original staging. So, despite the absence of the reader (or viewer of the work), the *Adventures* provides a unique understanding of the bodily expressed emotions and reactions of the acting persona, Richard Shusterman the philosopher, as they were, or might have been, in performing as the Man in Gold. Such emotions and reactions of the performer, together with our reactions to the once actual and multi-staged—and now described and photographically recorded—performances simultaneously constitute and celebrate the success of the performance as text.[4]

2   Somaesthetics as Metalanguage

In writing of the performance of the Man in Gold, Shusterman refrains from commenting at any length on what exactly is going on within himself, and, in general, leaves the matter to his readers and viewers to explore, in the media descriptions provided. But what we see and read inspires and evokes glimpses and resonances within our own imaginations of the real embodied performance itself. Our initial surprise at the silent philosopher, the Man in Gold who does not speak, is quickly dissipated by a deepening understanding that what is happening here, in the work, is in itself an entirely new kind of philosophical experiment. Certainly this kind of experiment must be one of the most challenging Shusterman could set for himself, and yet a powerful

---

4   See Hans Robert Jauss, *Toward an Aesthetic of Reception*, tr. Timothy Bahti, Introduction by Paul de Man (Minneapolis: University of Minnesota Press, 1982).

expression of his pragmatism, a philosophy whose center is precisely experimentalism. And with the performance of the Man in Gold, Shusterman seems even to test whether somaesthetics, as philosophical aesthetics of the body, may artistically, philosophically, "speak" without need of philosophical discursive explanation.

Some may think the discipline of aesthetics is relatively easy and open to everyone. For example, it is not uncommon to hear the question asked, in the end, aren't we simply discussing whether something is beautiful or not?[5] But things are much more complicated than that. Our first reactions to unprecedented events, or images, is typically evidence only of our culturally ingrained *mores*, our acquired notions and expectations, created and directed through time via geographical cultures and their educational practices; in other words, by each "specific" society with its unique culture. According to what I have called the peoples' pluralistic aesthetic "regionalisms,"[6] each "specific" society and its particular culture produces its own unique reactions to art, and to human "bodily" and "embodied" features, which typically remain unrecognized for their relevance, being thought of as mere "cultural" reactions.

Particular perceptions of beauty, for example, are all too often mistaken as universal aesthetic judgments. We need only mention the classical aesthetic values of proportion and symmetry in Greek and Roman sculpture and architecture, which continue to shape European and Western judgments of beauty. In thinking beyond the limits of this classical mindset, Shusterman's pragmatist experiment is at once aesthetic and scientific, a test to determine the success of a post-classical and embodied aesthetics. This test succeeds with Shusterman's own "somaesthetics," which is a freestanding philosophy that places the aesthetically everchanging and self-transforming body at its center. Shusterman's somaesthetics clearly reveals how the history of philosophy has too often ignored or repressed the centrality of the body for the mind and culture, in favor of a virtually disembodied view of the mind, and its effects; a tradition that should be revised beginning with the body and its neglected role

---

5 The "cultural" response is exemplified in all performance art in that especially this art form aims at extolling all the possible active "performativity" by staging the cultural, social, and political aspects of all kinds of body-politics. See Bezrucka, "Performing Arts/Performance Arts," in *Encyclopedia of Consumer Culture*, vol. 3, ed. Dale Southerton, (Manchester: Manchester University Press, 2011), 1079–1080.

6 See Bezrucka, *The Invention of Northern Aesthetics in 18th-Century English Literature* (Newcastle upon Tyne: Cambridge Scholars, 2017) where I mark the origin of this concept via Frances Grose's delimitation to only "regional" versions of aesthetic concepts (see 147–167), clearly asserting the cultural and nonuniversal value of beauty. See also Bezrucka, *Genio ed immaginazione nel Settecento inglese* (Valdonega: Università di Verona, 2002).

in thought and culture. Shusterman establishes this centrality of the body to all things with his figure and performance of the Man in Gold. As the Man in Gold performs, he embodies the unexpected; and, in the process, teaches us to welcome new ways of thinking and feeling, and of being within our ever-changing reality, which requires only provisional (and nonuniversal) solutions, for it to be constantly revised, according to our ongoing adaptation to actual situations.

As Friedrich Nietzsche in *The Birth of Tragedy* reminds us—with his privileging of the Dionysian over the Apollonian spirit—we must not forget that the body is the most neglected dimension of human life in the history of philosophy, a tradition that has always privileged the mind at the expense of the body, establishing itself as the secular social guardian over all human thoughts and passions. This was done, not only by controlling one's mental states, but also and primarily by controlling the body, its drives, its sexual life, and ultimately its gender, as Michel Foucault has written in his *History of Sexuality*.[7] Drawing on the writings of Nietzsche and Foucault and the pragmatists, Shusterman's project of somaesthetics counters this longstanding neglect of the body in philosophy, and the oppression of the body in society; and he does so in nontraditional ways. By "performing" his philosophy, by performing as the Man in Gold, Shusterman explores and celebrates variety, and celebrates too the involvement of the spectators themselves, those viewing the performance, delivering over to them an accountability for the interpretation of the performance of which they have become a part. Shusterman effectively involves the spectators critically in their own examination of the artistic event, and their place in it, much as playwright Bertolt Brecht theorized for his new theatre art-theory.[8]

3 Spectators and the Man in Gold

In the contemporary world cultural identity remains a major issue, evident in literature, in the protagonist's typical quest for one's own identity-characteristics, within a given cultural contextualization. In the *Adventures* only the skin color of the face tells us the Man in Gold is born from a white background, but even this feature may be interpreted as mere *maquillage*—and, apart from that, no

---

7 Michel Foucault, *The History of Sexuality*, vol. 1, An Introduction, tr. Robert Hurley (New York: Pantheon Books, 1978); see also Judith Butler, *Undoing Gender* (New York: Routledge, 2004).
8 On Bertolt Brecht's theatre see Walter Benjamin, *Understanding Brecht* (London: New Left Books, 1973).

further clues appear. By this strange void of identity markers, the Man in Gold in his tight golden costume is free to become, through the many reactions of people around him, what "they" consider him to be; indeed, the Man in Gold seems to absorb the spectators' various cultural projections and opinions about him. In evoking the "gut feelings" of viewers, the Man in Gold exemplifies their prejudices and their inconsistent, if not irrational, preconceptions. Indeed the unsuspecting contingent viewers who happen to encounter him willy-nilly react to this out-of-the-norm being, the Man in Gold, out of an epistemic void created by their confrontation with a body they have never seen before—a strange body, a silent body, a sexual body—and one to whom they react in various ways. Some ignore him, some are curious, some are irritated, some feel endangered and even see their own world crumbling to pieces, so much so that they feel, rather tellingly, compelled to call the police, exemplifying their need for reestablishment of law and order. This gamut of reactions to an unknown corporality, a man who does not speak, provides a unique compass for determining how various feelings regarding a different body, or even a different species, inevitably arise in an audience. Yet, despite their variety, such reactions all express a certain fear, as if the appearance of a man in gold should constitute an undefinable threat to their sociocultural standards and understanding, to the extent that they cannot recognize that what they are seeing is an art performance.

In his defenseless openness to others—in his condition of existential vulnerability—the Man in Gold, almost like a helpless target, or even a newborn baby that cannot possibly look after itself, opens himself to, and becomes, appropriately, a passive recipient of other peoples' identity hypotheses and related imagology.[9]

Spectators perceive and judge the Man in Gold as a jerk, a freak, an iconoclastic reactionary, a revolutionary, and even an extraterrestrial. They perceive the Man in Gold as the embodiment of what they themselves consider to be an outsider in relation to their socially normative system and all its related standards. In receiving and embodying the peoples' first impressions, the Man in Gold inhabits a vulnerable and even defenseless position of being quite simply what is different, or what is in itself considered to be "foreign."

Spectator reactions to the Man in Gold provide us thus with an insight into ourselves, an insight into how, all too often, we struggle to come to terms with

---

9 See Mark C. Taylor and Esa Saarinen, *Imagologies: Media Philosophy* (London: Routledge, 1994); and Joep Leerssen, "Imagology: History and Method," in *Imagology: The Cultural Construction and Literary Representation of National Characters: A Critical Survey*, ed. Manfred Beller and Joep Leerssen (Amsterdam: Rodopi, 2007), 17–32.

the unknown. But the Man in Gold seems to pose other problems, and reveal still other insights besides. Often when people do not understand something they try to conjure what that "something" is; so too with the Man in Gold. With his golden skin, and his silence, he poses first of all an ontological problem: Is he a new species? The Man in Gold also recasts in unique ways traditional epistemological problems, such as the problem of knowing other minds. How can we begin to know the mind of this strange being? Our typical methods of inquiry and cognitive practices of judgment are little help in framing an understanding such an individual. As a result of these difficulties, interpretation of the Man in Gold easily falls prey to "us-and-them" binary thinking, and labelling typical of "othering" practices. Nobody talks to the Man in Gold in a friendly manner, but each instead signals to him that barriers have been erected. In fact, some people even shout him away, and in doing so they reveal a pervasive frame of thought characterized by intolerance, prejudice, xenophobia, and cultural narrowmindedness with their correlated use of ethnic stereotypes.

The ontological value of this embodied performing-art experiment of one being, the Man in Gold, lies precisely in its power to generate various interpretations of such embodied otherness. So, while the Man in Gold is an active performer, and a passive receptor, being just what he is, the spectators are forced to react with surprise and interpretively respond to such a being, in an involuntary active way: they are forced to change their interpretive attitudes. Faced with the performance of the Man in Gold, the spectators are unwillingly drawn to use both their imagination and rationality (by the simple act of viewing) and compelled to exit their cultural comfort zone. To confirm the past reliability of these cultural comfort zones, the viewers react negatively to the figure of the Man in Gold. But such negative reactions to the Man in Gold also simultaneously reveal the spectators' epistemological limits, specifically their lack of openness to difference, their difficulty with adapting to change and variation; and their desire to maintain the "status quo."

4   Performance Arts and Performative Arts

This active involvement in the live experience also marks the borderline between traditional arts and performative arts.[10] If we go to a museum, typically we do not experience an aesthetic reaction like one experiences in front

---

10   RoseLee Goldberg, *Performance: Live Art 1909 to the Present* (London: Thames and Hudson, 1979, 2001); and Bezrucka, "Performing Arts/Performance Arts," *Encyclopedia of*

of a live work of performance art because we go to the museum in anticipation of a positive aesthetic emotion upon viewing one or several static works of art. These positive emotions are generally anticipated via expectations, and confined to pleasure in the beautiful, which we are certain to experience before our most beloved works of art. We can thus have an aesthetic emotion, and even a very strong aesthetic emotion, for example, being somatically overwhelmed as in instances of Stendhal Syndrome. But these sorts of aesthetic emotions cannot really be defined as extemporary happenings because, however powerful they may be, in having them, we are also simultaneously confirming what we had expected prior to viewing the object in question, even though the emotion may be stronger or weaker depending on various factors. In a live piece of performance art, by contrast, experiences come unexpectedly for the spectator, because the spectator—becoming an involved witness and thus a participant in the art-performance—is drawn into an unknown artistic realm, and thereby becomes vulnerable to change via a new aesthetic experience.

Such forced changes perplex the viewer by thrusting her from an otherwise relatively epistemologically inactive condition. This kind of sudden transformation occurs, for example, when the Man in Gold unexpectedly appears, forcing the viewer to activate within her mind new categories of perceptual judgment. The same may happen for a viewer at a performance of Serbian-American artist Marina Abramović such as *The Artist is Present* at the Museum of Modern Art in Manhattan, New York (March 14–May 31, 2010). Like the Man in Gold, Abramović creates conditions in her performance art that leave the audience at liberty, which, in turn, sets her at maximum risk, even putting her very life in danger. This kind of performance art is, of course, extreme, and inevitably leaves a strong mark on the spectator self-consciously participating in one of Abramović's borderless performances; in some contrast to Shusterman's performances as the Man in Gold, which are not acted out in a museum or an art institution, but in what may be called "reality contexts," achieving in these alternative contexts an augmented reality element of surprise.

The Man in Gold is both a live performer, and, at the same time, and revolutionarily so, a passive receptor of what others see and recognize him to be. In becoming the embodiment of the audience's unsolved issues, of those fears one does not want to acknowledge but which may all too easily be projected onto others (as is the case here), the Man in Gold serves as the material evidence of the "reading" or "evaluation" we usually make of people and the

---

Consumer Culture, vol. 3, ed. Dale Southerton (Manchester: Manchester University Press, 2011), 1079–1081.

attitude we assume in doing so: usually, by refusing their "otherness." The ontological weakness the Man in Gold has chosen to experience, through changing his body, effectively puts him in danger, so much so that he sometimes needs to flee the scene of spectators to protect himself. This is what happened at a five-star hotel in Cartagena, Columbia. People having dinner beheld a man dressed in a golden bodysuit walking through the restaurant, and considered the Man in Gold a real threat to conformity, and shouted at him to leave—all of which endangered the performance and the Man in Gold himself. As Shusterman narrates the event in Cartagena in the *Adventures*, the Man in Gold himself was changed by this painful experience. In becoming the passive victim of impromptu and extemporized reactions on the part of the audience, their very "getting out of control" crystallizes the fears and problems they have with all unexpected "otherness."

By revealing these fears the audience also reveals its perhaps unspoken struggle with the unknown, the unknown which they mark off and exclude from their perception-borders: all those images of otherness that do not fit within their national and cultural stereotypes. Of course, the Man in Gold hardly fits into any known or easily formulated category of reference for what is reasonable (visually, socially, or culturally), so, naturally his very presence destabilizes the diners in Cartagena, forcing their irrational reactions. But Shusterman, or the Man in Gold, receiving their reactions, embodying them, is himself forced to experience what it means to be a foreigner or an outsider in this city, someone who is not recognized as being "normal" or standard or typical or average, and for that reason is judged to be an enemy of the *status quo*. In other words, the Man in Gold is made to feel, perhaps, like an immigrant of sorts. Indeed, his "performed" and "lived" experience of displeasure, abjection, suffering, and otherness that fellow beings project and force the performer (and victim) to "embody," will, nevertheless, allow the performer to synthesize and analyze "otherness" also for others, provoking his audience to challenge and transcend both past and present gender and identity stereotypes.

But painful as the experience was for him, the scene at the Cartagena restaurant also provides the Man in Gold with a remarkably enriching opportunity to become another human being—and not just an experience of taking on an artistic role, but really inhabiting and embodying, in the most highly enriching cognitive somaesthetic kind of way.[11] For Shusterman, as a pragmatist philosopher in line with William James and John Dewey, one practical result of the

---

11 See Tzachi Zamir, "Philosophy and/or Performance: A Discussion of Richard Shusterman's *The Adventures of the Man in Gold*," *Journal of Aesthetic Education*, vol. 52, no. 4 (Winter 2018), 116–123, 120.

experience as the Man in Gold in Cartagena, has been a heightened awareness of the importance of the body as the center of a somaesthetic ethics. Such an ethics is marked especially by the value of openness to positive bodily experiences, which by virtue of bodily engagement alone, are conducive to a healthy cognitive and psychological development.

5 Spectators/Readers

Through this experimental performance of the Man in Gold, both spectators and readers "experience" certain cultural frames which, according to Jacques Lacan (and in contrast to Sigmund Freud), are not so much instinctual as the result of the interiorization of the outside culture, through a process Foucault in *The Archaeology of Knowledge* has linked to the power of the provisional "*episteme*" in which we live: "By *episteme*," writes Foucault, "we mean in fact, the total set of relations that unite, at a given period, the discursive practices that give rise to epistemological figures, sciences, and possibly formalized systems."[12]

The only similar experience that comes to mind (but not a coincidental one) may be one pertaining to "mask theory." In one particular psychological live-experience exercise, individuals are invited to wear masks and then to assume a stranger's personality. In wearing a mask, and assuming an alternate personality, the individual attempts to void oneself of one's "self." This experience of becoming another and voiding oneself is itself a unique type of somaesthetic experience always aimed at experiencing "otherness." But in Shusterman's own experimental performances as the Man in Gold, the happening is far more challenging because here an audience is implied, and this audience is an element which is not controllable by the performer, yet becomes a main feature of the performance without them knowing it.

It is exactly in the moment of void that precedes a "recognition" or the crystallization of a "new form," that the somaesthetic experience takes place. The Man in Gold is, for a moment, an ethical and political void which somehow needs to be filled with identity, ethnicity, and gender, with which and through which he would know himself and the world, and, in the process, experience the world through related forms of discrimination, racism, sexism, and other forms of identity and social discrimination. The experience of the Man in

---

12   Foucault, *The Archaeology of Knowledge & the Discourse on Language*, tr. A. M. Sheridan Smith (New York: Pantheon Books, 1972), 191.

Gold, as it appears in the pages of the *Adventures*, is at once ethical, social, cultural, and political; but it is also deeply pedagogical. After all, to be the "other," and to "incarnate" this otherness, for those who safely belong to the élite groups, is instructive and can be very illuminating. Perceived discrimination is not what some may call "discrimination on paper," but real discrimination, actual, felt discrimination, and it changes one's life—positively and negatively. As Shusterman writes in "Somaesthetics and the Body/Media Issue" (collected in *Performing Live*),

> Somaesthetics is devoted to the critical, ameliorative study of one's experience and use of one's body as a locus of sensory-aesthetic appreciation (*aisthesis*) and creative self-fashioning. It is therefore likewise devoted to the knowledge, discourses, practices, and bodily disciplines that structure such somatic care or can improve it. Though modern Western philosophy has largely slighted the body, if we put aside this prejudice and simply recall philosophy's central aims of knowledge, self-knowledge, right action, and quest for the good life, then the crucial philosophical value of somaesthetics becomes clear in several ways.[13]

Shusterman in the *Adventures* explores these various experiences of embodied art performances, whose cardinal point and political value lie in the fact that the performer willingly does not assert anything, but makes himself the vessel and vehicle of other peoples' meaning and will. In this sense, the live-value of the performance of the Man in Gold could not be greater.

The experiences of the Man in Gold are the embodiment of Shusterman's pragmatist aesthetics—embodied as a lived somaesthetics—which aims at a re-appropriation of the body, in contrast to the dematerialized aesthetic tenets of the tradition, from Plato's unity of truth-and-beauty to modern, regional, philosophical aesthetics. Against this tradition of separation of mind and body, detachment of art from life, Shusterman rejoins art, bodily experience, and aesthetic pleasure, and extends his project of pragmatist aesthetics and somaesthetics beyond the Western tradition to include Asian embodied forms of art and practice. As Shusterman writes in "Somaesthetics and Care of the Self: The Case of Foucault," "Recognition of somatic training as an essential

---

[13] Shusterman, *Performing Live: Aesthetic Alternatives for the Ends of Art* (Ithaca: Cornell University Press, 2000), 138.

means toward philosophical enlightenment and virtue lies at the heart of Asian practices of Hatha Yoga, Zen Meditation, and T'ai chi ch'uan."[14]

The body, too long forgotten by philosophy, is set here into its rightful and preeminent position, a position of extreme potentiality. As the Man in Gold teaches us throughout the pages of the *Adventures,* to be passive in reception hardly entails absence of thoughtful judgment, or suspension of philosophical inquiry and the drawing of conclusions.[15] The ethics and politics of somaesthetics is now clear. As Shusterman writes in "The Somatic Turn: Care of the Body in Contemporary Culture" (in *Performing Live*), "Philosophy's concern for knowledge, self-knowledge and right action are all bound up with its central overarching quest to live a better life. The pursuit of happiness implies attention to the body both as a locus and a medium of pleasures and as a tool for action."[16] The Man in Gold and his bodily performative art action successfully demonstrate that happiness is reachable, and that body-boundaries and demarcation lines can be put under cognitive siege and rethinking—simply by making them visible.

---

14   Shusterman, "Somaesthetics and Care of the Self: The Case of Foucault," *The Monist*, vol. 83, no. 4, *Philosophy as a Way of Life* (October 2000), 530–551, 532.
15   Shusterman, *Body Consciousness: A Philosophy of Mindfulness and Somaesthetics* (Cambridge: Cambridge University Press, 2008).
16   Shusterman, *Performing Live*, 169.

CHAPTER 10

The Golden Turn in Shusterman's Somaesthetics: The Magical Figure of the Man in Gold

Else Marie Bukdahl

Art does not reproduce the visible; it makes visible.
PAUL KLEE[1]

∴

1   Art and the Body

When Richard Shusterman's *The Adventures of the Man in Gold: Paths Between Art and Life* (2016) appeared, many scholars and artists were surprised and curious to see in the work photographs of the philosopher dressed in a golden suit.[2] Some were also curious about the relationship between the philosopher of pragmatism and aesthetics (one well known throughout the art world), and the mysterious figure appearing at the center of this work, i.e., the Man in Gold. Several reviewers lauded Shusterman's "philosophical tale" of the Man in Gold and explored this question of the relation between the two philosophers: one the one hand, Shusterman the philosopher who speaks and writes on aesthetics; and, on the other hand, the figure of the Man in Gold, who is also a kind of philosopher, but in contrast to Shusterman, one who does not speak or write. For those familiar with his work leading up to the *Adventures*, exploration of the relation would take a point of departure from Shusterman's project of "somaesthetics," with its revival of, and central focus on, "the soma," defined as the "living, purposive, sentient, perceptive body."[3] In fact, Shusterman advances

---

1 Paul Klee, *On Modern Art,* tr. Paul Findlay (London: Faber and Faber, Ltd., 1947), 51.
2 Richard Shusterman, *The Adventures of the Man in Gold: Paths Between Art and Life / Les Aventures de L'Homme en Or: Passages entre L'Art et la Vie,* photographs by Yann Toma (Paris: Éditions Hermann, 2016).
3 Shusterman, *Thinking through the Body: Essays in Somaesthetics* (Cambridge: Cambridge University Press, 2012), 141.

his project of somaesthetics precisely as a way of integrating the linguistic and the nonlinguistic dimensions of embodied human life. As Shusterman writes in *Thinking through the Body*,

> Somaesthetics offers a way of integrating the discursive and nondiscursive, the reflective and the immediate, thought and feeling, in the quest of providing greater range, harmony, and clarity to the soma—the bodymind whose union is an ontological given but whose most satisfying unities of performance are both a personal and cultural achievement.[4]

The body occupies an intermediary position between the discursive and nondiscursive, between the sensuous and intellectual, but not as a third thing synthesizing these two dimensions, rather as the ground of these dimensions, and the means to reintegrate them. Somaesthetics articulates paths of reintegration of the human body with itself, and the human body with its natural environment and social and cultural contexts. The melioristic cultivation of body consciousness, as Shusterman develops this view in *Body Consciousness: A Philosophy of Mindfulness and Somaesthetics*, is essential to this integration of the human form, in all its various dimensions, in particular, the integration of the physical and mental. As Shusterman writes, the "soma" in somaesthetics functions as "as a bridge between the spaces of inner self and outer nature, and between physical and mental events."[5] The individual bridges these spaces and integrates herself, writes Shusterman, by means of study but also and more importantly through creative and experimental practices that enable her to understand her body/mind through new aesthetic experiences. Like the soma, this concept of aesthetic experience is also central to his pragmatist and somaesthetic philosophy, as Shusterman writes in "A Philosopher in Darkness and Light: Practical Somaesthetics and Photographic Art." "Experience forms the generating core of my pragmatist philosophy, in theory and in practice. Most of my philosophical views derive from experiences outside the library, seminar room and the philosophical texts I have read." Experience, for Shusterman, is not a passive affair; there are passive elements to it, but it is primarily active. "Experience, for me," writes Shusterman, "implies experimentation, creative exploration and involvement."[6] In the

---

4   Shusterman, "Somaesthetics and the Revival of Aesthetics," *Filozofski Vestnik*, volume/Letnik XXVIII, Number/Številka 2 (2007), 149.
5   Shusterman, *Body Consciousness: A Philosophy of Mindfulness and Somaesthetics* (Cambridge: Cambridge University Press, 2008), 145.
6   Shusterman, "A Philosopher in Darkness and Light: Practical Somaesthetics and Photographic Art," translated into French as "Un Philosophe en ombre et en lumière," in *Lucidité: Vues de*

Adventures, Shusterman undertakes a radical experiment in aesthetic experience, in philosophy, and in art, by becoming a living and performing work of art, namely, the Man in Gold.

2 A New Concept of Visual Art

If experience implies creative experimentation, then, for Shusterman, this implies the exploration of boundaries, such as the boundaries traditionally separating the various disciplines, e.g., philosophy, literature, and the arts. Experience, writes Shusterman, "connotes the idea of experiments in transcending disciplinary boundaries." But perhaps the most important boundary to be transcended in Shusterman's philosophy is the boundary separating, on the one hand, the various practices and disciplines which are essentially discursive, and, on the other hand, the nondiscursive dimension of aesthetic experience. Too often, and too long, disparaged in philosophy, even in pragmatism, Shusterman throughout his work seeks to revive "the non-linguistic dimension of experience."[7]

This concept of "experience," in Shusterman's philosophy, is neither metaphysical nor ideological. Instead, "art as experience"—a phrase Shusterman borrows from pragmatist John Dewey—means that both the artist and the person experiencing the work of art operate on an open platform with a high level of visibility. The artist creates the work but must also engage in the aesthetic experience the work of art, and the public must be able to engage in its own aesthetic experience the artwork. This active aesthetic experience of the artwork, which entails interpreting the work's particular qualities, is how the work comes to fulfilment; not by creation but in aesthetic experience. The aesthetic experience is, therefore, an essential part of the work, so it is crucial that there is always an intense interaction between the artwork and the viewer, in the viewing experience.[8] This aesthetic experience of the work by the viewer is embodied and affective, and ideally intensely pleasurable and stimulating of interpretation.

---

l'intérieur / Lucidity: Inward Views," ed. Anne-Marie Ninac (Montréal: *Le Mois de la Photo à Montréal*, 2011), 280.
7 Lauri Väkevä, "Interviewing Richard Shusterman: Part I," *Action, Criticism, & Theory for Music Education*, Issue 1 (Spring 2002), vol. 1, 4.
8 Shusterman, "Intellectualism and the Field of Aesthetics: The Return of the Repressed?" in *Revue Internationale de Philosophie* 220 (2002), 331.

While these views present direct challenges to "the golden cage of autonomous art," several artists have responded favorably Shusterman's critiques, and incorporated these philosophical insights into their own works of art, and even invited him to participate in their exhibitions. In 1996, for example, artist Carsten Höller asked Shusterman to write the catalogue text for the provocative and interactive installation *House for Pigs and People* (1997), a collaborative work by Höller and Rosemarie Trockel for *documenta X*, in Kassel, Germany (1997). In Shusterman's *Pragmatist Aesthetics*, Höller had found a parallel to his own concept of the artist's interactive dialogue with the viewer and her surroundings, and the merging of art and experience with the aim of benefitting life. Shusterman's essay, in turn, analyzed Höller and Trockel's project from the perspective of pragmatism, while, at the same time, critically underlining some of the more traditional ideas of the aesthetics of visual art.

Originally, Höller had asked Shusterman to write on the installation because Höller's art had been inspired by Shusterman's philosophy of art. But after studying and writing on the Höller and Trockel installation, Shusterman soon discovered that other artists were also working to affect the entire body of the viewer, some of whom had also been inspired by his philosophical writings on artistic perception and the importance of corporeality in art, and its importance in all aspects of human life. Daniel Barber, for example, had similarly found inspiration in works like *Body Consciousness: A Philosophy of Mindfulness and Somaesthetics*, and applied this aesthetic theory to studio art practice.[9]

Inspired by his own aesthetic experiences at *documenta X*, Shusterman in his *documenta* text deepened his critique of "the crusty old dogma that firmly divides art from life and praxis," and the related closed world of galleries, i.e., "the white cube." The exposed artwork, writes Shusterman, demonstrates that a "concretely embodied reality" has been created, and reveals how "art can play a powerful role in changing our realities by changing: our perception, attitudes and consequent actions."[10] In connection with his criticism of the artworld's insularity, in the *documenta X* text, Shusterman also denounces contemporary aesthetics for being overly intellectual and for "emphasizing art as a symbol system or an object of mere cognitive interpretation, rather than an object of deeply felt experience and intense pleasure." Art has simply become too remote

---

9   Daniel Barber, "Somaesthetic Awareness and Artistic Practice: A Review Essay," review of Shusterman's *Body Consciousness*, in *International Journal of Education of the Arts*, ed. Liora Bresler, vol. 9, Review 1 (September 2008), 2; see also 6–8.

10 Shusterman's *documenta* text, "A House Divided," is reprinted in C. Höller and R. Trockel's *A House for Pigs and People / Eine Haus für Schweine und Menschen* (Koln: Verlag: Walter König, 1997), 31–32. See also the illustrations of the project.

and esoteric for most people to be able to enjoy it at all. As Shusterman writes, "the stress on the power and value of aesthetic experience is ... very important for the contemporary art world which seems to be losing its appeal for the general public because of its failure to create powerful aesthetic experience."[11]

Although Shusterman's philosophy has always emphasized the need for this kind of boundary-crossing between art and life, and had explored in practical performance somaesthetic disciplines such as the Feldenkrais Method, the Alexander Technique, *taijiquan*, and *zazen*, he had never performed in practice any "specific somaesthetic disciplines" involving visual art. So when asked about his "practical somaesthetics of visual art," Shusterman was unable to provide a satisfactory answer. Instead, he said that he lacked an "appropriate practical creative practice to work with."[12]

But that was about to change.

3 Somaesthetics and Somaflux Photography

A chance meeting in 2009 with renowned photographer Yann Toma helped Shusterman to resolve this problem, and their collaboration quickly became a turning point in his aesthetics and creative practice, imbuing both with new perspectives, orientations, and layers of meaning.[13] At the time, Toma was working with an original form of photography called "radiant flux," so he proposed that Shusterman take part as a performer. That was August 2009. Unfortunately, Shusterman's busy schedule meant delaying the shoot almost a year. Then in June 2010 Shusterman stepped beyond the intellectual comfort of detached philosophical analysis, and into art itself. It was then that Shusterman discovered what it was like to be an active part of the process of creating a work of art, experiencing the process with all his senses, his entire body. The experience would have a profound impact on Shusterman as a philosopher, radically altering his perception of art, especially regarding photography, performance, installation art, and collaboration.

In "A Philosopher in Darkness and in Light: Practical Somaesthetics and Photographic Art," Shusterman recounts how he was transformed, philosophically, beginning with his transformation into an artistic performer. It all started

---

11   Väkevä, "Interviewing Richard Shusterman: Part I," in *Action, Criticism, & Theory for Music Education*, 5.
12   Shusterman, "A Philosopher in Darkness and Light," 281.
13   The visual arts, generally, and photography especially, become increasingly prominent in Shusterman's somaesthetics.

when Toma asked Shusterman to wear a glittering gold bodysuit, which had been worn by Toma's parents in the Paris Ballet. Understandably hesitant to wear a tightfitting golden suit in front of a camera, Shusterman nonetheless got into costume and so began his metamorphosis into a new artistic character. Once Shusterman was in the golden suit, Toma danced around him with two lamps—first slowly, then quickly—holding the lamps like two golden wands, at once sensing and tracing the varying qualities of auratic light radiating from the golden suited figure who would soon be known as the "Man in Gold." In fact, Toma had to move quickly to ensure that only the tracings of the lights—and not Toma's own body tracing them—would be captured by the camera; and that only the visible aura of the Man in Gold would appear. As Shusterman recalls, "Yann was fully absorbed in understanding me, in feeling and responding to my energy," and how "a deep sense of mutual understanding was thus created between us through silent, corporeal communication." Within this corporal communication, between photographer and subject, Toma not only traced the aura of the Man in Gold but "also reshaped it with his own." But in reshaping the energy flows of the Man in Gold, as Shusterman recalls, Toma with his lights and sensitivity, was also "conversely reshaping his [own] energy flow through his encounter with mine."[14]

Toma calls the form of photography emerging from his collaboration with Shusterman "somaflux photography." In a still entitled *Somaflux* from the video performance *A Night with Richard Shusterman* (2010), we see the photographer at work moving quickly (and glimpsed darkly) around the Man in Gold (Figure 1). The darkness of the shot is essential to the creation of somaflux films and photographs (e.g., *Somaflux*, 2010) because otherwise the glowing aura of the Man in Gold is too difficult to capture with the camera. In fact, two sets of opposites, which are also "complementarities," as Shusterman describes them, are always in play in somaflux still photography: one set of opposites is "darkness and light," darkness as a setting, and Toma's glowing lights illuminating the aura of the Man in Gold; the other set of opposites is "fixity and flux," or stillness and motion, with the Man in Gold still in pose, and Toma moving quickly to trace light around the Man in Gold. Exploring the intervals of these "complementarities" of Toma's photography, Shusterman experienced a powerful liberation from what he calls his "habitual patterns and inhibitions of self-expression," even acquiring a new understanding of the complexity of relations holding among somaesthetics, photography, art, and life.[15]

---

14   Shusterman, "A Philosopher in Darkness and Light" (2011), 282–283.
15   *Ibid.*, 285 and 287.

FIGURE 1 Yann Toma, *Somaflux with Richard Shusterman performing as the Man in Gold*. Photographic Still from the film, *A Night with Richard Shusterman*. Paris, 2010
PHOTO COURTESY OF YANN TOMA AND RICHARD SHUSTERMAN

4 *Aesthetic Transactions* Exhibition, Paris 2012

While deeply engaged with this project with Toma, in 2011, Shusterman was also asked by his French colleagues Richard Conte and Sandra Laugier to curate an exhibition entitled *Aesthetic Transactions: Pragmatist Philosophy through Art and Life*, to be presented in 2012, at the Michel Journiac Gallery in Paris (May 24–June 6). This exhibit would celebrate the twentieth anniversary Shusterman's book *Pragmatist Aesthetics* (published simultaneously in English and French). The artists he selected to participate in the exhibition, including ORLAN, Carsten Höller, Tatiana Trouvé, Pan Gongkai, Luca Del Baldo, and Thecla Schiphorst, had all enriched Shusterman's life experience, and, in their own ways, they too had been inspired by Shusterman's concept of art as created and perceived through the body. Shusterman wrote the exhibition catalogue essay, "Aesthetic Transactions: Pragmatist Philosophy through Art and Life," and the entire catalogue, together with the choice of the artists to participate, reveals how Shusterman's own artistic experiences performing as the Man in Gold heightened and extended not only his understanding of visual art's specific character, and its intense language of form, but also the public's multifaceted embodied participation in the arts.

While several of the selected artworks in *Aesthetic Transactions* were performances (in kinship with the performances of the Man in Gold), all of the artworks were forms of performative expression; and the exhibition as a whole visually illustrated two main themes from *Pragmatist Aesthetics*, specifically, aesthetic experience as active not passive, and aesthetic analysis as participatory, in an impressive and contemplative manner. Within his catalogue essay for *Aesthetic Transactions*, Shusterman also revealed—no doubt inspired by his experiences as the Man in Gold—that visual-artistic interpretation can convey insights that discursive language cannot; or, at least, not as intensely. With regard to the first main theme (articulated in the catalogue), Shusterman writes that "aesthetic experience is not a passive ... disembodied contemplation but rather involves the active somatic engagement of purposive perceptual discrimination. Artworks are not only created through somatic action; their reception also involves the soma's sensorimotor acts of perception and response." And with regard to the second main theme, Shusterman writes that "the philosopher's most useful role in aesthetics ... should be that of an actively engaged participant concerned with improving aesthetic experience by heightening perception and enriching creativity and meaning."[16]

Höller's contribution to *Aesthetic Transactions*, entitled *The Pinocchio Effect* (1994, 1999, 2003), expanded the art field by showing how visual art applies not only to vision, but to all the senses, including proprioception, despite visual art's seemingly nontactile nature; and, how in the process, art can succeed in engaging the viewer in new ways.[17] At the same exhibition, Paris-based artist Tatiana Trouvé's *Polder* installations (2011) created an intensely embodied experience, yet without any presentation of a body, rather, entirely through the language of art, in particular, through "the extensive but meticulously detailed leather wrappings and lacings that simultaneously cover and reveal the metal skeleton." The French multimedia artist ORLAN also exhibited at *Aesthetic Transactions* a photograph from her *5th Surgery Performance, Operation-Opera* (1991). As Shusterman writes in *Aesthetic Transactions* catalogue of ORLAN's work, "Her cosmetic surgeries are undertaken not to achieve

---

16   *Aesthetic Transactions: Pragmatist Philosophy through Art and Life*, curated by Shusterman, 3, L'Imprimerie Elkotec, Palaiseau, Paris Mai (2012), 12–13.
17   See Shusterman's nuanced description of Höller's installation in *Aesthetic Transactions*, 16–18, fig. 11.

a particular surgical result but to appreciate the transactional experiential process of remaking the self as a performative expression of individual freedom."[18]

The Chinese painter and installation artist Pan Gongkai also exhibited at *Aesthetic Transactions* in Paris 2011, with an ink painting and a film of his 2011 Venice Biennale installation, *Snow Melting in Lotus*. Drawing from the rich resources of classical Confucianism (central to Pan Gongkai's orientation), Shusterman in *Aesthetic Transactions* highlights "the notion of an ethics of harmony in which ethical education rests on the twin aesthetic pillars of art and ritual."[19] Pan Gongkai's artworks involve a continuing dialogue between tradition and innovation, in both Chinese and Western art and philosophy, including somaesthetics. His exhibition in Paris invited viewers to a magical and engaging visual interplay between the traditional subject matter of the lotus and the traditional technique of ink painting with the use of modern computer technology that is a key part of his installation. In Pan Gongkai's computer-generated imagery, a printed text about western aesthetics falls like snowflakes to the ground over the painted lotuses still standing proud on walls of the corridor that forms the installation.

Interactive technology artist Thecla Schiphorst also showed at the exhibition with her work *Tendrils* (2010). Schiphorst created what Shusterman describes in the *Aesthetic Transactions* catalogue as "a responsive, kinetic wearable artwork," a form of "interactive garment that responds to being touched, both when touched locally by direct contact on the garment's surface," and when "touched collectively through remotely transmitted signals from an iPhone Touch App or that are delivered through a network link to wearable armbands that are part of the *Tendrils* network." Schiphorst's *Tendrils*, writes Shusterman, is almost "a second living skin, tender and sensitive in its own reactions of shivering and quivering, yet also incorporated into the wearer's somatic experience." As a "second living skin," *Tendrils* bears close aesthetic proximity to Shusterman's own glittering "second living skin" worn by the Man in Gold.

Some of the exhibiting artists at *Aesthetic Transactions* invited Shusterman to participate as a performer in their various artistic processes, thereby creating original and collaborative works. Artist Luca Del Baldo, for example, invited Shusterman to pose semi-naked for a portrait painting. Following the session, and the exposing of the finished portrait, Shusterman reflected in the *Aesthetic Transactions* catalogue on "the pragmatist values of experimentation and meliorist striving, the aesthetic experience of collaborative creation, and even the cognitive gains from exploring new practices that provoke new sensations,

---

18   Shusterman, *Aesthetic Transactions*, 18–22, figs. on 14 and 17.
19   *Ibid.*, 21.

spur new energies and attitudes, and thus probe one's current limits and perhaps transcend them to transform the self." Shusterman adds that if his work as the Man in Gold had not liberated him from "some deep inhibitions," he would never have entertained the idea of posing semi-naked "for a painting like Del Baldo's nor had the courage to exhibit it in public."[20]

The Man in Gold himself was also included in the exhibition, providing a fresh opportunity to reveal his significance for Shusterman's understanding of the relationship between art and life, and the exploration of the relation between the art of living and the art of the artworld. The Man in Gold was present in three forms at *Aesthetic Transactions*: still photographs, projections of three films of past performances, and a surprise impromptu visit of the Man in Gold himself (https://aesthetictransactions.webs.com). Commenting more generally on the Man in Gold, Shusterman describes him as "an embodied projection" and "an incorporated extension" that has succeeded in shaping, enriching, and transforming both Shusterman's own life and work and the connection between them. The Man in Gold has provided Shusterman's philosophical aesthetics with a new understanding of "the aesthetic experience of artistic creation," which would come to play a prominent role in his later philosophical works, while, at the same time, extending his "experience into new roles and contexts," and providing him a richer understanding of "self and self-knowledge."[21]

In short, this expression of his identity as the Man in Gold and the opportunity of being a genuine collaborator in artistic creation augmented Shusterman's concept of visual art through the curating of the show with the five artists. The exhibition visualized the possibility of combining art and philosophy through a new perspective, one of creating together instead of existing separately.

5   Photography and Performance

Being the Man in Gold also expanded Shusterman's philosophy of photography. In "Photography as Performative Process," published in *Thinking through the Body* (2012), Shusterman sets in focus not the material photograph, but the performance of photography as a fine art; not the end result, but the "performative process" as an end in itself, on with its own unique creative dimensions, difficulties, and aesthetic pleasures. Why has the focus in philosophy of photography, asks Shusterman, almost always been on the photograph itself, or

---

20   *Ibid.*, 23, fig. 24, 29 and 32, fig. 28.
21   *Ibid.*, 31–32, illustration on 33.

the subject or object in the photograph, rather than, for example, on the art of taking pictures, or the art of performing as a subject before the camera, or the whole interactive relationship of the photographer and the subject and the setting. These sorts of questions had not, in fact, arisen for Shusterman either, at least not until he had begun working with Toma and performing as the Man in Gold. Only then did Shusterman look seriously into the performance process of photography and theorize this in his aesthetics. Through this work, he and Toma discovered that the subject's posing and movements can be as important as the photographer's camerawork; and both agreed that collaboration is vital to the art. Even if first person testimony is hardly the standard approach to philosophical aesthetics, such a perspective is justified, writes Shusterman in "Photography as Performative Process," particularly regarding "experimental dimensions of making and appreciating art."[22]

Toma is probably most famous for his creation of the artistic genre of "Radiant Flux," from which the Man in Gold himself emerged. In his *Somaflux* collaborative performances with the Man in Gold, writes Shusterman, Toma "tries to capture and visually represent"—both in still photographs and video— "the invisible aura of the person posing for him," and succeeds in rendering intensely visible what is normally invisible.[23] In so doing, writes Shusterman, Toma "is drawing or painting with light."[24] The roots of this form of photography are to be found in the "space writing" of Man Ray [as in his *Space Writing (Self-portrait)* (1935) (Figure 2)], and in "light drawing," which can be seen in Gjon Mili's photographs of Pablo Picasso in the South of France in 1949 for *Life Magazine*.[25]

Toma's *Somaflux* photography and films with the Man in Gold are more performative than these other forms of "space writing," as they involve more dancing in their drawing of light, a style of dancing that expresses strong liberating

---

22   Shusterman, *Thinking through the Body*, 243.
23   Ibid., 254.
24   Ibid., 255.
25   Ibid. See also Jenna Lawson, "Painting with Light: History of Light Painting," for a discussion of light painting photographers, including Frank Gilbreth and Lillian Moller Gilbreth, Man Ray, Pablo Picasso, Andreas Feininger, Jozef Sedlák, and Kamil Varga (https://jennalawsonfmp.blogspot.com/2011/05/history-of-light-painting.html). While the technique was invented by Frank Gilbreth and Lillian Moller Gilbreth in 1914, beginning around 1935 Man Ray was the first artist to work in the new medium of "space writing," or "light painting photography." As Jeanna Lawson writes in "Painting with Light," "in 1935 Man Ray set up a camera and used a small penlight to create a series of swirls and lines in the air." See also "Behind the Picture: Picasso 'Draws' with Light," *Life Magazine* (January, 1949) (https://time.com/3746330/behind-the-picture-picasso-draws-with-light/).

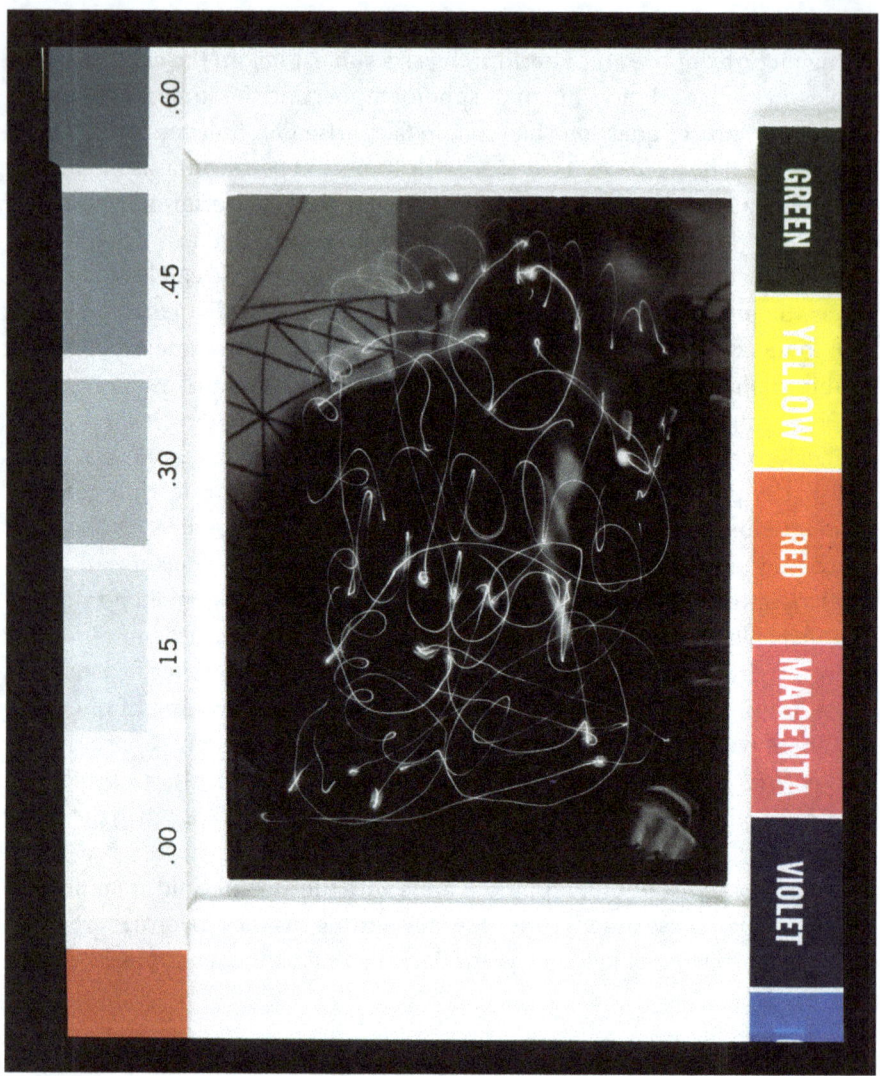

FIGURE 2　Man Ray, *Space Writing (Self Portrait)*, 1935. Gelatin silver print on paper. 8.1 × 5.9 cm
BOWDOIN COLLEGE MUSEUM OF ART, BRUNSWICK, MAINE MUSEUM PURCHASE, LLOYD O. AND MARJORIE STRONG COULTER FUND, AND THE ARTIST RIGHTS SOCIETY. COURTESY OF BOWDOIN COLLEGE OF MUSEUM OF ART

mental forces. Because Toma's photography is intrinsically performative, the subject of the process, namely, the Man in Gold, cannot be separated from the activity of being photographed. The entire artistic process, of photographer and subject, is interwoven by an extremely complex network of intricate paths of communication. As Shusterman writes, "among the most powerful and aesthetic dimensions of our performative process was the nonverbal somatic communication between us; the way we reciprocally sensed and responded to each other's energy" and "the artistic intentions and sensibility these movements expressed." Shusterman adds that "as Toma probed and traced my energy he also reshaped it with his own, while conversely reshaping his own energy by probing and processing mine." This shared "experience of common exploration" and heightened awareness, as a form of artistic "co-creation," continues Shusterman, changed them both in powerful ways.[26] For both Shusterman and Toma, the collaborative process of photography deepened their understandings of visual art and extended their range of thought on the art of photography, and the philosophy of photography.

Shusterman would also find his aesthetic experiences, and understanding of the arts, to be deepened by ongoing dialogue with the other artists of *Aesthetics Transactions*. For example, a year after the Paris exhibit, Shusterman explained, in discussions with Pan Gongkai in Beijing (March 24, 2013), how performing as the Man in Gold revealed new ways of bringing art and philosophy together. As Shusterman writes,

> This integration of making art and doing philosophy together in the performance of the same individual, is one reason I like the Wen Ren (文人) tradition in China—the intellectual thinking and the making of art are brought together to nourish and enrich each other so that the individual who combines these practices is improved.[27]

Other artists, as much as the Man in Gold himself, have taught Shusterman that "art, like philosophy, extends the range of one's thinking." But if art, like philosophy, extends the range of thought, philosophy, especially when it enters freely and openly into the arts, also expands the range of creative thought in artists.

In the same dialogue, Pan Gongkai asked Shusterman, "What is the relation between the art of living and the art of the artworld?" Shusterman answered: "Art is a way of exploration of oneself. In making art one expresses oneself, and this self-expression helps you better to know yourself so you can improve yourself or cultivate yourself better, not simply for yourself but for your family, your university, your community."[28] And for Shusterman himself,

---

26 Shusterman, *Thinking through the Body*, 259–260.
27 Pan Gongkai, "Dialogue with Richard Shusterman on Philosophy, Art, Life," *Journal of Somaesthetics*, Issue on *Somaesthetics and Visual Art*, vol. 1, no. 1 (2015), 47.
28 Ibid., 50.

when he wears the golden suit, he has also the opportunity not only to revive the tradition of practicing philosophy as a way of life, but also to perform art as a new way of exploring oneself, to explore his creative limits and vital force (or *qi* in Chinese), and to discover paths of self-improvement (or what Shusterman calls meliorism). In exploring himself, as Shusterman himself notes, he is also exploring a long tradition found in Eastern philosophy and Western philosophy. The Socratic wisdom, "Know thyself," is central to ancient Greek philosophy, but, as Shusterman writes, that wisdom also bears close resemblance to the Chinese philosophical ideas of "xing shen (省身), self-examination and xiu shen (修身) self-cultivation." "In the Confucian *Analects*," writes Shusterman, "you learn to examine yourself three times a day. Art is a form of self-cultivation and self-examination."[29]

Pan Gongkai in his dialogue then turns to Shusterman's own unique form of artistic cultivation with his performances as the Man in Gold, highlighting parallels to the Chinese tradition of ink painting, and Pan Gongkai's own ink painting, in particular.

> In Chinese painting practice, there is something in common with your performance [as the Man in Gold] but with a lot of differences. In Chinese painting, the action is very subtle, only very small movements with one hand, or a few fingers, not like big dancing. The action of movement in my ink painting is almost the biggest kind of movement in this artistic form.[30]

6 The Royaumont Abbey: A Mysterious Birth

Shusterman's the *Adventures* chronicles the "adventures" of the Man in Gold, who appears in different parts of Europe, North America, and South America. The *Adventures* is an original and complex intertwining of two styles of writing, i.e., philosophical autobiography and poetic fictional discourse. Through both of the styles, the Man in Gold appears as a living human being with great sensitivity, even many surprising mood changes, various and often unpredictable desires, a love of beauty, and deep and unsettling fear of unpleasant and unpredictable situations. Throughout these adventures new paths between art and life are revealed, as new connections between art and life are explored.

---

29 *Ibid.*, 51. Pan Gongkai mentioned the relevance of Wang Ruiyun work in "developing self-cultivation through art," and her "theoretical background for self-cultivation, mostly Zen" (52–53).

30 Pan Gongkai, "Dialogue with Richard Shusterman," 59.

These explorations appear in Shusterman's written text of the work about the Man in Gold, but they also appear in Toma's photographs of the Man in Gold, found throughout. Sometimes lying silent in the dark, other times moving around in the evening or daylight, the Man in Gold seems always to be surrounded by an enchanted atmosphere that draws the viewer into his magic circle, a glowing being with a sensitive heart, someone we want to know.

But knowing him is difficult, even apparently for Shusterman himself. The Man in Gold's genealogy remains obscure, and obscure even partly to him. The Man in Gold does not know his father; although, happily, he knows (or, at least, thinks he knows) his mother. His mother is the tiny dancing goddess Wu Xiaoxing, who, through a series of seductive human incarnations, has captured his heart. The Man in Gold is born fully mature, a paradoxical being in many ways. He is young and old, and communicates not through language but by silent and somatic "posture, gesture, and acture." Shusterman explains:

> The Man in Gold eschews discursive language, recognizing it as the glory of philosophy but also an imprisoning source of its oppressive folly—its one-sidedness. He expresses himself instead in posture, gesture and acture, to emulate the dancing beauties that he loves and learns from incarnations of the divine Wu Xiaoxing.[31]

Devoid of personal name or history or the confines of language (though he is capable of language), the Man in Gold enjoys an incredible freedom from these things. In performing as the Man in Gold, Shusterman also enjoys an incredible freedom from those things, for in becoming this other kind of being, his "ordinary mind or self goes away." He is "cleansed" from his "ordinary self," and "free to perceive differently." Such liberation, for the philosopher, is also powerfully melioristic; for it is, writes Shusterman, "a liberation of self that is also, in some ways, a self-enrichment through new perceptions."[32]

Naturally, writes Shusterman, the Man in Gold tires of the philosopher's ongoing critical and analytical descriptions and explanations, "in dry, unimaginative philosophical prose." The Man in Gold "wants his story told as he lived it," and continues to live it, and he lives through his performance and aesthetic experience, which are not at all discursive. So, despite his natural inclination to language, Shusterman has done his best in the *Adventures* to honor the wish of the Man in Gold, and tell his story in the way he would have it told.[33] To this

---

31 Shusterman, *Adventures*, 58.
32 Pan Gongkai, "Dialogue with Richard Shusterman," 74.
33 Shusterman, *Adventures*, 14.

end, Shusterman explains that he has lent his body as "the somatic medium for the Man in Gold's gestural communication." But this communication is much more dramatic, expressive, and suggestive than verbal language can convey. Only the photographical language of Toma's photos and films of the Man in Gold can capture those experiences in their full presence and intensity.[34]

The Man in Gold was born in the medieval abbey of Royaumont, which is surrounded by a romantic garden. That is where Shusterman's first performances with Toma "the crucial midwife for his birth" took place. For many hours, and long into the night, recalls Shusterman, he posed in a dark chamber in the abbey, sometimes lying down without moving, sometimes even drifting into sleep. In these "moments of lost consciousness," however, writes Shusterman, "the Man in Gold's own consciousness was coming to the fore, stimulated by Yann's dynamic light."[35] But birth is never easy, and in his struggles, and in his fears of the dark room, the Man in Gold escaped to the garden, Toma following close behind. Shusterman narrates this early event in sensual and evocative language so the reader can almost smell the flowers, and experience the Man Gold's dancing and dramatic movements, and the liberation they produce. The passage almost appears to have been taken from a novel and is marked by a joyful atmosphere full of tension and intensity.

> After a few hours of posing, I could no longer stay motionless. Some inner force compelled me to quiver and shake with irresistible energy. It wanted out; it wanted light ... I shot through the chamber door, running down the long corridor and steps leading out to the courtyard, following a seductive scent to the Abbey's enchanting gardens in full June bloom. ... In the flowering garden, rich in fragrance, sun and movement, I lost my sense of Self, as the Man in Gold possessed me, absorbing for himself the full light of self-consciousness and expressing his manly will of independence ... the Man in Gold began to dance around the garden. Inventing choreographic narratives based on the venue's affordances and energies, he leaped over shrubs, knelt to smell the tiniest of flowers, and refreshed his sweating face and hands with water from the pond.[36]

The Man in Gold got his name later that day, and still later launched his peregrinations through Europe, North America, and South America, all the while

---

34 *Ibid.*, 19.
35 *Ibid.*, 28.
36 *Ibid.*, 30–32.

THE GOLDEN TURN IN SHUSTERMAN'S SOMAESTHETICS   193

FIGURE 3   Yann Toma, *Somaflux with Richard Shusterman performing as the Man in Gold: Currents of the Seine*, 2012
PHOTO COURTESY OF YANN TOMA AND RICHARD SHUSTERMAN

his horizons expanding through the immediacy of his sensuous experience and direct contact with nature and human nature.

The Man in Gold arrived in Paris in June 2012 in connection with the *Aesthetic Transactions* exhibition. Besides his brief surprise appearance at the opening, Toma arranged a secret nocturnal performance in the heart of Paris on the left bank of the Seine (Figure 3).

If we compare the stills from one of the scenes in this movie with Shusterman's description, we see the differences between the verbal and visual discourse; and we can also perceive and feel the atmosphere as fictional. Shusterman writes:

> The sculptures along the quai fascinated the Man in Gold, who happily posed and played around them, excited by the flowing water with its brightly dancing reflections of street lamps and the lights of tourist boats gliding up and down the river. The boats especially enchanted him; he

yearned to board them so he could wed his movement with the river's flow, merge with the water which he felt as his essence.[37]

7 The Dunes and the Sea of Northern Jutland

The last of the adventures of the Man in Gold recounted in the book was in Northern Jutland, Denmark. On Sunday 25th June 2014, Toma and Shusterman arrived in Aalborg, the largest city in this part of Denmark. Denmark is a prominent place for somaesthetics, and one of the many homes of the Man in Gold.[38] Over the years, in the course of Shusterman's lectures at Aalborg University (and its affiliated institutions in Copenhagen), and through collaborations with other artists, the topics of somaesthetics and the Man in Gold have emerged with considerable frequency, ultimately leading to the founding of *The Journal of Somaesthetics*, based in Aalborg University.[39] But perhaps the most surprising work of somaesthetics to emerge from Shusterman's work in Denmark was *The Adventures of the Man in Gold*.

I had the honor of being the first Dane to host the Man in Gold in my home. It was in my own rustic cottage by the beach, in the northernmost part of Denmark, where the Baltic and the Nordic seas meet in frequently rough seas beyond green dunes lined with fields of seductively scented flowers. The sound of the strong winds and the rhythmic movements of the waves are constant, and the strong daylight seemed somehow to have prevented the Man in Gold from appearing. Then suddenly, as Shusterman himself poetically describes the scene, the Man in Gold was there.

> Yann looked up at the heavens, wondering if his friend had arrived by riding the gentle clouds rather than the rough waves (for both elements share his beloved watery essence). Then, kissing the golden guest between the

---

37 *Ibid.*, 68.
38 When the University of Aalborg, in the Northern part of Denmark, invited Shusterman to be visiting professor in 2013, it afforded the Man in Gold an opportunity to connect with a new academic and cultural environment and to work with a number of contemporary artists. Unfortunately, the university failed to formalize this appointment due to Danish immigration restrictions, but Shusterman gained an enduring connection to the Department of Art and Technology at Aalborg University, while at the same time expanding his work to Aalborg University's institutions in Copenhagen.
39 See, for example, Gongkai's "Dialogue with Richard Shusterman on Philosophy, Art and Life" and Peng Feng's article "Somaesthetics and its Consequences in Contemporary Art," *Journal of Somaesthetics*, vol. 1, no. 1, Somaesthetics and Visual Art (2015), 42–107.

FIGURE 4 Yann Toma, *Somaflux with Richard Shusterman performing as the Man in Gold: Sunset in Vesterklit*, 2014
PHOTO COURTESY OF YANN TOMA AND RICHARD SHUSTERMAN

eyes to energize his *qi* [energy flow], Yann raised his hands in benediction and bellowed (in his special shaman voice) *"L'homme en or!"*[40]

The Man in Gold soon began to dance in the dark dunes amidst flashes of light that tore the darkness and turned the dunes into a magical landscape (Figure 4). I followed the captivating dance of the Man in Gold to a quiet place and found him deep in meditation, astonished by the very landscape he had created. Attending this performance, as a real artistic event, heightened my senses and awareness, and created dynamic suspense, like nothing else (Figure 4).[41]

The next morning, after having slept in my cottage, the Man in Gold indicated his wish to visit two artists, the Viking Queen and her husband the King of Mighty Stones. The Man in Gold had looked forward to meeting with these art colleagues for the first time, and to learning more about art, especially the

---

40 Shusterman, *Adventures*, 82.
41 Ibid., 82.

creative process, and the relation between art and life, and to new opportunities to gain access to the sensory experience of reality. Laura DiSumma-Knoop highlights this particular meeting with the two artists, as it is recorded in the book, *The Adventure of the Man in Gold*, claiming that moment to be "the moment in which the book advances what I take to be its strongest and most innovative point: that philosophers can create and that they are entitled to artistic expression."[42]

The final chapter of the *Adventures* is titled "The Magic Vessels of the Viking Queen." I now make way for the Queen herself, Marit Benthe Norheim, the very Viking Wizard Queen of Shusterman's tale. I will leave it to the two artists to describe the Man in Gold's marvelous adventures in their artworld.

8 The Artists of Pink Rock Castle, by Marit Benthe Norheim

Richard Shusterman in the last chapter of the *Adventures*, "The Magic Vessels of the Viking Queen," identifies two sculptors Claus Ørntoft as the "King of Mighty Stones" and "Magical Master of the Lions," and Marit Benthe Norheim as "The Viking Wizard Queen." I write now as the Viking Wizard Queen of "Pink Rock Castle" in North Jutland, Denmark,[43] and of our honored guests, the philosopher Richard Shusterman, the photographer Yann Toma, and the mysterious Man in Gold. By inviting the Man in Gold to inhabit his body, Shusterman opened himself to a strange and difficult possession, difficult even for him to understand. In the *Adventures* Shusterman even asks why he continues to allow such possession; after all, life would probably be easier if he didn't. But Shusterman acknowledges that there is no ultimate philosophical answer; only a sense that perhaps this possession "had to be."

> Why did I open myself up to this strange possession? I am not certain of the answer. Having long been taught by philosophy's modes of critical thinking and the even more potent surprises of life, I am skeptical of the certitude of self-knowledge and the capacity to penetrate one's true and deepest motivations. We are masters of self-deception.[44]

---

42 Laura T. Di Summa-Knoop, "A Review of Shusterman and Toma's *The Adventures of the Man in Gold: Paths Between Art and Life: A Philosophical Tale*," *Newsletter of the American Society for Aesthetics*, vol. 38, no. 2 (Summer 2018), 5 (https://cdn.ymaws.com/aestheticsonline.org/resource/resmgr/newsletters/38.2.pdf). I will leave it to the two artists to describe the Man in Gold's marvelous adventures in their art world.

43 Ibid., 84.

44 Shusterman, *Adventures*, 8.

FIGURE 5 Yann Toma, *Somaflux with Richard Shusterman performing as the Man in Gold: The Lion's Altar.* Hirtshals, North Jutland, Denmark, 2014
PHOTO COURTESY OF YANN TOMA AND RICHARD SHUSTERMAN

In his alter ego of the Man in Gold, Shusterman simply *is* the artwork, created with the assistance of Toma the "midwife" photographer. But *why* he is the Man in Gold, and how the Man in Gold experiences the world through the philosopher, Shusterman cannot say. These things lie beyond the reach of reason.

As an artist myself, it is spellbinding to read the philosopher's tale, observing how fluidly Shusterman slides into and out of his two personas, Shusterman the philosopher, and the Man in Gold, their realities, and their different ways of being in the same world. I say "as an artist" because I find it easy to identify with these two modes of aesthetic experience, namely, finding inspiration in a feeling of being possessed, as if by a spirit that takes control of me as an instrument for the creation of art. Somehow, the artwork seems to know more than I, and so much more that sometimes it can take years to understand what that artwork wanted to convey through me. This kind of experience of becoming an "instrument" or "channel" of art, and an attendant feeling of "divine inspiration," are not easy things to explain; and explanations are not always welcome subjects in our rational world.[45]

---

45   Ibid., 14.

In thinking back on the Man in Gold's wonderful visit, I remember one particular summer day in our garden. I had been watching Richard and Yann engaged in a photography shoot. The photographer with his dynamic energy prepared his camera and lighting while the philosopher quietly disappearing into himself and preparing to change his identity into the Man in Gold. Soon they began to move in synchronicity, a kind of dance and performance, the Man in Gold in his performance before the camera, and the photographer in his own dynamic performance before the subject. The Man in Gold would leap and then strike a pose, holding it perfectly motionless, while the photographer would focus his camera, and then quickly whirl about his subject, tracing the aura of the Man in Gold with golden light.[46] The photographical performance appeared to be very intense and seemingly physically exhausting. Eventually they had to take a break.

Searching for a place to rest, the Man in Gold found a giant, flat, granite slab in our carving yard, still warm from summer sun. Upon touching the textured surface of the granite slab, the Man in Gold felt a warm surge of magical energy and stretched out upon it to rest in rejuvenate (Figure 5).[47] The slab later became one of a number of slabs that Claus used in his sculptured public square titled *Small Tectonic Space*, located by the sea in Hirtshals, not far from where we live. Claus likes to invite people to use the giant granite composition as a place to rest, play, or reflect (Figure 6).

We live in the far north of Denmark, with all its wild and windy weather. In sculpting the square, Claus sought to give expression to this area of the north, by shape and texture of the granite, and the natural play of darkness and light on the stone. As Claus writes,

> The sea and nature around Hirtshals demands interaction between mighty forces. The sculpture writhes in baroque fierceness and after dark, the over 400 tons of granite plates float on light while smoke seeps out between the cracks. In principle, the square is one slab of granite, which the sculptor has cleaved into 44 pieces. The benches have been pressed into undulating motion from whole oak planks.[48]

Shusterman describes Claus in the *Adventures* both as King of Mighty Stones and as the Magical Master of Lions. He is Magical Master of Lions because he sculpted from granite three lions for the Queen of Denmark. In presenting

---

46 *Ibid.*, 82.
47 *Ibid.*, 106; photograph on 108–109.
48 Claus Ørntoft, *Skulpturelle rum* (Sculptural Spaces, 2019), 4.

THE GOLDEN TURN IN SHUSTERMAN'S SOMAESTHETICS 199

FIGURE 6   Claus Ørntoft, *Small Tectonic Space*. Granite slabs and sculpture are floating on light and smoke after dark. Hirtshals, North Jutland, Denmark, 2016
PHOTO COURTESY OF EIGIL KIRKEGAARD

the lions to the Queen, at an unveiling entitled *Three Lions and Nine Hearts* (May 2013), Claus's speech described the different phases of his creative process, and how in sculpting the lions he bore always in mind the involvement of nature and the viewer (Figure 7), which are also essential elements in Richard Shusterman's philosophy of art. Claus writes (here translated from the Danish):

> The Queen asked me to look at the park before we met for the first time. Her Majesty was concerned that the solution be site specific. That it wasn't just something that looked as if it had simply fallen out of the sky, but related to the site in terms of its content as well as architectonically. That is just up my street! I walked around the park and pondered. Seeing as it was the Queen who had approached me, I thought a lion would be fitting. The figure of the lion has always been a feature of my production, because I have always been interested in the Romanesque stonemasons who built the early granite churches in Denmark and used the Animal as Emblem and Animal as Narrative. Those stonemasons had never seen a

lion before, but they understood the tale of the strongest animal, powerful and difficult to control. It is protective, as we can see in baptismal fonts, but also with great powers that one had to be wary of. I kept circling around the theme of the lion—and SAW a lion standing abandoned in the large—in inverted commas—empty, park space. I looked at other possible solutions, but the idea of the lion kept resurfacing without any obvious way that I could use it. Then I realized that there are actually three lions in the Royal Coat of Arms. I suddenly saw a simple solution that would fulfill all the requirements: The solution would have a clear relationship to the location and, within the coat of arms, which I had taken as my starting point, had free movement, both in terms of content as well as architectonically. The lions occupy the area in front of the palace with ease, and make it their territory. They create direction in the space and the spaces in between them without actually touching the park. Thus, the three lions have leapt out of the coat of arms in a free interpretation. The hearts are scattered around them and create an oblique reference to the coat of arms. And there are also three lions on the palace's gable! When I got the idea, I thought that it would be three triumphant lions that occupied the park and that it would be easy! But when I went from idea to process, I quickly realized that creating triumphant lions was an impossible task, because in my world it would represent perfection and would become a postulate. And that it thus had to be a process towards triumph. Later in the process I realized that these are three lions in the midst of a process.[49]

Both Claus's lions and my sculptures of the human body and boats form central parts of Shusterman's last chapter, "The Magic Vessels of the Viking Queen." My sculpture of a nude woman, in fact, is also a crucial character in the *Adventures*, because she is the woman with whom the Man in Gold falls in love.[50] In the tale, she is Wanmei, a Chinese goddess. In creating her, I have wondered often who she is, but, like Claus and like Shusterman himself, consider the viewer of the artwork to complete it. At our home, once Shusterman had metamorphosed into the Man in Gold, he too was now a work of art, but

---

49 Ørntoft, *Three Lions and Nine Hearts* (I/S Stenshede, 2013), richly illustrated. The speech was given for the unveiling of the sculptures in May 2013, 5–7. See also in the same book articles by Claus Ørntoft, ("The process—sketches and models"), Birgit Jenvold ("About the exhibitions"), and Else Marie Bukdahl ("To see a World in a Grain of Sand").
50 Shusterman, *Adventures*, 1.

FIGURE 7   Claus Ørntoft, *Three Lions and Nine Hearts*, 2012. Granite, Marselisborg Palace Park, Aarhus, Jutland
PHOTO COURTESY OF CLAUS ØRNTOFT

a work of art who was also a viewer of art, and one who felt deeply for this particular sculpture. Through the Man in Gold, and through Shusterman's tale, I came to know her better, the sculpture, I mean, and something perhaps of her background in Asia and fiction.

As a child I lived in India. I started school in Norway at the age of seven. But by then, I was convinced that I was half Indian. I had so many stories to tell. My experiences of the world were not those of Norway. This division, I suspect, and this need to narrate one half of my mind to the other, and the other to the first, would form me as an artist and a story teller, from a very early age. Later in life, I see the many ways Asian societies cherish public spaces, as places to gather and eat and share their experiences. That love of open public spaces has stayed with me over the years and continues to shape the way I think about art, and the kinds of sculptures I create. In that respect, and I suspect many others, my sculptures and boats, although made in Denmark and residing there are also very Asian.[51]

The concept of passage, or travel, often between two very distant places, is also essential to my work. I suspect my own inner division informs this aspect of passage and distance as well, just as certain divisions and experimental syntheses seems to inform Shusterman's philosophical explorations in the *Adventures*. He too is divided: one the one hand, he is a philosopher of art who travels widely; on the other hand, he is an artist and a work of art, who also travels widely in his many adventures. The theme of mobility, or travel, appears in several of my sculptures, and in each of them I continue to see and feel representations of emotions. I see in my boats representations of the emotions because emotions themselves are so mobile: they arrive and they depart and they make their presence felt in such powerful ways, like ships coming to land, and leaving again; or like automobiles that drive past us, seemingly driving through us, often slowly, sometimes fast, and often with great size and force. But not always do emotions rush past us and through us; and not always do they arrive without warning. Sometimes we seem to know they are coming; we can even "see" them coming on the horizon. Sometimes we are able to prepare ourselves and "climb into them," as it were, never in full control, but at least partly directing their course; sometimes we are able to take the helm and sail, and through such sailing we feel free.

---

51   Marit Benthe Norheim, "*A Sailing Sculptural Installation with Direct Social Participation, Artistic Exchange and Incorporated Music, Journal of Urban Culture Research,* published jointly by Chulalongkorn University, Thailand, and Osaka City University, Japan, vol. 7 (2013), 79.

FIGURE 8   Marit Benthe Norheim, *Life-boats*. Three sailing sculptures in ferrocement, 2017
            PHOTO COURTESY OF CLAUS ØRNTOFT

In the *Adventures* the Man in Gold is a deeply emotional being, and in the last chapter of the work he climbs upon, and into, the "Magic Vessels of the Viking Queen," which he experiences as vessels for feeling strong and unique emotions. I call the vessels *Life-boats*. They are sculptural installations in ferrocement, designed to invite and engage direct social participation and artistic exchange; and they incorporate music by composer Geir Johnson (Figure 8).[52] The three Life-boats are sailing sculptures. They are CE certified canal boats and they are and seaworthy: they sail with captains and crews. Their subject matter is a three-part portrait of women, in different universal stages and conditions (young womanhood, pregnancy, and old age).[53]

52 Else Marie Bukdahl analyzed the relation between Shusterman's somaesthetics and the projects of Marit Benthe Norheim in several articles including *The Camping Women* and *The Life Boats*. See her article "New Visual Dialogues and New Art Projects with a Social and Melioristic Goal in the Urban Space and at Sea," *Journal of Urban Culture Research*, published jointly by Chulalongkorn University in Thailand and Osaka City University, Japan, vol. 8 (Jan.–June 2014), 73–77.
53 Ann-Dorte Christensen and Marit Benthe Norheim, *A Shipload of Women's Memories, Narratives across Borders* (Aalborg: Aalborg University Press, 2017), 113.

In cities where they dock, the public can board the three Life-boats and experience the installations from the inside. The insides of the Life-boats are artistically designed, and nautical in nature. From the outside of each Life-boat, and from the inside, one sees and learns of each of the three women's identity, her narrative. Each is woman is titled, or subtitled, with a kind of name, drawn from the indoor word-identification game called "My ship is loaded with ..."

> *My ship is loaded with Memories*—the aging woman floats on her stomach with her rear end making up the cabin. She carries 19 figureheads on her back which are emblematic portraits of living women over the age of 70 who have in common that they come from different cultures and have related to other cultures than their own.
>
> *My ship is loaded with Life*—the pregnant woman floats on her back with her stomach as the cabin. Her interior will be filled with self-portraits drawn directly on the walls.
>
> *My ship is loaded with Longing*—the young woman lies on her side, with her hip as the cabin and with a treasure chest decorated with pearls and glass into which people can post letters describing their hopes, dreams and longing. The three *Life-boats* are always sailing together.

My ship is loaded with Longing was the first ship finished. It was resting outside my studio when the Man in Gold climbed aboard and into her hull, followed by the photographer, exploring her entire bodily form. At the time, I was still in the process of creating *My ship is loaded with Life*. The Man in Gold climbed aboard this ship too, still in roughly modelled concrete sculpture. The photographer was there too and delighted in photographing the Man in Gold upon the woman ship, playing with the proportions of a giant grey rock woman and a comparatively small golden man (Figure 9).

As I beheld the Man in Gold inside the giant woman, I considered then, as I had considered in creating the Life-boat, how each human being is created inside a woman. In forming a woman of vast size and power, seaworthy and capable of carrying many human beings, I reflected on how we are all very much the same kind of being; and in seeing the Man in Gold inside this woman, I saw him too as one of us, a physical being made from a physical being, despite descriptions of the mind as detached from the body in much of western philosophy, and which Shusterman has sought to overcome throughout his writings. But in observing the Man in Gold, I also saw a being who unlike us, a man, a philosopher, an artist, but also a living work of art, a being who was, in some sense, a living and glowing sculpture. Perhaps that partly explains

FIGURE 9   Yann Toma, *Somaflux with Richard Shusterman performing as the Man in Gold: Ship of Longing*, 2014
PHOTO COURTESY OF YANN TOMA AND RICHARD SHUSTERMAN

his powerful attraction to one of my sculptures of women, a nude slightly smaller than the size of the Man in Gold. I sculpted her at the Norwegian Art Academy while a student. I had been experimenting with the transparency of the material, thinking of this transparency as representative of her fragility. When the Man in Gold found her near the end of the corridor of the studio, along one of the back rows, Toma was there to photograph the interaction, man and woman, darkness and light, life and art, sculpture and performance, stillness and motion, all complementing one another.[54] With Toma's lighting, the sculpture's golden aura glowed, and as it glowed so too did the aura of the Man in Gold, and soon they melted together, the Man in Gold and the woman he would name "Wanmei" (Figure 10).[55] The nature of their attraction was somewhat mysterious, but perhaps not entirely. As Shusterman writes in the *Adventures*, "The Man in Gold fears being misunderstood, not only because

---

54   Shusterman, *Adventures*, 112.
55   See photographs of Wanmei in Shusterman's *Adventures*, 115–116, and front cover.

FIGURE 10 Yann Toma, *Somaflux with Richard Shusterman performing as the Man in Gold: The Look of Love*, 2014
PHOTO COURTESY OF YANN TOMA AND RICHARD SHUSTERMAN

misunderstandings spur the scorn of rejection, but also because they betray and sully the love that is his hope and mission."[56] In Wanmei, the Man in Gold, a man and artwork, felt he was truly loved and understood, and he too felt that he truly understood and loved the artwork and woman Wanmei.

9 The Birth of a New Artwork and New Literary Work

I, Else Marie, return now to give not only a very short description of the *Adventures* as a philosophical tale but also concluding remarks about the birth of a new artwork and a new literary work. Shusterman has called the *Adventures* a philosophical tale and there is a parallel to the long history in the literary world. But he does not use the works of his predecessors as models. Rather, they can be considered earlier parallels to his book in Voltaire's philosophical tale *Candide* (1759), Diderot's *Rameau's Nephew* (1761–62), and Milan Kundera's

---

56 Shusterman, *Adventures*, 64.

Identity: A Novel (1998). As in Shusterman's book, there are continuous transitions between the real and the fictional world that reveal general philosophical issues.[57]

In his intense encounter with the world of visual art and particularly his impressive performances as the Man in Gold, Shusterman has provided new conditions for solving fundamental relations between existential and aesthetic questions. In Yann Toma's magical photos, performances, and films, which are characterized by highly evocative artistic qualities, the Man in Gold has succeeded in revealing these new conditions. When encountering the Man in Gold in the glittering appearance, one is reminded of Shakespeare's famous words, "We are such stuff as dreams are made on," because dream and reality are interwoven in the adventures of this fictional magical figure. Through his rhythmical, nonverbal body language, he has opened numerous doors to a new understanding of artistic creation, the connection between art and life and the body-mind relation. The Man in Gold has succeeded in what Rainer Maria Rilke calls bringing "into *oeuvre* the form of things whose seal has not been broken."[58]

The *Adventures*—an original version of a philosophical tale—proves that Shusterman has become an "an excellent writer of poetic prose."[59] The many often surprising transitions in the book between the real and the fictional world reveal new developments of key issues in his somaesthetics, among others his concept of body-mind awareness, the difference between the language of form and verbal language, and the very intense active relationship between the

---

57   The adventures of the Voltaire's fictional character Candide also contain real events like the disastrous year of 1755 combined with basic existential conditions. But contrary to Shusterman, Voltaire created his philosophical tale as a consistently humorous and ironic tale that expresses philosophical views, particularly the view that this world is not the best of all possible worlds. The *Adventures* also contains parallels to Diderot's *Rameau's Nephew*. This work is a fictional and humorous philosophical conversation between Diderot (not in fact Diderot himself, but with some elements from his life) and the famous composer Rameau's nephew (a fictional figure, but with some traits from the real world), which also makes continuous transitions between the real and the fictional world, revealing general philosophical issues. Diderot's work is a richly faceted fictional critique of those who argued against the Enlightenment. Milan Kundera's *Identity: A Novel* is a modern philosophical tale that also has certain features in common with the *Adventures*. Like Shusterman, Kundera blends reality, fantasy, satire and philosophy and confronts the reader in a different way with a large range of questions about our identity, which is indeed a central theme of the *Adventures*.

58   Quoted by Merleau-Ponty in *The Primacy of Perception* (Evanston: Northwestern University Press, 1964), 188.

59   Stefán Snævarr, "Shusterman and the Man in Gold," *The Nordic Journal of Aesthetics*, no. 54 (2017), 92.

viewer and the artwork. Shusterman has succeeded in bringing the biographical, philosophical, and fictional parts of the *Adventures* into a narrative and stylistic unity, in which the photos of the magical recreation of the Man in Gold's performances visualize how bodily interaction with the surrounding world creates new somaesthetic experiences and new meaning. The Man in Gold's unpredictable experiences in the enchanted experiential visual space created by Yann Toma's magical photographic tools have been transformed in the *Adventures* into a literary, philosophical, and poetic world that inspires us to think, feel, and create in new ways.

CHAPTER 11

On Shusterman's Somaesthetic Practice: The Case of the Man in Gold

Yang Lu

1   Who Is the Man in Gold?

Who is the Man in Gold? Is there any relation between *The Adventures of the Man in Gold* and literary classics such as *The Adventures of Tom Sawyer, The Adventures of Huckleberry Finn*, or *The Adventures of Tintin*? As the Chinese translator of this fantastic reflection of Richard Shusterman's own performative experience of somaesthetics, I begin my answer with the beginning of my encounter with this work. It was in May 2017, at a somaesthetics symposium hosted by Fudan University, Shanghai, after Shusterman had delivered his keynote speech with its introduction of his newly published book *The Adventures of the Man in Gold* to his Chinese audience, that I spoke with the philosopher of somaesthetics whom I had admired for many years. The work is an adventure of a mature individual, Shusterman explained to me, a work about a person who is mature in both his mind and body, but who remains in many aspects innocent and misunderstood, in some ways similar to Antoine de Saint-Exupéry's *The Little Prince*.[1] Moreover, Shusterman continued, there is an extraterrestrial aura to the Man in Gold, because of his extraordinary golden skin and strange behavior that recalls the Little Prince's unearthly existence.

The comparison of the Man in Gold and the Little Prince attracted me. For Shusterman's book portrays how performative art conducted by an accomplished philosopher can initiate philosophical contemplation on how to return to our original, more innocent nature. That same evening, under the starry night sky, gazing through the huge glass vault of the university tower's coffee shop, we had a friendly conversation about childhood and literature. Many children think and dream about the Little Prince, and many adults continue to think and dream about children's literary genres like fairytales. Shusterman referenced the famous Danish writer Hans Christian Andersen, whose children's stories include "The Little Mermaid," "The Emperor's New

---

1   Antoine de Saint-Exupéry, *The Little Prince* (New York: Reynal & Hitchcock, 1943).

Clothes," and "The Golden Treasure." That Danish connection helps explain why in 2013, three years after the birth of the Man in Gold, Shusterman as Visiting Professor at Denmark's Aalborg University, invited his friend the photographer Yann Toma to join him in the northern tip of Denmark to photograph another performance of the Man in Gold. Shusterman wanted to continue there his explorations of the experiences of the Man in Gold in photographic images, and the idea of the Man in Gold as expressing philosophy without words. Philosophy, said Shusterman, could communicate through storytelling and images rather than in abstract metaphysical discourse dictated from commanding elitist heights. Philosophy, Shusterman continued, could then be brought closer to a more popular readership in the manner of Saint-Exupéry's *Little Prince*. The result was Shusterman's *The Adventures of the Man in Gold* whose title and spirit recall Mark Twain's *The Adventures of Tom Sawyer* and *The Adventures of Huckleberry Finn*, and George Remi's *Adventures of Tintin* as well.

2   The Abbey in France

Prior to the "birth" of the Man in Gold, and the book that records his adventures, it has not been at all unusual for performative art to constantly seek out variety in fantastic new forms. Yet it is indeed extraordinary for a distinguished philosopher to put himself in a golden body stocking and inhabit an "extraterrestrial" character to engage in a continuous artistic performance, which also reveals a strangely "other" identity. It was in the summer of 2010, as Shusterman writes in the *Adventures*, that he met Toma at the famous Royaumont Abbey, not far from Paris, where the Man in Gold was born. In the *Adventures* Shusterman writes of his deep appreciation for the beauty of the Abbey, with its austere, medieval, Cistercian buildings, and his admiration for the Abbey's more recent devotion to the arts and sciences, having over the years hosted many important intellectual and artistic events. As Shusterman notes, in this very Abbey, Continental and Anglo-American philosophers have met to try to reconcile or overcome their deep divergences. And it is here, appropriately, for a philosopher steeped in both Anglo-American and Continental philosophy, that Shusterman donned the golden body stocking, worn by Toma's parents in the Paris Opera, and Toma set up his camera and lighting equipment to photograph the transformation of Shusterman into the Man in Gold using the photographer's distinct auratic lighting effects. Shusterman himself, however, did not, at the time, understand that the shooting would turn out to be quite so dramatic. As Shusterman recalls in the *Adventures*,

> I was expecting to be photographed in my own clothes, but Yann had other ideas: he pulled out a plastic bag with a pair of identical glittering gold body stockings and asked me to put one on. They were, he explained, costumes used by his parents who, in the 1970s, had starred in the Paris Opera Ballet.[2]

Shusterman looked at the body stocking and wondered: How could his 60 year-old philosopher's body get into this glitzy skintight garment? Half-hoping that the bodysuit would not fit, Shusterman discovered, surprisingly, it fit him well. After some hours of motionless posing in their third session in a dark chamber in one of the Abbey's wings, Shusterman found himself seized by an irresistible urge to burst into movement. He shot through the chamber's door and ran down a long corridor leading into the Abbey courtyard. Shusterman the philosopher, inside a glittering gold body stocking, had begun metamorphosing, mysteriously, into another kind of man, one no longer satisfied to pose in a dark, hidden room, or to submit to confinement and or the manipulation of others. Now, he sought to go forward, to adventure in the world, perhaps not unlike Shusterman himself, the globetrotting philosopher. After wandering the grounds, the man in the golden body stocking returned to the private wing where invited guests at the Abbey were having lunch on the terrace. When the Abbey's owner exclaimed in surprise, "L'homme en Or!" which is French for "The Man in Gold!" the new man had been given a new name, a titular name, that then and still distinguishes the Man in Gold from Shusterman the academic philosopher.

3   Private Redemption

Shusterman decided to publish the *Adventures* in France, and in both English and French, because of the Man in Gold's French origin. The French publisher of the book asked Shusterman to add a Preface to serve as a philosophical introduction, because Shusterman was known as a philosopher not a fiction writer or performance artist. In the Preface, Shusterman points out that the *Adventures*, which contains color photographs, intertwines the detailed narration of a Western philosopher with the unique unearthly vision of the Man in Gold and its ineffable Daoist mysteries. Moreover, beyond its philosophical,

---

2 Richard Shusterman, *The Adventures of the Man in Gold: Paths Between Art and Life* (Paris: Éditions Hermann, 2016), 21.

literary, and aesthetic aims, the *Adventures* is a deeply personal effort at redemption through art, for the moral flaws and failures and regrets of the philosopher. Shusterman frankly explains how his painful moral lapse, which involved a photography session, came to function for him as a lesson in the power of photography, and as a stimulus to atone for his failing through photographic art. The lapse

> involved an odd episode in September 2009 that initially seemed insignificant but proved life-changing. As the sun began to set after a long romantic afternoon, the bewitching woman in my company confessed (perhaps to further enchant me) that though she admired my aesthetics more than any contemporary alternative, there was something it sorely lacked: the artist's perspective. Like most philosophy of art, my theory, she rightly remarked, was totally dominated by the observer's or interpreter's point of view. My aesthetics would be more complete by including also the artist's experience. ... I acknowledged the truth of her critique. But how could I achieve the artist's perspective, I asked, having no artistic training? Her almond eyes sparkled mischievously as she handed me her camera, opened her white shirt and lay back on the bed, her naked chest half-exposed. 'Take a few shots of me like this; do your artistic best; and I'll then give you instructional critique. If the images are good enough, I'll let you keep the best one as a keepsake and inspiration to go further in adopting the artist's perspective.' Inept and inexperienced with cameras, I did not even use the proper settings and ended up taking a few short video clips rather than stills. After reviewing for me their merits, she selected one and, as promised, uploaded it to my computer.[3]

Shusterman forgot about the video clip in his computer, until his wife accidently discovered it weeks later. A good marriage was unhappily undone. By openly recounting his transgression, Shusterman expresses his regret to the wife he loved, who is also the mother of their beloved child, who remains the apple of the philosopher's eye. Among all the other factors described in the Preface as inspiring the *Adventures*—e.g., the question of how somaesthetics applies to contemporary art, the exciting experience of collaborating with Toma, and the desire to see aesthetics from the point of view of the artist—Shusterman's confession is especially instructive for understanding the allegorical meaning of the story of the Man in Gold. For the work is not only a pragmatist's philosophical

---

3 Shusterman, *The Adventures of the Man in Gold*, 10–11.

demonstration of how somaesthetics can transcend the academy and enter the world of performative art; *The Adventures of the Man in Gold* is also a quest for atonement and redemption, a philosopher's quest for self-knowledge and self-improvement by exposing his flaws before the world.

4   Shusterman and Merleau-Ponty

According to Shusterman, his somaesthetics is different in three ways from phenomenologies like Maurice Merleau-Ponty's developed in *Phenomenology of Perception*, in which the body also forms a central perspective that structures the philosophical system and is celebrated as a sentient, purposive and skilled subjectivity. As Shusterman writes in *Thinking through the Body: Essays in Somaesthetics*,

> First, rather than seeking to reveal an alleged primordial, foundational, and universal embodied consciousness that (in Merleau-Ponty's words) is 'unchanging, given once and for all,' and 'known by all men' in all cultures and times, I claim that somatic consciousness is always shaped by culture and thus admits of different forms in different cultures (or in different subject positions within the same culture). Second, somaesthetics is interested not merely in describing our culturally shaped forms of somatic consciousness and modes of somatic practice, but also in improving them. Third, to effect such improvements, it also includes practical exercises of somatic training rather mere philosophical discourse.[4]

In short, for Shusterman, somaesthetics is more than the theoretical affirmation of the significant role the body plays in all perception. Somaesthetics is a practical philosophy for developing the body to become what it is and can be. In addition to writing and lecturing on somaesthetics, Shusterman's many practical body consciousness workshops, given all over the world, initiate, guide, and cultivate, personal somaesthetic practice and performance.

Already in the late 1990s, Shusterman wrote about the radical implications of the new media age. A most surprising and contradictory phenomenon in this age, he says, is the heightened concern for the body when its actual presence seems no longer so necessary for communication because of our developed

---

4   Shusterman, *Thinking through the Body: Essays in Somaesthetics* (Cambridge: Cambridge University Press, 2012), 4.

telecommunications. "One striking paradox of our new media age is its heightened concentration on the body," writes Shusterman in "Somaesthetics and the Body/Media Issue." "As telecommunications render bodily presence unnecessary, while new technologies of mediatic body construction and plastic cyborg-surgery challenge the very presence of a real body, our culture seems increasingly fixated on the soma, serving it with the adoring devotion once bestowed on other worshipped mysteries."[5] It is no wonder, then, in our modern metropolitan culture, that fitness centers are replacing churches and museums as places we go for edification, if not salvation. For the philosopher behind the Man in Gold, the phenomenon of contemporary culture's fixation on the body requires extended philosophical critique—not to deny the importance of embodiment, but to redirect our efforts of somatic cultivation toward more productive, healthier, and democratic ways.

5 Body Consciousness

In *Body Consciousness* Shusterman provides an etymological explanation of the word "somaesthetics."

> The term 'soma' indicates a living, feeling, sentient body rather than a mere physical body that could be devoid of life and sensation, while 'aesthetic' in somaesthetics has the dual role of emphasizing the soma's perceptual role (whose embodied intentionality contradicts the body/mind dichotomy) and its aesthetic use both in stylizing one's self and in appreciating the aesthetic qualities of other selves and things.[6]

This is rather a modest interpretation of the meaning "somaesthetics." Shusterman is fully aware of the resistance his somaesthetic theory may encounter, and which it has already encountered. As Shusterman himself has said, why advocate any more attention to body consciousness? Is not our culture already suffering too much from a monstrously overgrown body consciousness which even infects fields like philosophy, which traditionally are devoted to the mind? Furthermore, as Shusterman admits, thanks to the information revolution, today we are surrounded by increasing signs, images, and simulacra. Why,

---

5   Shusterman, *Performing Live: Aesthetic Alternatives for the Ends of Art* (Ithaca: Cornell University Press, 2000), 137.
6   Shusterman, *Body Consciousness: A Philosophy of Mindfulness and Somaesthetics* (Cambridge: Cambridge University Press, 2008), 1–2.

then, should we devote our limited attention to our own somatic experience? Isn't it better to let our body be as it is and act as it does, without the guidance of somaesthetic discipline or theory or other forms of critical reflection?

Shusterman, however, endeavors to prove that the "soma" in somaesthetics refers not merely to body as flesh, but also to embodied subjectivity with mental and even spiritual life. To the posed questions above, Shusterman replies that the soma (properly understood) constitutes the foundation, or core, of our human identities. The soma not only forms the first perspective and medium for our interaction with the world, but also, by constructing needs, habits, interests, pleasures, and capacities, determines our fundamental choices of goals and methods, even if they may appear in one's unconscious behavior. The process of somaesthetic cultivation includes the construction of spiritual life as well, although not in the sense of the disembodied spirit of the traditional mind/body dualism. As Shusterman writes in *Body Consciousness*,

> If (in Husserl's words) 'the Body is ... the medium of all perception,' then body consciousness surely warrants cultivating, not only to improve its perceptual acuity and savor the satisfactions it offers but also to address philosophy's core injunction to 'know thyself,' which Socrates adopted from Apollo's temples at Delphi to initiate and inspire his founding philosophical quest.[7]

Here Shusterman indicates that the body (or what he designates as the soma) is not only an object we perceive in the world, but also the subjective sensibility that perceives and experiences that world. This idea of the soma provides the key to understanding Shusterman's own somaesthetic practice, in its various forms and disciplines.

6 Shusterman and the Man in Gold

The performative artistic practice of the philosopher is far from a simple journey. In the *Adventures* Shusterman relates how the Man in Gold caused him to be censured and almost arrested. Waiting with his nine-year old daughter at

---

[7] Shusterman, *Body Consciousness*, 3. Shusterman references Edmund Husserl's *Ideas Pertaining to a Pure Phenomenology and to a Phenomenological Philosophy*, Second Book: *Studies in the Phenomenology of Constitution*, tr. R. Rojcewicz and A. Schuwer (Dordrecht: Kluwer, 1990). Here Husserl writes: "The Body is, in the first place, the *medium of all perception*; it is the *organ of perception* and is *necessarily* involved in all perception" (61).

New York's LaGuardia airport on their way to board a flight to Montreal, they were looking at some unedited digital files of the Man in Gold's Royaumont adventures. Suddenly a stern-looking female TSA security guard approached them and told the philosopher to close his laptop immediately, because she believed he was showing pornographic images. Shusterman attempted to explain that the images were artistic and involved no nudity or lewd gestures at all, and that the child was his own beloved daughter. But none of it helped. The TSA security guard threatened the philosopher to say that if he did not remove the material straightaway, she would call the police to arrest him. The incident provoked in Shusterman abiding fears not only about how the Man in Gold would be received, but also how the Man in Gold would affect the reputation and image of the philosopher whose body he inhabited. If a New York City airport refused to tolerate the Man in Gold, and saw him as disturbed, then what anger or violence would he provoke in places far more culturally conservative? As Shusterman continues in the *Adventures*,

> How sinister would I myself seem by my intimate bond with him? I needed to underline the distinction between myself and the Man in Gold, without denying our connection. In all future films of the Man in Gold my name is therefore omitted from the title to indicate that the adventures are those of the Man in Gold, even if the name of Richard Shusterman must appear somewhere in the credits. The Man in Gold has no identity papers; he has no nationality. A citizen of no country on earth, he may be regarded in some sense as extraterrestrial.[8]

What he writes here is more a lamentation than a philosophical argument. Shusterman apparently prefers to keep a certain distance from the Man in Gold, even though the Man in Gold inhabits Shusterman's body. This preference or attitude seems to derive from two reasons. One is a worry that too close an identification with the bizarre and unconventional Man in Gold will spoil Shusterman's philosophical reputation and what remains of his family life. The other is that a separation with the Man in Gold allows Shusterman to maintain his separate identity as the narrator of the tale of a strangely wordless, sensitive philosopher-alien so that he is able to construct an adult philosophical fairytale about him, one resembling that of the Little Prince. The Man in Gold appears as an individual who emerges on the scene as an enigmatic figure who

---

8   Shusterman, *The Adventures of the Man in Gold*, 40–42. The phrase "future films" in this quotation refers to films following Shusterman's first film entitled *A Night with Richard Shusterman* (2010).

seems to descend to this planet from another world, and nowhere seems to find in our world the same beauty and love that he desperately seeks. Instead, the Man in Gold typically encounters misunderstanding and aggressive taunting, which cause him to flee instantly in fear. These oppositional poles of what he seeks and what he fears create the essential tension of his character and the underlying engine of the narrative of his adventures.

7 Daoism and the Man in Gold

Shusterman admits that his book the *Adventures* is influenced by Daoist philosophy. In fact, five times in the text of the *Adventures* Shusterman cites the teachings of Laozi, the ancient Chinese philosopher. From these words of Laozi, Shusterman draws a powerful conclusion: "In the union of the world, the female always gets the better of the male by stillness."[9] For Laozi, the founder of Daoism, the Dao constitutes the absolute beginning of the universe in that all beings have causes and conditions that must derive from a necessary foundation. However, this foundation of being cannot be itself a being. Therefore, the Dao that can be talked about is not the true, constant Dao; and the name with which it can be named cannot be its true and constant name. With the couplet expressing this idea, Laozi begins his five thousand words *Dao de Jing*, two thousand six hundred years ago. For Shusterman, the fact that the Man in Gold does not utter words, does not affirm philosophical propositions, reveals a Daoist wisdom. In the words of Laozi, cited in introducing the Man in Gold and his mysterious birth, "One who knows does not speak; one who speaks does not know."[10] "If the Man in Gold sometimes communicates his thoughts through Richard Shusterman," writes the author, "[Shusterman] feels both difficulty and reluctance to translate those thoughts into words." In short, although Shusterman admires and perhaps prefers to be a philosopher without words, like the Man in Gold, yet he remains needful of words to tell the story of his hero's adventures. In this way, the fictional tale of the Man in Gold—because it is based on real performances, with and of the body of the philosopher—combines with the book's confessional Preface to suggest a paradox that seems to haunt philosophy in all its literary forms. On the one hand, lies philosophy's performative helplessness to faithfully capture nonverbal factual reality through verbal representations. But, on the other hand, this

---

9   Laozi, *Tao de Ching*, tr. D. C. Lau (London: Penguin, 1963), Ch. 61. See Shusterman, *The Adventures of the Man in Gold*, 114.
10 Shusterman, *The Adventures of the Man in Gold*, 19.

very helplessness and mediating veil of words reveals (albeit through creative fictions) a more captivating and insightfully meaningful interpretive vision of the real. If this complexity implies a fundamental, dialectical tension in philosophy, then might it suggest a way of interpreting the dialectic of theory and practice in somaesthetics?

CHAPTER 12

Somaesthetics and Cinema: The Man in Gold in the Film *Walk the Golden Night*

Jerold J. Abrams

> Photography is truth. And cinema is truth at twenty four frames per second.
> JEAN-LUC GODARD, *Le Petit Soldat* (1963)

∴

1   Introduction

Richard Shusterman's book *The Adventures of the Man in Gold: Paths Between Art and Life, a Philosophical Tale* is a rich experimental work of somaesthetics and philosophy of photography. Shusterman narrates the work in English, French, and Chinese, as a literary autobiography of his adventures performing live as the character known as "the Man in Gold." Paris photographer Yann Toma records these adventures in full color somaflux photographs of the Man in Gold in Europe and South America, which appear throughout the text. These adventures along "paths between art and life" transform art into life, and life into art; while also transforming philosophy into photography, and photography into philosophy; all within "a philosophical tale," which is both fictional and nonfictional, and an exploration of the relation between fiction and nonfiction. As an exploration of the relations and limits of these spheres, the *Adventures* also travels a recursive path, a path back into itself, by raising philosophical questions about itself. As a strange and difficult-to-categorize hybrid of philosophy, still photography, cinema, sculpture, drawing, architecture, autobiography, performance art, science fiction, and detective mystery, the sheer internal diversity and complexity of the *Adventures* inevitably raises the question of philosophical self-consciousness, of what kind of work it is.

While on location in Cartagena, Columbia, Toma and Shusterman also shot a short, silent, color, moving picture of the Man in Gold entitled *Walk the Golden Night* (2011), a still from which also appears in the *Adventures*, along

© JEROLD J. ABRAMS, 2022 | DOI:10.1163/9789004468801_014

with stills from Toma's films *Château* (2010), *A Night with Richard Shusterman* (2010), and *Lights in the Dark* (2011). If the *Adventures* raises questions about itself as a work of philosophy, then *Walk the Golden Night* also seems to raise questions about itself as a film. But while the *Adventures* poses these questions from within the genre of science fiction, *Walk the Golden Night* seems to pose its own philosophical questions from within the genre of the detective mystery, in a tradition shaped very deeply by Orson Welles's *Citizen Kane* (1941). Like *Citizen Kane*, *Walk the Golden Night* is ambiguously a documentary and a feature fiction film, a detective's investigation into the life and mind of a mysterious man, pursued as a seemingly unknowable subject, and yet whose unknowable nature ultimately reflects the unknowability of every other individual, such as one watching the film. The answer to the question of the meaning of the last uttered word by Charles Foster Kane (Orson Welles), "Rosebud," is no more knowable than the mind of the Man in Gold who speaks no words at all, or the nature of the film, *Walk the Golden Night*. And yet, this very ambiguity of the film, *Walk the Golden Night*, as a detective mystery that inevitably points back into itself, and provides no ultimate resolution, also reveals the philosophical self-consciousness of the film, again, in the tradition of *Citizen Kane*, but also as an experimental and silent art film, in the tradition of Andy Warhol's *Empire* (1964).

2 The *Camera Obscura* and the Midwife Analogy

In the first chapter of the *Adventures*, "A Mysterious Birth," set in the Royaumont Abbey, Shusterman recalls "the Man in Gold's birth in a dark chamber of the abbey's institutional wings."[1] The birth of the "embryonic persona"[2] of the Man in Gold from a "dark chamber" suggests multiple meanings. First, biologically, any man is born of the "dark chamber" of a womb. Second, the imagery of a "dark chamber" also suggests a photographer's dark room. Third, the word "camera" descends from "*camera obscura*," which refers to devices that pass an image through a pinhole, and cast them onto an opposing plate where they appear upside down; and *camera obscura* is Latin for "dark chamber." So, the Man in Gold, born of a "dark chamber," would appear to be born *of* the camera, or born of the *camera obscura*. Of course, the Man in Gold does not appear

---

1 Richard Shusterman, *The Adventures of the Man in Gold: Paths Between Art and Life, A Philosophical Tale*, English and French, English to French translation by Thomas Mondémé, with Somaflux Photography by Yann Toma (Paris: Éditions Hermann, 2016), 17.
2 *Ibid.*, 20.

upside down in photographs in the text of the *Adventures*, or in the film *Walk the Golden Night*; he is not inverted like an image cast by a *camera obscura*. But a kind of inversion may be seen in the *Adventures* insofar as Toma as photographer appears to have passed Shusterman through a kind of philosophical *camera obscura* sufficient to invert the figure from a relatively detached and discursive scholar into a somaesthetically engaged and nondiscursive performing artform: namely, the Man in Gold.

Fourth, the Man in Gold is "conceived" within the chamber of Shusterman's mind, and the mind itself may be thought of as a "dark chamber" where thoughts are "born." From the dark chambers of the mind and the camera, within the dark chamber of the abbey, the philosopher "gives birth to himself" in the new and "fully adult form" of the Man in Gold. To "give birth to oneself" may seem bizarre, but, in fact, that image has a long tradition in philosophy.[3] For example, Heraclitus describes the universe both as a glowing "fire everliving" and a "child" that perpetually gives birth to itself.[4] Similarly, in Friedrich Nietzsche's philosophical novel, *Thus Spoke Zarathustra*, the character Zarathustra speaks of giving birth to himself as "a dancing star."[5] Synthesizing this tradition in new form, Shusterman in the *Adventures* speaks of himself as giving birth to himself as a "creature of light."[6] But even though he gives birth to himself as the Man in Gold, this birth requires a "midwife." "The crucial midwife for his birth was Yann Toma, who remains his ever-present companion and protector," writes Shusterman in the *Adventures*.[7] As the imagery of giving birth to oneself as a "creature of light" recasts imagery from Heraclitus and Nietzsche, the image of a "midwife" to a philosopher recasts Plato's midwife analogy from the *Theaetetus*. Socrates (whose mother was a midwife) is himself now kind of midwife: he is a philosophical midwife to young philosophers like Theaetetus who are "pregnant" with thought, which can only be delivered by philosophical dialogue.[8] As Socrates delivers thought by question and answer, the photographer Toma acts as midwife to deliver from the philosopher Richard Shusterman a new kind of art which is a synthesis of photography and philosophy. As Socrates, with a philosopher's discerning ear, listens to questions from

---

3 *Ibid.*, 18.
4 Heraclitus, Fr. XXXVII, in *The Art and Thought of Heraclitus*, ed. Charles H. Kahn (Cambridge: Cambridge University, 1979), 45.
5 Friedrich Nietzsche, *Thus Spoke Zarathustra*, tr. Walter Kaufmann (New York: The Modern Library, 1995), 12.
6 Shusterman, *Adventures*, 94.
7 *Ibid.*, 20.
8 Plato, *Theaetetus*, in *The Complete Works of Plato*, ed. John M. Cooper, assoc. ed. D. S. Hutchinson (Indianapolis: Hackett, 1997), 150a–151b, 167–168.

Theaetetus and guides him in the delivery of his thought, Toma, with a photographer's discerning eye, observes an emerging golden aura hovering about the philosopher. "With uncanny intuition," writes Shusterman, "Yann sensed a mysterious artistic form hovering as an energetic aura around Shusterman's nomadic soma and yearning to emerge in vivid bodily form."[9] Seeing the "energetic aura," Toma quickly prepares the camera in the dark chamber of the abbey for photographical delivery of the new form of art. Shusterman recalls the experience in the "delivery room."

> Yann guided the unsuspecting philosopher to the delivery room he prepared there and provided the birthing equipment: camera, lights, and body suit. His midwife role is mystically unending; for every time the Man in Gold comes to life, Yann must be there to provide his golden, energizing skin.[10]

The "golden, energizing skin" is one of two bodysuits originally worn by Toma's parents in the Paris Opera Ballet of the 1970s. Once inside the golden skin, one philosopher becomes another: the philosopher of art Richard Shusterman, who speaks and writes his philosophy, becomes the silent philosopher known as the Man in Gold, and whose philosophy is performed and experienced as a living work of art.[11]

Plato's midwife analogy from the *Theaetetus* also appears synthesized, within the *Adventures*, with his "myth of the metals" from the *Republic* III. Here Socrates explains that philosophers are born with "golden" natures, in contrast to those born with silver natures (i.e., natural guardians), and those born with bronze natures (i.e., natural craftspeople); and precisely because of their golden natures, philosophers are fated to great struggle and suffering in youth. Plato describes this struggle and suffering in his celebrated "myth of the cave," in *Republic* VII, with the young philosopher attempting to escape a vast underground cave, a kind of cinematic dark chamber, toward the golden light of the sun.[12] In the *Adventures* Toma the photographer-as-midwife assists in the birth of a golden philosopher from the dark (and cave-like) chamber of the Abbey. Upon emergence from this chamber, "the Abbey's wise and wizardly mistress" Marie-Christine Daudy names the glowing figure "the Man in Gold."[13]

---

9 Shusterman, *Adventures*, 20.
10 Ibid., 20 and 21.
11 Ibid., 21.
12 Plato, *Republic* III, 415a–417b, 1050–1052.
13 Shusterman, *Adventures*, 34.

3 Genius and the Photographical Situation

In general, philosophers of photography take their subject matter to be the material form of the photograph. But, according to Shusterman in "Photography as Performative Process," there are more things in photography than are dreamt of in our philosophy, and among these is the performative art of actually taking photographs. Unfortunately, writes Shusterman, "photography's somatic dimension of dramatic, somatic, performative process" has been "occluded by our one-sided concentration on the photograph itself."[14] Occlusion in photography means to conceal one thing with another, within a photograph; but Shusterman uses the term to indicate how actual photographs, as one dimension of the art, have concealed another dimension of the art, specifically, the art of taking photographs, which is itself a fine and performing art like theatre or ballet or the symphony. As any of these arts requires certain elements, e.g., a symphony requires a stage, musicians, instruments, a conductor, and an audience, Shusterman enumerates four elements of what he calls the "photographical situation:" namely, the photographer, the camera, the subject, and the setting; together these four form a complex, dynamic, performative, and ontological-aesthetic sphere.

These four elements of the photographical situation are also essential to the *Adventures*, with Toma as photographer with his camera, Shusterman as subject, and the settings which are various. But the elements of the photographical situation also appear to synthesize themselves in a dynamical manner: the subject synthesizes with the camera becoming a hybrid of philosopher and photography, who is in turn affected by his various settings, and the always present photographer. With this transformation of the subject and the photographical situation, a further change is also effected; for while a subject, e.g., a philosopher, is separable from the photographical situation, the Man in Gold appears to be inextricable from the photographical situation, a golden "creature of light" whose existence seems to depend on the art of photography.

As the imagery of the golden philosopher and the philosopher's midwife both descend from ancient Greek philosophy (and specifically Plato), so too, in part, does the scene in the *Adventures* of the delivery of a genius first beheld as a glowing aura. As Shusterman writes in "Genius and the Paradoxes of Self-Styling," "As for the notion of genius, in deriving from the Latin and Greek words (*gignĕre* and γίγνεσθα) for begetting and being born, it suggests

---

14   Shusterman, *Thinking through the Body: Essays in Somaesthetics* (Cambridge: Cambridge University Press, 2012), 243.

a natural distinction or native-born endowment of the self."[15] Beyond this ancient terminology, Shusterman continues, "the ultimate roots of genius go deeper and further back—to the supernatural, to the Greek notion of *daimon* (δαίμων or δαιμό-υιου) denoting a 'tutelary god or attendant spirit allotted to every person at his birth, to govern his fortunes and determine his character.'"[16] Ralph Waldo Emerson in "Demonology" revives this ancient concept of the "demon" as a unique and powerful spirit allotted to each individual at birth; and Shusterman invokes Emerson's view that each individual possesses (or is possessed by) a "genius or good daemon," one that "might even in some cases be preternaturally heard and seen," and "when seen, appearing as a star immediately above the head and attached to the head of the person whom it guided."[17] As Shusterman writes in the *Adventures*, Toma, with his "uncanny intuition," beheld about his subject a glowing golden demon, appearing as a "mysterious artistic form" and an "energetic aura." From that moment on, and beginning with his role as midwife, Toma would become what Shusterman describes as the "ever-present companion and protector" of the Man in Gold. Of course, to be an "ever-present companion and protector" is also one of the functions of the "*daimon*" or "genius," in Shusterman's "Genius and the Paradoxes of Self-Styling," the *daimon* as a "tutelary god" or "attendant spirit."

Toma attends the Man in Gold as a photographer, following him, capturing him in moments of stillness and motion, revealing his nature as "a creature of light." Several of Toma's somaflux photographs in the *Adventures* show the Man in Gold amidst glowing lines of light, using "light-drawing" photography, a form of the art which "echoes the etymological origins of 'photography.'"[18] The word "photography," in Greek, means "light-drawing," so Toma's photographs, which depict lines of light, may be seen as "light-drawings" in two ways: first, they are light drawings because they are photographs; and, second, they are photographs of drawings of light.[19] For example, in the two-page spread color photograph, *Currents of the Seine* (2012), the Man in Gold stands by the Seine with his hands extended toward a large concrete public

---

15 Shusterman, "Genius and the Paradoxes of Self-Styling," in *Performing Live: Aesthetic Alternatives for the Ends of Art* (Ithaca: Cornell University Press, 2000), 204.
16 Shusterman, *Performing Live*, 204.
17 Ralph Waldo Emerson, "Demonology," in *The Early Lectures of Ralph Waldo Emerson*, vol. III, ed. Robert E. Spiller and Wallace E. Williams (Cambridge: Harvard University Press, 1972), 160. See Shusterman, *Performing Live*, 204.
18 Shusterman, *Adventures*, 22.
19 Ibid., 94.

work of art, spray-painted with graffiti. Golden streams of light seem to emit from the hands of the Man in Gold, and to fall upon the public work of art at the point of the graffiti markings. Whether the Man in Gold is creating this graffiti or erasing it or coloring it in, or perhaps even sensing it, or "photographing it" through some unique capacity (given his nature as a "creature of light"), these things remain ambiguous in the photograph, as ambiguous as the Man in Gold himself.[20]

Toma also attends the Man in Gold by photographing him in moving pictures, which may be truer to the nature of the Man in Gold than still photography, at least in some ways. If photography is essential to the nature of the Man in Gold, and movement is essential to the nature of any living creature, in addition to photography, then the nature of the Man in Gold would appear to be something closer to cinematography than still photography. The word photography, as we've mentioned, means light-drawing; and "cinematography" is a portmanteau of "cinema" and "photography." The word "cinema" derives from the Greek word κίνημα (and κινώ), meaning "moving." So, cinematography means "moving light-drawings" or "drawings of light in motion." Of course, the Man in Gold does not (and cannot) appear moving in still photographs, but he does appear as a moving being in the short film *Walk the Golden Night*.

4   *Walk the Golden Night* and *Citizen Kane*

Walk the Golden Night opens in a street corridor in Cartagena at night.[21] The Man in Gold stands on the sidewalk of the empty street. He gazes into the camera with mild unbothered curiosity while streetlamps glow like giant electric torches, their gleam eclipsing their glass casings; the imagery of these shots recalls the pooling starlight in post-impressionist Dutch painter Vincent van Gogh's *Starry Night* (1889), and *Starry Night Over the Rhone* (1888). The Man in Gold moves through the corridor beholding its form and the lights. Then the Man in Gold leaves the street corridor, and walks toward the restaurant, where he remains for only moments, rebuffed by some rude diners, before fleeing to the fortified perimeter, as Shusterman records the scene in the *Adventures*. Upon reaching the city's ramparts, the Man in Gold ascends the wall's stairs, stands on the wall's walkway, and gazes upon the moon and "the quiet moonlit

---

20 Ibid., 66–67.
21 As Shusterman recalls in the *Adventures*, "By evening Yann had coaxed a hesitant Man in Gold to risk a late-night stroll in Cartagena's city center." *Ibid.*, 50–52.

sea."²² The Man in Gold then descends the stairs of the wall to a large cuboid concrete and iron cage in the middle of a grassy field. The cage appears to safeguard a manhole for accessing electrical lines or waterways, but the Man in Gold seems to see something else. As he grasps the cage, the structure glows brighter and brighter with seemingly heatless incandescence. The Man in Gold himself also glows brighter and brighter and with the same brilliant colors. He gazes into the camera as if the camera somehow understood what was happening, even if the viewer does not. Suddenly the Man in Gold turns and runs into the distance; and the film ends.

Walk the Golden Night is difficult to interpret because its subject matter is strange, and because there is no dialogue. Once it has ended, any viewer may reasonably wonder what kind of film *Walk the Golden Night* is. Clearly the film is an experimental art film, and clearly the subject is the same Man in Gold from the *Adventures*; but that work is both fiction and nonfiction, and philosophy and photography, and exactly which genre of fiction, or how many genres of fiction it is, is one of the questions that the *Adventures* poses in relation to itself. *Walk the Golden Night* also raises the question of its genre. On the one hand, the film appears to be a documentary about the Man in Gold. On the other hand, the film appears to be a short fiction film. In either case, the film appears to be a detective investigation, with the photographer following the

---

22   *Ibid.*, 52. A still from the film *Walk the Golden*, of the Man in Gold standing atop the wall and gazing at the moon, also appears in the *Adventures*: "Somaflux with Richard Shusterman Performing as the Man in Gold: Photographic Still from the film *Walk the Golden Night*, 2011." This photograph of the Man in Gold (a golden alien-being beholding the Moon) recalls one of the most historically relevant and brilliant photographs of all time, *A Man on the Moon*. On July 20, 1969 astronaut and Apollo 11 Commander Neil Armstrong, with his 70-millimeter Hasselblad Electric Data Camera (EDC), photographed fellow astronaut Edwin E. "Buzz" Aldrin standing near their lunar module, the *Eagle*, in the Sea of Tranquility, on the moon. In the photograph, *A Man on the Moon*, Aldrin seems an otherworldly being. His human physical shape is lost beneath the bulbous white spacesuit, and his face entirely disappears behind the shimmering sheet of gold of his spherical helmet's Lunar Extravehicular Visor Assembly (LEVA); this giant golden eye reflects everything in its mirror, including the camera itself and the photographer/astronaut, Armstrong. To any alien beholding the golden eyes of the visors, one photographing the other, in one of the more difficult photographical situations in history, Aldrin and Armstrong would appear strange creatures; perhaps resembling Toma and the Man in Gold on the wall in Cartagena. Standing in the dark beneath the moon, a silent photographer records a silent, golden, alien being gazing at the moon, and into the camera; and neither one, Toma nor the Man in Gold, apparently, at home in this world, each apart from everyone else, each a viewer of space and one another, like astronauts from another world, calmed by the calm moonlit sea, but like the Sea of Tranquility in *A Man on the Moon*, the moonlit sea of Cartagena in *Walk the Golden Night* was not the sea of his "tranquil home" far from Earth.

mysterious subject through the corridors of the city of Cartagena at night; and in neither case is any resolution provided to the mystery of the Man in Gold. And yet because the film seems at once an unresolved investigative documentary and an unresolved mystery plot, a third investigation also appears within the film, which is neither fictional nor documentary but philosophical in the form of the film's investigation of itself.

The eye of the camera itself has always had a strange and ambiguous quality. On the one hand, the camera eye reveals reality in a way clearer than any other medium of visual art. On the other hand, the viewer of a film knows the reality depicted, while crisp and vivid like nothing else in art, is not reality. The eye of the camera also has a powerful and penetrating detective quality: it seems to see all, and does so from a hidden perspective, as unseen by the audience as a private eye following a suspect at night through the labyrinthine corridors of a city. The camera waits, sees, investigates, follows, quietly, and ultimately reveals what it sees, like a detective or a philosopher, detached, discerning, objective. Welles understood this power of the camera and placed its investigative and philosophical power at the center of his masterpiece, *Citizen Kane* (in a manner that still rightly stuns viewers with awe). *Citizen Kane* is a fictional documentary-styled journalistic investigation of the life of the journalist and newspaper man, Charles Foster Kane, the film drawing its complex genre of investigative journalism partly from the profession of its subject.

The detective mystery at the center of the film is the meaning of Kane's last spoken word before dying, "Rosebud." Does "Rosebud" mean pain of loneliness and lost youth, followed by existential darkness in adulthood, crystallized in pure childhood memories of riding a sled named "Rosebud," the very word "rosebud" being a metaphor for beginnings? Or perhaps the meaning of Kane's last word, "Rosebud," can never be known. Perhaps Kane's life, like any man's life, must remain forever a vast labyrinthine mystery, and any attempt to sum up anyone's life with confidence in the meaning of his or her last words is doomed to failure. This particular view appears in the film: "I don't think any word can explain any man's life. No, I guess 'Rosebud' is just a piece in a jigsaw puzzle. A missing piece" (*Citizen Kane*). These two interpretations of "Rosebud" are mutually exclusive, as philosopher of film Noël Carroll writes in "Interpreting *Citizen Kane*" (in Carroll's *Interpreting the Moving Image*).[23] Assuming the latter interpretation, that "Rosebud" is a "missing piece" in a "jigsaw puzzle" that can never be completed, one may also wonder whether even Kane himself, if

---

23 Noël Carroll, *Interpreting the Moving Image* (Cambridge: Cambridge University Press, 2010), 153–165.

he were alive, could put together the pieces of the jigsaw puzzle of his life, and explain the true meaning of "Rosebud."

In the *Adventures* Shusterman raises this kind of question in regard to his transformation, in a work that documents and investigates the experiences of the Man in Gold who inhabits the philosopher. In *Citizen Kane*, following the death of the investigative journalist Kane, his friends and colleagues undertake an investigation into the man, attempting to understand just one word, "Rosebud." But in the *Adventures*, it is Shusterman himself, as a living philosopher, investigating himself as another being, and what exactly led to his transformation, and how it all happened, and continues to happen. But Shusterman openly admits the difficulty of the investigation, and considers the impossibility of resolution. "Why did I open myself to this strange possession?" asks Shusterman. "I am not certain of the answer." Just as Kane's life, and the meaning of "Rosebud" may remain forever a mystery (which, I think, they must), so too may the Man in Gold remain forever a mystery, even to Shusterman himself. No final answer is forthcoming; and if any does, still, it should be treated with suspicion. After all, writes Shusterman in the *Adventures*, "we are masters of self-deception."[24] Each individual masters this art of deceiving himself, even the Man in Gold.

Understanding the Man in Gold and Kane requires some preliminary understanding of the origins of the modern detective, photography, and the *flaneur*, which are all interrelated and emerge at about the same time in early-to-mid-nineteenth century. During this time, French printmaker Louis-Jacques-Mande Daguerre (1787–1851) was developing his "Daguerreotype" camera,[25] and around the same time, a certain kind of individual who came to be known as the *"flaneur"* also appeared in European cities like Paris. According to Walter Benjamin in "The Paris of the Second Empire in Baudelaire" the *flaneur* is a silent, detached spectator who walks the city, often at night, while observing the activities of others. Soon these two phenomena, the *flaneur* and the camera, became one: the private, voyeuristic eye of the *flaneur*, and the private, voyeuristic eye of the camera; and their combination (in life and in literature) gave rise to the amateur detective, the "private eye."[26] In literature, that fusion

---

24 Shusterman, *Adventures*, 9.
25 English photographer Thomas Wedgewood (1771–1805) is widely regarded as one of the earliest pioneers in modern automated photography with his experiments in photochemical impressions.
26 Walter Benjamin, *Selected Writings*, vol. 4, 1938–1940, tr. Edmund Jephcott and Others, ed. Howard Eiland and Michael W. Jennings (Cambridge: Harvard University Press, 2003): "Photography made it possible for the first time to preserve permanent and unmistakable traces of a human being. The detective story came into being when the most

took brilliant form with Edgar Allan Poe's "The Murders in the Rue Morgue" (first published in *Graham's Magazine*, 1841), in which amateur detective Auguste Dupin and his friend (the narrator) walk the city of Paris at night and solve a murder mystery. Poe's story quickly became the model of a new genre, one admitting of seemingly endless variation, from Sir Arthur Conan Doyle's *The Adventures of Sherlock Holmes* to Welles' *Citizen Kane* to Shusterman's *The Adventures of the Man in Gold* and *Walk the Golden Night*.²⁷

Shusterman discusses the figure of the *flaneur*, along with Benjamin's analysis, in "The Urban Aesthetics of Absence: Pragmatist Reflections in Berlin." Here Shusterman philosophically reconstructs the emergence of the *flaneur* as a natural reaction to the "bursting saturation of city presence."²⁸ Overwhelmed by complexity and activity, the *flaneur*, writes Shusterman, detaches into "absence," separating from the city even while remaining within it, and now simply observes: "the *flaneur* distances himself from the crowd by his absence of practical purpose and urgency."²⁹ A variation of this figure of the *flaneur* appears in both the *Adventures* and *Walk the Golden Night*: the individual who walks the city, silently, observing all, like a camera, while another individual, the photographer, equally silent, also walks the city, and observes (and even seems to investigate) the Man in Gold observing the city. Unlike the *flaneur* separated from social activity, with his camera capturing in visual images others within the city, the Man in Gold does not carry a camera; but he is himself a kind of camera (rendering him a unique kind of *flaneur*), and one who is always attended by the photographer Toma, with his camera (rendering him, too, a unique kind of *flaneur* because he is a photographer following a man who is also a camera).

---

      decisive of all conquests of a person's incognito had been accomplished. Since that time, there has been no end to the efforts to capture [*dingfest machen*] a man in his speech and actions" (27).

27   Following Benjamin, Susan Sontag also explores this strange evolution from *flaneur* to detective/photographer in *On Photography* (New York: Farrar, Straus, & Giroux, 1973, 2005): "The photographer is an armed extension of the solitary walker reconnoitering, stalking, cruising the urban inferno, the voyeuristic stroller who discovers the city as a landscape of voluptuous extremes" (42–43). The photographer is "armed," writes Sontag, with a camera that shoots and captures the "unofficial reality" lurking behind the "façade of bourgeois life," as if modern society like a criminal had covered its tracks imperfectly, leaving clues here and there, waiting to be found and followed. Upon tracking down these clues, writes Sontag, "the photographer 'apprehends'" the hidden reality "as a detective apprehends a criminal" (42–43).

28   Shusterman, "The Urban Aesthetics of Absence," in *Performing Live*, 106.

29   *Ibid.*, 106.

This kind of combination, of Toma and the Man in Gold, is unique within the tradition of detective literature and cinema, not because two silent *flaneurs* walk and photograph the city at night, but precisely for the deepening integration of the *flaneur*, the detective, the camera, and the subject photographed and investigated. Still, even if *Walk the Golden Night* may be understood as part of this tradition (as I think it should), the limits of this interpretation must also be acknowledged. After all, in detective literature and cinema, plot is everything; while, in *Walk the Golden Night*, arguably, there is no plot. There is no crime, no statement of a puzzle to be solved, no suspects, no interviews of suspects or witnesses, no discovery and no demonstrative reveal; there can't be (because there is no dialogue). By contrast, in *Citizen Kane*, which is also a unique variation of the tradition, the plot is the investigation of the mind of Kane after he has died, naturally (in stark contrast to most detective mysteries); the plot is a maze and a puzzle, beginning with a clue, "Rosebud," that leads the investigation through interviews and camera reels, but ultimately delivers the problem into the hands of the viewer who must choose one of the two solutions, as Carroll articulates them in "Interpreting *Citizen Kane*."

On the other hand, there *is* a mystery in, and to, the film *Walk the Golden Night*, and one no less philosophical than that of *Citizen Kane*, even if more difficult to see; yet bearing resemblance to the mystery of *Citizen Kane*, and indeed all great detective mysteries. For in any great mystery a detective investigates and explores a vastly intricate puzzle, but in all great detective mysteries the detective, or the work in question, will investigate the vastly intricate puzzle of the mind of the detective himself, or the mind of his suspect, or very often both. "The Murders in Rue Morgue" is a murder mystery but it is also an investigation of the mind of Dupin; just as *A Study in Scarlet* is an investigation of the mind of Sherlock Holmes; just as *The Maltese Falcon* is an investigation of the mind of Sam Spade; or *Citizen Kane*, quite explicitly, is an investigation of the mind of Charles Foster Kane; and *Walk the Golden Night* and the *Adventures* are investigations of the mind of the Man in Gold. All of these works are adventures through the labyrinths of the mind.

But the *Adventures* and the *Walk the Golden Night* are also philosophical mysteries because they are adventures through the labyrinths of themselves, not unlike Andy Warhol's *Brillo Boxes* or his film *Empire* (1964). Like *Walk the Golden Night*, *Empire* is also an experimental and strange film. It has no cuts, no sound, no color, no action, and no characters, at least, no *human* characters. The whole film is just one continuous shot (at 485 minutes, over eight hours at long) of the Empire State Building, taken from the window of another skyscraper, a kind of Hitchcockian *Rear Window*-like detective investigation, from window to window. *Empire* holds the viewer's attention by the size and stillness and silence of its subject, a film as silent and still (and sublime) as the Empire State Building itself. As Arthur Danto writes in "The Philosopher as Andy Warhol" (in *Philosophizing Art*), the philosophical genius of the film lies in its paradoxical and self-conscious nature. Any film is a moving picture, in contrast to a still photograph, but *Empire* is a film without moving pictures, so that it raises the question of its visual difference to a still photograph of the Empire State Building, and thereby effectively enters the sphere of philosophy, by entering into philosophy's recursive space of self-consciousness.

Walk the Golden Night analogously raises the question of its nature by inhabiting an experimental space between art and life, being both a form of art, and the record of a man's life, but a man who is simultaneously, and paradoxically, a being of art, and, therefore, a man who is a man and not a man. *Walk the Golden Night* also inhabits a strange space between philosophy and film because it is a film about a philosopher transformed into a different kind of philosopher, and whose mode of doing philosophy is not the traditional linguistically expressed form of the genre, but the silent aesthetic exploration of experience, as silent and visual as still photography or pre-talkie moving pictures, all recorded cinematically (and silently) by Toma. *Walk the Golden Night* inhabits yet a further and no less strange space between documentary film and fiction film, as a documentary-like film of a partly fictional world that does not exist apart from the medium of documentary filmmaking. In viewing *Walk the Golden Night*, one simply cannot discern the film as art or life, fiction or nonfiction, investigative documentary or mystery plot, about a man who is mysteriously both a philosopher and photography itself.

5 Emerson, Mood, and the Camera

In "Thought in the Strenuous Mood: Pragmatism as a Philosophy of Feeling," Shusterman reconstructs the tradition of pragmatism as a philosophy of feeling (or mood), from C. S. Peirce's category of "firstness" (as feeling), to William James's study of thought as pervaded by mood, e.g., what James calls "the strenuous mood,"[30] to John Dewey's view of "the immediate qualitative feeling of background mood" as "the foundation of his aesthetics" and "his entire theory of experience and coherent thought."[31] Ultimately, however, Shusterman finds pragmatism's central idea, that mood is at the core of thought, to emerge a

---

30 Shusterman, "Thought in the Strenuous Mood: Pragmatism as a Philosophy of Feeling," *New Literary History*, vol. 43, no. 3 (Summer 2012), 433–454.
31 *Ibid.*, 441.

generation before Peirce and James, in Ralph Waldo Emerson's transcendentalist philosophy and its central concepts of mood, temperament, genius, art, and "strenuously spirited" creativity.[32]

In developing his philosophy, Emerson drew from many sources in the tradition such as David Hume's view in the *Treatise of Human Nature* that "reason is, and ought only to be the slave of the passions,"[33] Immanuel Kant's transcendentalist view in the *Critique of Pure Reason* that the mind constructs its own experience, and the movement of romanticism (which subordinates reason to imagination and art), combining all of these with a great admiration for the new art of photography. In Emerson's philosophy, each individual mind is a kind of living transcendental camera, which sees the world from own its own unique perspective. "And so why not draw for these times a portrait gallery?" writes Emerson in his *Lectures on the Times*. "Let us paint the painters. Whilst the Daguerreotypist professor, with camera-obscura and silver plate, begins now to traverse the land, let us set up our Camera also, and let the sun paint the people."[34] The camera-mind "traverses the land," writes Emerson, and photographs the world; but, in photographing the world, this camera-mind also simultaneously "paints" as it photographs, with the "colors" of its moods. The human creature, writes Emerson in *Nature*, is a "transparent eyeball"[35]—which refers to the transparent eyeball-like lens of a camera; and this transparent eyeball sees and thinks and records everything with (and through) feeling. Nothing beheld with the transparent eyeball is simply *there* in itself, but the mind shapes all things it sees and experiences all manner of moods, with love, with heartbreak, or the strenuous mood. "Nature always wears the colors of the spirit," writes Emerson in *Nature*, "To a man laboring under calamity, the heat of his own fire hath sadness in it. Then, there is a kind of contempt in the landscape felt by him who has just lost by death a dear friend."[36] There is no fire or landscape in itself, but only a fire or landscape beheld with emotional eyes.

In what is arguably his masterpiece, "Experience," Emerson provides perhaps his best statement of his romantic and photographic transcendentalism, once again defining the mind as a camera lens which colors its shots with mood, while creating for itself a dreamlike cinematic experience. "Life

---

32   *Ibid.*, 448.
33   David Hume, *A Treatise of Human Nature*, ed. L. A. Selby-Bigge, 2nd ed. text rev. P. H. Nidditch (Oxford: Clarendon Press, 1978), 415.
34   Emerson, "Introductory Lecture," in *Collected Works of Ralph Waldo Emerson*, ed. Robert E. Spiller and Alfred R. Ferguson (Cambridge: Harvard University Press, 1971), vol. I, 170.
35   Emerson, *Nature*, in *Collected Works of Ralph Waldo Emerson*, vol. I, 10.
36   *Ibid.*, 10–11.

is a train of moods like a string of beads," writes Emerson, "and, as we pass through them, they prove to be many-colored lenses which paint the world their own hue, and each shows only what lies in its focus."[37] Shusterman advances a similar view in "Thought in the Strenuous Mood:" "Mood colors our sensibility giving experience its basic tonality."[38] Moods "color" experience, for Shusterman, as for Emerson, and experience of the world changes with mood; almost like changing the colored filters on a camera, or changing one lens for another—and, once again, there simply is no perspective of the world as it is in itself; there is never perspective without one (or some) of these filters or focal lengths or unique lenses or varying apertures or shutter speeds. "We have learned that we do not see directly, but mediately," writes Emerson, "and that we have no means of correcting these colored and distorting lenses which we are, or of computing the amount of their errors. Perhaps these subject-lenses have a creative power; perhaps there are no objects."[39] Human beings are transparent eyeball cameras whose mooded lenses artistically create their own experiences of objects, whatever the objects may be (if they exist at all).

As Stanley Cavell writes in "Thinking of Emerson," Emerson's essay " 'Experience' is about the epistemology, or say the logic, of moods."[40] Cavell further develops this view in "Finding as Founding: Taking Steps in Emerson's 'Experience,' " claiming that "Experience" lays the ground of "something like a priori categories of human life," in moods, which are essential to the construction of all experience.[41] In the same year that he published "Thinking of Emerson" (1971), Cavell also published *The World Viewed: Reflections on the Ontology of Film*. In that book, Cavell gives a fine description of a scene of trench warfare from Kubrick's *Paths of Glory*, which renders the camera's

---

37   Emerson, "Experience," in *Essays: Second Series, Collected Works of Ralph Waldo Emerson*, vol. III, ed. Joseph Slater, Alfred R. Ferguson, and Jean Ferguson Carr (Cambridge: Harvard University Press, 1984), 30.

38   Shusterman, "Thought in the Strenuous Mood," 439.

39   Emerson, "Experience," in *Essays: Second Series*, 43. Emerson in "Experience" describes these moving pictures as dreams: "Dream delivers us to dream, and there is no end to illusion" (30). Each dream is an "illusion," a cinematic, constructed, emotional dream, and each gives rise to the next, and the next. See also Emerson's "Illusions," in *The Conduct of Life*, in *Collected Works of Ralph Waldo Emerson*, vol. VI, ed. Barbara L. Packer, Joseph Slater, Douglas Emory Wilson (Cambridge: Harvard University Press, 2004): "We wake from one dream into another dream," writes in his later essay "Illusions" (167).

40   Stanley Cavell, "Thinking of Emerson," in Cavell's *Transcendental Etudes*, ed. David Hodge (Stanford: Stanford University Press, 2003), 11.

41   Cavell, "Finding as Founding: Taking Steps in Emerson's 'Experience,' " in *Transcendental Etudes*, 119.

perspective emotional, in a way that closely recalls Emerson's "Experience," and Cavell's analyses of that essay.

> It is sometimes said, and it is natural to suppose, that the camera is an extension of the eye. Then it ought to follow that if you place the camera at the physical point of view of a character, it will objectively reveal what the character is viewing. But the fact is, if we have been given the idea that the camera is placed so that what we see is what the character sees *as he sees it*, then what is shown to us is not just something seen but a specific *mood* in which it is seen. In *Paths of Glory*, we watch Kirk Douglas walking through the trenches lined with the men under his command, whom he, under orders, is about to order into what he knows is a doomed attack. When the camera then moves to a place behind his eyes, we do not gain but forgo an objective view of what he sees; we are given a vision constricted by his mood of numb and helpless rage.[42]

In the trench scene, Kubrick uses what Alfred Hitchcock calls "pure cinema," which is a set of three shots: first, an objective shot of the character; second, a subjective shot from behind the eyes of that character (at whatever he sees); and third, another objective shot of the character (from the same or a similar position as the first shot). This "pure cinema" shot sequence establishes a viewer, an object seen by the viewer, and the viewer's emotional reaction to an object, and thereby, according to Hitchcock, creates an idea for the viewer of the thought of the character, and very often the emotionally charged thought of that character. In *Paths of Glory* Kubrick shows Colonel Dax (Kirk Douglas) walking the trench, from an objective perspective—taken from a backward-dollying camera (first shot)—then the camera looks from behind Dax's eyes to behold the men about to die (second shot); and then the camera returns to the objective perspective (third shot), thereby revealing Dax's "mood of numb and helpless rage," as Cavell describes it.

Like Kubrick's *Paths of Glory* trench sequence, *Walk the Golden Night* also forgoes the objectivity of the camera, in Cavell's sense, by setting the camera behind the eyes of a character, namely, the photographer Toma, to see the Man in Gold. But, in contrast to *Paths of Glory*, *Walk the Golden Night* does not use the technique of "pure cinema," so the that the viewer does not see an emotion register in the eyes of the photographer, Toma (who never appears onscreen).

---

42 Cavell, *The World Viewed: Reflections on the Ontology of Film*, Enlarged Edition (Cambridge: Harvard University Press, 1979; original edition, 1971), 129.

But *Walk the Golden Night* does reveal the mood of the photographer in other ways. For example, the photographer is a walker and viewer following another walker-viewer, which renders the photographer a kind of detective with a mooded perspective characteristic of a detective. The photographer's mood is steady and focused and strenuous; it is the mood, apparently, of an investigation. The mood also appears to be contemplative and even dreamlike because so many shots are saturated with golden light, an almost liquid-like flowing glow. The strenuous and focused detective's mood arises naturally from the very medium of the camera, especially a camera silently following a silent subject at night; but the dreamlike quality of the film also seems to be natural to cinema.

6 Langer, Danto, and *Walk the Golden Night*

According to Susanne Langer in "A Note on the Film," "Cinema is 'like' dream in the mode of its presentation: it creates a virtual present, an order of direct apparition. That is the mode of dream."[43] Glowing images float before the eyes, one thing becoming another, and strangely so, as in a dream. If the medium itself is "dreamlike," then some films, like *Walk the Golden Night*, seem to explore this medium with seemingly self-consciously dreamlike images. In fact, *Walk the Golden Night* seems to be a self-consciously dreamlike film in several ways. First, following Langer, any film is dreamlike and "apparitional" (or ghostly) because of its glowing and moving "virtual present." Second, the character of the Man in Gold seems to be apparitional in the film; and indeed Shusterman in the *Adventures* even describes the Man in Gold as an "apparition" with an "invisible aura." Third, the film has no dialogue, like very many dreams. Fourth, set at night in the city, the streetlamps and the concrete portal pooling golden light both add a haunted quality to the film, not quite a nightmare, but certainly dreamlike. Fifth, the unseen photographer's camera seems to float eerily forward, following, like an apparition.

This camera technique of the first-person forward-moving perspective is also intrinsically philosophical. In his essay on "Moving Pictures" Danto calls this technique "kinetification," and identifies it as both ghostly and philosophical.[44]

---

43 Susanne Langer, *Feeling and Form: A Theory of Art* (New York: Charles Scribner's Sons, 1953), 412.
44 According to Danto in "Moving Pictures," in *Philosophizing Art: Selected Essays* (Berkeley: University of California Press, 1999), "Where photography opens up a new dimension is when, instead of objects moving past a fixed camera, the camera moves among the objects fixed or moving" (228).

Kinetification is philosophical, writes Danto, because it "seems to overcome, at least in principle, the distance between spectator and scene, thrusting us like movable ghosts into scenes that a kinetic photography locates us outside of, exactly like disembodied Cartesian spectators."[45] If, in modern philosophy, the subject is separated from the world, then a version of that division appears in cinematic experience, with the viewer outside of and set in opposition to a world displayed on a screen. But camera kinetification seems to synthesize the viewing subject and the screened object (as if by some Kantian cinematic schematism), for when the camera moves forward through a world, the viewer (carried along with that kinetified perspective) feels as if she has been "thrust" into the screen, writes Danto, like a "disembodied Cartesian spectator," and a "movable ghost," entering a portal of light, to explore the world of the film from the inside.

Danto's main example in "Moving Pictures" is Jean Alexandre Louis Promio's film *Panorama du Canal Grande* (1896, Venice): "When the early cameraman strapped his apparatus to a gondola and rolled the film while riding through the canals of Venice, it was his philosophical achievement to thrust the mode of recording into the scenes recorded in a remarkable exercise of self-reference."[46] *Panorama*, writes Danto, is "a remarkable exercise of self-reference," and an early "philosophical achievement," because Promio's camera kinetification "thrusts the mode of recording into the scenes recorded," with two movements of the mind of the viewer. First, the film thrusts the viewer's projected imagined form into the film (like a "movable ghost"); and second, once this happens, the viewer is also suddenly aware of the presence of the camera within the film. Of course, the viewer does not see the actual camera, but she is made to "see" the powerful presence and effect of the camera, sufficient to carry her into the screen, and thereby synthesize subject and the object; and with that synthesis, she also beholds the film's capacity for self-reference. The film effectively refers to itself by "pointing" the viewer's attention to the invisible (and ghostly) presence of the camera filming the film, and by "pointing" the viewer's attention to the camera's power to inject her imagination into the film, and expel it, and render her aware of this motion, in one incredibly complex movement. As Danto writes in "Moving Pictures," speaking of films like Promio's *Panorama* and François Truffaut's *Stolen Kisses*, "Film becomes in a way its own subject; the consciousness that it is film is what the consciousness is of."[47]

---

45   Danto, "Moving Pictures," in *Philosophizing Art*, 229.
46   *Ibid.*, 229.
47   *Ibid.*, 230. According to Danto in "Moving Pictures," François Truffaut's *Stolen Kisses* also achieves self-referentiality through kinetification. Toward the end of the film, the camera

But Promio's philosophical achievement in *Panorama*, as Danto describes it in "Moving Pictures," is quite different to Warhol's philosophical achievement in *Empire*, as Danto describes it in "The Philosopher as Andy Warhol." Both films are philosophically self-conscious, and both films achieve self-consciousness by engaging the viewer in questions of the self-contradictory nature of the film being viewed. But these two films achieve self-consciousness through self-contradiction in quite different ways. *Empire* achieves philosophical self-consciousness as a moving picture without moving pictures (or at least minimal movement). *Panorama*, by contrast, achieves philosophical self-consciousness in a moving picture by moving the camera, and thereby moving the viewer and not moving the viewer through the film. *Empire* is "aware of itself" because it is and is not a moving picture; while *Panorama* is "aware of itself" because the viewer is and is not outside the film, and therefore is and is not viewing the film as a film.

Like *Panorama*, and in contrast to *Empire*, *Walk the Golden Night* also achieves a form of philosophical self-consciousness by kinetification. The camera moves (more or less) throughout the film, and generally moves forward, following the Man in Gold who also moves (more or less) throughout the film. The camera moves forward with a ghostly quality, floating along steadily, in its haunted fashion, with a quality recalling Kubrick's early use of the Steadicam in his nightmarish ghost story, *The Shining* (1980). As the camera moves forward, in *Walk the Golden Night*, the viewer seems to enter the film, and to be carried along like a "movable ghost," in Danto's sense. She too follows the Man in Gold as he walks the golden night, but the viewer herself does not seem to walk, so much as to float like a ghost, through the film, as if in a dream. Of course, this "disembodied Cartesian spectator" of *Walk the Golden Night* also remains outside the film, as an embodied spectator considering her strange and ghostly experience, even as she is drawn into the film through kinetification. She is then both inside the film and outside the film, in Danto's sense, a subject outside an object, and a subject inhabiting that object—an aesthetic experience as wonderfully self-contradictory as a dream.

No other form of art quite achieves this paradoxical aesthetic experience as cinema, and no technique of cinema quite invites this experience as "kinetification." In fact, this kind of aesthetic experience categorically separates film, for example, from theatre. As Danto writes in "Moving Pictures" of

---

sees through the detective's eyes and then "the camera literally climbs the stairway with an eye and a lubricity of its own and pokes into one bedroom after another in search of the lovers, as in one of Truffaut's films" (*Ibid.*). Danto does not name the film, but it is *Stolen Kisses*.

experiences of kinetification, "We are within scenes that we also are outside of through the fact that we have no dramatic location, often, in the action that visually unfolds, having it both ways at once, which is not an option available to the audiences of stage plays."[48] A viewer in the audience at a play is not onstage interacting with the players; nor does she feel as if she had somehow left her seat to levitate and float forward into the portal of the stage, and inhabit her own unique character position, as the theatre-equivalent of an Emersonian "transparent eyeball," let alone "having it both ways at once," in Danto's sense, i.e., being in the audience and being onstage at the same time.

On the other hand, precisely because film projects the viewer into the screened world, the aesthetic experience of a film can closely resemble (in some ways) the aesthetic experience of architecture. As Danto writes in "Moving Pictures," with kinetification, "cinema approaches the proper apprehension of architecture, which is something to be not merely looked at but moved through, a quality that, in turn, the architect will have built into his structure."[49] Of course, again, there's a fundamental difference between these two aesthetic experiences, the interior of architecture, and the interior of a film: for even as a viewer explores the interior of a film, she remains outside the film, in a manner closed off to architecture. So, the aesthetic experience of architecture is not paradoxical (at least, not in the same way) as film kinetification.[50]

A further paradoxical aesthetic experience appears in *Walk the Golden Night*, and this one too achieved by kinetification. As *Panorama* creates for the viewer a unique imagined aesthetic feeling of gliding along the liquid streets of Venice, *Walk the Golden Night* creates for the viewer a similar aesthetic experience of gliding along the streets of Cartagena. But, in doing so, *Walk the Golden Night* also creates a strangely ghostly aesthetic experience of gliding and walking at the same time, as the camera glides (like an apparition), but somehow with a human gait. On the one hand, the kinetified perspective is quite human because it appears at the eye-level of a man walking forward on a street; on the other hand, the perspective is somewhat nonhuman because of its impossibly liquid-smooth gliding quality. And yet, despite the strangely

---

48   Ibid., 229.
49   Ibid.
50   An aesthetic experience of film whose camera moves continuously through an architectural space, for example, Alexander Sokurov's fine film, *Russian Ark* (2002), is another matter entirely.

self-opposed perspective of floating and walking, or a gliding gait, once the viewer is kinetified, thrust into the film as a movable ghost, that very perspective may also be viewed as a somaesthetically idealized perspective. The height and gait, and the context of the perspective, encourage the viewer to inhabit a human perspective, but then with the ghostly smooth forward movement, the viewer finds herself idealizing her own walking perspective; she finds herself inhabiting an idealized version of herself. She finds herself within the film walking upright and aligned, poised and focused, calm and at ease, floating easily forward with grace and elegance.

Unlike some filmmakers today who jerk the camera this way and that, and jar the attention of the viewer, the camera in *Walk the Golden Night* neither pulls side-to-side suddenly nor bounces nor bobbles, but enters the viewer into its perspective, partly by kinetification, and partly its somaesthetically idealized movement, as if the limbs and joints of her frame had been aligned and steadied to glide as they should. As she floats through the film, the viewer sees what lies outside her, but she also feels with her internal sensations of "proprioception" and "kinaesthesia," sensations Shusterman in "Somaesthetics and Architecture" identifies as "important for the appreciation of architecture as an environment through which we move and orient our bodies, maintaining a dynamic equilibrium as we navigate entrances, corridors, and staircases."[51] These same sensations, proprioception and kinaesthesia, are also important for our appreciation of cinema, through which we also move, although in a different way, "maintaining a dynamic perceptual equilibrium," in Shusterman's sense, as we navigate, for example, the corridors and the restaurant of Cartagena, and finally the staircase of the ramparts by the sea, in *Walk the Golden Night*.

---

51   Shusterman, "Somaesthetics and Architecture," in *Thinking through the Body: Essays in Somaesthetics* (Cambridge: Cambridge University Press, 2012), 226 (see also 9). Shusterman acknowledges the importance of Johann Wolfgang Goethe's aesthetics in "Baukunst," in *Ästhetische Schriften 1771–1805*, ed. Friedmar Apel, in *Sämtliche Werke*, vol. 8 (Frankfurt: Deutscher Klassiker Verlag, 1998), 368. See also Shusterman, "Somatic Style," in *Thinking through the Body*: "Proprioception concerns the inner sensations and resulting cognition of the position, posture, weight, orientation, balance, and internal pressures of one's body, while kinesthetic perception more specifically relates to perceived changes in such feelings of posture, orientation, pressure, and equilibrium that arise through bodily movement" (330).

7   The Film's Ending

The ending of *Walk the Golden Night* is the strangest and finest sequence of the film. After descending the Cartagena ramparts to the ground, to take hold of the iron bars of the portal rising from the grass, the Man in Gold glows brighter and brighter. There seems to be no way to say exactly what is happening in this sequence, especially as light seems to flood the shot as if welling up from the ground through the portal. But perhaps this scene may be set in relation to the early sequence in the restaurant. If the Man in Gold had entered the restaurant to dine, but then fled in fear of rude customers, perhaps here he has found what he needs. Perhaps here at the portal in the ground, he has found something like food and drink appropriate to "a creature of light," as Shusterman describes the Man in Gold in the *Adventures*. A creature of light and photography might not consume human food anyway; so, perhaps the Man in Gold at the portal is drinking or somehow absorbing (as if through his hands and his eyes) the golden luminescence rising and pooling from the portal. Perhaps the portal descends deep into the earth's crust to some underground lake of shimmering cinematic light, possibly even the same substance pooling at the hands of the Man in Gold in Toma's somaflux photograph *Midnight Fire on the Dunes* (2014) or *Currents of the Seine* (2012), in the *Adventures*. Perhaps what is happening at the end of *Walk the Golden Night*—though one can no more know, than one can know the meaning of Charles Foster Kane's "Rosebud"—is that the Man in Gold, as a being of cinematography, has found a well of phosphorescent ink, and once sufficiently filled with this liquid light, he is ready to draw in moving pictures of light. Standing at the well, and turning to the distance, the brightly glowing Man in Gold now sprints into the darkness, his form seemingly overwhelming the frame with blasts of light. The blasts vibrate and then still in black, and the film ends.

PART 3

Shusterman in His Own Words

∴

CHAPTER 13

Somaesthetics, Pragmatism, and the Man in Gold: Remarks on the Preceding Chapters

Richard Shusterman

1

Having read the twelve chapters written for this collection and generously dedicated to the critical study of my work in philosophy and somaesthetics, I must now undertake the task of commenting on them. It is not an easy endeavor. I am very grateful for what I have learned from the contributing authors' interpretive and critical insights, but somewhat overwhelmed because their essays cover such a broad range of topics, both in philosophy and beyond. They include issues of ontology, phenomenology, aesthetics, hermeneutics, pragmatist philosophy, ethics, philosophy of mind and body, the nature of the self, and philosophy as a way of life. Besides these philosophical topics, we find psychoanalysis, politics, rap music, literature, and the visual arts of photography, film, sculpture, and performance art. I acknowledge the blame for this scatter lies in my own diversity of interests. Faced with such a variety of topics and different styles (from the systematically polemical to the personal and poignantly evocative), I doubt if I could compose an attractively well-structured essay of response that would do justice to all this variety of commentary while still maintaining a compelling unity of theme and tone. I also feel this collection already has too much of me in it and needs no more, even if (to my great pleasure) a considerable number of the articles focus instead on the Man in Gold. Despite my anxieties about composing a text of response to the previous twelve essays, I know this book's genre demands it, as does professional courtesy to the high-quality scholars and artists whose contributions grace this book.

I will try, however, to keep my remarks brief and avoid detailed polemics and quibbling. If one of my philosophical heroes, John Dewey, defined philosophy as "a criticism of criticisms," he did not mean to encourage an attitude of choleric fault-finding towards earlier critique, but rather to highlight philosophy's "generality ... [of] discriminating judgment."[1] The contributors will forgive

---

1 John Dewey, *Experience and Nature* (1925), in *John Dewey: The Later Works, 1925–1953*, vol. 1, ed. Jo Ann Boydston (Carbondale: Southern Illinois University Press, 1981), 298.

me if I fail to address all their points in my response. We know each other well enough to continue to debate the details of subtle differences beyond the covers of this book, so that we can spare our readers needless tedium. My text is primarily interested in clarifying misconceptions and exploring interesting questions emerging from the previous chapters, not in winning philosophical arguments. Rather than trying to organize my comments in terms of general themes, I will simply arrange them according to the book's order of texts that editor Jerold Abrams has ably constructed. Before beginning with Abrams' useful introduction, I should note that the book's title *Shusterman's Somaesthetics: From Hip Hop Philosophy to Politics and Performance Art* aptly recalls an early collection, *Shusterman's Pragmatism: Between Literature and Somaesthetics* (2012), thus reinforcing the fact that somaesthetics is a continuation rather than a departure from pragmatism while highlighting its interdisciplinary scope which pragmatism also inspires.

Abrams is right to identify Richard Rorty and Arthur Danto as key influences in my philosophical thought. I was lucky enough to know them personally and benefit from their kindness, but also from critical debate with them. If Rorty introduced me to pragmatism and encouraged me to move to America to study it more closely, then Danto taught me how to do aesthetics by working from concrete contemporary artworks and movements. Of course, Andy Warhol's *Brillo Boxes* belonged to a somewhat different artworld than the hip-hop and country music I explored in the 1990s, but Danto's work on pop art and in art criticism were exemplary for me. Abrams does not mention another intellectual mentor, whose influence on my philosophical development was equally great, Pierre Bourdieu. He not only opened my eyes to the sociopolitical dimensions of aesthetics and of philosophy in general (which helped me see the limits of analytic aesthetics), but he also changed my life by inviting me to spend a year at his research center in Paris (in 1990) and thus introducing me to European intellectual culture.

My debates with Bourdieu were more severe than those I had with Rorty and Danto (perhaps because he had a more contentious personality), but he ultimately taught me a lesson in intellectual magnanimity commensurate with his academic greatness.[2] Although *Pragmatist Aesthetics* was severely critical of his arguments against the very legitimacy of popular art and popular aesthetics, Bourdieu overcame his initial anger at my critique and introduced my book (which was still in manuscript form and mostly in English or unpolished

---

2   For an account of those debates, see Richard Shusterman, "Bourdieu and Pragmatist Aesthetics: Between Practice and Experience," *New Literary History* 46, 3 (2015), 435–457.

French) to his publisher, Jerome Lindon of Minuit. The book was published (shortened by three chapters) as *L'art à l'état vif: la pensée pragmatiste et l'esthétique populaire* a few months before the original version of *Pragmatist Aesthetics* appeared with Blackwell. I believe that this French translation (because of its more popular format and the broad media coverage it received) was what initiated European interest in the book and established my connection with European intellectual life that has been so rewarding both philosophically and personally. Some of my experiments in thinking originated in Europe. That is where the concept of somaesthetics first took shape and appeared in print in 1996, in my book *Vor der Interpretation* (Vienna Passagen Verlag, 1996), which—like its first, French version, *Sous l'interprétation* (Paris: L'éclat, 1994)—does not exist in English. My first practical workshops in somaesthetics were in Europe, and the Man in Gold was born in France, and the *Adventures* was first published in Paris. Before beginning my comments on the chapters, I pause here to acknowledge the excellent work of all the translators (many of them fine theorists in their own right) who have made my work more accessible and more attractive to more people.

The book's first two chapters, by Stefan Snævarr and Alexander Kremer, focus on the pragmatism-somaesthetics connection, and these chapters relate interestingly to each other. Snævarr worries that my pragmatism wrongly disregards ontology and fails to supply even "a minimal pragmatic ontology." Kremer instead devotes considerable effort to outlining my ontological outlook by quoting extensively from an article, "What Pragmatism Means to Me: Ten Principles," where my basic ontological principles are outlined.[3] These principles include "the changing, open, and contingent nature of reality" that implies both the possibility for human action to change aspects of reality and the need for philosophical fallibilism, since changes in reality can falsify established beliefs. With respect to human reality and the human self, Kremer explains my "non-reductive, embodied naturalism" and "emergentism" according to which mental life emerges from but is not reducible to physical elements while also being shaped by social forces. He does so by again citing extensively from the same article. There is no point in repeating Kremer's points and quotations here, as they are evident in his chapter.

Instead, let me respond to Snævarr's charges of inconsistency with respect to essentialism and dualism. Pragmatists like myself distinguish between two senses of "essential." One is the foundational notion denoting an essence

---

3 The article first appeared in English, but in a French publication: *Revue Française D'Études Américaines* 124 (2010), 59–65; and there is no other English version available, though it was also published in French, Portuguese, and Chinese translations.

that is both necessary and sufficient for the concept in question and that is so not only under currently existing circumstances but also necessarily and always. This concept of essential belongs to the fixed, foundational ontology that pragmatism rejects. But "essential" can mean simply necessary (or at least crucially important) but not sufficient under existing circumstances. In this sense, a pragmatist can say that embodiment is essential to human life, even if we can perhaps imagine that individuals may someday exist without our characteristic human embodiment but whom we would nonetheless classify as human beings. In this sense, we can see that one's soma is essential to the self but that merely having a soma is not sufficient to constitute what we would consider a full-fledged self or person; a neonate has a soma but does not have full-fledged self.[4] Moreover, the soma is not a dualist combination of *Leib* and *Körper* but a single entity that, in different circumstances and from different perspectives, exhibits capacities that phenomenologists have divided between those German concepts, thus reinstating a dualism similar to the one they often reject in Descartes.

Kremer is certainly correct in noting that Rorty drew me closer to pragmatism by suggesting I read Dewey (I was already reading Rorty's neopragmatism). However, the Dewey he recommended was not *Art as Experience* but rather *Reconstruction in Philosophy*. I later learned that Rorty disliked *Art as Experience* (which he rarely cites or discusses), not only because it built centrally on the concept of experience, which Rorty rejects but also because it treats aesthetics as a field of philosophical inquiry, which Rorty regards as "another of Kant's bad ideas."[5] Not surprisingly, Rorty opposed somaesthetics for its recognizing the philosophical import of nonverbal experience and the cognitive aspects of somatic feelings and action. Kremer is surely correct in insisting that somaesthetics is not merely a form of aesthetic theory but that it includes general ontological, epistemological, ethical, and political dimensions that he identifies with a full-fledged philosophical vision or what he calls "a philosophy."

However, there is an important sense in which somaesthetics is also more than a philosophy. Although I initially preferred to conceive it, in the 1990s, as within the field of philosophy, I recognized from the outset (with the

---

4 Snævarr should recognize that I do not regard the soma as fully constituting the self because he well knows (and wittily interprets) my work with the Man in Gold, who takes my soma but has a different self. See Stefán Snævarr, "Shusterman and the Man in Gold," *Nordic Journal of Aesthetics*, 54 (2017), 86–92.
5 Richard Rorty, "Response to Richard Shusterman," in *Richard Rorty: Critical Dialogues*, ed. M. Festenstein and S. Thompson (Cambridge: Polity Press, 2001), 153–157.

pragmatist spirit of fallibilism and openness to change) that where it belongs depends on how it develops, and this depends on the community of somaesthetic researchers. "That community, not this individual, will best define its precise disciplinary home and limits," I wrote.[6] I soon happily realized (thanks to the way other disciplines began to apply it) that somaesthetics should be an interdisciplinary field of inquiry, practiced somewhat differently in different disciplinary and transdisciplinary contexts, and concerned with different aims and methods though sharing to some extent certain foci, concepts, and values. One of the disciplines outside philosophy where somaesthetics has inspired rewarding research and practice is the field of Human-Computer Interactive Design or HCI, in which I too have ventured to collaborate with a number of experts in the field. Particularly noteworthy in somaesthetic HCI is Kristina Höök and her research team based in Sweden's Royal Institute of Technology, whose work includes not only research papers but also exciting design prototypes like the "Soma Mat" and the "Breathing Light."[7] Of course, these interdisciplinary efforts recognize the philosophical roots of somaesthetics as well as the role of practical somaesthetic workshops in nourishing the design process.

Leszek Koczanowicz clearly recognizes that somaesthetics has grown from a philosophical to an interdisciplinary project, and he creatively expands the range of its melioristic thrust by envisioning its possible role for political theory and praxis through a microphysics of political emancipation based on concrete somaesthetic practices of transgression in everyday life. These acts need not be dramatic or criminal to provide "a niche of freedom" through "resistance of the concrete against an abstract and oppressive ideology" that typically

---

6   Richard Shusterman, "Somaesthetics: A Disciplinary Proposal," *The Journal of Aesthetics and Art Criticism* 57, 3 (1999), 299–313.
7   See Kristina Höök et al., "Somaesthetic Design," *Interactions*, vol. 22 (July–August 2015), http://interactions.acm.org/archive/view/july-august-2015/somaesthetic-design; "Somaesthetic Appreciation Design," *CHI '16: Proceedings of the 2016 CHI Conference on Human Factors in Computing Systems* (May 2016), 3131–3142, https://doi.org/10.1145/2858036.2858583; and Kristina Höök, *Designing with the Body: Somaesthetic Interaction Design* (Cambridge: MIT Press, 2018). My textual contributions to the field are in Richard Shusterman, "Somaesthetics" in *The Encyclopedia of Human-Computer Interaction* (2014), https://www.interaction-design.org/literature/book/the-encyclopedia-of-human-computer-interaction-2nd-ed/somaesthetics. Wonjun Lee, Youn-kyung Lim, and Richard Shusterman, "Practicing Somaesthetics: Exploring Its Impact on Interactive Product Design Ideation," in *Proceedings of the 2014 Conference on Designing Interactive Systems* (New York: ACM, 2014), 1055–1064, Doi: 10.1145/2598510.2598561; and Sara Eriksson, Kristina Höök, Richard Shusterman, et al., "Ethics in Movement: Shaping and Being Shaped in Human-Drone Interaction," in *Proceedings of CHI 2020*, paper 549, 1–14. https://dl.acm.org/doi/abs/10.1145/3313831.3376678.

oppresses by instilling obedience and tacit acceptance of its values, largely through inculcation of somatic norms of conduct and appearance. Such concrete acts of transgression can afford an emancipatory joy that may stimulate further efforts of emancipation. Of course, as I have repeatedly argued, transformative somaesthetic praxis by individuals in everyday life should not be a substitute for collective political action, but should work alongside and help inspire collective and institutional praxis of reform. Through somaesthetic cultivation, individuals can develop a greater sense of their somatic power and capacities for action that in turn inspires more confidence for engaging in collective activism and resistance.

Somaesthetics, moreover, can help individuals monitor their emotional reaction to oppression so that they can choose the right moment or form of transgressive resistance. The political value of such somaesthetic awareness and control is often neglected, even in thinkers who understand the corporeal dimensions of oppression. I have shown how Frantz Fanon, for example, recognizes that colonialist oppression creates in the colonized natives a buildup of angry "muscular tension that finds outlet regularly in bloodthirsty explosions" of murder and tribal warfare that are politically unproductive, but he fails to consider how somaesthetic control could channel that anger into more effective acts of political resistance.[8] There is a *phronesis* of transgressive action, and improved somaesthetic awareness and self-monitoring contribute to such practical intelligence.

My early passion for hip hop, which Max Ryynänen's essay discusses, derived not only from its musical rhythms but also from progressive rap's lyrics and their political and philosophical messages of activist transgression for emancipatory progress toward greater democracy. In the 1980s and early 1990s before "gangsta rap" began to dominate the scene, knowledge rap seemed to me a paradigm for contemporary pragmatist aesthetics by combining deeply embodied artistic expression with philosophical thinking and progressive political and pedagogical praxis. Hip hop also expressed itself as a whole way of life, which I interpreted in terms of the ancient idea of philosophy as an art of living. As pragmatist aesthetics and the philosophical art of living were the two prime themes that led me to somaesthetics and that were central to my study of rap, it is not surprising that some early interpreters of my somaesthetic project

---

8   Frantz Fanon, *The Wretched of the Earth*, tr. Constance Farrington (New York: Grove Press, 1963), 54. I develop this argument in detail in "Somaesthetics and Politics: Incorporating Pragmatist Aesthetics for Social Action," in *Beauty, Responsibility, and Power: Ethical and Political Consequences of Pragmatist Aesthetics*, ed. Leszek Koczanowicz and Katarzyna Liszka (Amsterdam: Rodopi, 2014), 4–18.

(including the always insightful Martin Jay) took rap as its paradigm.[9] Even if my study of Western somatic therapies and Asian somatic disciplines were equally inspirational and perhaps ultimately more formative for my studies of body consciousness, rap was surely decisive for my appreciation of the political import and transgressive joy of somaesthetic experience.

As Ryynänen notes, in the early 1990s I was active in a hip hop project of cultural politics, involved in *JOR Quarterly: The Journal of Rap Expression and Hip Hop Culture*, a Philadelphia-based rap fanzine (one of rap's first magazines). The journal was founded in 1991 by the black civil-rights activist George Ware, who believed African-American music could be helpful in building black pride, gaining broader social recognition for African-American culture, and thus bringing greater sociopolitical power for African Americans. Ware helped create the Black Music Association before creating *JOR Quarterly*, for which I regularly wrote a column as "Rich Frosted," the only white brother in the mix. The distance between the academic community and the local rap community was enormous at that time, yet George Ware's home was within short walking distance from my office at Temple University, located in the black ghetto of North Philadelphia. Working and grooving with his crew in collaborative action toward emancipatory progress was pleasurably rewarding, because it made my philosophical work seem more real by connecting it with community action for a common cause. I suspect it also had a pinch of that joy from transgression that Koczanowicz discusses in the microphysics of everyday life. In any case, rap offered the shared enjoyment of dancing together, providing evidence for my view that somatic pleasure is not necessarily a private, individualist affair, a view that led one commentator to describe my aesthetics and politics as advocating for "a *con-sensualist* society rather than a merely consensual one."[10]

With Tonino Griffero's essay we turn sharply away from the aesthetics and somaesthetics of meliorist activism and submit ourselves to a "pathic aesthetics" of passive quietism. Griffero's interest in somaesthetics, though polemical, is genuine because of the overlap between somaesthetics and the new phenomenology of aesthetics and the body to which he adheres. The Italian translation of *Body Consciousness* appeared in a book series he edits, and he also arranged for translations of some of my articles in publishing projects

---

9   Martin Jay, "Somaesthetics and Democracy: Dewey and Contemporary Body Art," *The Journal of Aesthetic Education* 36:4 (2002), 55–69.
10 Antonia Soulez, "Practice, Theory, Pleasure, and the Problems of Form and Resistance," *The Journal of Speculative Philosophy* 16, 1 (2002), 3.

related to his phenomenological interests. I am happy to see him welcomed in this collection because his polemic usefully highlights, by contrast, the active, meliorist dimension of somaesthetics. Griffero works in the German "new phenomenology" tradition, inspired by Hermann Schmitz and best known in Anglophone philosophy through Gernot Böhme whose influential work on the concept of atmosphere I found very useful and who has been a friendly critic of somaesthetics, faulting it for what he sees as its overly tolerant pluralism.[11]

These phenomenological approaches to the body focus on the body as *Leib*, while somaesthetics treats the human soma as its core concept. The soma is not simply a perceiving embodied subjectivity but a material, active entity that is located in the physical world and that can stylize, to a certain extent, its material and performative form to express its values. This basic difference has important consequences, such as somaesthetics' concern (in theory and practice) for material matters such as fashion, food, and somatic appearance. When Griffero claims that disciplined cultivation of the material body (*Körper*) such as bodybuilding "is fairly useless," one wonders for whom he is speaking and whether this is not the traditional phenomenological voice of the European, male intellectual who speaks for all humanity and for all times. In my relatively limited experiences of bodybuilding, there were also rich cognitive gains for my perceiving subjectivity. This discipline even gave me new sensations and perceptions of the body as *Leib* that were not devoid of implications for my philosophical theorizing.

Leaving aside such critiques deriving largely from the difference between soma and *Leib*, somaesthetics seems to have two key flaws, according to Griffero's "pathic" perspective. The first is pragmatist meliorism, its recognition that despite the impressive range of our ordinary somatic abilities and knowledge, there are sometimes problematic occasions (whether through injury, aging, disease, bad habits, or special circumstances or goals) when one's established abilities and knowledge require improvement to handle those problems and achieve a better outcome or quality of life. The pathic approach instead advocates "a wise passiveness" of mere acceptance as "the best path to our atmospheric harmony with the world," an acquiescent resignation that contrasts with what William James advocated as pragmatism's "strenuous mood"

---

11   I appeal to Böhme's concept of atmosphere in "Somaesthetics and Architecture: A Critical Option?" in *Thinking through the Body*. For his critique of somaesthetics, see Gernot Böhme, "Somästhetik—sanft oder mit Gewalt," *Deutsche Zeitschrift für Philosophie*, 50:5 (2002), 797–800. Böhme explains Schmitz's "pathic concept of the body," in "The Concept of Body as the Nature We Ourselves Are," *The Journal of Speculative Philosophy* 24, 3 (2010), 224–238.

of action. In other words, instead of any effort to improve our somatic skills with training or new learning, Griffero claims our everyday activities which constitute "a strategically unprepared and unplanned art of living ... seems to us entirely sufficient." Who is this "us" for whom no melioristic body training is necessary? It cannot include the elderly and infirm, who need to learn new skills of balance and body alignment to compensate for the strength and neural sensitivities they have lost. Nor is ordinary exercise sufficient for competing or amateur athletes who are striving to improve their performance; nor for actors and musicians who seek to improve their playing through improved somatic use. (My work as a somatic therapist has surely made these needs for meliorism more evident than if I had confined my somaesthetic work to reading and writing; so have my injuries and the growing disabilities of aging.) I cannot agree with Griffero's claim that "my melioristic perspective inevitably excludes the unique and deep pleasure of feeling our vulnerability, and thereby ignores the rich pathic aesthetic possibilities that our weakness, and even our illness, may and do sometimes provide." I have in fact explicitly argued for the pleasures of illness and vulnerable fragility, while noting that these pleasures provide also cognitive benefits and can deepen through improved attention (meliorism again).[12]

The second key flaw Griffero sees in somaesthetics is the role it gives to action. Somaesthetics shares the pragmatist notion of experience as intrinsically active as well as passive. As Dewey famously characterized it, experience is a relation of both "doing and undergoing, outgoing and incoming energy."[13] It seems wrongly one-sided to take a purely "pathic" approach to the body, to aesthetics, or to life in general. Living is an activity that essentially involves breathing and other somatic actions; even what we call passive perceiving involves action. Simply to see our surroundings, we must open and focus our eyes. In order to taste, even as passively as possible and even if someone is kind enough to feed us like a baby, we need to open our mouths.

Dorota Koczanowicz's insightful essay on "Eating as an Activity" admirably makes this point about tasting while instructively demonstrating somaesthetics' gastronomical meliorism. This involves more than explaining how we can learn to taste better (i.e., with more acuity and greater pleasure—cognitive and sensory—accruing from such acuity) by more attentively and skillfully

---

12   Richard Shusterman, "Pleasure, Pain, and the Somaesthetics of Illness: A Question for Everyday Aesthetics," in *Paths from the Philosophy of Art to Everyday Aesthetics*, ed. Oiva Kuisma, Sanna Lehtinen, and Harri Mäcklin (Helsinki: Finnish Society for Aesthetics, 2019), 201–214.
13   John Dewey, *Art as Experience* (Carbondale: Southern Illinois University Press, 1987), 54.

performing our chewing and swallowing while coordinating them with our breathing and smelling and other somatic activities involved in ingesting food and drink. This gastronomical meliorism is also an issue of cultural politics: to raise the status of our eating experience to the legitimacy and quality of aesthetic experience, so that the mere *act* of eating becomes an *art* of eating imbued with cultural meaning and affording shared social pleasures. This art is not limited to the rich and sophisticated who dine on caviar and truffles. Costly delicacies and service are not necessary for artful eating. I witnessed this art most powerfully in the humble context and simple fare of a Zen cloister in rural Japan.[14] The melioristic thrust of somaesthetic gastronomy extends to issues of health and hunger. Bad eating habits caused by somaesthetic indifference and corrupted tastes often result in obesity and related diseases. Reforming our eating habits could contribute to a more equitable global food distribution and healthier ecology, for example, by reducing the demand for meat and the use of plastics in food packaging and implements.

2

The next six essays of this book focus on the Man in Gold. As readers of his *Adventures* know, I am reluctant to speak for him. But since he is a "philosopher without words" who is very close to me, I feel obliged to explain him as best I can, especially here in response to these chapters about him. I am pleased that so many thoughtful critical readers share my fascination for his mysterious being and his dramatic entry into my life, which transformed my aesthetic theory and practice in astonishing ways. Jerold Abrams' fascination proved powerful enough to generate two perceptive essays rich in imaginative interpretations with intriguing philosophical and artistic intertextual connections. Unable to decide which of the essays was best for this book, we finally decided to include them both as bookends to Part 2's treatment of the Man in Gold.

The connections Abrams draws between Danto, Warhol, and my work with the Man in Gold are insightful and pregnant with meanings, too many and too deep to elaborate properly here. Let me focus on the theme of transfiguration. Danto uses the term in a broader sense than the biblical account of

---

14 Richard Shusterman, *Thinking through the Body: Essays in Somaesthetics* (Cambridge: Cambridge University Press, 2012); and "Somaesthetics and the Fine Art of Eating," in *Body Aesthetics*, ed. Sherri Irvin (New York: Oxford University Press, 2016), 261–280.

Jesus's transfiguration, which is the basis of Raphael's famous painting with that title, which Hegel and Nietzsche philosophically interpret. In Danto's art theory, transfiguration refers to the Christian notion more precisely defined as transubstantiation, where the Eucharist wafer and wine miraculously become Christ's body and blood. From the beginning, Danto affirmed the artworld's power to transform the ontological status of ordinary objects like Brillo boxes or bicycle wheels into the higher ontological status of artworks. Ordinary objects thus are "latent artworks waiting, like the bread and wine of reality, to be transfigured, through some dark mystery, into the indiscernible flesh and blood of the sacrament."[15] *This* transformation is a change of substance, but the biblical transfiguration is more a visual affair. In the transfiguration episode (recounted in the gospels of Matthew 17, Mark 9, and Luke 9, and the Second Epistle of Peter) Jesus takes disciples Peter, James, and John "into a high mountain apart by themselves," where he is visually transfigured before their eyes and then approached in conversation by the long-dead Moses and Elias. This inspires Peter to speak to Jesus, offering to construct tabernacles for each of the three prophets. But suddenly a bright cloud overshadows them all, while a voice declares "This is my beloved son," causing the disciples to cower in awe till Jesus calms them. Here the transfiguration is a visual change to intensified light and shining brightness. In the gospel of Matthew, when Jesus "was transfigured," "his face did shine as the sun, and his raiment was white as the light;" while Mark simply reports "his raiment became shining, exceeding white as snow." Luke, like Matthew, notes "his countenance was altered, and his raiment was white and glistering." Because it happened at night (Luke noting Jesus's companions "were heavy with sleep"), the transfiguration's shining light would emerge all the brighter through the surrounding darkness.[16]

The transfiguration of the Man in Gold is interesting to consider in this Christian context, because one could interpret his story as exemplifying transfiguration in both the strict sense and the deeper sense of transubstantiation, in other words, not only a visual change through illumination but a change of substance or identity. Clearly, the Man in Gold has a visible aspect of transformative light that shines brightly on the background of darkness and gives his countenance and raiment a special aura. Indeed, this transfiguration through

---

15 Arthur Danto, "The Artworld," *Journal of Philosophy*, 61 (1964), 571–584.
16 All New Testament quotations here are from the King James Version. I provide a more detailed account of the different notions of transfiguration in "Art as Religion: Transfiguration of Danto's Dao," in *Danto and His Critics*, 2nd ed. Mark Rollins (Oxford: Blackwell, 2012), 251–266; and *Chemins de l'art. Transfigurations, du pragmatisme au zen*, tr. Raphaël Cuir (Paris: Al Dante, 2013).

light in darkness gives him birth, and, in this sense, defines his identity. But what is that identity? On one interpretation, the Man in Gold is the transubstantiation of the philosopher Richard Shusterman, enjoying a different ontological identity than the philosopher. But what is that ontological status? Is the Man in Gold an artwork, and would this constitute an ontological elevation that makes him superior to the philosopher? Or, instead, is the Man in Gold, as the imaginative creation of two people (Shusterman and Yann Toma), only a fictional entity with no real substantive identity, only a borrowed existence in the performances of Shusterman and the photographs, films, and texts relating to those performances. I cannot resolve these questions here; perhaps they are ultimately unresolvable or not worth resolving. The uncertainty of who (or *what* he is) certainly forms part of his charm, but also creates much of the discomfort his live appearance often arouses.

I am very grateful for Abrams' introduction of Philip K. Dick's golden man as a counterpart character to use (through comparison and contrast) in interpreting the Man in Gold. Although Dick's most famous novel has a prominent role in one of my key essays,[17] I was unaware of *The Golden Man* until Abrams brought it to my attention. If I had known it back in 2010 when the Man in Gold first emerged, I doubt if I would have had the courage to write a whole book about him or welcome him (so named) into my life and work. Abrams does such a fine, detailed job comparing the two figures that I dare not take the space here to extend the comparisons further. I would however like to highlight one point that relates back to Jesus and to what Abrams describes as Emersonian transfiguration. Although the Golden Man, like the Man in Gold, is attacked for his difference from ordinary humans, we have no sense that he physically and emotionally suffers from his rejection as the Man in Gold does. Even when imprisoned and shot at, the Golden Man remains invulnerable and untouched. In contrast, the Man in Gold's anguish and vulnerability are central to his story and explain his life of wandering. If he is (as Abrams describes him with Emerson's words) "a divine pilgrim" who "stands in the world ... [and] feels himself its native king," he is a persecuted pilgrim whose feelings of kingship (if he could feel them) are steeped in suffering and scornfully mocked by his tormentors, the way Roman soldiers mocked Jesus as "King of the Jews." Like Jesus, the Man in Gold brings a message of love but the powers of the world hate him for it; and his "happy end" involves departing this earth with a love-filled ascent to heaven. Although ancient Daoism is the explicit mythological

---

17 I use the concept of an "empathy box" from Dick's *Do Androids Dream of Electric Sheep?* (the source of the film *Blade Runner*) in Richard Shusterman, "The End of Aesthetic Experience," *The Journal of Aesthetics and Art Criticism* 55 (1997), 29–41.

framework for the extraterrestrial nature of the Man in Gold, it is not hard to read other mythologies into his story, including that of a science fiction hero, as Abrams portrays him.

Diane Richard-Allerdyce's Lacanian reading of the Man in Gold is also a splendid gift. I could almost feel the Man in Gold swelling with joy in being so deeply understood, because truly to understand his message of love is to see and love its beauty, and to communicate its loving message further, through words he cannot use. Adroitly applying Lacanian notions of the Real, the Symbolic, and the Imaginary, but also his concepts of the Mirror Stage and the "third term," she is able to convey what seem to me the deepest, most personal and affective layers of the work's meaning. Portraying *The Adventures of the Man in Gold* as a testimony of love's precious ambiguities, its indissoluble tangle of hopes, torments, and joys, of union and loss, she deftly explains how the story challenges both the autonomy of the individual and the unity of the self. Richard-Allerdyce moreover compellingly expresses the book's joy of liberatory boundary crossing (akin to the joy of transgression mentioned earlier) and its celebration of indeterminacy, hybridity, and a paradoxical *jouissance* that is both a forgetting and a remembering of self. We find here not only the familiar complementarity of gain and loss but also their contradictory identity: the loss of the philosopher's sense of self is in fact a gain of another self that was earlier lost in the formation of the philosopher-subject and was unconsciously mourned by him. With the Man in Gold, this lost self emerges from the repressed darkness of a primordial, palpable but inarticulable loss where the Lacanian realms of the Real and the Imaginary seem to overlap. This joy foregrounded through obscure loss gleams enigmatically, just like the illuminated images of the Man in Gold shine from the darkness. If Richard-Allerdyce sees the Man in Gold as a forgotten but now "remembered part of the author's being (rather than a projection or alter ego)," I would then ask in (the spirit of the book's complex hybridity and indeterminacy), why not both?

The concept of projection is central to Yvonne Bezrucka's chapter, but her intriguing application of this concept does not present the Man in Gold as the projection of the narrator's (secret, forgotten, or imagined) self. Instead, focusing less on the plotline of the book than on the performances it documents, Bezrucka sees the Man in Gold's projective function as a provocative stimulus for the real-life observers of his performances to project their own cultural and personal prejudices in their spontaneous reactions to him. Because of his strange appearance that strips him of the typical social "identity markers" through which we perceive and react to people, the Man in Gold creates an "epistemic void" or empty screen onto which those who encounter him project or reveal their own values and the limits of their sympathy and openness to difference. I know that his striking "embodied otherness" has often led sensitive Europeans to see him as symbolizing the many foreign migrant and refugee "others" who face persistent prejudice and socio-political rejection in European nations. The Man in Gold thus performs an epistemic and ethical function of making people more aware of their prejudices and intolerance, which, as Bezrucka perceptively notes, provides an experimental way of practicing philosophy through embodied performance that instructs both the performer and the audience. The performer here, who otherwise enjoys a privileged life of acceptance and security, can get a small taste of "existential vulnerability" and "defenseless openness to others." Although the Man in Gold is active in movement and gesture, Bezrucka rightly notes an important passive aspect of his activity in which, rather than self-assertion, he silently "makes himself the vessel and vehicle of other people's meaning and will." Other readers of the *Adventures* will instead see the Man in Gold as the active possessing force that takes the performer (and the story's narrator) as his vessel or vehicle.[18]

Vessels play an important role in the Man in Gold's adventures, even in the literal sense of concrete, material vessels. The chapter written by Else Marie Bukdahl, with textual supplements by Benthe Norheim that include a passage by Claus Ørntoft, offers images of those concrete vessels as well as photos of other sculptures by this Danish artist couple, whom I met through Else Marie. (I cannot help but use her Christian name, and those of Claus and Benthe, because of our intimate friendship nourished through the lovely days and nights I spent in their homes and our shared experience with the Man in Gold.) This chapter is special because its authors actually witnessed the Man in Gold, and sheltered him with sympathy and love. Else Marie's text usefully puts the Man in Gold in the larger context of my work in philosophy and the arts, with its method of transactional experiential inquiry, including my experience of curating an art exhibition in Paris.[19] Yann Toma exhibited photographs and videos of the Man in Gold at that Paris show, but my artistic transactions with Benthe and Claus, that Benthe so beautifully describes, came later. They were

---

18   We need not presume an absolute or vitiating contradiction between the performer and narrator acting to present the Man in Gold and instead being possessed by him. Perhaps there is rather an interpenetration of roles and energies, a blurring of influence, a blending of the active and passive that defines our experience.

19   See Richard Shusterman, "Transactional Experiential Inquiry: From Pragmatism to Somaesthetics," *Contemporary Pragmatism*, 12 (2015) 180–195. The art show at Galerie Michel Journiac was titled *Aesthetic Transactions: Pragmatist Philosophy through Art and Life*, with a catalogue of the same title. Its website is more easily accessible: http://aestheticvtransactions.webs.com/.

so generous in their welcoming of the Man in Gold—providing the most precious props for the climax of his quest in the *Adventures*—that I included their artistic biographies at the back of that book, along with Yann's.

The salient hybridity of the *Adventures* includes the multiplicity of its contributors. The art of Claus and Benthe was a powerful inspiration to the artistry of that book, contributing not only to its images but to its imaginative atmosphere and magical mood. It therefore seems important for a fuller understanding of the Man in Gold to have the testimony of those who not only know him by personal acquaintance but also can best explain the artworks with whom he interacted. Why do we not have similar testimony by Yann Toma, who is so extremely close to the Man in Gold as to be essential to his existence? I have often asked Yann to write up an account of his thoughts and feelings concerning the Man in Gold, a text that I could ponder by myself or share with others interested in the *Adventures*, such as readers (and authors) of this book. Yann always agreed, but never in fact provided one. I refrain from pressing him about this reticence, because I sense his reluctance to testify or to explain his silence. How to account for it? My best explication is that Yann is playing the Man in Gold's role of refusing verbal expression and thus insisting that his visual art amply expresses his experiences and understandings of the Man in Gold—and his feelings for him. We can see in the *Adventures* that Yann loves him. Indeed, as many commentators recognize, love is a key theme of the book, not only romantic love but also the love of art and the affectionate, creative love among collaborating artists. Love, perhaps, is also the deep, motivating force that created the book. Euripides long ago claimed, "Love [Eros, the god or his power] surely teaches a poet, even the one who was previously uninspired."[20]

The following chapter by Lu Yang is very welcome and helpful for several reasons. First, it elaborates and complicates the interpretation of the theme of love in the *Adventures* by highlighting love's errant dangers and misdeeds. Building on the painfully frank confession in the book's preface that relates to a secret love outside the narrating author's marriage, which, when discovered through photography, led to the end of his marriage, Yang convincingly interprets the book as tale of sin, punishment, and redemption. If the narrating author (a philosopher of art) sinned through too much love, by loving beyond the limits set by marriage, then his punishment was loss of love through the ruin of his marriage, whose ruin came through a photographic image. The reaction to this loss of love was the birth of Man in Gold, a creature

---

20   Cited in Claud Calame, *The Poetics of Eros in Ancient Greece*, tr. Janet Lloyd (Princeton: Princeton University Press, 1999), 199.

of photographic art, who wanders the world seeking love and finally finds it in a work of sculptural art and the supportive, nurturing love of artists (Yann Toma and the author's Danish friends). If we take this interpretive line further in a psychoanalytic direction, the Man in Gold who possessed the narrating author to write his book is the projection of the author's unconscious, an imaginary counterpart of the narrating author's subconscious, miserably sorry self. If the Man in Gold is a strange, lonely creature desperately seeking love but repeatedly punished by disappointment and rejection until the happy ending of union with the sculptural Wanmei among a loving community of artists, what does this imply for the narrating author?[21] One reading is that redemption of the loss of traditional social bonds of family (wife and daughter) comes through the alternative, more imaginative, and more tolerant world of art.

However, as Richard-Allerdyce's penetrating proposal suggests, there may be deeper, unconscious losses of forgotten selves lurking beneath the narrative. In the story, the Man in Gold thinks Wanmei may be an avatar of his imagined goddess mother, Wu Xiaoxing. Is the mourned loss of love motivating the tale, the love of the narrating author for his lost wife, or of other failed romances (long forgotten and perhaps too many or too embarrassing to remember), or is it the loss of a mother's love? The Man in Gold was born five years after the death of the narrating author's beloved mother. Was that death the painful, forgotten loss of love that spurred him to take on the Man in Gold, or did the forgotten pain of losing a mother's love come earlier: in childhood, in the forced separation of nursery school, in the birth of a younger sibling, in the loss of the mother's breast through weaning, in the realization of being an individual separate from one's mother? To pursue these questions risks turning this critical discussion of a book into a clinical one of psychoanalyzing an author; that is inappropriate here.

This book is fortunate to have Lu Yang's chapter because it speaks to the reception of the Man in Gold in China (as described by the *Adventures* expert Chinese translator) but also indicates the enthusiastic Chinese reception of somaesthetics in general. All of my authored books on somaesthetics and pragmatism have been translated into Chinese (except for the latest one published in 2021).[22] Despite this warm reception of my somaesthetic texts and ideas,

---

21   Wanmei's material existence as a sculpture is important. The desiring love of the Man in Gold for Wanmei (visually represented in his luminous embrace) is not the objectification of a real woman but the humanizing spiritualization of an object, a statue.

22   That book is Richard Shusterman's *Ars Erotica: Sex and Somaesthetics in the Classical Arts of Love* (Cambridge: Cambridge University Press, 2021). The Chinese reception of my work includes a book on pragmatism and somaesthetics that exists only in Chinese, as it was constructed and translated from a series of lectures given at Fudan University in 2017.

I have been unable to do my usual work of practical somaesthetics in China. In contrast to Japan and South Korea and several European countries where I have often given practical somaesthetic workshops in body consciousness, I never managed to arrange one in China, despite my desire to do so. I do not know (and will not risk probing) the precise reasons for China's apparent reluctance to host this practical work: there may be political, ideological, academic, or merely bureaucratic factors. It is therefore important and appropriate that Lu Yang titles his chapter on the Man in Gold "On Shusterman's Somaesthetic Practice" because the *Adventures* is the only dimension of that practice that China has witnessed, apart from some film clips of the Man in Gold that have been projected there. However, the *Adventures* is where Chinese intellectuals can best understand the Man in Gold, not only through the book's images and story, but also through the grace of Lu Yang's translation. His highlighting of Daoism is a third reason why Lu Yang's chapter is particularly useful, as Daoist themes and mystery pervades the *Adventures*, which also includes key quotes from the legendary Laozi, founder of Daoism. I should confess, however, that unlike the quotes from Laozi, the Daoist goddess Wu Xiaoxing and the divine Wanmei (believed to be her avatar) are the fictional products of the narrating author of the *Adventures*, inspired no doubt by earthly beauties he has known and by the imaginative vision of the Man in Gold.

In the final chapter of Part 2, Jerold Abrams analyzes certain performative, photographical aspects of the Man in Gold to develop a remarkable interpretation of his filmic existence, whose presence in the *Adventures* is significantly diminished by the book's print format, which allows only a few stills from the movies about him. Abrams is indeed the first to provide an extended critical discussion of the Man in Gold in film. There are only six movies starring the Man in Gold, and *Walk the Golden Night*, the sole one available in its entirety on Vimeo, is the focus of Abrams' impressive chapter. His wide-ranging analysis relates this film to influential movies and theorists in fascinating ways that enrich the film's meaning through interpretation while preserving its strange mystery. He recognizes that this film, like the Man in Gold himself and his book *Adventures*, resists clear classification into familiar forms or genres, floating instead in a mysterious in-between space. Abrams deftly portrays how *Walk the Golden Night* hovers between "documentary film and fiction film," "a detective film ... and ... a science fiction film." I cannot dispel the mystery and strangeness of this film, as I did not make it. Yann Toma filmed it with the camera of an iPhone 4 late on a Saturday night in Cartagena in a series of fairly long shots, and his student Elliot Storey then edited the film in Paris. I might have edited it differently; perhaps beginning the film with some of its current closing shots of the Man in Gold absorbing the powerful streams of light (that Abrams well describes) and thus creating a visual narrative suggesting the luminous arrival and energizing of the Man in Gold for his Cartagena adventure.

Abrams' comparing *Walk the Golden Night* to *Citizen Kane* is humbling, almost to the point of shame. It is true that these films share a sense of fictional documentary and unresolved, even unresolvable, mystery. One might wonder what mystery for the Man in Gold could be the counterpart to Kane's enigmatic dying word "Rosebud?" If I had to suggest such a mystery, the one that haunts me would be the real identity of "Wanmei" (who is visually absent from *Walk the Golden Night* and appears only at the end of the book *Adventures*, after the Cartagena episode that forms the basis of the film). We more or less know who she is for the Man in Gold: the imagined, erotically desired avatar of his presumed mother, the Daoist goddess Wu Xiaoxing. But who might she be for the narrating author whose words gave these divinely beautiful women their identities and names? The implied identification of mother goddess and erotic target suggests the primal sin of incest—desired if not performed. Does this extend to the narrating author, who certainly loved his mother and perhaps never got over her death in 2005? Was he seeking her in another world through the Man in Gold? I do not know, and the Man in Gold cannot say. His wordless silence is an apt reminder to end here my words of response.

CHAPTER 14

On the Path of Somaesthetics: An Interview with Richard Shusterman

Yanping Gao

The following interview was conducted online in the spring of 2020 because of COVID-19. The interviewer, Yanping Gao, is Associate Professor at CASS, and the author of *Winckelmann's Vision of Greek Art* (Peking University Press, 2016). She is also coeditor of China's journal *International Aesthetics*. The notes were added in editing the interview for publication in this book.

YANPING GAO:
Perhaps we should begin by noting that we are doing this interview online instead of in-person as originally planned, at the international somaesthetics conference scheduled for May 7–8, 2020 in Shanghai, at the Somaesthetics Center of East China Normal University. The conference, of course, has been cancelled. I do not think it's the right time to ask you how somaesthetics relates to the COVID-19 crisis; our scientific knowledge of the virus is still too limited and uncertain for good answers to such questions. But our plan to interview at the Shanghai conference leads into the first questions I'd like to ask you, whether or not you wish to address the COVID-19 question. Your aesthetic theories have been very influential in China. The Shanghai somaesthetics center is one example, but one could also mention the books, articles, and doctoral theses about your pragmatist aesthetics and somaesthetics, as well as published interviews in Chinese academic journals which are more numerous than your interviews published in English. You have no formal training in Chinese or Chinese philosophy. How did you come to be so deeply engaged with Chinese thought and how do you see the role of scholarly interviews (like this one) in your philosophical work?

RICHARD SHUSTERMAN:
I agree that our scientific knowledge of COVID-19 is still inadequate to draw extensive and confident conclusions, but I would not want to avoid this issue entirely, so let me suggest a few simple and perhaps already obvious points. The most repeated instructions to mitigate

the spread of the virus insist on three key points: social distancing, more frequent and more thorough washing of hands, and the wearing of face masks that cover the mouth and nose. All these demands involve suddenly and radically changing our deeply entrenched bodily habits, and this in turn calls for greater somaesthetic awareness and self-knowledge to ensure better somatic self-control. Enhanced body consciousness enables better monitoring of one's distance from others and restraining our naturally felt impulses to shake hands or embrace those dear to us, as we (through habit) automatically tend to do. Better body awareness enables more mindfulness of proper handwashing, and can help us learn to be more somatically comfortable wearing face masks and to talk more effectively through them. In the West where mask wearing for health reasons is far less common than in East Asia, we need to transform our aesthetic perception concerning the mask-wearing faces of others, so as not to judge mask wearers as weird or menacing in some way. Certainly at the outset of the crisis, such feelings of aesthetic unease or psychological discomfort in seeing masked faces created an unpleasant atmosphere that troubled personal interaction in public places. Moreover, enhanced body consciousness could play a helpful role in diagnosis, particularly in self-diagnosis. In situations where mass testing is impossible or impractical, one must fall back on personal judgment of one's health. Individuals with greater mastery of body consciousness can better recognize subtle symptoms of illness in themselves before being tested and can then take appropriate measures of self-quarantine or getting tested and treated by medical staff. What seems an asymptomatic condition may later reveal itself as symptomatic, and spur the individual toward a sharper and more penetrating level of somaesthetic awareness.

That is all I should say now with respect to this virus that ruined our original interview plans. But as for interviews, they are much easier to conduct in writing through email than through the traditional "live" in-person meeting format. The live interview is much more enjoyable in its initial recording stage. But, at least in my experience, it takes a great deal of time to edit, because my spontaneous oral answers always seem less precise and cogent (when I see them transposed in written form) than texts that I compose directly in writing. Transcribed oral communication is probably less precise or effective because its original oral utterance relies on contextual and somatic clues (like gesture) to convey one's meaning more accurately and cogently. Those clues are missing when one does an interview by email, so this interview method although initially less fun is ultimately more efficient.

There are two main reasons why I appreciate the interview form in doing philosophy. First, some of the questions the interviewer raises can be refreshingly surprising. An interview can bring me to think of interesting points that relate to my work but that I never regarded as so related and that I would never have otherwise considered without the stimulus of a question. In philosophy's standard form of the academic article or book, the philosopher decides the limits of discourse and thus can focus solely on that with which she is fully familiar and comfortable while avoiding any aspect of the topic that she feels is inconvenient or too difficult to address. Nothing unfamiliar enters the circumscribed world of her thought. The questions imposed by an interviewer can enlighten and stimulate by piercing that protective circle.

The second reason I think interviews are useful is that they encourage a simpler, more direct, and therefore often clearer formulation of one's philosophical views. I mean "clearer" not in the sense of sharper accuracy or more systematic elaboration but rather in the sense of easier to understand. Because interviews are a less formal way of doing philosophy (where one does not need to write in the official academic style and cite all the relevant books, articles, and authorities in order to satisfy the academic gatekeepers for standard scholarly publications), the philosopher need not mince her words. She can speak spontaneously and unguardedly in her own voice without having to qualify her opinions to make them palatable to those in charge and without having to express them in formal academic style. I like this sort of freedom and informality because it encourages not only more spontaneity of thinking and dialogical exchange, but also a refreshing pithiness of direct statement. If I were making these same points in an academic journal article on the metaphilosophy of philosophical interviews, it would probably take me many more words and would require an elaborate setting up of the problem with a review of the relevant literature. It is more energizing to get right to the point. This is true, I believe, not only for the philosopher making the point but also for the interviewer and the eventual readers. That directness, clarity, and more accessible readability are very useful for conveying one's work effectively to a broader audience. I think this is especially true for foreign audiences for whom my interviews are often translated. It is usually far easier to translate the direct dialogical text of an interview (whether oral or written) than the complex syntax and semantics of academic prose, subtly nuanced and qualified as it must be to meet prevailing academic standards. Moreover, when I know that the interview will appear in a language that most of my colleagues (and I) cannot read, I tend to feel even freer and probably answer more imaginatively.

YG: But now please return specifically to my question concerning China, where you've published many interviews and dialogues with philosophers and literary theorists, and even with the renowned Chinese painter Pan Gongkai. How did you get involved with Chinese thought?

RS: Paradoxically, my journey into Chinese intellectual life began with a relationship with Japanese culture that was not particularly intellectual. In 1992 through a romantic relationship with a Japanese-American artist, I got to know her family who maintained a home (not far from New York City) that was rich in the beautiful traditional Japanese culture of everyday life: fine Japanese cuisine and furnishings, tatami floors, pretty gardens and flowers, and graceful refinement of manners. Up until then I had always viewed Asian culture as alien and unappealing. But through this largely aesthetic, affective relationship I became enchanted with Asian culture and its somaesthetic dimensions. Of course, this attitude might be criticized today as a form of sexist orientalism; but an attitude of fascination and desire for the Other is not always or necessarily exploitative. It can generate deeper transcultural understanding, and I hope this has always been the case in my encounter with East-Asian culture.

My first acquaintance with East Asia was with Japan and Korea. My book *Pragmatist Aesthetics* was published in Japan three years before it appeared in Chinese, and as a result I was invited by Hiroshima University to spend a year there as special research professor. (The book's Korean translation also preceded its Chinese version.) I soon learned that Japanese culture was grounded in Chinese thought of which I knew nothing. That changed when a professor from Peking University wrote to ask me if he could translate my book *Pragmatist Aesthetics* into Chinese. I agreed and promised to write a preface for the translation, because I regard books as tools of communication that can be more effective if they have prefaces that can contextualize their use in a different culture. To write that preface, I began to study Chinese philosophy, guided (through email correspondence) by Roger Ames, whom I am proud to recognize as my unofficial teacher in this field. Another translation contract soon followed, this time for *Practicing Philosophy*. That meant I had to study enough Chinese philosophy to write two substantial, contextualizing prefaces. I was very encouraged and pleased by what I read, noting the important ways that Chinese thought converged with themes in pragmatism and somaesthetics. This, of course, inspired me to read further, as did the need to write prefaces for further translations of my books into Chinese, including one book that does not exist yet in English but was based on a special series of lectures I delivered at Fudan University in May 2017. You probably know this book better than I do, because you not only translated it but also helped me put it together from various preliminary texts, lecture notes, and transcripts. For that work I sincerely thank you, and I should also here acknowledge my debt to the many scholar-translators who have made my books available in different languages.

YG: I think that your Chinese translators and the Chinese readership in philosophy and aesthetics would also like to thank you. Somaesthetics has been very popular among Chinese academics. All your works in this field but also your other major works have been translated into Chinese. Your writings have helped Chinese scholars to realize that Chinese culture has its own valuable traditions of embodiment that are worth exploring and reviving. How do you explain this popularity and what are the main inspirations you received from the Chinese tradition?

RS: My work has indeed been fortunate with respect to its Chinese reception. I am very happy that besides the publication of my texts and the extensive commentary on them, there is now a Somaesthetics Center at Shanghai's East China Normal University. I was initially surprised by the enthusiastic reception of my work in China, but now I believe I understand some of the reasons for it. Successful reception in a foreign country's intellectual field depends on the existence of positive and productive affinities between the work and influential elements in that foreign field or tradition. I can list five important affinities that I think made my work attractive to Chinese academics.

First, pragmatism has affinities with Marxism, which is the major, if not also the official, philosophy in communist China. Like Marxism, pragmatism is a naturalistic philosophy that emphasizes practice and the idea of transforming material realities rather than just theorizing about them. Both these philosophies of practice direct themselves toward democratic meliorism. Second, pragmatism is a philosophy that emphasizes change. Marxism (with its Hegelian-inspired notion of historical dialectic) is likewise a philosophy of change, but so is classical Chinese philosophy, which has its roots in the ancient *Yijing* or *Book of Changes*. A third affinity relates to respect for the body in philosophy. Classical Chinese philosophy recognizes the body's centrality in multiple ways, whether through the Confucian concern for its use in ritual and the arts or through the Daoist concern with disciplines of breathing and other body techniques. Because my work in somaesthetics (but also in pragmatist aesthetics) highlights the body and other material realities, Chinese theorists see it as opposing the dominant Western idealist tradition and as having affinities with Marxist materialist approaches. A fourth affinity is my concern for popular aesthetics, which converges not only with the Marxist emphasis on respecting and serving the common people, but also with the appreciation of popular arts that we can find in classical Chinese thought. Pluralism constitutes a fifth affinity between my work and classical Chinese philosophy, and it is from classical Chinese philosophy that the Chinese influence on my thought has been the strongest.

I have learned a great deal from both Confucianist and Daoist texts, particularly with respect to the five themes I mentioned above, but also with respect to the basic idea of philosophy as a way of life, something that one practices in everyday living rather than in mere theorizing through academic writing and teaching. The ideal of self-cultivation that is ethical, aesthetic, and somatic and that contributes to one's social environment beyond the self is an ideal central to my vision of pragmatist philosophy and somaesthetics. I tend to cite Confucian texts more often than Daoist texts in my philosophical writing because Confucian claims and quotations are easier to fit into a coherent chain of reasoning. But I feel the spirit of my work is as close or probably even closer to Daoist thought. In my most recent book, *The Adventures of the Man in Gold*, a philosophical tale rather than a standard philosophical treatise, Laozi is the only philosopher directly quoted, and indeed repeatedly quoted, and the book even quotes him also in traditional Chinese characters rather than merely in English and French or in the modern, simplified Chinese characters.[1]

---

1 Richard Shusterman, *The Adventures of the Man in Gold: Paths Between Art and Life* (Paris: Éditions Hermann, 2016).

Having noted the influence of Confucianist and Daoist texts, I should not neglect to mention the third important Chinese religious and philosophical tradition, that of Buddhism. Here the influence on my thought has been only indirect and more practical than theoretical. It has been only indirect because the Buddhist influence on my philosophical thinking came through my experience with Zen Buddhism in Japan, Zen having evolved from Zen Buddhism. The influence was more practical than theoretical because my study in the Zen dojo near Takehara focused on meditation techniques and their resultant experiences rather than theoretical philosophical questions. But I do not regard such practical influence as less important. I am a philosopher of experience. Most of my philosophical ideas come from experiences outside of the reading and writing of texts. My Zen experiences were deeply transformative for my thinking about body consciousness, as was my professional practice as a body therapist in the Feldenkrais Method. Finally, to return to the influence of Chinese culture, I should note my appreciation for its literati tradition of poetry, calligraphy, and ink-wash painting that beautifully exemplifies the classical Chinese ideal of aesthetic and ethical self-cultivation through artistic embodiment. I've written one essay on the ink-wash painting tradition, a tradition that is still vibrant in contemporary Chinese art, but I should emphasize that the Chinese influence on my thinking originated from philosophy not from the arts.[2]

Although reluctant to do so, I feel obliged to add another line of thought regarding the reception of my work in China. It concerns the international political context of the circulation of intellectual ideas, which we beauty-loving theorists prefer to ignore because it is too often too ugly. If there had not been good political relations between China and the United States in the first seventeen years of this century, I do not think that my books (as authored by an American pragmatist philosopher) would have been welcomed as they were. Perhaps they might not have been thought to be worth publishing. They may not even have been published. We should not forget that there are factors other than quality that influence the circulation of ideas, and those factors extend beyond academic and commercial and local political considerations to include international politics and its weaponization of culture. I should say no more.

---

2 Richard Shusterman, "Somaesthetics and Self-Cultivation in Chinese Art," in *Transformative Aesthetics*, ed. E. Fischer-Lichte and B. Wihstutz (London: Routledge, 2017), 83–109.

YG: Yes, let us leave the issue of international politics and return to philosophy. One could say that humanities research in the past three decades has been experiencing an "affective turn." In your recent book, *Act and Affect*, which you kindly noted that I edited and translated and which is currently published only in Chinese, the theme of affect is also central. How do you assess the role of "affect" in your own philosophy, both with respect to somaesthetics and to pragmatism in general? Does your notion of "affect" relate to affect in Deleuze or to Spinoza's philosophy which inspired Deleuze?

RS: One of the key aims of that book, *Act and Affect*, is to highlight that feeling is essential to action but also to thinking. Pragmatism is usually understood as a philosophy of action; the very term pragmatism derives from the Greek word for action. Critics of pragmatism often argue that it is too narrowly practical and focused on action, ignoring other important aspects of human existence. My book demonstrates how pragmatism can also be understood as a philosophy of feeling. It shows how the major pragmatist philosophers insist on the importance of feeling as the motor of action, as a crucial factor for structuring perception and thought, and as a key tool for ethical progress to a more caring and democratic society. Although the book is not yet published in English, the original germ of its argument appears in an article "Thought in the Strenuous Mood: Pragmatism as a Philosophy of Feeling."[3]

As for my understanding of affect, there are, indeed, some similarities between my philosophical views and those of Deleuze, but also some notable differences. I should mention an article that systematically compares my somaesthetics to Deleuze's philosophy of the body. It was published in a book on Deleuze and pragmatism, and it makes some useful points though it also involves some misinterpretations of my views. But I will not go into correcting them here.[4] Before responding to your question about affect, I should note that Deleuze and I share two important philosophical orientations. One is a respect for the idea of experience in philosophy, including nonlinguistic experience. This differentiates us from a very large group of philosophers

---

[3] Richard Shusterman, "Thought in the Strenuous Mood: Pragmatism as a Philosophy of Feeling," *New Literary History* 43, 3 (2012), 433–454.

[4] W. Małecki and S. Schleussner, "'What affects are you capable of': On Deleuze and Somaesthetics," in *Deleuze and Pragmatism*, ed. S. Bowden, S. Bignall and P. Patton (London: Routledge, 2015), 216–234.

who reject the notion of experience for philosophical thinking and insist on dealing only with conceptual entities or what can be formulated in language. Both Deleuze and I are particularly interested in the revelatory power of extraordinary experiences, including powerful aesthetic experiences, but he seems to see these experiences (as do Bergson, Blanchot, and Foucault) as revealing a superior realm of reality and as ontologically superior to ordinary experience whereas I am reluctant to leap to that conclusion. I instead see the revelatory power of extraordinary experiences as revealing previously unrecognized aspects of the same world we encounter in ordinary experience rather than some higher metaphysical realm. Such special or limit experience provides a heightened view of the real rather than a view of a higher reality.

The second orientation that Deleuze and I share can be described as a pragmatic stance. We both tend to understand what things are in terms of what they can do rather than in terms of a fixed material structure or essence. There is in this attitude a recognition of change rather than fixity and an appreciation of a melioristic dimension of philosophy. I think we share a faith, or at least a hope, that a better understanding can improve experience and one's manner of living and that philosophy can provide for better understanding by inventing new concepts rather than simply clarifying or defining old ones. The project of somaesthetics could be understood in this way, as a concept to improve our understanding and experience, most notably our somatic experience. Deleuze and I share the view that changing one's body practices can also produce new and better ways of understanding and living. Of course, Deleuze's recommended somatic transformation—becoming a body without organs (a very mysterious notion that seems extremely remote from our physiological body and whose examples come from drug addiction, hypochondria, and other problematic somatic behavior)—appears to be very different and more limited than the range of body practices on which somaesthetics focuses.[5]

---

5 G. Deleuze and F. Guattari derive their notion of the body without organs from Antonin Artaud who wrote in his play *To Have Done with the Judgment of God*, "When you will have made him a body without organs, then you will have delivered him from all his automatic reactions and restored him to his true freedom." Somaesthetics locates our unfreedom not so much in our organs, without which we could not act, but instead in our automatic unthinking habits that are largely produced by the institutions whose subjugating power

The notions of change and meliorism find expression in the concept of affect, which both Deleuze and I regard as involving changes in the body. One's body is continuously affected by other bodies (human and nonhuman) it encounters, and it reciprocally affects other bodies in the world. I am particularly concerned with those changes that influence our feelings and perceptions in ways that we either notice or could notice if we paid proper attention; not all modifications of the body reach the level of consciousness or promote thought or action. Deleuze takes his notion of affect from Spinoza's theory of emotion. Spinoza defines emotion as "the modifications of the body, whereby the active power of the said body is increased or diminished," and he notes "that the body can be affected [or modified] in many ways" that increase or diminish its power, but also in ways that do not influence the body's power in an appreciative way.[6] Spinoza thus has a bodily theory of emotion.

My concern with affect did not originally derive from reading Spinoza but from reading William James who was famous for his somatic theory of emotion (where emotion always involves some sort of motion or changes of the body) and from reading contemporary neuroscience that followed James in recognizing the somatic dimension of emotion and also thinking. Recently, in rereading Spinoza, I find that his views are extremely pertinent for somaesthetics. In fact, I believe his views on body-mind unity anticipate my idea of the soma. As you may recall, I define the soma as the sentient, living, purposive body, that is, an embodied subjectivity or body-mind. The soma includes both the body as a perceiving, conscious subjectivity and the body as a material thing in the world; it embraces both what Germans distinguish as the subjective, perceiving *Leib* and the material bodily object or *Körper*. The soma is thus a concept that expresses the essential ontological unity of what we call body and mind. Spinoza boldly asserts that same ontological unity. He writes "that mind and body are one and the same thing, conceived first under the attribute of thought, secondly, under the attribute of extension."[7] That one thing I regard as the soma. Moreover, in arguing that the soma is capable

---

shapes our subjectivity and that require critical somaesthetic reflection in order to reveal and overcome them.

6   Benedict de Spinoza, *Ethics*, in *The Chief Works of Benedict de Spinoza*, vol. 2, tr. R. H. M. Elwes (London: George Bell, 1884), 130.
7   *Ibid.*, 131.

of perception and purposive action, I find support in Spinoza's argument that no one has convincingly proved that our bodies are incapable of such things because no one has succeeded in fixing "the limits to the powers of the body."[8] Furthermore, the somaesthetic idea that our powers of thought depend on the body's powers and therefore that we might improve our cognition through improving our somatic condition, similarly finds support in Spinoza's affirmation "that the mind is not at all times equally fit for thinking ... but according as the body is more or less fitted for ... this."[9] When I introduced "somaesthetics" as a new name for certain old ways of thinking, I was conscious that many of its key ideas had already been expressed in the long history of philosophy East and West, but I did not highlight Spinoza. I'm happy to take this opportunity to acknowledge him as an important precursor to somaesthetics' advocacy of the unity of the soma as body-mind and to the importance of somatic power for our mental powers.

YG: Most scholars identify you as a body philosopher, the originator of somaesthetics, but the body was not at all part of your original field of research in which you established your international reputation in philosophy. That field was analytic literary theory. Your first two articles were on "The Anomalous Nature of Literature" and "The Logic of Interpretation," and your first article in *The Journal of Aesthetics and Art Criticism* (with which you have been closely associated) was "Aesthetic Blindness to Textual Visuality."[10] Your first book focused on literary criticism, while the second was devoted to T. S. Eliot; and literary topics appeared quite frequently in your articles and books until the early 2000s.[11] Thereafter, you seem to have lost your interest in literature, concentrating instead on the philosophy of the body and moving closer to the visual arts. You have published dialogues with visual artists, essays on visual art theory and art criticism

---

8 *Ibid.*, 132.
9 *Ibid.*, 133. In the book's philosophical preface, Kant and Nietzsche are mentioned once, and in the tale itself there is one passing mention of Plato, but of no other philosophers apart from Laozi.
10 Richard Shusterman, "The Anomalous Nature of Literature," *British Journal of Aesthetics* 18 (1978), 317–329; "The Logic of Interpretation," *Philosophical Quarterly* 28 (1978), 310–324; and "Aesthetic Blindness to Textual Visuality," *Journal of Aesthetics and Art Criticism* 41 (1982), 87–96.
11 Richard Shusterman, *The Object of Literary Criticism* (Amsterdam: Rodopi, 1984); and *T. S. Eliot and the Philosophy of Criticism* (New York: Columbia University Press, 1988).

(including a catalogue for an art show you curated in Paris), and you also created a series of works in performance art and video, as the Man in Gold, which resulted in a book. You have even experimented in cinema with documentary films about your work.[12] Is there any specific reason for this departure from literature and your movement toward visual art?

RS: That is a very interesting question. My concern for the body was already evident in *Pragmatist Aesthetics* (1992), and it became crucial through my project of reviving the idea of philosophy as an art of living in *Practicing Philosophy* (1997), where I introduced the term "somaesthetics." But let me try to explain the apparent trajectory from literature to visual art that you mention in terms of my educational background. Trained as an Austinian-Wittgensteinian analytic philosopher, I believed aesthetics suffered from making essentialist generalizations about what is common and special to all the arts. Because that essentialist approach generated either distortive inaccuracies or empty, abstract formulas about what art is, I thought it better to begin by theorizing from a narrower, sharper focus by concentrating on one art form. Literature was not only the art I knew best; it was also the art that shared the same medium as philosophy—namely language. Indeed, it is sometimes difficult to determine the boundary between literature and philosophy. Plato's best dialogues are both philosophy and literary art, as are the essays of Montaigne, Bacon, and Emerson, and the fictional philosophical tales of Voltaire and Diderot.

Now, having noted this literary genre of the philosophical tale, let me suggest that rather than having left literature aside, I have, in the end, returned to it in a deeper, fuller way by producing a literary work of philosophical fiction that incorporates my adventures in visual art and that reflects philosophically on its own strange hybrid status. This book, *The Adventures of the Man in Gold*, is bilingual; includes fact and fiction; and is composed of text and illustrations from the performances of the Man in Gold as photographically captured by the artist Yann Toma, my collaborator in this artistic project. Yann is

---

12 The art show was *Aesthetic Transactions* at Galerie Michel Journiac, Paris (2012); for more information see https://aesthetictransactions.webs.com. The documentary film *Philosophical Encounters with Richard Shusterman* is directed by Pawel Kuczynski (Delos Films, 2013). Another documentary, entitled *The Man in Gold: Exposure and Self-Knowledge*, directed by Pawel Kuczynski (for Delos Films) is scheduled for release in 2021.

only one example (probably the richest) of how I came to engage with visual art through personal contacts with artists. Having encountered my philosophical writings on subjects other than visual art, some intellectual artists sought to involve me in their visual art projects, and this drew me ever closer to the visual arts. Carsten Höller, Tatiana Trouvé, ORLAN, and Pan Gongkai are key examples, and they all participated in the Paris art show I curated. Something similar happened with the documentary film; its director, Pawel Kuczynski, proposed this film project because he knew my philosophical work. And through the fascinating experience of shooting the film I improved my understanding of cinema and gained a deeper appreciation of the art of acting.

Experience is a key concept in my pragmatist aesthetics and somaesthetics because I believe in the value of learning from the practical, embodied experience of doing and then reflecting on that practical experience. My work in somaesthetics would have been greatly impoverished if it had not been nourished by my practical experience in various body disciplines, especially my professional training and work as a Feldenkrais practitioner. As you know, I teach somaesthetics not only through lectures but through practical workshops.

YG: Yes, I know you are a Feldenkrais practitioner, and I participated in one of your two-day practical workshops in Denmark. You have also written about the Alexander Technique (which Dewey studied), and bioenergetics. These body practices form part of the somatic movement of so-called "new age" culture that was strongly influenced by Asian thinking and spirituality. You too have been influenced by Asian culture and spirituality, at least in terms of your experience with Zen. Is this convergence of your interests in the body and Asia merely a coincidence?

RS: I should preface my answer by putting things in historical perspective. The Alexander Technique was invented and widely practiced long before the new age. Alexander's books began appearing already in 1910, and John Dewey became his pupil in 1916, but what we call new age culture did not really take hold until the 1970s. Many movements advocating attention to the body and techniques of somatic or psychosomatic improvement appeared in the West long before the new age. William James was an influential participant in the physical culture movement of the 1890s. My initial exploration of the somatic techniques and theories of Alexander, Feldenkrais, and Bioenergetics was not related to any interest in Asian culture. It was inspired by dancer friends who were, indeed, my first inspiration for the somatic turn in my thinking, including my transformation from a typical analytic philosopher focused on language to a pragmatist philosopher concerned also with nondiscursive or nonconceptual forms of understanding. The inspiration for this turn was decidedly experiential. The powerful, transformative, enlightening bodily experiences I had with these dancers convinced me of the need to take the body more seriously in my philosophical explorations and to appreciate forms of cognition and communication that are not discursive. I began studying Western body practices in the late 1980s and early 1990s long before I knew anything about Asian philosophy, though through my dancer friends I did experiment with yoga and *taijiquan*. I began my professional Feldenkrais training in 1998, but I did not begin studying Asian philosophy until after the year 2000 when I was obliged to prepare prefaces for two books of mine that were being translated into Chinese and were eventually published in October 2002. The academic year of 2002–2003 was also the period I spent in Japan and studied Zen with Master Inoue Kido. Of course, it is certainly true that my interest in Asian philosophy and its associated somatic techniques reinforced my conviction in the importance of the soma and my recognition of the spiritual dimensions of somatic cultivation and body consciousness. I should also admit that my closest dancer friend was thoroughly steeped in the new age spirit and was a passionate yoga practitioner and instructor. Perhaps some of her enthusiastic new age feeling rubbed off on me (at least enough to experiment with *taijiquan* and yoga), but my focus was primarily Western somatic methodology because it seemed more scientific and suitable to my analytic and pragmatist method of thinking at that time. To be honest, I was also suspicious and uncomfortable about what I perceived as the uncritical superficiality of new age thinking and of its knowledge of Asian philosophical traditions. I did not know those traditions myself, but I did not believe that my new age dancer friends really knew those philosophies in an adequate way either. One of my reasons for spending a year in Japan and studying Zen in a remote Japanese dojo was to try to escape the limits of Western new age orientalism. I was not satisfied with new age orientalism or "Upper West Side Buddhism," as Arthur Danto characterized the American reception of Zen inspired largely by D. Z. Suzuki and his seminars at Columbia University in New York. In one of our textual exchanges, I contrast my own Zen experience with the New York (apparently new age) version that Danto imbibed, a contrast Danto himself recognized.[13]

YG: Your ideas of body consciousness and somaesthetics are defined as covering perception from all the bodily senses, but your work seems to focus particularly on proprioception. Why?

RS: Somaesthetics is indeed concerned with all the bodily senses. Moreover, I understand sensory perception as essentially transmodal. In other words, we perceive not through the separate action of the different senses, each separately providing their own distinct sensory input that the mind then combines; we instead perceive through our senses working together from the outset to deliver an integrated sensory perception. The perception of a particular sensory modality thus involves other senses. With taste and smell this transmodal nature is most obvious, but transmodality pertains throughout the realm of sensory perception.

There are two reasons why my writings in somaesthetics highlight proprioception. First, this sense modality has long been neglected. Since ancient times, we typically speak of the five senses: sight, hearing, smell, taste, and touch, thus ignoring proprioception and its related sense of kinaesthesia or the sense of movement. Proprioceptive input, however, is essential for proper regulation of posture and movement and consequently for all the other sensory perceptions that depend on the proper control of our posture and movement (such as steadying the head and directing the eyes to stabilize and orient the gaze for seeing). The ignoring of proprioception contributes to neglect of the body because the proprioceptive sense is focused on the body itself rather than external things. This, then, is the second reason somaesthetics should highlight proprioception. Proprioception is a distinctively somaesthetic sense because it concerns perception of one's own body rather than external objects, whether we perceive those objects through the distant senses of sight and hearing or the more proximate senses of smell, taste, and touch. With proprioception we sense the body itself as we feel it from the inside, perceiving our posture and balance in rest and in movement

---

13 Richard Shusterman, "Art as Religion: Transfigurations of Danto's Dao," in *Danto and His Critics*, ed. Mark Rollins, 2nd ed. (Malden: Blackwell Publishing, 2012), 249–266. For Danto's response, see 308–310. The exchange appears in French in my *Chemins de l'art: Transfigurations, du pragmatisme au zen* (Paris: Al Dante, 2014) to which Danto provides the book's "Afterword."

through sensory input about the position or tension of our muscles, tendons, and joints. Proprioception (together with the sense of bodily heat and pain) belongs to what neuroscience distinguishes as the distinctively somaesthetic form of sensory perception, and the neuroscientists locate its cerebral processing in what they identify as the somaesthetic cortex.

YG: Your somaesthetics seems focused on perfecting somatic perception and performance. Is there a somaesthetics for disabled people?

RS: That is a very useful question. One of the early worries that people expressed about somaesthetics was that it was essentially designed to serve (and to favor) the beautiful, strong, healthy, and youthful members of society while disregarding or demeaning those with somatic difficulties. Even people who were very sympathetic to my work in aesthetics (such as Arthur Danto) initially expressed this concern about privileging the somatically superior and degrading the physically disabled. One way I respond to this worry is by insisting that somaesthetics is essentially designed for disabled people because all people are disabled in some way. What I mean by this perhaps puzzling statement is that we all have a certain degree of somatic malfunctioning at some point in time (whether it is because of an illness, an injury, excessive fatigue, a bad habit, or simply the increasing decrepitude of old age). As I explain in *Body Consciousness* (Cambridge University Press, 2008), somaesthetics does not agree with the way that Maurice Merleau-Ponty and other thinkers sort people into two simple categories of the disabled and the normal. In the first category, we find brain-damaged or otherwise severely physically impaired individuals who suffer from pathological somatic incapacities, such as the patient Schneider whom Merleau-Ponty repeatedly discusses. In the other category belong the rest of us "normal" people whose bodily functioning Merleau-Ponty describes as miraculously flawless and spontaneous. Instead, I argue that we all suffer (at certain times, in various ways, and to different degrees) from various bodily malfunctions or disabilities (headaches, backaches, stiffness, lethargy, flawed motor habits, injuries, arthritis, etc.). In *Thinking through the Body* (Cambridge University Press, 2012), I discuss a series of these malfunctions or disabilities that are connected with somatic habits or muscle memory and that I describe as the somaesthetic pathologies of everyday life.

The more disabled one is the more one needs the intelligence of somaesthetic thinking to overcome one's bodily disabilities and limits in order to perform the tasks that one needs or wishes to perform. When one is young, healthy, and uninjured, one's mere strength is often enough to get the somatic job done. However, when a person is somatically disabled in some way (even if merely through the ailments and weakness that typically come with injuries, sickness, and old age), somatic intelligence is needed to circumvent the disabling condition. It is therefore not surprising that both Alexander and Feldenkrais suffered from somatic disabilities and that precisely these disabilities inspired them to explore the body mechanics for developing methods to overcome those disabilities through alternative ways of using the body. There is a larger lesson here for our understanding of disability. What we label (and mourn) as disability can be enabling as well as disabling; it can teach us new ways of seeing and doing things. At the very least it can instruct us in patience. In the same way, although somaesthetics is concerned with improving our health and our pleasure, it also recognizes that there are valuable things to learn through illness and pain that pleasure and health cannot teach us as effectively or deeply. I have not yet given this dimension of somaesthetics as much attention as it deserves, but I make a start in a recent article on "Pleasure, Pain and the Somaesthetics of Illness."[14]

YG: Will your next book be devoted to pain and disability? I should not conclude this interview without a forward-looking question regarding your next book.

RS: My next book should appear before this interview because it is already in production. One could say it concerns an area where pleasure and pain, ability and disability commingle or intertwine in significant ways, but where, one hopes, the positivity of performative abilities and pleasures predominate. The book concerns the somaesthetics of erotic love, which the ancient poet Sappho already recognized as "bittersweet" and a "giver of pain" as well as pleasure. There are, of course, the pangs of erotic desire and the various pains that sometimes occur in lovemaking (especially in some of its more intense and tempestuous forms). There are also obvious forms of erotic disability, which include perceptual and ethical insensitivity to the needs and feelings of one's lover but also various physical (and aesthetic) flaws

---

14 Shusterman, "Pleasure, Pain, and the Somaesthetics of Illness: A Question for Everyday Aesthetics," in *Paths from Philosophy of Art to Everyday Aesthetics*, ed. O. Kuisma, S. Lehtinen and H. Mäcklin (Helsinki: Finnish Society of Aesthetics, 2019), 201–214.

in one's lovemaking performance. This forthcoming text (the third of my books on somaesthetics with Cambridge University Press) is titled *Ars Erotica: Sex and Somaesthetics in the Classical Arts of Love*.

The topic of lovemaking is extremely sensitive, and its study seems untimely and unwelcome in today's cultural climate, especially in academic humanities research. Although sex is an obvious topic for somaesthetic research, I always feared that devoting an extensive study to eroticism (given its associations with the evils of sexism, carnality, predatory violence, and patriarchy) would somehow discredit the reputation of somaesthetics. That is one reason why this book took a very long time to write, and why I distance my arguments by making them through historical examples of erotology in a variety of premodern cultures rather than engaging in contemporary analysis. The book examines the potential of erotic love to provide somaesthetic experiences that are richly cognitive and ethically ennobling as well as aesthetically rewarding. It thus suggests the possibility of a different approach to sex education. However, the topic of lovemaking remains troublingly awkward for me to talk about, and I can easily imagine that my discussing it could make you feel very uncomfortable (even though you are only reading my words far away in Beijing), so let me conclude our interview now by thanking you for your questions and your interest in my philosophical work.

Abbreviated Bibliography and Filmography of Richard Shusterman

Books

The Object of Literary Criticism. Amsterdam: Rodopi, 1984 (revised French edition, *L'Objet de la critique littéraire*, 2009).
Aesthetics: Vol. 5 of Sources for the Study of Philosophy in High School. Ed. R. Shusterman et al. Jerusalem: Ministry of Education, 1986 (in Hebrew).
T. S. Eliot and the Philosophy of Criticism. London and New York: Duckworth and Columbia University Press, 1988.
Analytic Aesthetics. Ed. R. Shusterman. Oxford: Blackwell, 1989.
The Interpretive Turn: Philosophy, Science, Culture. Ed. R. Shusterman, J. F. Bohman, and D. R. Hiley. Ithaca: Cornell University Press, 1991.
Pragmatist Aesthetics: Living Beauty, Rethinking Art. Oxford: Blackwell, 1992. Second edition. New York: Rowman and Littlefield, 2000; with a new introduction and additional chapter. Translated into 14 languages: French, German, Finnish, Portuguese, Polish, Japanese, Korean, Chinese, Spanish, Slovak, Hungarian, Romanian, Italian, and Russian.
Sous l'interprétation. Paris: Éditions de l'éclat, 1994. Translated into German.
Practicing Philosophy: Pragmatism and the Philosophical Life. New York: Routledge, 1997. Translated into German, French, Chinese, Polish, and Japanese.
La modernité en questions. Ed. R. Shusterman, F. Gaillard, and J. Poulain. Paris: Cerf, 1998.
Interpretation, Relativism, and the Metaphysics of Culture. Ed. R. Shusterman and Michael Krausz. New York: Humanity Books, 1999.
Bourdieu: A Critical Reader. Ed. R. Shusterman. Oxford: Blackwell, 1999.
La fin de l'expérience esthétique. Tr. Jean-Pierre Cometti. Pau: Presse Universitaire de Pau, 1999.
Performing Live: Aesthetic Alternatives for the Ends of Art. Ithaca: Cornell University Press, 2000. Translated into German, Chinese, Korean, and French.
Surface and Depth: Dialectics of Criticism and Culture. Ithaca: Cornell University Press, 2002. Translated into Chinese.
The Range of Pragmatism and the Limits of Philosophy. Ed. R. Shusterman. Oxford: Blackwell, 2004.
O stuze I życiu. Od poetyki hip-hopu do filozofii somatycznej. Wroclaw: Alta 2, 2007. A collection of articles by R. Shusterman, and interviews with him, selected and translated into Polish by Wojciech Małecki.
Aesthetic Experience. Ed. R. Shusterman and Adele Tomlin. New York: Routledge, 2008.

Body Consciousness: A Philosophy of Mindfulness and Somaesthetics. Cambridge: Cambridge University Press, 2008. Translated into French, Polish, Korean, Chinese, Portuguese, German, and Italian.

Soma-esthétique et architecture: une alternative critique. Genève: Haute Ecole d'Art et Design, 2010. *Thinking through the Body: Essays in Somaesthetics*. Cambridge: Cambridge University Press, 2012. Translated into Hungarian, Polish, and Chinese.

Aesthetic Transactions: Pragmatist Philosophy through Art and Life. Paris: Galerie Michel Journiac / L'éclat, 2012. Catalogue of the art show by that name at Galerie Michel Journiac, Paris, France. May 24, 2012–June 6, 2012. Curated by R. Shusterman.

Stili di vita: Qualche istruzione per l'uso (with Roberta Dreon and Daniele Goldoni). Milano: Mimesis Edizioni, 2012.

스타일의미학 *Aesthetics of Style* (in Korean). Ed. R. Shusterman and Hyijin Lee. Seoul: Book Korea, 2013. Volume includes the Korean translation of "Somatic Style," translated by Lee Hyijin.

Chemins de l'art: Transfigurations, du pragmatisme au zen. Afterword by Arthur Danto. Tr. Raphaël Cuir. Paris and Brussels: Al Dante/Aka—Cellule éditoriale de l'Académie royale des beaux arts de Bruxelles, 2013.

Szómaesztétika és az élet művészete. Kremer Sandor. Budapest: Jate Press, 2014. Collection of four essays, translated from English, with a specially written preface.

The Adventures of the Man in Gold / Les Aventures de l'homme en or. Tr. Thomas Mondemé. Paris: Hermann Éditions, 2016. With images by photographer Yann Toma.

Aesthetic Experience and Somaesthetics. Ed. R. Shusterman. Leiden/Boston: Brill, 2018.

《情感与行动：实用主义之道，商务印书馆2018年8月》 *Act and Affect: Paths of Pragmatism*. Tr. Yanping Gao. Shanghai: The Commercial Press, 2018. Volume based on Shusterman's May 2017 "Summit Lectures" at Fudan University, Shanghai.

(With Satoshi Higuchi and Gunther Gebauer) 《身体感性と文化の哲学：人間・運動・世制作》 (In English as *Philosophy of Somaesthetics and Culture: Human Being, Movement, Worldmaking*). Tokyo: Keiso Shobo, 2019.

Bodies in the Streets: The Somaesthetics of City Life. Ed. R. Shusterman. Leiden/Boston: Brill, 2019.

Ars Erotica: Sex and Somaesthetics in the Classical Arts of Love. Cambridge: Cambridge University Press, 2021.

Films

Château. Richard Shusterman performing as the Man in Gold. Cinematography by Yann Toma. 2010.

A Night with Richard Shusterman. Richard Shusterman performing as the Man in Gold. Cinematography by Yann Toma. 2010.

Lights in the Dark. Richard Shusterman performing as the Man in Gold. Cinematography by Yann Toma. 2011.
Walk the Golden Night. Richard Shusterman performing as the Man in Gold. Cinematography by Yann Toma. Edited by Elliot Storey. 2011.
Golden Parisian Nights. Richard Shusterman performing as the Man in Gold. Cinematography by Yann Toma. Edited by Elliot Storey. 2012. 6:10 minutes.
Philosophical Encounters with Richard Shusterman. Directed by Paweł Kuczyński. Produced by Delos Films. 2013. A three-part educational documentary: *Encounter One: The Role of a Philosopher*, *Encounter Two: Making a Difference*, and *Encounter Three: Looking Ahead*. Each of the three parts is approximately 30 minutes. Encounter One: *The Man in Gold*. Written/directed/edited by Pawel Kuczyński. Camera by Piotr Rejmer, Marcin Ściegliński, Paweł Kuczyński. Music by Lucas Janu. Produced by Delos Films. 2021. 58 minutes.

Books about Shusterman

Embodying Pragmatism: Richard Shusterman's Philosophy and Literary Theory. Ed. W. Małecki. Frankfurt: Peter Lang, 2010.
Shusterman's Pragmatism: Between Literature and Somaesthetics. Ed. D. Koczanowicz and W. Małecki. Amsterdam: Rodopi, 2012.
Delin Liu. *A Study on Shusterman's New Pragmatic Aesthetics*. Jinan: Shandong University Press, 2012. 刘德林：《舒斯特曼新实用主义美学研究》，济南：山东大学出版社，2012.
Mao Chongjie. *Three Faces of Pragmatism: On John Dewey, R. Rorty and R. Shusterman's Philosophy, Aesthetics and Cultural Politics*. Beijing: Chinese Academy of Social Sciences Press, 2009. 毛崇杰著：《实用主义的三副面孔：杜威、罗蒂和舒斯特曼的哲学、美学》，北京：社会科学文献出版社，2009年.
Mitek-Dziemba, Alina. *Literatura i filozofia w poszukiwaniu sztuki życia: Nietzsche, Wilde, Shusterman*. Katowice: Wydawnictwo UŚ, 2011.
Wei Shuanxi. *The Somatic Turn and The Transformation of Aesthetics: On Shusterman's Somaesthetics*. Beijing: Chinese Academy of Social Sciences Press, 2016. 韦拴喜：《身体转向与美学的改造：舒斯特曼身体美学思想论纲》，北京：中国社会科学出版社，2016.
Wang Yaqin, *Research on Richard Shusterman's Somaesthetic Thought*. Beijing: Chinese Academy of Social Sciences Press, 2020. 王亚芹著:《具身化：理查德·舒斯特曼身体美学研究》.北京: 中国社会科学出版社，2020.

Name Index

Abramović, Marina 172
Alexander, Frederick Matthias 12, 69, 97, 181, 273, 277
Alighieri, Dante 92
Altindere, Halil 77
Ames, Roger 264
Aristotle 11, 78, 136, 145n56
Austin, J. L. 57, 272

Baraka, Amiri 80
Barber, Daniel 180
Baumgarten, Alexander 44, 86, 87
Beethoven, Ludwig von 91
Bennich-Björkman, Li 67
Bergson, Henri 269
Berleant, Arnold 112, 113
Blanchot, Maurice 269
Bloom, Harold 47
Böhme, Gernot 88, 90, 250
Boltanski, Luc 65–66
Borgmann, Albert 103
Borradori, Giovanna 5
Botha, Catherine F. 153, 154, 156
Bourdieu, Pierre 65, 68, 244
Brecht, Bertolt 169
Brennan, Tim 81
Brillat-Savarin, Jean Anthelme 116–117
Brown, James 80
Bulgakov, Mikhail 72
Buruma, Ian 61

Carroll, Noël 227, 230
Cartagena, Colombia 143, 146, 173–174, 219, 225–227, 238–240, 259–260
Cavell, Stanley 233–234
Clark, Gordon Matta 111
Coleridge, Samuel Taylor 16
Confucius 50, 59, 70, 185, 190, 266–267
Cratylus 136

Daguerre, Louise-Jacques-Mandé 228, 232
Danto, Arthur 127–135, 231, 235–238, 244, 252–253, 274–276
Darby, Derrick 83
Darwin, Charles 9, 45, 54, 55

Daudy, Marie-Christine 222
David, Jacques-Louis 6
Davidson, Donald 45
Del Baldo, Luca 183, 185–186
Delacroix, Eugene 6
Deleuze, Gilles 268–270
Dennett, Daniel 45
Dewey, John 2–3, 5, 9–12, 23, 29–32, 42, 44–51, 55–56, 68–69, 75, 78–80, 82, 84, 94–95, 98–99, 113, 114, 135, 173, 179, 231, 243, 246, 251, 273
Di Summa, Laura 153–154, 196
Dick, Philip K. 18, 126, 137, 254
Dickens, Charles 47

Eliot, T. S. 1, 3, 271
Ellington, Duke 105
Emerson, Ralph Waldo 3, 4, 11, 47, 80, 238, 272
  "Beauty" 16
  and "demon" 224
  "Experience" 232–234
  "Literary Ethics" 18, 126, 134–137, 143
  and Man in Gold 135, 143, 145n56, 153, 156, 158
  and mood 231–234
  Nature/*Nature* 232
  Possession 16
  Stanley Cavell on 3, 4, 11, 16, 18, 47, 80, 126, 134–135, 137, 143, 145, 153, 156, 158, 224, 231–234, 238, 254, 272
  Transfiguration 134–135, 143, 254
Engels, Friedrich 65

Fanon, Frantz 248
Feldenkrais, Moshe 13, 32, 181, 267, 273, 274, 277
Fish, Stanley 92
Ford, Harrison (Rich Deckard) 137
Foucault, Michel 32–34, 42, 54, 62–63, 68–69, 71, 103–104, 154, 169, 174–175, 269
Freud, Sigmund 174

Galen 106
Goldfarb, Jeff 67

NAME INDEX

Gongkai, Pan   183, 185, 189–190, 264, 273
Guru   83

Habermas, Jürgen   35–36
Hayes, Isaac   80
Hegel, G. W. F.   4, 9–10, 43, 127–129, 253, 265
Heidegger, Martin   153
Heldke, Lisa   108–109, 113
Heraclitus   93, 135–136, 221
Hitchcock, Alfred   230, 234
Höller, Carsten   180, 183–184, 273
Höök, Kristina   247
Hume, David   108, 232

Jacobs, David   92
James, William   4, 11, 44–45, 49, 55, 68, 78, 96, 100, 173, 231, 232, 250, 270, 273
Jameson, Frederic   77
Jaspers, Karl   57
Jesus (Mathew, Mark, Luke, and John)   72, 253–254

Kant, Immanuel   2, 44, 79, 88, 94, 112, 232, 236, 246
   on "taste"   79
Kirstinä, Väinö   74–75
Knowles, Alison   111
Korsmeyer, Carolyn   110–113
Kristjánsson, Kristjan   40, 41
KRS-One   83
Kubrick, Stanley   233–234, 237
Kuehn, Glenn   113
Kundera, Milan   47, 206–207

Lacan, Jacques   18, 150–162, 164, 174, 255
   mirror stage   160
   third term   157–158
Langer, Susanne   235
Laozi   19, 135, 217, 259, 266
Largus, Scribonius   106
Lefebvre, Henri   64
Lemke, Thomas   62
Locke, Alain   75, 82

Margolis, Joseph   25, 41, 43
Marino, Stefano   150, 153, 156, 162
Markham, Pigmeat   80
Marvin, Gladney   74–75

Marx, Karl   65, 265–266
Mead, George Herbert   68–69
Mencius   70
Merleau-Ponty, Maurice   23, 25–29, 31–32, 42, 52, 54, 68–69, 95, 113, 213, 276
Messi, Lionel   39–40
Mili, Gjon   187
Mitchell, Juliet   161
Montaigne, Michel de   3, 11, 54, 272

Nietzsche, Friedrich   3, 11, 33, 54, 80, 100, 102, 108, 145, 145n56, 156, 169, 221, 253
Norheim, Marit Benthe   19, 126, 127, 146–147, 162, 196, 202–203, 256

ORLAN   183–184, 273
Ørntof, Claus   19, 146–147, 162, 196, 256

Peirce, Charles S.   2, 44–45, 49, 55, 78, 231–232
Perullo, Nicola   113
Petronius   106
Picasso, Pablo   187
Plantinga, Alvin   37–38, 39n56
Plato   16, 93, 108, 114, 157, 175, 221–223, 272
Plessner, Helmuth   25, 28
Poe, Edgar Allan   229
Promio, Jean Alexandre Louis   236–237
Proust, Marcel   4, 102
Pryba, Russell   113
Putnam, Hilary   45

Rabinow, Paul   63
Ragland-Sullivan, Ellie   162–163
Ray, Man (photographer)   187–188
Ricœur, Paul   30, 30n24, 64
Röhrig Assunção, Matthias   62
Rorty, Richard   1–5, 13, 44–45, 47–49, 57, 93, 135, 244, 246
Rose, Jacqueline   160
Rose, Nikolas   63
Russell, Bertrand   1, 1n1, 57, 113

Santayana, George   5, 11
Sartre, Jean-Paul   57
Schiphorst, Thecla   183, 185
Schmitz, Hermann   88, 90, 99, 250
Scott, Ridley (*Blade Runner*)   137

Scott-Heron, Gil   80
Sellars, Wilfred   2
Shelby, Tommie   83
Shelley, Mary   145
Shusterman, Richard
  on Arthur Danto   5–18, 126–135, 231, 235–238, 244, 252–253, 274–276
  on John Dewey   2–5, 9–12, 23–24, 29–32, 42, 44–51, 55–56, 68–69, 75, 75n2, 78–84, 94–95, 98–99, 113–114, 135, 179, 231, 243, 246, 251, 273
  on Hip Hop   4, 17, 74–78, 83–85, 244, 248, 249
  on the Man in Gold   17–19, 32, 59, 125–148, 191–199, 243–246, 252–260, 266, 272
  on pragmatism   1–5, 25–31, 44–47, 48–51, 53–57, 59, 76, 78, 80, 84, 88, 91, 93, 109, 113, 115, 150, 154, 156, 168, 177, 179, 180, 231, 244, 245–247, 250, 265, 268
  on popular art   4, 10, 76–85, 131, 244, 266
  on somaesthetics   12, 24–25, 32, 39, 48–59, 71, 101, 114–121, 167–169, 175–176, 178, 181–182, 185, 213–215, 239, 246–253, 258, 261–278
  on Richard Rorty   1–5, 13, 25, 44–49, 57, 93, 244, 246
Simmel, Georg   110
Simonides of Keos   166
Socrates   16, 50, 54, 106–107, 215, 221–222
Spinoza, Benedict de   268, 270–271

Spoerri, Daniel   111
Straus, Erwin   88
Suzuki, D. Z.   274

Telfer, Elizabeth   113
Toma, Yann (photographer)   14, 19, 126–127, 133, 135, 138, 140–141, 143, 146n60, 147, 149, 151, 154, 158–162, 166, 181–183, 187–189, 191–198, 205–208, 210, 212, 219–225, 226n22, 229–231, 234, 240, 254, 256–257, 259, 272
Trockel, Rosemarie   180
Trouvé, Tatiana   183–184, 273
Truffaut, François   236

van Gogh, Vincent   225
Voltaire   206–207, 207n57, 272

Ware, George   76, 76n5, 249
Warhol, Andy   5–6, 9–10, 19, 126, 129–133, 220, 230–231, 237, 244, 252
Weber, Max   61
Welles, Orson (*Citizen Kane*)   220, 227–229
West, Cornel   83
Whitman, Walt   23, 29, 47
Wittgenstein, Ludwig   26, 26n10, 57, 156, 272

ya Salaam, Mtume   77, 77n8, 81

Zamir, Tzachi   157, 162–163
Žižek, Slavoj   158

Subject Index

Aesthetic Transactions   183–186, 193, 272
affect (see also mood)   268–270
Alexander Technique   12, 97, 181
analytic aesthetics   1, 5
architecture   98–99, 238–239
atmospheres   89–90, 99, 102
aura (surrounding Man in Gold)   147, 166n2, 182–183, 198, 205, 209, 224
autobiography   151

beauty   150, 168
biopower   62–63, 71
Brillo Boxes (work by Andy Warhol)   7–9, 126, 129–130, 131–133, 230

camera   138–139, 143, 146n60, 159, 182, 198, 223, 226n22, 227–229, 229n27, 231–232, 234–235, 235n44, 236–237, 236n47
camera obscura   220–222
Chinese philosophy   19, 261–262, 264–266
COVID-19   261–262

daimon   224
Dao de Jing (standard format is *Daodejing*)   217
Daoism   217–218
Denmark   146, 194, 198–200
disability   276–277
documenta X/documenta   111, 180–181

Empire (film by Andy Warhol)   131, 133, 230–231, 237
ethical vegetarianism   109
experience, aesthetic (as nondiscursive)   136
Extraterrestrial; alien (Man in Gold as)   137, 170, 209–210, 216, 255

fairy tale (the *Adventures* as genre)   196, 198, 220, 272
Feldenkrais Method   13, 181
fiction   154, 157, 211, 226
film   131
flaneur   228–230

genius   223, 231, 235–236
Golden Man, The (novella by Philip K. Dick)   126, 137–147

habits   98
hatha yoga   176
historicism   134

identity (and identification)   53, 181–182, 186, 265–267
interview (as genre)   263–264, 273–276

jouissance   150

kinaesthesis (aesthetic sense)   239
Körper and *Leib*   27–29, 34–35, 39, 49, 95, 250

light-drawing (technique in photography)   140–141, 152–154
Little Prince, The (by Antoine de Saint-Exupéry)   209–210, 221–222

Marxism   265–266
materialism   37–39
mood (in Shusterman's somaesthetics)   231

narrative self   32

Osteria Francescana (restaurant)   114, 126

pathetic aesthetics   86–91
performance art   171–174, 182–183
popular art   4, 10, 76n6, 78, 82, 94, 131, 244, 266
popular culture   81–82, 89–90, 93–94
possession (artist's feeling of being possessed)   17, 151
postmodernism (in art and culture)   77, 81, 83–84, 88–89, 92
pragmatist aesthetics   61–64, 68–69, 71, 76, 87–90, 91–94
private redemption   211–213
proprioception (aesthetic sense)   239

rap (Hip Hop)   74–85, 91–92
recycling, music (in Hip Hop)   17–18, 82–85
Royaumont Abbey   190, 192, 210, 220

sculpture   138–139, 151, 159, 214–216
self-fashioning   3–4, 15–16

silence, nonverbality (of Man in
    Gold)   143, 148
soma   12, 24–25
somaesthetics
    architecture   98–99, 104, 108, 135, 139,
        238–239, 250
    Asian thought   50, 58–59
    atmosphere   18, 87, 89, 90, 93, 98, 99,
        102–104
    COVID-19   261
    Dewey's body-mind   29–31
    disability   19, 276–277
    eroticism   161, 277–278
    meliorism   13, 18, 19, 24, 32, 44, 48, 51, 62,
        71, 96, 100–105, 178, 185, 190, 191, 203,
        247, 249–252, 265, 269–270
    normative   12, 24, 31–32, 34, 104n84, 115, 170
    phenomenology   87–90, 95, 113, 127–128,
        213, 215, 243, 249, 250
    proprioception   19, 52, 117–119, 184, 239,
        239n51, 275

somapower   61, 63, 65, 67, 69, 71–72
somatic attention   96–97
the art of eating   106, 110–113, 114–120,
    177, 189n27
the art of living   51
three dimensions   12, 52
Somaflux photography   181–182, 187–188
somapower   61–73

taijiquan [T'ai chi ch'uan]   176, 181
taste (as aesthetic judgment)   106–114, 118–
    120, 122–126, 131–132
transfiguration   127–136, 138, 143, 147, 150,
    252–254

Yijing (Book of Changes)   266
yin and *yang*   155, 167

zen/chan Buddhism   12, 133, 176, 181, 267,
    273–274

www.ingramcontent.com/pod-product-compliance
Lightning Source LLC
Chambersburg PA
CBHW071158300426
44113CB00009B/1249